William Kingston

How Britannia Came to Rule the Waves

William Kingston

How Britannia Came to Rule the Waves

ISBN/EAN: 9783954272174
Erscheinungsjahr: 2012
Erscheinungsort: Bremen, Deutschland

www.maritimepress.de | office@maritimepress.de

Bei diesem Titel handelt es sich um den Nachdruck eines historischen, lange vergriffenen Buches. Da elektronische Druckvorlagen für diese Titel nicht existieren, musste auf alte Vorlagen zurückgegriffen werden. Hieraus zwangsläufig resultierende Qualitätsverluste bitten wir zu entschuldigen.

Contents

Chapter One.

Introductory Remarks.

Rome was not built in a day, nor has the glorious British Navy attained its present condition except by slow degrees, by numerous trials and experiments, by improvements gradually and cautiously introduced, and by the employment of a vast amount of thought, energy, and toil. We are apt to forget when we see an elaborate machine, the immense quantity of mental and physical exertion it represents, the efforts of the united minds perhaps of many successive generations, and the labour of thousands of workmen. I propose briefly to trace the progress which the British Navy has made from age to age, as well as its customs, and the habits of its seamen, with their more notable exploits since the days when this tight little island of ours first became known to the rest of the world.

Some writers, indulging in the Darwinian theory of development, would make us believe that the ironclad of the present day is the legitimate offspring of the ancient coracle or wicker-work boat which is still to be found afloat on the waters of the Wye, and on some of the rivers of the east coast; but if such is the case, the descent must be one of many ages, for it is probable that the Britons had stout ships long before the legions of Cæsar set their feet upon our shores. I am inclined to agree with an ancient writer who gives it as his opinion that the British were always a naval people. "For," says he, in somewhat quaint phraseology, "as Britain was an island, the inhabitants could only have come to it across the ocean in ships, and they could scarcely have had ships unless they were nautically inclined." The same writer asserts that the Britons had vessels of large size long before the invasion of the Romans, but that they either burnt them to prevent their falling into the hands of the invaders, or that they were destroyed by the Romans themselves, who then, adding insult to injury, stigmatised the people as mere painted barbarians, whose sole mode of moving over the waters of their coasts and rivers was in wicker baskets covered with hides — the truth being, that these wicker-ribbed boats were simply the craft used by the British fishermen on their coasts or streams. How could the hordes that in successive ages crossed the German Ocean have performed the voyage unless they had possessed more efficient means of conveyance than these afforded? I must, therefore, agree with the aforesaid ancient writer that they had stout ships, impelled by sails and oars, which were afterwards employed either in commercial or piratical enterprises. The Britons of the southern shores of the island possessed, he says, wooden-built ships of a size considerably greater than any hide-covered barks could have been. It is very certain that many hundred years before the Christian era the Phoenicians visited the coasts of Cornwall and Devonshire, and planted colonies there, which retain to the present day their ancient peculiarities and customs, and even many names of common things. It is probable that these colonists, well acquainted as they were with nautical affairs, kept up their practical knowledge of shipbuilding, and formed a mercantile navy to carry on their commerce with other countries, as well as ships fitted for warfare to protect their ports from foreign invasion, or from the attacks of pirates.

Many English nautical terms at present in use are clearly of Phoenician origin. Davit, for instance, is evidently derived from the Arabic word *Davit*, a crooked piece of wood, similar in shape to that by which the boats of a vessel are hoisted out of the water and hung up at her sides. The word Caboose was the name given by the Phoenicians to the temple dedicated to the god of fire, whom they worshipped, built on the decks of their vessels; when a purer faith was introduced, it being found convenient to cook dinners in the no longer sacred *Caboose*, the name being retained, Blackie the cook took the place of the officiating priest. Caboose is at the present day the name of the kitchen-house on the deck of a merchant-vessel. Many other terms even now used by seafaring people are derived directly or indirectly from the same far-distant origin, as are several of the customs observed at the present day. I may mention some of them by-and-by.

Ships of the Ancients.

The ancient Greeks and other Eastern nations had ships of considerable size many hundred years before the Christian era. The earliest mythical stories describe long voyages performed by vessels of far more complicated structure than the simple canoe. The ships engaged in the Trojan war each carried a hundred and twenty warriors, which shows that at the period referred to they could not have been of very small dimensions. Although they might have been open, they had masts and sails, and were propelled by rowers sitting on benches, while the oars were fastened to the sides of the ship with leathern thongs. Some were painted black, others red. When they arrived at their destination, the bows were drawn up on shore; or when on a voyage, they at night anchored by the stern, with cables secured to large stones. At an early period they had round bottoms and sharp prows. We hear of ships with three ranks of rowers, called triremes, B.C. 700, and long before that time biremes, or ships with two ranks of oars, had been introduced. In the time of Cyrus, long sharp-keeled war-ships were used, having fifty rowers, who sat in one row, twenty-five on each side of the ship. About B.C. 400, the practice of entirely decking over ships was introduced; Themistocles induced the Athenians to build a fleet of two hundred sail, and to pass a decree that every year twenty new triremes should be built. The Greeks even at that period, however, seldom ventured out into the open sea, steering in the daytime by headlands or islands, and at night by the rising and setting of different stars.

The Greeks possessed ships of war and merchant-vessels. That a war-galley was of large size may be inferred from the fact that she carried two hundred seamen, besides on some occasions thirty Epibatoe — literally, marines, trained to fight at sea. These war-vessels moved with wonderful rapidity, darting here and there with the speed of a modern steam-vessel. The ordinary war-ships were triremes, or had three banks of oars. The merchant-vessels or transports were much more bulky, had round bottoms, and although rowers were employed on board, yet they were propelled chiefly by their sails. After the time of Alexander, vessels with four, five, and even more ranks of rowers became general, and ships are described with twelve and even thirty ranks of rowers and upwards — but they were found of no practical use, as the crew on the upper benches were unable to throw sufficient power into the immensely long oars which it was necessary to employ.

Fully B.C. 500, the Carthaginians invented the quadremes, and about B.C. 400, Dionysius, first tyrant of Syracuse, whose ambition was to create a powerful navy, built numerous vessels of the same description, unused till that time by the Greeks. The rowers in these ships, with numerous banks of oars, could not have sat directly one above another, as some suppose; but the feet of those on the upper tier must have rested on the bench or thwart on which those immediately below them sat. Thus the tiers of oars were probably not more than two feet, if so much, one above another; and supposing the lowest tier was two feet above the water, the highest in the quadremes could not have been more than ten feet, and even then the length of the oar of the upper tier must have been very great, and it must have required considerable exertion on the part of the rower to move it. The most interesting part, however, of an ancient ship to us at the present day was the beak or rostra. At first these beaks were placed only above water, and were formed in the shape of a short thick-bladed sword, with sharp points, generally three, one above another, and inclining slightly upwards, so that they might rip open the planks of the vessels against which they ran. They were sometimes formed in the shape of a ram's head fixed to the end of a beam; and hence in modern days we have adopted the name of rams, which we give to ships of war built on the same principle.

After a time these beaks were fixed on to the bow of the ship below the water, and were thus still more dangerous to other ships, when they could strike an antagonist on the side. The bow of a ship was generally ornamented by the head of some animal, such as a wild boar or a wolf, or some imaginary creature placed above the rostra. On both sides of the prow were painted eyes, such as are seen on the bows of boats and vessels in the Mediterranean at the present day. The upper part of the prow was frequently ornamented with a helmet covered with bronze. The steersman or pilot was looked upon as the chief in rank among the crew, and after him there came an officer whose duties were similar to those of the boatswain, as he had the care of the gear and command over the rowers. The stern or puppis, from which we derive the term poop, was elevated above the other parts of the deck, and here the helmsman had his seat, sheltered by a shed frequently adorned with an image of the tutelary deity of the vessel. Sometimes he had a lantern hanging in front of him, probably to enable him to see the magic compass, the use of which was kept secret from the rest of the crew. A circular shield or shields also ornamented the stern. Behind the helmsman was placed a slight pole on which flew the dog-vane, to show the direction of the wind. In the centre of the ship was a raised platform on a level with the upper part of the bulwarks, on which in battle the soldiers took their stand to hurl their darts against the enemy.

TRIREME.

The quadremes and quinqueremes carried from three to four hundred rowers, and a ship belonging to Ptolemaeus Philopater is described as carrying four thousand rowers. From the surface of the water to the top of the prow was forty-eight cubits, or seventy-two feet, and from the water to the top of the stern fifty-three cubits, or nearly eighty feet; she had thus sufficient room for forty ranks of rowers, and the oars of the uppermost rank were thirty-eight cubits or fifty-seven feet long, the handles of which were weighted with lead, so as to balance the outer part, and thus render the long oars manageable. The lower parts of the holes through which the oars passed were covered with leather. Till the invention of the rudder, vessels were steered by two large oars, one on either side of the stern, with very broad blades. Ships were also furnished with long poles, by which they could be shoved off the ground. The triremes were fitted with two masts, and so were even smaller vessels; the larger had three masts, the largest of which was nearest the stern. They were usually of fir; and the head of the lower mast, which is at present called the top, was in the shape of a drinking cup. Some of these tops were of bronze; the largest held three men, two in the next, and one in the smallest; and breast-works

11

ran round them to defend the occupants from the darts of the enemy. They were also furnished with tackles for hoisting up stones and weapons to hurl at the foe. Above the main-mast was a top-mast or topgallant-mast, called the distaff; the yards were hoisted up much as in the present day, and were secured by parrels or hoops to the mast. They were fitted with topping-lifts and braces. Each mast carried two square sails, and in after days the Romans introduced triangular sails. Though they generally ran before the wind, they were also able to sail on a wind, though probably not very close-hauled.

Ships were supplied with weather-boards, or broad belts of canvas, to keep out the sea, and were surrounded, also, by lines of ropes one above another, to prevent the seamen from being washed overboard. Sometimes these breast-works were made of skins or wicker-work, and in bad weather were raised to a considerable height above the bulwarks. It is said that Anacharsis, upwards of 500 B.C., if he did not invent, greatly improved the form of anchors, which were already made of iron. The anchor had generally two flukes or teeth, and was then called bidens; but sometimes it had only one. We use the same

ROMAN MERCHANT-VESSEL.

12

terms as the ancients, to cast anchor or weigh anchor, whence the latter term is equivalent to set sail. Each ship had several anchors; that in which the Apostle Paul sailed, we know, had four, and others had eight. The largest and most important anchor was denominated "the last hope," hence, when that failed, arose the expression "the last hope gone." A buoy was used fixed to the anchor by a rope, to show the spot where it lay.

The Romans possessed no war fleets till the year B.C. 260, when a fleet of triremes was built to oppose the Carthaginians. Many of them having been sent to the bottom, however, by the quinqueremes of that people, the Romans built a hundred of the latter-sized ships from the model of a Carthaginian vessel wrecked on the coast of Italy. The Romans must have had very large merchant-vessels to enable them to transport the enormous monoliths from Egypt which they erected in Rome. These vast stones, also, could not have been got on board and brought up the Tiber without considerable mechanical appliances.

The construction of their ships differed but slightly from that of the Greek vessels; they had turrets on the decks of their larger men-of-war, and employed a variety of destructive engines; so that in battle the soldiers on board fought much as they did when standing on the walls of a fortress. Of one thing I am sure, that no correct drawings of ancient ships have come down to us, if any such were really made; those on medals, cameos, and such as are painted on walls, are probably as far removed from the reality as a Thames barge is from a dashing frigate. They give us, certainly, the different parts of the ship, and from them we may form a pretty correct idea of what a ship really was like. Certain it is, however, that ships were built of prodigious size, and if not equal to a line-of-battle ship of late days, they must have been as large as, if not larger than, the *Great Harry*, and probably quite as well able to encounter as she was the boisterous seas. Long before the Christian era, ships boldly struck across the Mediterranean, and even passing through the Pillars of Hercules, coasted along the shores of Iberia and Gaul, and thence crossed over to Britain, or coasted round the African continent.

Advanced as the ancients were in architectural knowledge, there is every reason to suppose that they were equally capable of building ships to answer all their requirements, either for war or commerce. They were probably thus not only of great size, but well built, and were certainly finished and ornamented in an elegant and even a magnificent manner, far superior to that of many ages later. The mistaken notion as to the size of the ships of the ancients arises from the supposition that because merchantmen of the present day are smaller than men-of-war, that they were so formerly — the reverse, however, being the case. Men-of-war were generally long, narrow vessels, constructed for speed, to carry only fighting men, with a small quantity of provisions; whereas merchantmen were built of considerable beam and depth to stow a large quantity of cargo. A Phoenician vessel was able to afford accommodation to 500 emigrants, with provisions for a long voyage, besides her crew, while her masts were formed of the cedars of Lebanon.

Nautical Customs derived from the Ancients.

Among the best-known customs of the ocean is the ceremony that takes place when ships cross the line. That, however, like many others of olden days, is getting somewhat into disuse. Few of those who have witnessed it, probably, have suspected that its origin dates as far back as the times of the Phoenicians. As the ship approaches the imaginary band which encircles the globe, a gruff voice hails her from alongside, and demands her name and nation, whence she is from, and whither she is bound. These questions being answered, she is ordered to heave to, when no less a person than old father Neptune himself, with his fair wife Amphitrite, and their attendant Tritons, climb up over the bows, and take possession of the fore-part of the deck. Neptune generally wears a crown formed out of a tin saucepan, with a flowing beard, a wig of oakum, and a robe composed of some gay-coloured petticoat-stuff, stored up for the occasion, or a piece of canvas, with curious devices painted on it, while he carries in his band a trident, made out of a harpoon or a boat-hook. The fair Amphitrite, who is more commonly known on board as Bill Buntline, the boatswain's mate, is habited, like her lord, in the gayest of gay attire, with a vast profusion of oakum locks, and bows of huge proportions, although it must be confessed that she has very little to boast of in the way of feminine delicacy or personal beauty, while the Tritons are at all events very odd-looking fish.

The captain, surrounded by his officers, with the passengers behind him, stands on the poop, and a spirited conversation, not altogether destitute of humour, generally takes place between him and Neptune — when the monarch of the main demands that every one on board who has not before crossed that portion of his watery realm where the ship then floats, shall be brought before him. None, whatever their rank, are excused. Those who at once consent to pay tribute are allowed to escape without undergoing any further ceremony, but those luckless wights who refuse or have not the wherewithal to pay are instantly seized on by the Tritons, lathered with pitch and grease, shaved with a rusty hoop, and soused over head and ears in a huge tub, while from all quarters, as they attempt to escape from the marine monsters, bucketfuls of water are hove down upon them. Uproar and apparent confusion ensues; and usually it requires no little exertion of authority on the part of the captain and officers to restore order.

We might suspect, from the introduction of the names of Neptune and Amphitrite, that this curious and somewhat barbarous custom must have a classical origin. There can be no doubt that it is derived from those maritime people of old, the Phoenicians. Ceremonies, to which those I have described bear the strongest similarity, were practised by them at a very remote period, whenever one of their ships passed through the Straits of Gibraltar. That talented writer, David Urquhart, in his "Pillars of Hercules," asserts that the Phoenicians and Carthaginians possessed a knowledge of the virtues of the loadstone, and used it as a compass, as did the mariners of the Levant till a late period.

The original compass consisted of a cup full of water, on which floated a thin circular board, with the needle resting on it; this was placed in a small shrine or temple in front of the helmsman, with a lantern probably fixed inside to throw light on the mysterious instrument during the night. The most fearful oaths were administered to the initiated not to divulge the secret. Every means, also, which craft could devise or superstition enforce was employed by the Phoenicians to prevent other people from gaining a knowledge of it, or of the mode by which their commerce beyond the Straits of Hercules was carried on, or of the currents, the winds, the tides, the seas, the shores, the people, or the harbours. A story is told of a Phoenician vessel running herself on the rocks to prevent the Romans from finding the passage. This secrecy was enforced by the most sanguinary code — death was the penalty of indiscretion; thus the secret of the compass was preserved from generation to generation among a few families of seamen unknown to the rest of the civilised world. The ceremonies, especially, were kept up, though in a succession of ages they have undergone gradual alterations.

The lofty shores which form the two sides of the Straits of Gibraltar were known in ancient days as the Pillars of Hercules. Here stood the temple of the god, and hither came the mariners before launching forth on the more perilous part of their voyage, to pay their vows, and probably to bind themselves by oaths to conceal the secrets to be revealed to them. Perhaps in all cases the temple on shore was not visited, but, at all events, the oaths were administered to the seamen on board, ablutions were performed, and sacrifices offered up. The introduction of Christianity did not abolish these observances, and through the ignorance and superstition of the mariners of those seas they were for century after century maintained, though the motive and origin were altogether forgotten.

A traveller, who wrote as recently as the seventeenth century, describes a ceremony which took place on board a ship in which he was sailing, when passing through the straits. Just as the two lofty headlands were in sight on either side of the ship, an old seaman came forward with a book, and summoning all those whose names he declared not to be registered in it, made them swear that they in future voyages would compel their fellow-seamen to perform the same ceremonies in which they were about to engage. Behind him appeared a band of veteran seamen dressed up in a variety of fantastic costumes, with a drum and other musical instruments. These forthwith seized on all whose names were not registered as having before passed through the straits, and dragging them forward, thrust them into tubs, and soused them thoroughly with water. No one was altogether exempt, but those who had before passed were allowed to escape a like process by the payment of a fine.

These same mariners, when they extended their voyages to the southern hemisphere, very naturally postponed the ceremony which they were in the habit of performing on passing the straits, till they crossed the line. They also, not altogether abandoning classical allusions, changed the name of their *dramatis personae*. Hercules, who had no connection with the ocean, whatever he might have had to do with the Straits of Gibraltar, had to give place to Neptune, the long-honoured monarch of the main, and Amphitrite was introduced to keep him company. We recognise in the duckings, the sacrificial ablutions, and in the shaving and fining, the oaths and the penalty.

When the hardy seamen of Great Britain first began to steer their ships across the line, they were undoubtedly accompanied by pilots and mariners of the Mediterranean. These, of course, taught them the ceremonies they had been in the habit of performing. The English, as may be supposed, made various additions and alterations suited to their rougher habits and ideas, and what at one time probably retained somewhat of the elegance of its classical origin, became the strange burlesque it now appears.

Another nautical custom still in vogue is also derived from remote antiquity. At the present day, with doubtful propriety, in imitation of the rite of baptism, we christen a ship, as it is often called, by breaking a bottle of wine on her bows as she glides off the stocks. The custom is of thoroughly heathen origin. A similar ceremony was practised by the ancient Greeks when they launched a ship. We ornament our vessels with flags; they decked theirs with garlands. At the moment the ship was launched forth into the deep the priest of Neptune raised to his lips a goblet of wine, and after quaffing from it, he poured the remainder out as a libation to his deity. The modern Greeks still perform the ceremony much in the manner of their ancestors. Clearly, the custom we have of breaking a bottle of wine is derived from the libations of the ancients. In most instances, at the present day, the ship is named at the moment she is launched by a young lady, who acts the part of the priest or priestess of old.

Of late years a religious service is usually performed at the launch of a man-of-war. The heathen libation is not, however, omitted, and the whole ceremony presents a curious jumble of ancient and modern forms suited to the tastes of the day. Still we are bound heartily to pray that the gallant sailors who will man the stout ship may be protected while in the performance of their duty to their country; and, still more, that they may be brought to a knowledge of the Gospel.

The Greeks invariably gave feminine names to their ships, choosing, whenever possible, appropriate ones; while the less courteous Romans bestowed masculine names on theirs. Though we may not have followed the Greek rule, we to the present day always look upon a ship as of the feminine gender.

The mariner's compass, the most important instrument used in navigation, demands further notice. The magnet, or loadstone, was known to the ancient Greeks many centuries before the Christian era. The legend runs, that one Magnes a shepherd, feeding his flocks on Mount Ida, having stretched himself on the ground to sleep, left his crook, the upper part of which was made of iron, lying against a rock. On awaking, and rising to depart, he found, when he attempted to take up his crook, that the iron adhered to the rock. Having communicated this extraordinary fact to some neighbouring philosophers, they called the rock after the name of the shepherd, Magnes, the magnet.

The Chinese, of still more ancient date, so their traditions affirm, discovered a mountain rising out of the sea possessing an intensity of attraction so great that the nails and iron bands were drawn out of their ships, causing their immediate wreck. Those sea-arabs whom we call Phoenicians had, at a very early date, made use of their knowledge of the property of the loadstone to turn towards the North Pole; though, like many other discoveries, as I have just mentioned, it was kept a profound secret among a select few, and concealed from the public by having an air of religious mystery thrown over it. Lumps of loadstone formed into balls were preserved in their temples, and looked upon with awe, as possessing mystic properties. With these round stones the point of a needle was rubbed, as often as it required fresh magnetising.

I have already described the compass used by the Phoenicians, and how, long after Islamism had gained the ascendency, it was possessed by their descendants. At length the secret was divulged, and it came into general use among the mariners of the Mediterranean in the tenth and eleventh centuries. Its original form was unaltered for nearly four centuries, when, in 1502, Flavio Gioja of Positano, near the town of Amalfi, on the coast of Calabria, a place celebrated for its maritime enterprise, improved upon the primitive rude and simple instrument by suspending the needle on a centre, and enclosing it in a box. The advantages of his invention were so great that his instrument was universally adopted, and hence he gained the credit of being the inventor of the mariner's compass, of which he was only the improver.

Long before the compass was used at sea, it had been employed by the Chinese to direct the course of their caravans across the desert. For this purpose a figure, placed in a waggon which led the caravan, was so constructed that the arm and hand moved with perfect freedom, the magnetic needle being attached to it; the hand, however, pointed to the south, the negative end being fixed in it. The Chinese also used a needle which was freely suspended in the air, attached to a silken thread, and by this means they were able to determine the amount of the western variation of the needle. It is possible that both the Chinese and Arabs discovered the magnetic powers of the loadstone, although the latter in their long voyages may have allowed the knowledge they possessed to have been drawn from them by the astute Chinese; or, *vice versa*, the Arabs may have obtained the knowledge which the Chinese already possessed, and kept it secret from the western nations. We all remember the wonderful adventures of Sinbad the Sailor, as narrated in the Arabian Nights — how the ship in which he sailed was attracted by a magnetic mountain, which finally drew all the iron bolts and nails out of her. Now it happens that the author places Sinbad's mountain in the same part of the world in which the Chinese say their magnetic mountain exists. Ptolemy, in his geography, also describes a magnetic mountain existing in the Chinese Seas. We may therefore, I think, come to the conclusion, that the mariner's compass was known to the ancients long before the Christian era, and that although disused for centuries, the knowledge was never altogether lost.

Chapter Two.

Early English Ships (from A.D. 600 to A.D. 1087.)

We Englishmen undoubtedly derive a large portion of our nautical spirit from our Saxon ancestors, the first bands of whom came to the shores of our tight little island under those sea-rovers known as Hengist and Horsa, invited by the helpless Britons to defend them from the attacks of the savage Picts and Scots. The enemies of the gallant heroes I have named were apt to call them pirates; but as might made right in most sublunary affairs during those dark and troubled ages of the world's history, they looked upon the roving commissions they had given themselves as perfectly honourable and lawful, and felt no small amount of contempt for the rest of mankind who chose to stay at home at ease by their firesides, while they were ploughing the ocean in search of plunder and glory. I suspect that they had a strong preference for the former.

After the Saxons had driven the ancient inhabitants of the island out of the more fertile portions of the country, and had made themselves, according to their notions, pretty comfortable in their new homes; they, in a little time, in their turn, were sadly pestered by foreign invaders. These were the Danes. Those hardy sons of the North, still more wild and fierce than the Saxons, and still less scrupulous in their proceedings, pleased with the appearance of the country which they had come over to look at, settled themselves in every nook and corner of Old England in which they could haul up their ships, and find a resting place for their feet. I cannot help feeling a great respect for those old sea-kings. They were heathens, and we must judge of them by the light which they possessed, and not by any standard acknowledged in the present civilised world. Bold, enterprising, and sagacious, their own country confined and barren, they looked on the wide ocean as the only worthy field for the employment of their energies. They loved it for itself, too; they were born on it, or within the sound of its surges; they lived on it, they fought on it, and it was their wish through life to die on it, as if only on its boundless expanse their free spirits could be emancipated from this mortal coil. This same spirit still exists and animates the breasts of the officers and men of our navy, of our vast mercantile marine; and, though mentioned last, not certainly in a less degree of the owners of the superb yacht fleets which grace the waters of the Solent, of the Bay of Dublin, of Plymouth Sound, of the mouth of the Thames, and indeed of every harbour and roadstead round our shores. No people, unless animated by such a spirit, would go to sea simply for the love of a sea-life as do our yachtsmen. We may depend upon it that they are the lineal descendants of those old sea-rovers, somewhat more civilised and polished certainly, differing as much in that respect, it is to be hoped, from their remote ancestors as do their trim yachts, which will go nine knots or more within four and a-half points of the wind, from the tubbish-looking sturdy craft of the Danes, which had no idea of sailing any way except dead before the gale.

There was something barbarously grand in the notion of the old Norse kings which induced them, when worn out with age and fatigue, to sail forth into mid-ocean, and then, lighting their own funeral pile, to consume themselves and the stout ship they loved so well in one conflagration. Seriously, however, we must not forget that they were influenced by a very terrible and dark superstition, and be thankful that we live in an age when the bright beams of Christianity have dispelled such gross errors from this part of the globe. I cannot help fancying that the late Lord Yarborough, that chief of true yachtsmen, had somewhat the same feeling I have been describing, refined and civilised of course, when, his vessel, the *Kestrel*, being in Malta harbour, he found death approaching, and ordered her to be got under weigh, to stand out to sea, that he might breathe out his spirit surrounded by that element on which he had so long made his home, and in which he so truly delighted.

The tribes, now so closely united, which make up the British race, were the most maritime people of their time, and it is not, therefore, surprising that we should now possess strong nautical propensities. The Normans, it must be remembered also, who afterwards conquered England, were descended from the same bold sea-rovers, though, having paid sundry visits to Paris, where they learned to write poetry, to sing, and to dance, with many other accomplishments, they had wonderfully improved in civilisation since the days of their ancestors, of whom I have been speaking. Still the same enterprising spirit animated their bosoms, afterwards to shine forth with splendour, when their descendants became the leaders of numberless exploring expeditions to all parts of the world, and of the victorious fleets of Old England.

There is no doubt, as I have shown, that the English possessed trading vessels, if not also ships, built exclusively for war, from a very early period.

The first regular war-fleet, however, which we hear of was one built by our great King Alfred, to protect his dominions from the attacks of the Danes.

He designed a ship from the model of those used by the Greeks, Romans, and Carthaginians, similar to the Maltese galley employed down to a very recent date in the Mediterranean. His ships are said to have been twice as large as any vessels of war used by other nations at that period. They were large galleys, propelled by sixty oars, with a deck above that part where the rowers sat. On the deck stood the fighting men and mariners, who managed the sails, for they had masts and sails as well as oars. There were besides probably small towers or breast-works at the stern and bow to contribute to their means of attack and defence. These ships were built of well-seasoned materials, commanded by experienced officers, whom the king had collected from all quarters, and manned by expert seamen. The commanders were ordered to go forth in quest of the Danes, to attack wherever they encountered them, and to give no quarter; orders which were strictly obeyed, and which for the time were most efficacious in clearing the coast of pirates. In consequence of the ease with which the ships were moved through the water, and from their being always able to keep the weather-gauge, as likewise from the strange appearance which they presented to their enemies, Alfred's commanders were not afraid of attacking twice or thrice their own number of the enemy, and invariably came off victorious. Indeed they had nearly the same advantage over the Danes which a steamer at the present day has over a fleet of Chinese junks. Alfred, it is said, caused surveys to be made of the coasts of Norway and Lapland, and sent out ships to the polar regions in search of whales.

I have met with an old writer, who describes a far more remarkable achievement than any of these. He was a monk, of course, and his knowledge of geography we may suspect was rather limited, when he tells us that in the reign of Alfred a voyage was performed to the Indies by the way of the north-east — that is to say, round the north of Asia — under the command of a certain monk, Swithelm, who, as his reward, was made Bishop of Sherburn. The mission was undertaken to aid the Christians of a place called Saint Thomas, on the continent of India, and we are assured that the curiosities which were brought back, and are fully described, are exactly like the productions found in India, when it became more fully known. The expedition, if it ever took place, must have proceeded down the African coast and round the Cape of Good Hope. If so, the seamen of Britain, with a monk as their commander, succeeded in an enterprise which, having been totally forgotten, immortalised Bartholomew Diaz as the discoverer of the Stormy Cape full six centuries afterwards. We must not place more faith in the narrative than it deserves, but one thing is certain, that if any long or perilous voyages were performed, the prints of ships pretending to be those of the days of King Alfred found on tapestries, old illustrated histories and other works are not slightly incorrect. When a boy, I used very strongly to suspect that if a ship had ever been built after the model of the prints exhibited in the History of England, she would either, as sailors say, have turned the turtle directly she was launched, or have gone boxing about the compass beyond the control of those on board her; but as to standing up to a breeze, or going ahead, I saw that that was impossible. I have since discovered, with no little satisfaction, when examining into the subject, that the verbal descriptions of the ships of those days give a very different idea to that which the prints and tapestry work do, which so offended my nautical instincts.

Large substantial vessels, we may depend on it, existed in those days, and though encumbered with much top hamper, and rigged only with square sails, they did not carry the high towers nor the absurdly cut sails which they are represented to have done in all the illustrated histories I have seen. The celebrated galleys of King Alfred are described by an old writer as very long, narrow, and deep vessels, heavily ballasted on account of the high deck on which the soldiers and seamen stood above the heads of the rowers. Of these rowers, there were four to work each oar, and as there were thirty-eight oars on a side, there must have been upwards of three hundred rowers to each vessel. Whether these vessels had more than one mast is uncertain. From their want of beam they would have run much risk of turning over had they attempted to sail except directly before the wind. They moved with great rapidity; and in an engagement off the Isle of Wight, they ran down the Danish vessels in succession till the whole fleet of the enemy was either sunk, driven on shore, or put to flight.

The navy of England still further increased during the reign of Alfred's immediate successors, till, in the time of King Edgar (A.D. 957), it had reached the number of three thousand six hundred ships at least, "with which," as say his chroniclers, "he vindicated the right claimed in all ages by the sovereigns of this island to the dominion of the seas (meaning the seas surrounding England), and acquired to himself the great title of *The Protector of Commerce.*"

This navy was divided into three fleets, each of twelve hundred sail, which he kept in constant readiness for service, one on the eastern coast, another on the western, and a third on the northern coasts of the kingdom, to defend them against the depredations of the Danish and Norman pirates, and to secure the navigation of the adjacent seas; which, that he might the more effectually do, he, every year after the festival of Easter, went on board the fleet on the eastern coast, and sailing westward with it scoured the channel of pirates; and having looked into all the ports, bays, and creeks between the Thames' mouth and Land's End, quitted this fleet and sent it back, and going on board the western fleet did the like in those parts, as also on the coasts of England, Scotland, and Ireland, and among the Hebrides or Western Islands, where being met by the northern fleet, he went on board the same, and came round to the Thames' mouth. Thus encompassing all his dominions, and providing for the security of their coasts, he rendered an invasion impracticable, and kept his sailors in continual exercise. This he did for the whole sixteen years of his reign.

May our rulers ever possess the wisdom of Alfred, the greatest of England's kings, and by the same means preserve inviolate the shores of our native land.

It would have been well for Old England had all its monarchs imitated the excellent example set by King Edgar, and had never allowed any decrease in the naval establishment. Let the present generation do as he did, with the modifications changed times and circumstances have introduced, and then, although we may not be able correctly to troll forth "*Hearts of oak* are our ships," we may sing truly —

> "*Iron coats wear our ships,*
> *Lion hearts have our men;*
> *We always are ready;*
> *Then steady, boys, steady;*
> *We'll fight and we'll conquer again and again.*"

King Edgar appears to have been the last great naval sovereign of the Saxon race. When his son Ethelred, by the murder of his brother Edward, came to the throne, his navy was so neglected that the Danes made incursions with impunity on every part of the coasts of England, and in the year A.D. 991, they extorted no less a sum than 10,000 pounds from that wicked monarch, or rather from his unfortunate subjects (who, depend upon it, had to pay the piper), as the price of their forbearance in refraining from levying a further amount of plunder.

This circumstance might have served as a strong hint to the English of those times to keep up the strength of their navy, but it does not appear to have had any such effect; and even that wise monarch, Canute the Great, had only thirty-two ships afloat. We find, however, that when Harold, son of Earl Godwin, was striving to maintain his claim to the crown of England (A.D. 1066), he fitted out a numerous fleet, with which he was able to defeat his rivals. Now, as we are elsewhere told that one of these rivals alone had a navy of three hundred sail, his must have been of considerable magnitude. After his death, at the battle of Hastings, his sons and several of his chief nobility escaped in the remnant of their fleet to the coasts of Norway, and gave no little annoyance to the Norman Conqueror, William.

It must be remembered that the Duke of Normandy, as he was then styled, had, to bring over his army, nine hundred transports; but he burnt them when he landed, to show his own followers, as well as the Saxons, that he had come to die or to conquer.

Such is a very brief account of the navy of England up to the time of the Norman Conquest.

It is more easy to describe what the ships of those days were not like than to give an exact description of them. Certainly the ships represented on tapestry, on seals, or on coins are very unlike any piece of naval architecture which ever had existence. Every seaman knows how impossible it is for an ordinary landsman to draw anything like a faithful representation of a ship, however picturesque a production the thing might appear to him. We are bound, therefore, to look with grave suspicion on the performances of the draughtsmen of those early days; who had but a poor idea of drawing the objects they had constantly before their eyes.

Our artist has given a fair representation, I suspect, of what a ship was in those early days. She probably had another mast aft, and some more head sail of a square shape. What are called fore and aft sails were not generally used till comparatively modern times. She looks as if she really was fitted to cross the channel, to carry a number of men, and even to contend with heavy seas. The tall masts, heavy rigging, and large tops, on which a number of men could stand and fight, had not then been employed on these northern seas.

I have hitherto spoken only of the war-ships of those early days. There were, however, merchant-ships which traded to far-distant shores. They were probably good wholesome craft, of somewhat tub-like form, of about the size of a vessel of the present day of one hundred to one hundred and fifty tons, rigged with two or three big sails, with one bank of oars, and manned by a hardy and numerous crew, who patiently waited for the coming of a fair wind before they ventured to make sail; and who, though generally addicted to hugging the shore, yet at times ventured to stand out into the boundless ocean, guided alone by the stars. The mercantile marine was encouraged in every way by the wiser sovereigns of the Saxon race, as the nursery of those stout seamen who would prove the best bulwarks of their country against foreign invasion.

We now come to a fresh epoch in the history of Old England; but as no writer of those days has thought fit to enlighten us as to naval affairs, our knowledge of them is meagre and unsatisfactory.

Literature, in that iron age, was chiefly confined to monastic cells; we hear of bishops becoming warriors, and leading their armies to battle on the field, and it is recorded that there were other monks besides Swithelm who took to the profession. Probably some sailors, after growing weary of cutting throats on the high seas, and other acts of piracy, assumed the easy and dignified position of monks, and endowed their monasteries with their wealth; but then it may be questioned whether they were likely to have been able to read, much less to write.

William of Normandy had, for some time, too much to do on shore in keeping his new subjects in order, to attend to affairs afloat; but he at length was compelled to build and fit out a fleet to defend his kingdom from the attacks of the Danes, instigated by the sons and followers of Harold. He, after much consideration, hit upon a new plan for raising a fleet, and it is a point of history worthy of recollection. He exempted five of the principal ports of the kingdom from all taxes, impositions, or burdens, on condition that each should fit out, man, and support a certain number of vessels for a certain period. They were Dover, Romney, Sandwich, Hastings, and Rye, and were thence called the Cinque Ports.

Though others were afterwards added, the name has ever since been retained. It appears by Doomsday Book that Dover, Romney, and Sandwich, severally, were to provide *twenty* vessels each, with *twenty-one* men, provisioned for *fifteen* days at their own charge. After that time the crews were to be supported by the Crown.

Another document states that, besides the twenty men, there is to be a master of the mariners, who is to receive sixpence a-day, a constable, who is to receive a like sum, and each mariner threepence a-day. These five ports, with other smaller ones attached to them, provided in all 57 ships, 1187 men, and 57 boys, one boy being on board each ship. These boys were called gromets. A gromet is now the name given to a ring of rope used sometimes to slide up and down the mast, and I conclude, therefore, that the duty of these boys was to swarm up the mast, and set and furl the lighter sails.

In the reign of King John (A.D. 1217), Herbert of Burgo, the captain of Dover, hearing of an invasion intended by Lewis the Elder, son of the King of France, in favour of the discontented barons, assembled in the king's name forty tall ships from the Cinque Ports, and took, sunk, and discomfited eighty sail of Frenchmen in a gallant engagement on the high seas. These ports did great service under Henry the Third and Edward the First. Among other brave deeds, they fitted out one hundred sail, and encountered two hundred sail of Frenchmen with such success, that they effectually ruined the navy of France. Many years happily passed before that country recovered the loss of her men and ships. I will give a fuller account of this action further on. Numberless are the tales of a like description to be told.

Besides the twenty-three mariners which these warships of the Cinque Ports carried, there were on board a considerable number of fighting men, knights, and their retainers, armed with bucklers, spears, and bows and arrows. They also used slings and catapults, and perhaps stink-pots, like those employed by the Chinese at the present day, as well as other ancient engines of warfare. That ships of war were capable of holding a considerable number of men, we learn from the well-known account of the death of the brave young Prince William, son of Henry the First. When crossing the channel from Normandy, in an attempt to make his ship get ahead of that of his father, he kept too close in with the shore, and consequently ran on a rock called the Shatteras. He might have been saved; but hearing that his sister, the Countess of Perche, still remained on board, he ordered the boat in which he was escaping to put back to rescue her. On arriving alongside, so large a number of people jumped into the boat, that she was swamped, and all were lost. On this occasion two hundred people perished, only one, the ship's butcher, escaping to the shore, and through him the sad tidings were known. Now, if we turn to any old illustrated History of England, we shall find, probably, a print professing to describe this very event. Yet, on examining it, we shall see that the vessel is not large enough to carry twenty people, much less two hundred. The artists either made their sketches from river barges, or row-boats, or drew a ship from one they saw at a distance, and having altered and adorned her to suit their own fancies afterwards, put a crew on board, utterly forgetful of the proper proportions between the ship and the men.

In the reign of the son and successor of William the Conqueror, William the Second, called Rufus, the first great crusade against the Saracen possessors of the Holy Land was commenced, in the year 1095. To aid in that extraordinary expedition, a large fleet was fitted out in England, and placed under the command of the Earl of Essex. The ships, as they had a long voyage to perform, and a number of armed men and provisions to carry, must have been of considerable size. As the use of the mariner's compass was unknown to them, they must have coasted round the shores of France, Portugal, and Spain, before they entered the Mediterranean.

The Atlantic in those days was not likely to be more tranquilly disposed than it is at present, and thus the mariners must have been expert and brave, and the ships well found, or they would not have performed the voyage in safety. We know that the Crusaders had horses, but they probably were transported from the neighbouring shores of the Mediterranean, and any favourite war-steeds which came from England were conveyed across France. Neither Henry the First nor Stephen, from A.D. 1100 to 1135, maintained a navy, properly so-called, but on the few occasions that they required ships, they hired them of the merchants, called on the Cinque Ports to supply them, or had them built for the purpose.

Probably all vessels in those days carried oars, or long sweeps, to assist them in calms, and in going in and out of harbours; but many craft of considerable burden depended solely on oars for moving at all. There appears to be much difference of opinion as to how these oars were worked when there were several tiers, and I therefore return to the subject already touched on in the first chapter. It is most probable that there was one space, or between decks, devoted entirely to the rowers. This space was fitted with a succession of rows of benches one higher than the other, but not one above another. That is to say, that the bench immediately higher than the first was placed in the interval between it and the one behind it, so that the rowers sitting on this higher bench had their feet pressed against the bench below them, others on the tier above having their feet on their bench. As the tiers were higher and higher in the vessel's sides, the oars would be longer and longer, and would project far beyond the lower ones; indeed, they would become sweeps, and probably the inner part of each would extend completely across the vessel, and thus the upper oars on the same tier would not be opposite to each other. The lowest tier would perhaps be pulled only by one or two men, and as the tiers rose in height, and consequently the oars in length, more men would be added. Then, again, the lower tiers would have many more oars than the upper, and consequently even more men would be seated on the lower than on the upper benches. This, I think, is the best solution as to the difficulty regarding the mode in which the rowers of a large galley were placed. The hold and the deck immediately below the rowers was thus left for cargo and stores, and perhaps for sleeping-places, while the deck and forecastle, and aftercastle or poop above them, were free for working the sails and for righting. The officers, and perhaps the crew, slept under the poop and forecastle, and in other buildings on deck, as is the case on board many vessels at the present day, only the forecastles and poops were more like those of a Chinese junk than of any modern European craft.

Henry the Second, in the year 1171, collected or built a fleet of four hundred ships of great size, for the purpose of carrying over his troops for the conquest of Ireland, which country he annexed to the English crown. These ships, as no enemy was to be encountered on the ocean, were merely transports.

Richard the First, of the Lion Heart, who began to reign 1189, fitted out a fleet, which, when assembled in the port of Messina in Sicily, in the year 1189, ready to carry his army to the shores of the Holy Land, consisted of sixteen capital ships of extraordinary burden (occupying the position of three-deckers), one hundred and fifty ordinary ships of war, and fifty-three galleys, besides vessels of less size and tenders. In his passage to Acre, known also as Ptolemais, he encountered a huge vessel of the Saracens, laden with ammunition and provisions, bound for the same place which was then besieged by the Christian army. She was called the Dromunda, and her size was enormous. Though she appeared like some huge castle floating on the sea, Richard ordered his galleys to attack her, and as they approached, they were received by showers of missiles, Greek fire, and other horrible combustibles. It was no easy task to board so lofty a ship, but the king urged on his men, some of whom, jumping overboard, swam to the rudder, to which they secured ropes, and thus gained the power of steering her. The most active now climbed up her sides, but were driven back by the overwhelming number of her defenders. The galleys were next ordered to try the effect of their beaks; retiring to windward, and setting all their sails, as well as working away with their oars, they bore down on the Dromunda with such force and velocity, that their iron beaks pierced the sides of the monstrous ship, which instantly began to sink, and out of fifteen hundred officers and men who composed her company, the whole, with the exception of fifty-five, were drowned. These latter were chiefly officers, none of the common men being received on board the galleys.

SINKING OF THE DROMUNDA.

It is very evident that the art of shipbuilding must have made considerable progress in that part of the world, when a ship of such a size could be constructed. The Dromunda could scarcely have been less in size than a fifty-gun ship in Nelson's day.

We here see the effect produced by rams, much in the way it is proposed to employ them in modern warfare. There will, however, be this difference in a naval battle of the future, that both sides will be provided with these formidable implements of warfare. Before Richard reached Acre a fierce naval engagement had taken place between the besiegers and the besieged. The latter came out of port with their galleys two and two, preserving a similar array in their advance. The Crusaders prepared to receive them, moving to a distance, so that they should not be denied free egress. The Crusaders then disposed their ships in a curved line, so that if the enemy attempted to break through they might be enclosed and defeated. In the upper tiers the shields interlaced were placed circularly, and the rowers sat close together, that those above might have freer scope. The sea being perfectly calm, no impediment was offered to the blows of the warriors or the strokes of the rowers; advancing nearer to each other, the trumpets sounded on both sides, and mingled their dread clangour. First, they contended with missiles, but the Crusaders more earnestly plied their oars, and pierced the enemy's ships with the beaks of their own. Soon the battle became general; the oars became entangled, and the combatants fought hand to hand.

There was one English galley which, through the rashness of the crew, got close alongside an enemy, who set her in flames with their Greek fire. The Saracens on this rushing in at all parts, the rowers leaped into the sea, but a few soldiers remained through desperation. Those few overcame the many, and retook their half-burned ship. The weapons used were swords, axes lances, arrows, and other missiles, as well as engines for casting large stones; and both Saracens and Christians employed that burning oil commonly called the Greek fire, which is said to consume both flint and iron. It was the invention of the seventh century, and was long used with terrific effect by the Greeks, who called it the liquid fire. It is supposed to have been composed of naphtha, pitch, and sulphur, with other ingredients. It was propelled in a fluid state through brazen tubes from the prows of vessels and from fortifications, with as much facility as water is now thrown from the fire-engine; igniting the moment it was exposed to the air, when it became a continuous stream of fire, carrying with it torture and destruction. Water increased its power, and it could only be extinguished by vinegar or sand; while, in addition to its other horrors, it emitted a stifling smoke, loud noise, and disgusting stench. Tow dipped in it was fastened to the heads of arrows, which thus became carriers of unquenchable flame. It was kept in jars or large bottles. It was probably introduced into England before the time of Richard the First, for in 1195 a payment was made by the king for carrying Greek fire and other implements from London to Nottingham.

Fire-ships were, indeed, of far earlier date than the days of Richard the First. We find them in use among the Tyrians in the time of Alexander the Great. It is related that at the siege of Tyre, when a mole was being constructed to join that city to the continent, the inhabitants, having loaded a large ship heavily by the stern with sand and stones, for the purpose of raising her head out of the water, and having filled her with all sorts of combustible matter, they drove her violently with sails and oars against the mole, when they set fire to her, the seamen escaping in their boats. The mole being in a great measure built of wood, with wooden towers on it, was by this device utterly destroyed. Thus we see that the Tyrians invented and successfully employed fire-ships before the Christian era. We are apt to consider many other discoveries modern which were known to the ancients. For instance, an Italian author, some three centuries ago, describes a ship weighed in his time out of the lake of Riccia, where it had lain sunk and neglected for above thirteen hundred years. It was supposed to have belonged to Trajan.

He observed, he says, "that the pine and cypress of which it was built had lasted most remarkably. On the outside it was built with double planks, daubed over with Greek pitch, caulked with linen rags, and over all a sheet of lead, fastened on with little copper nails."

Here we have caulking and sheathing together known in the first century of the Christian era; for, of course, the sheet of lead nailed over the outside with copper nails was sheathing, and that in great perfection, the copper nails being used instead of iron, which, when once rusted in the water by the working of the ship, soon lose their hold, and drop out.

Captain Saris, in a voyage to Japan in the year 1613, describes a junk of from eight to ten hundred tons burden, sheathed all over with iron. As in the days of the Plantagenets the country had not the advantage of possessing a Board of Lords Commissioners of the Admiralty, nor, indeed, any office in which the records of the ships built, altered, re-built, or pulled to pieces were kept, or, indeed, any naval records whatever, we are without the means of ascertaining what special improvements were introduced either in shipbuilding or in the fitting or manning of ships during each particular reign. Indeed, for several centuries very slow progress appears to have been made in that art, which ultimately tended to raise England to the prosperous state she has so long enjoyed.

Chapter Three.

The Navy in the days of the Plantagenets — from A.D. 1087 to A.D. 1327.

William Rufus, in 1087, had scarcely a vessel which deserved the name of a ship of war. The trade of the country, however, was carried on by small craft, of which there were great numbers; there remained also some of the transports of former years, but William when expecting the invasion of his kingdom by his brother Robert, found to his sorrow that he possessed no ships of sufficient size to compete with those of the Normans. Being unwilling to weaken his land forces by sending them on board such ships as he possessed, he engaged all the large trading-vessels of the country, and invited mariners to embark in the transports. He gave commissions, also, to all the traders to sink, burn, and destroy every Norman vessel they could meet with, and offered considerable rewards for every successful action. Besides this, he published proclamations inviting all private persons to fit out vessels on their own account, encouraging them with the promise of similar rewards. Numbers of traders accepted the commission, and the sea swarmed with privateers. They were of small size, but were manned by bold seamen, who encouraged one another by their numbers. Robert, who was aware that the English had no fleet, not expecting any resistance at sea, thought only of loading his transports with as many men as they could carry. His ships were therefore ill-prepared for action, being overloaded with men, and he little expected any opposition from the small ships of the English.

The latter, meantime, obtained exact intelligence of the movements of the Normans, while they kept secret their own forces and plans. The Normans at length sailed, and had no time to laugh at the smallness of the English ships before they began to quake at their numbers. The latter bore down upon them like a pack of hounds on a stag, and, encouraged by the promised rewards, fought with the greatest fury. In vain the Normans attempted to fly; they were overtaken and overpowered by the multitude of their assailants. The number that perished by the sword and drowning was astonishing; those who attempted to escape were overtaken, and shared the fate of the others; and but few got back to Normandy with the news of their defeat. Never was a sea-fight in which personal courage was more nobly exhibited; never a more complete victory, nor ever, apparently, slighter means of obtaining it.

The Normans called the English pirates, but they were properly privateers, and the original armament to which they were united, though a poor one, was a royal force. William punctually paid the promised rewards.

People were generally too pleasantly employed in those mediaeval days in knocking their neighbours on the head, or in storming and demolishing their castles, and other similar pastimes on shore, to attend to any subject so unromantic as shipbuilding or navigation.

Still the monarchs of the Plantagenet race had ships of their own; but their chief notion of keeping up a navy was by laying taxes on the seaports, on commerce, and on the fisheries, thus crippling the surest means by which a fleet could be maintained. The chief naval events of the intermediate reigns have been described in the preceding chapter.

John, we are told, had a naval establishment of ships and officers, with certain boards for its government. He had not many vessels, however, as he chiefly depended on the Cinque Ports to furnish him with ships, while he laid an embargo on merchant-vessels in case of necessity; and turned them into ships of war. He must have had a great notion, however, of keeping up the dignity of England on the ocean, as he passed an ordinance that all ships should lower their topsails to the English flag; a custom which was preserved for many centuries. Foreigners, however, did not always show themselves willing to conform to the custom, and it was more than once the cause of quarrels between England and other nations. Still, even at the present day, English men-of-war do not salute foreign ships in that or any other way, unless the latter pay the compliment to them first, or at the same time.

Philip Augustus of France having attacked his ally, the Earl of Flanders, the king fitted out a numerous fleet, which he placed under the command of the Earl of Salisbury, giving him directions to destroy rather than to capture any of the enemy's ships. The Earl of Salisbury observed his instructions, and followed the movements of the enemy, waiting for an opportunity to bear down upon them. The French ships, amounting to more than nine hundred sail, moved slowly over the sea, he watching them vigilantly, and bearing the reproaches of his officers, who thought him deficient in courage. On the third day a slight storm having thrown the French fleet into confusion, the earl bore down upon them. The winds had so terrified the French that they were in no condition to stand before a furious enemy. The English, who were far better sailors, were in high courage, and so furiously assaulted the French ships that in a short time upwards of a hundred were sunk, many more running on shore, while scarcely forty got back to the ports of France.

Another important action, before-mentioned, occurred in this reign. Prince Louis, afterwards Louis the Eighth, to whose father Pope Innocent had made a liberal present of England without consulting its inhabitants, had set sail from Calais at the head of a large army, convoyed by eighty large ships of war. Hubert de Burgo, with a great baron, Philip D'Albiney, as his lieutenant, assembled all the ships they could from the Cinque Ports, though the whole did not amount to more than half that of the French fleet. The latter was under the command of Eustace the monk, who had formerly been in the pay of John, but had lately transferred his services to Louis. The English ships were armed with strong beaks, like those of the Roman galleys, and their mode of attack consisted, as of yore, in charging the vessels of the enemy, and endeavouring to pierce their sides with their iron rams. They were impelled chiefly by oars, but also carried sails, to enable them to bear down with greater speed on the enemy; hence the importance of obtaining the weather-gage. The two fleets came in sight of each other in the Straits of Dover, on the 24th of August, 1217. The English admirals having by their skilful manoeuvres obtained the weather-gage, bore down on the enemy with irresistible force. In addition to other means of offence, they had brought on board a number of barrels of unslaked lime; on nearing the enemy they poured water on the lime, so as to slake the whole mass, and the smoke thus created being borne by the wind into the faces of the French, prevented them from seeing the operations of the foe till it was too late to avoid them. The English boarded, their first endeavour being to cut away the rigging and halliards of the French ships, when the masts and sails went over the side. Most of the French knights, preferring death to imprisonment, leaped overboard. Throwing their grapnels on board, the English made a furious onslaught on the enemy, the crossbow-men and archers, under Sir Philip D'Albiney, discharging their bows and arrows, did immense execution. Out of the whole fleet, fifteen only escaped. De Burgo's great aim, however, was to obtain possession of the traitor Eustace, and diligent search being made, the quondam ecclesiastic was found in the hold of one of the captured vessels, when he was immediately killed. The French fleet was put to flight, the crews of those which escaped landed on the Kentish coast. The victory prevented Louis from obtaining further reinforcements from France, and showed the English barons, who had hitherto adhered to his cause, that it would be hopeless to attempt the subjugation of England. They, therefore, at once made their peace with the king, and Louis was glad to get off by renouncing all claim to the English crown. We now come to the long reign of Henry the Third, A.D. 1216. Frequent expeditions were fitted out on his demand by the Cinque Ports, and by other maritime towns, while merchant-vessels were occasionally pressed into his service to carry him and his troops over to France. The king himself also possessed a fleet of some importance, one of his ships carrying, besides the commander and officers and the regular fighting men, fully thirty mariners. Many merchant-vessels of the present day of eight or nine hundred tons, do not carry a larger crew. In those days we read that a number of piratical vessels, both British and of other nations, scoured the ocean, and committed great depredations both along the coast and on the peaceable merchantmen who sailed up and down it.

The great object of the commander of a fleet in those days was to gain the weather-gage, then to bear down under all sail in order to strike the broadsides of the enemy's ships; when the one generally attempted to board the other, if not to throw stink-pots into their antagonists' vessels, or what were called fire-works, a sort of hand grenades; and sometimes slaked lime to blind the foe with the vapour. With this object in view the admiral manoeuvred his fleet for hours together, rowing and sailing. As guns, when they first came into use, carried no great distance, they were not fired till ships got close together. Ships in action very frequently caught fire and blew up, and sometimes locked in a deadly embrace, were destroyed together. Trumpeters had an important part to play, not only to make signals, but to create as much noise as possible. The good ship called the *Matthew Gonson*, of the burden of three hundred tons, whereof was owner old Master William Gonson, paymaster of the king's navy, fitted out at this time for a voyage to the islands of Candia and Chio to bring back wine and other produce, besides the hundred men of her company, had six gunners and four trumpeters. Probably men-of-war had many more such musicians.

CANNON AS AT FIRST USED.

Edward the First, A.D. 1272, ordained various laws and ordinances for the government of his navy, which was now, though still furnished chiefly by the maritime ports, better organised than hitherto. He claimed, also, the right of England to the sovereignty of the narrow seas, asserting that from time immemorial it had been undisputed. About the year 1290, the pennant used at the present day by all ships commissioned by officers of the Royal Navy was first adopted.

In the reign of Edward the Second no important maritime event occurred, though squadrons were occasionally sent away on various services.

It is only by examining carefully into the details given by historians of the naval combats which took place in those ages, that we can hope to form a correct guess as to the size and construction of a ship, and the method of manoeuvring her. We are now coming to a very important epoch in naval matters, the reign of Edward the Third. 1327, when the mariner's compass was discovered, or rather became known in Europe, and cannon were first introduced on board ships.

Edward gained the title of "The King of the Sea," and raised the naval glory of England to a higher pitch than it had ever before attained by his many victorious combats on the ocean. The greatest naval engagement which occurred during the middle ages was that known as the battle of Sluys, when Philip the Sixth sat on the throne of France. The English fleet consisted of only 260 ships fit for warfare. The French, whose fleet amounted to no less than 400 sail, lay securely, as they thought, in the harbour of Sluys. Edward embarked on board the cog *Thomas*, commanded by Richard Fyall, and attended by several noblemen. A cog was a craft larger than those usually designated ships — the cog *John*, which is spoken of, had a crew of eighty-two men, and probably she carried besides a considerable number of knights and soldiers. Many ships of the English fleet must have been of small size. Froissart says that the French fleet consisted of 140 large ships, besides hanquebos with 35,000 men on board, Normans, Picards, and Genoese. The masts of so numerous an assemblage of vessels, as they were seen in the harbour of Sluys, resembled rather a forest than a fleet. Of these ships, nineteen were remarkable for their enormous size. Besides other implements of warfare, quantities of large stones were stored in the tops and also in small boats hoisted to the mast-heads, to be hurled on the assailants. The French had secured their ships together by chains, to prevent the English from breaking through them. Among the ships in the leading rank was the *Christopher*, full of Genoese archers, with the *Edward, Katherine, Rose*, and other large cogs which had formerly been captured from the English.

Edward had perfect confidence in the valour and prowess of his seamen and men-at-arms, and, notwithstanding the superiority of the enemy in numbers, he resolved to open a passage through them. Having ordered all his ships to be in readiness, he placed the strongest in the front, and filled those which were at each end of the line with archers. Also between every two ships of archers he placed one filled with men-at-arms. He likewise ordered another line to be formed on the side, as a body of reserve, and filled those ships also with archers, that they might be ready to support or relieve any most requiring aid.

The English fleet approaching the haven of Sluys in the manner described, found the French already lying in order of battle, in three divisions, waiting for them. The English having gained the advantage of the wind and sun by their dexterity and management, the king ordered the signal for engaging to be given. The Normans, perceiving the English to tack as they did to get the wind, thought that they were taking to their heels, and began to triumph. But they soon found out their mistake, and, being able seamen and brave combatants, prepared for the fight. They began the battle by advancing with the *Great Christopher*, and, with a vast noise of trumpets and other instruments, attempted to break the line, to come at the ship in which they supposed the British king to be. They were received with a general shout, and during continual huzzas the English poured such showers of arrows from their long bows into the enemy's ships as soon covered their decks with dead and wounded men, and put the whole fleet into general consternation. The *Great Christopher* was taken in the beginning of the battle, and all who were in her were either killed or made prisoners. The English, on this, filled her with archers, and sent her to annoy the Genoese ships, which formed part of the French fleet. And now death and destruction appeared on every side in their most terrible array. The very air was darkened with arrows, and the hostile ships rushing together, the men-at-arms engaged in close fight.

The English, taking advantage of the confusion into which they had put the French at the beginning of the fight, soon boarded them with the help of their grappling-irons, and pursuing their good fortune, obtained a complete victory, though a most bloody one, as their loss amounted to 4000 men killed and wounded. Great numbers of the French sailors desperately threw themselves into the sea, and submitted to a certain death rather than abide the repeated showers of English arrows; what also might have contributed more to this desperate resolution was that, on board the ships captured in the heat of battle, no quarter was given. The engagement lasted from eight in the morning till seven at night. The loss on the French side was enormous, 230 of their ships being captured; only about 30 having escaped. According to the Frenchmen's account of the battle, they lost two admirals, Bauchet, who was killed in action, and De Kernel, who was taken prisoner. King Edward behaved during the whole action with the most inimitable courage and conduct; regarding neither danger nor fatigue, he was always present where the battle raged the hottest.

During the night thirty French ships, endeavouring to escape, were attacked by the English, and on board of one of them, the *James of Dieppe*, after she had been engaged the whole night with the Earl of Huntingdon, 400 dead bodies were found. Certain old writers remark that the rostrum or beak used by the Romans could not have existed in the English ships, nor was the manoeuvre employed by which one ship attempts to break the oars of another. From this they conclude that the English fleet must have consisted of high-sided ships, worked chiefly by sails. Probably, however, they had oars also.

It is said that nearly 30,000 men were killed in this memorable battle. So apparently irretrievable was the disaster to the French that none of King Philip's counsellors had the courage to inform him of what had occurred. At length they bethought them of employing the court fool to communicate the disastrous intelligence. Accordingly, that dignified individual took an opportunity of remarking to the king that he considered the English arrant cowards.

"Why so, Master Wisdom?" asked Philip.

"Why does your Majesty ask? because they had not the courage to leap into the sea and be drowned as our brave Frenchmen did the other day, when your Majesty's ships went to the bottom."

In 1350 the warrior king, on board his cog *Thomas*, led his fleet to attack the Spaniards, who had ventured into the British Channel; he was accompanied by Edward, the Black Prince, and numerous great personages, with nearly four hundred knights. The king, attired in a black velvet jacket and beaver hat, took post on the bow of his ship, eagerly looking out for the enemy. As they did not appear, to beguile the time he caused his minstrels to play a German dance, and made Sir John Chandos, who had recently introduced it, to sing with them. From time to time, however, he looked aloft at the man stationed in the top of the mast to announce the approach of the Spaniards. At length they were seen, numbering forty large ships, denominated carricks; strong and handsome were they to behold — each mast was adorned with rich standards and banners, and their tops filled with soldiers and missiles. They, however, it was evident, wished to avoid an action, but the king, leading his fleet, stood down upon them till he reached a heavy ship, when, reckless of consequences, he ordered the helmsman to lay her aboard. So violent was the blow that the masts of the cog *Thomas* went over the side, the men in the top were drowned, and the ship sprang a dangerous leak. The Spaniard sheering off, Edward grappled another enemy; but now the cog *Thomas* sinking, the king and his crew took possession of the prize. In her he pushed into the thickest of the fight. The Prince of Wales' ship, also nigh to sinking, had grappled her huge adversary, when the Earl of Lancaster arriving and shouting, "Derby to the rescue!" boarded and obtained possession of the Spaniard, throwing all who resisted into the sea. Scarcely had the prince and his followers got on board the prize, when his own ship foundered. Sir Robert de Namur having grappled with a huge ship was carried by her out from among the fleet; the two combatants were rapidly leaving the rest of the ships astern, when Sir Robert's valet, Hannekin, bravely cutting the halliards of the principal sail, the English, taking advantage of the confusion, boarded and drove the Spaniards into the sea. Thus the Spanish fleet was completely beaten, and twenty-six large ships captured.

The British seem to have been as prone in those days as at present to seek for victory by laying the enemy on board and trusting to the strength of their own arms. At present, instead of battle-axes and clubs, or spears, or two-handed swords they have a fondness for their cutlasses and pistols. In the days, before Britannia could loudly roar with her thunder, naval combats were carried on with all the noise and hubbub the men on either side could create with their voices, as also with the braying forth of trumpets and beating of gongs and drums, in the hope of thus striking terror into the hearts of their enemies. How great is the contrast between such a naval engagement as has been described and one at the present day. In solemn silence the crews grimly stand at their guns, stripped generally to the waist. Not a sound is heard, not a word spoken, except perhaps one hearty cheer, a response to the captain's brief address. Slowly and steadily the hostile fleets approach each other till the signal is given to commence the deadly strife, and then in a moment, like fierce monsters awakened from sleep, they send from their cannons' mouths a quick succession of terrific roars, fire, and smoke, which laugh to scorn all the trumpet braying and shouting of our ancestors.

After the famous battle of Crescy, King Edward laid siege to Calais with a fleet of 738 ships, having on board 14,956 mariners, each of whom received 4 pence per diem. Of these ships, no more than 25 belonged actually to the king. The latter carried about 419 seamen only, which was not more than 17 seamen to each ship. Some, however, had 25 seamen, and others less. Many of the ships furnished by the maritime ports were larger than the king's. The total cost of the war, which lasted one year and 131 days, was 127,101 pounds, 2 shillings 9 pence, for even in those romantic days people could not knock each other on the head free of all charge, it must be remembered. The mention of that 127,101 pounds 2 shillings 9 pence also shows that their accounts must have been kept with most praiseworthy exactness.

Only great nations, to whom victory has generally been awarded by the God of battles, can afford to talk of their defeats. Though in most cases successful, Edward's arms met with a severe repulse before Rochelle, to the relief of which place he had sent forty ships, under the young Earl of Pembroke. "They were encountered by a French squadron of forty sail of capital ships," we are told, "besides thirteen able frigates, well manned, and commanded by four experienced officers. The earl was taken prisoner, and nearly every ship was captured or sunk." Though employed by France, they were Spaniards, supplied by the King of Castile. In addition to the large number of men-at-arms on board the Spanish ships, whose weapons were crossbows and cannon, large bars of iron and lead were used. The Spaniards bore down upon the small English ships with loud shouts and great noise; the English shouted in return, but were unable to climb up the lofty sides of the Spaniards. In the first day of the battle the Spaniards lost two barges, and the next day the earl's ship was attacked and captured by four large Spanish ships full of soldiers, while most of his fleet were either taken or destroyed.

Our national pride will make us examine narrowly to discover the cause of this disaster. In the first place, the earl, though brave, was inexperienced; then some of those forty French ships were larger than the forty English ships, and the able frigates were quick rowing galleys, full of men-at-arms, who must have done much mischief. The French on this occasion also made use of balistas and other machines for throwing bars of iron and great stones, to sink the English ships. They had also in another way got ahead of the English, for they had provided themselves with cannon, which the latter had not as yet got. This was the first naval engagement in which such engines of destruction were employed.

History is read by the naval and military man, and indeed by any one, to very little purpose, unless facts like these are not only carefully noted, but duly acted on; unless we take warning by the errors and neglects of our predecessors. It is not only necessary to be well-armed in appearance, but to be as well armed in reality, as those are with whom we may possibly be called to fight. It is wise not only to adopt new inventions likely to be of service, but if possible to have them already in use before they are adopted by our enemies. The gun of those days was a thick tube of wood, bound together with iron hoops, and probably could send a shot of three or four pounds little more than two or three hundred yards with very uncertain aim. What a contrast to the "Woolwich Infant" of the present day, with its shot of several hundredweight, whizzing for five miles or more through the air, with almost a certainty of hitting its object at the termination of its journey.

Chapter Four.

Ships and Commerce to the reign of Henry the Seventh — from A.D. 1327 to A.D. 1509.

In the early part of the reign of Edward the Third, the French introduced cannon on board their ships, chiefly in consequence of which his fleet, under the young Earl of Pembroke, as I have described, was defeated before Rochelle. He took care, however, that this should not again occur, and by the year 1338 he appears to have introduced them on board most of his ships, and by the end of his reign no ships of war were without them. Their employment, of course, effected a great change in naval warfare, but a far greater revolution was about to take place in the whole system of navigation, by the introduction of the mariner's compass. I have before stated that if not discovered it was at all events improved by Flavio Gioja, of Amain, in the kingdom of Naples, about A.D. 1300. It was soon discovered that the needle does not point, in all places, truly to the North Pole, but that it varies considerably in different degrees of longitude, and this is called the variation of the needle. It has also another variation, called the declination, or dip. The cause of these phenomena is still utterly unknown. The means of steering with almost perfect accuracy across the pathless ocean, gave a confidence to mariners, when they lost sight of land, which they had never before possessed, and in time induced them to launch forth in search of new territories in hitherto unexplored regions. The English were, however, too much occupied with foreign wars or domestic broils to attend much to navigation. We hear of a certain Nicholas of Lynn, a friar of Oxford, who, A.D. 1360, just sixty years after the use of the compass became known, sailed in charge of certain ships to visit and explore all the islands to the north of Europe. He, it is said, returned and laid before King Edward the Third an account of his discoveries in those northern regions, but what they were or what benefit resulted from them, history does not tell us. Father Nicholas's knowledge of navigation was probably somewhat limited and not very practical, and it is just probable that his voyage was not so extensive as it was intended to be; but that, having the pen of a ready writer, he drew on his imagination for a description of the countries he was supposed to have surveyed. At all events, we hear of no voyage undertaken at the sovereign's instigation till nearly two centuries later.

In the reign of Edward the Third, the Island of Madeira is said to have been discovered by a certain Lionel Machin, a citizen of London. The young citizen had been paying court to a lady, Arabella Darcy, whose father indignantly refused his suit; and not without reason, if we may judge of his character by his subsequent conduct. He collected a band of rovers and pursued the fair Arabella, who had gone to live in the neighbourhood of Bristol. He had fixed his eyes on a ship ready prepared for sea, the crew of which were on shore. Securing the lady, he carried her on board the ship, cut the cables, and made sail to the southward, without leave of the captain or owners. He met with due punishment, for, having made the then unknown island of Madeira, and he and Arabella having landed, the ship was driven to sea by a gale, leaving the two alone. She soon died of starvation, and when his companions ultimately returned, they found him in a sinking state, and buried him by the hapless damsel's side. A Portuguese captain hearing from the English pirates of the discovery of the island, sailed thither, and took possession of it in the name of his sovereign, Don John, and the infant Don Henry.

This account of Machin's adventures is doubted by many, but at all events it must be said that it is very much in accordance with the style of doing things in those days. Richard the Second began to reign A.D. 1377. Although probably no improvement took place in shipbuilding during his reign, it is not altogether destitute of nautical exploits. The maladministration of Government at the latter period of his grandfather's life, left the people in a discontented state, and this induced the French to make a descent on the English coast with a fleet of fifty ships, commanded by the Admiral de Vienne. They plundered and burnt Rye in Sussex, levied a contribution of a thousand marks on the inhabitants of the Isle of Wight, and finished off by burning Plymouth, Dartmouth, Portsmouth, and Hastings.

They were sufficiently long about these proceedings to enable the Abbot of Battle to fit out a fleet, with which he met them off Winchelsea, and completely defeated them. Their example was, however, followed by a body of Scotch pirates, who, with a number of ships under a Captain Mercer, ravaged the east coast of England. The Government, occupied with the coronation of the king, paid no attention to these insults.

Indignant at this state of things, a wealthy and truly patriotic citizen and merchant of London, John Philpot, at his own expense, fitted out a fleet manned by a thousand men, and set sail in person in quest of the pirate. He succeeded in coming up with him, and in bringing him to action, when he not only completely defeated him, but made him prisoner, capturing his entire fleet, as well as retaking all his English prizes, and fifteen richly-laden French and Spanish vessels. On his return, instead of being thanked, the gallant Philpot was tried for a misdemeanour, but so entirely did he succeed in vindicating his character, and so evident were the services he had rendered to the public, that he ultimately received the thanks and honours which were his due.

These circumstances should be borne in mind, for people of the present day are apt to fancy that the shores of Old England, since the time of the Danes perhaps, have ever been free from insult and annoyance, whereas we see that our neighbours across the channel have managed, whenever they have had the opportunity, without being so very seasick, to effect a very considerable amount of both one and the other.

A fleet, also, was sent to take possession of Cherbourg, which had been mortgaged by the King of Navarre to the English. The expedition was under the command of Philip and Peter Courtray. It was, however, encountered by a far superior Spanish squadron, which the English attacked with great fury, but Philip Courtray was severely wounded, and his brother Peter, who was taken prisoner with a number of knights and gentlemen, was never again heard of, numbers also losing their lives. While a large fleet under the Duke of Lancaster sailed to retrieve the loss, and was laying siege to Saint Malo, the French were ravaging the coasts of Cornwall. While, also, the Duke of Buckingham was in France, a fleet of French and Spanish galleys sailed up the Thames as far as Gravesend, which they plundered and burnt, as well as other places on the Kentish shore. Leaving the Thames, they sailed along the west coast, plundering and burning as they went. They were, however, met by a west country fleet, fitted out to attack them, and pursued to the Irish coast, where many were captured, and their prizes retaken. Still a sufficient force escaped to plunder and burn Winchelsea on their return.

On the accession of Charles the Sixth to the throne of France, he resolved to put in execution a scheme formed by his father to drive the English out of France by invading England itself. For this purpose, he purchased of various nations a fleet of 1600 sail to carry across an immense army which he had raised for the purpose. To defend his kingdom, Richard raised an army of 100,000 men, horse and foot, and equipped a fleet, placed under the command of the Earls of Arundel and Nottingham. Portsmouth and Plymouth fitted out small fleets of privateers, which sailed up the Seine, and made many prizes. Although there was no general engagement, the French fleet were cut off in detail, and in consequence of the strenuous efforts made by the English, the intended invasion was abandoned.

Henry the Fourth began to reign A.D. 1399. The French, in 1402, sent a fleet to assist Owen Glendowyr with an army of 12,000 men. They put into Milford Haven, and plundered the neighbourhood; but a fleet fitted out by the Cinque Ports, under Lord Berkley and Harry Percy, arrived there in time to capture fourteen of them before they had time to make their escape.

The principal admiral in this reign was Admiral Beaufort. He was styled Admiral of all the King's Fleet, both to the north and west; and among many other offices, he held those of Constable of Dover Castle and Warden of the Cinque Ports.

The fifth Henry, with whose name the famous victory of Agincourt over the French will ever be associated, began to reign A.D. 1413. He was so much occupied with his wars in France for the greater part of his reign, that he paid but little attention to naval affairs beyond obtaining the transports necessary to convey his armies across the channel. While he was carrying on his conquests in France, part of the French fleet came over and blockaded the English ships collected at Portsmouth and Southampton, and made an attempt to land on the Isle of Wight. They were, however, driven back with loss. Henry had, in the meantime, taken possession of Harfleur on the Seine. He was besieged by the French both by land and sea. The king accordingly despatched his brother the Duke of Bedford with a fleet of 500 ships, containing 20,000 men, to the relief of the town. They found the enemy's fleet, in which were several large Genoese carracks, lying before the haven of Harfleur, and pressing the siege with all possible vigour. As no relief could be given to the town without forcing a passage through the French fleet, an engagement was unavoidable. The English began the attack, and though the French maintained the fight for some hours, they gave way at last, and were totally defeated. Five hundred vessels were taken or sunk, together with five of the Genoese carracks, and nearly 20,000 men are reported to have been killed. The

whole English fleet entered the port in triumph, and carried a season-
able relief to the town.

GENOESE CARRACK.

Another important naval battle was fought during Henry's reign. Before he commenced his great and successful expedition to Normandy,
which province he regained for the crown of England, after it had
been lost for 215 years since the reign of King John, he despatched the
Earl of Huntingdon with a fleet of about 100 sail to scour the seas, that
his transports might cross without molestation. At this time the Duke
of Genoa had, in consequence of a treaty made with France, supplied
the French government with a squadron, consisting of eight large
carracks, and as many galleys, which had on board 600 crossbow-

men, under the command of John Grimaldi. These had united with the French fleet, consisting of 100 tall ships, and commanded by the Bastard of Bourbon. The Earl of Huntingdon speedily came up with the united fleets of France and Genoa at the mouth of the Seine. The engagement was long and desperate; the Genoese sustained the brunt of the engagement, their ships being larger and better formed than the French. One carrack especially, commanded by Lawrence Foglietta resisted the attacks of seven English ships. The English ships, it appears, were furnished with stages, which could be let down on the decks of the vessels they were attacking, so as to form a bridge across into them. Foglietta's ship was at length disengaged from her enemy by the dexterity of a sailor, who cut the cordage with which the stage had been secured to her side. Notwithstanding, however, all the efforts of the Genoese, who are in this instance their own historians, the French and they were completely defeated. John de Franguemont, the son of the vice-admiral, was slain, the Bastard of Bourbon was taken prisoner, and four, if not six, of the Genoese carracks fell into the hands of the English. On board of the carracks was a sum of money, the wages of the whole fleet for three months, the English accounts say for six months. They also assert that three carracks were taken and three sunk. This was a great victory, and it is evident that the enemy were numerically superior to the victors. This is the only account I have met with in which mention is made of stages or bridges used by the English to enable them to board the ships of the enemy. The carracks spoken of were undoubtedly large and powerful ships compared to those in general use at that period. The Genoese were at that time, and for long continued, the first maritime people in Europe, and from their shipwrights and seamen, as well as from the captured ships, the English obtained many of the improvements which were soon afterwards brought into the art of shipbuilding in England.

Henry died on the 31st of August, 1422, aged thirty-three years, worn out with the fatigues of his late campaign in Normandy. He had reigned nine years, five months, and eleven days.

I have before me a curious history in verse relating to navigation and nautical affairs, written during the reign of Henry, entitled *De Politia conservativa Maris*. The author, in his preface, urges the importance of England maintaining the dominion of the channel.

"The true process of English policy,
Of utterward to keep this regne in
Of our England, that no man may deny,
Nor say of sooth but it is one of the best,
Is this that who seeth south, north, east, and west,
Cherish merchandise, keep the Admiralty
That we be masters of the narrow sea.

Who can here pass without danger and woe?
What merchandise may forby be ago?
For needs him must take trewes every foe:
Flanders, and Spain, and other, trust to me
Or else hindered all for this narrow sea."

The whole poem is very curious, and full of information respecting the commerce of England in those days. It shows us how extensive it had already become, and how much alive the British merchants were to its importance, although the monarchs and chief nobles, madly engaged in civil wars or foreign conquests, did their utmost to destroy it, instead of endeavouring to protect and improve it. The more we study history, the more we shall be convinced that England owes her present greatness and prosperity to the enlightened energy and perseverance of her merchants and manufacturers, and the seamen of the mercantile marine.

Without them her brave armies and navies could not have been created or maintained, nor won the renown which England proudly claims.

"From Spain," says our poetical author, "we import figs, raisins, wine, dates, liquorice, oil, grains, white pastil soap, wax, iron, wool, wadmolle, goat-fell, kid-fell, saffron, and quicksilver.

"From Flanders, fine cloth of *Ypre and Curtike*, fine cloth of all colours, fustian, linen cloth; for which England returns wool and tin.

"From Portugal, always in unity with England, we obtain wine, osey, wax, grain, figs, raisins, honey, cordmeynes, dates, salt, hides.

"With Bretaigne we deal in salt, wine, crest cloth, and canvas; but this is only of late years, for the Bretons were noted pirates, and greatly interrupted the navigation of this kingdom, both by taking the merchant-ships and plundering and burning the towns on the sea-coast, till Edward the Third granted letters of reprisal to the inhabitants of

Dartmouth, Plymouth, and Fowey, which obliged the Duke of Bretaigne to sue for peace and engage for the future good behaviour of his subjects."

Here we have an example of the advantage of allowing people who possess the sinews of war to take care of themselves. We may depend on it they will, in most instances, give a good account of their proceedings.

The same principle may be applied to our larger colonies at the present day, and we may have little fear that if attacked they will maintain their independence, and the honour of the British name.

"We trade with Scotland for felts, hides, and wool in the fleece; and with Prussia, High Germany, and the east countries for beer, bacon, almond, copper, bow-staves, steel, wax, pelt ware, pitch, tar, peats, flax, cotton, thread, fustian, canvas, cards, buckram, silver plate, silver wedges, and metal.

"From Genoa we import most of the articles which we now procure from Africa, and which come in large ships called carracks, such as cloth of gold, silk, black pepper, and good gold of *Genne* (Guinea)."

Our author does not at all approve of the articles which were imported from Venice and Florence. They were very similar, in some respects, to those which now come from France, and without which, most undoubtedly, we could do very well.

> *"The great gallies of Venice and Florence*
> *Be well laden with things of complacence,*
> *Allspicery and of grocer's ware,*
> *With sweet wines, all manner of chaffare;*
> *Apes and japes, and marmusets tailed,*
> *Nifles and trifles that little have availed,*
> *And things with which they featly blear our eye,*
> *With things not enduring that we buy;*
> *For much of this chaffare that is wastable,*
> *Might be forborne for dear and deceivable."*

On the death of his father, August, 1422, the unfortunate Henry the Sixth, when not a year old, was proclaimed King of England and heir of France, and when eight years of age he was crowned both in London and Paris. No improvements in naval affairs were introduced during his inglorious and disastrous reign. The chief battle at sea was fought by a fleet under the command of the famous king-maker, the Earl of Warwick. In the Straits of Dover he encountered a fleet of Genoese and Lubeck ships laden with Spanish merchandise, and under the convoy of five carracks. Of these he captured six, and sunk or put to flight twenty-six more, took numerous prisoners, and slew a thousand men, while his prize-money amounted to 10,000 pounds, an enormous sum in those days, when the whole revenue of England did not exceed at one time 5000 pounds.

The Earl of Warwick was soon afterwards, with his fleet, instrumental in dethroning Henry, and placing Edward of Lancaster on the throne, under the title of Edward the Fourth. It was not, however, till the victory of Tewkesbury placed the crown securely on his brows that Edward was able to turn his attention to naval affairs. In the year 1475, having resolved to make war on France, he collected at Sandwich five hundred flat-bottomed vessels, in which he purposed to carry his army across the channel. He succeeded, indeed, in transporting them to the French coast, but the King of France suing for peace, and undertaking to pay a large tribute to England, he returned home. By similar means he brought the King of Scotland to submission. He granted many privileges to merchants trading to foreign countries, and encouraged commerce by every means in his power.

It is scarcely necessary to allude to the reign of his son, poor young Edward the Fifth, who had worn the crown but two months, when it was grasped by his uncle, Richard the Third, who was crowned at Westminster on the 5th of July, 1483.

When threatened with an invasion of England by the Earl of Richmond, he kept a powerful fleet in readiness to defend the shores of his kingdom. On hearing, however, that the earl had been driven off the coast, he very unwisely laid up most of his ships, and disbanded the greater part of his army. On discovering this, the sagacious earl immediately embarked all the forces he could collect in a few transports, and, landing at Milford Haven, gained the battle of Bosworth, which placed the crown of England on his head, and in which Richard lost his life.

Since old Nicholas of Lynn's expedition to the northern regions of the world in the reign of Edward the Third up to this period, no voyages of discovery had been performed under the patronage of Government; and probably but little, if any, improvement had taken place in marine architecture. A new era was about to commence, which was to see the establishment of England's naval glory. Other European nations were at that time far in advance of our country as regarded all affairs connected with the sea. It was a period rife with maritime adventure and enterprise. Men began to perceive that there were other achievements more glorious than those which the sword could accomplish, more calculated, at all events, to bring wealth into their coffers.

It was now that the ardent, bold, and sagacious spirit of Columbus devised the scheme for reaching India by the west, which resulted in the discovery of a new world. In 1485, having fully instructed his brother Bartholomew in his intended project, he sent him to England in order that he might apply to Henry, under the belief that the king would at once embrace his proposals. Unfortunately, he fell, it is said, into the hands of pirates, who stripped him of all he had; and on his reaching England in poverty he was attacked with a fever, which caused a still further delay. When he recovered he had to raise funds for his purpose by making and selling maps, and thus it was not till 1488 that he was in a condition to present himself before the king. He was, however, then well received, and an arrangement was made by which Christopher Columbus was to proceed on a voyage of discovery under the flag of England. Circumstances occurred to prevent the accomplishment of this plan, and Henry lost the glory he would have gained as the supporter of one of the greatest and truest heroes who has ever figured on the page of history. This honour was reserved for Ferdinand and Isabella of Spain, who, on the 17th of April, 1492, signed the articles of agreement with the Genoese navigator at the little town of Santa Fé, in the kingdom of Grenada.

The squadron prepared for this expedition, which was to prove of such mighty importance to the world in general, consisted but of three vessels, carrying in all but 120 men. I will describe them, as they give us some idea of the vessels of that period, and which were considered fit, by the mariners of those days, to contend with the stormy winds and waves they would in all probability have to encounter on so long a voyage. There was, first, the admiral's ship, called by him the *Santa Maria*, a carrack, or a ship with a deck. The second was the *Pinta*, commanded by Martin Alonso Pinçon; and the third the *Minna* of which Viconte Yannes Pinçon was master. These two were carvels, which are described as open vessels without decks. I suspect, however, that they must have been nearly, if not entirely, decked over — in fact, that they were what are now called flush-decked vessels, while probably the carrack was a frigate-built ship, or, at all events, a ship with a high poop and forecastle. Supposing the carrack to have earned sixty men, and the carvels thirty each, how could all the necessary stores, provisions, and water have been stowed away for those thirty, unless in a vessel of good size? or how could they have been protected from wet unless below a deck?

Carvels were strongly built craft, and we still speak of a vessel being carvel, or ship-built. I therefore do not hold to the idea that the two consorts of Columbus's ship were little better than open boats, but believe that they were stout, well-formed vessels, not so utterly unworthy of the great sovereigns who sent forth the expedition. Right honoured was the little town of Palos, whence it sailed on Friday, 3rd August, 1492.

Henry, although he had lost this great opportunity of increasing his renown, wisely perceived that in no way could he more effectually gain the respect of his subjects and consolidate his power than by affording every encouragement to naval enterprise, and to the extension of commerce. He therefore gladly listened to a proposal to search for certain lands said to exist in the north-west, made by John Cabot, a Venetian by birth, settled at Bristol. A commission, signed in 1496, was granted to him and his three sons, Lewis, Sebastian, and Sanctius, who were skilful in navigation and cosmography.

The record is as follows: — "The King, upon the third day of February, in the thirteenth year of his reign, gave licence to John Cabot to take six English ships, in any haven or havens of the realm of England, being of the burden of 200 tons or under, with all necessary furniture; and to take, also, into the said ships, all such masters, mariners, and subjects of the King as might be willing to go with him."

The expedition sailed early in the year 1497, and reached the coast of Labrador, Newfoundland, in June of the same year. There is some doubt whether the father, John, was alive at that time, so that the more celebrated Sebastian has the credit of the discovery. At all events, he performed several successful voyages in the same direction, and made many important discoveries. Thus, though the Spaniards claim the honour of being the discoverers of the middle portion of the great continent of America, there can be no doubt that the English were the first visitors to its northern shores, where many millions of their descendants are now established.

Henry, with his usual sagacity, saw the advantage of having a fleet of ships exclusively fitted for war, instead of drawing off those which might be well calculated for the purposes of commerce, but were not, from their construction, suited to stand the brunt of battle. He could not but perceive, besides this, that by employing the merchant-vessels, as had before been done, for the purposes of fighting, he crippled the merchants in their commercial pursuits, and prevented them from supplying him with the sinews of war. He desired also to have a permanent fleet ready, should war break out, to protect the coasts of his kingdom from foreign invasion. The first ship he built was called the *Great Harry*. She cost 14,000 pounds. She had four masts, a high poop and forecastle, in which were placed numerous guns, turning inboard and outwards. She had only one tier of guns on the upper-deck, as ports were not used in those days. She was, however, what would now be called frigate-built. She was burnt by accident at Woolwich in 1553. The *Great Harry* may properly be considered the first ship of what is now denominated the Royal Navy. There is a model of her in

56

Somerset House, and there are numerous prints of her which give a notion of what she was like. Few seamen of the present day, I fancy, would wish to go to sea in a similar craft. I certainly used to doubt that such a vessel could have ventured out of harbour at all, till I saw the Chinese junk which was brought to the Thames all the way round from China, and which, in appearance and construction, is not very dissimilar to what, from her model, the *Great Harry* must have been, except in point of size. She probably did not measure much less than 1000 tons; she must have been, therefore, about the size of a modern frigate.

Chapter Five.

Establishment of the Royal Navy of England — from A.D. 1509 to A.D. 1558.

No sovereign of England was ever proclaimed with more universal joy than was Henry the Eighth, when, at the age of eighteen, he succeeded to the throne of his father, A.D. 1509. Tyrant and despot as he became at home, he did not neglect the interests of commerce, while he maintained the honour of England abroad. He made very great improvements in the work his father had commenced. By his prerogative, and at his own expense, he settled the constitution of the present Royal Navy. An Admiralty and Navy Office were established, and commissioners to superintend naval affairs were appointed by him.

Regular salaries were settled for admirals, vice-admirals, captains, and seamen, and the sea-service at this time became a distinct and regular profession.

In 1512, Henry, having entered into a league with Spain against France, fitted out a fleet under the command of Sir Edward Howard, Lord High Admiral, and by an indenture, dated 8th of April of that year, granted him the following allowance: — For his own maintenance, diet, wages, and rewards, ten shillings a-day. For each of the captains, for their diet, wages, and rewards, eighteenpence a-day. For every soldier, mariner, and gunner, five shillings a-month for his wages, and five shillings for his victuals, reckoning twenty-eight days in the month. But the admiral, captains, officers, and men had also further allowances, under the denomination of dead shares. I doubt whether the naval officers and men of the present day would be satisfied with a similar amount of pay. Certainly the mariners of those days had more dangers and hardships to encounter than have those of the present time under ordinary circumstances. That year Henry's fleet consisted of forty-five ships, of which the largest was the *Regent*, of 1000 tons; the two next in size being the *Sovereign* and the *Mary Rose*, of about 500 tons each.

THE REGENT AND CORDELIER

War was now declared against France, and the English fleet put to sea under the command of Sir Edward Howard. It carried a considerable body of land forces, under the command of the Earl of Dorset, which were landed at the Port of Passages, in Spain. Afterwards, being reinforced by a number of stout ships, the admiral sailed for Brest, in the hopes of encountering the French. Sir William Knevet had command of the *Regent*, and Sir Charles Brandon, who had sixty of the tallest yeomen of the Guard under him, commanded the *Sovereign*. The fleet arrived off Brest just as the French fleet, consisting of thirty-nine sail, was coming out of the harbour. On seeing the enemy, Sir Edward made the signal for an immediate engagement. Scarcely was the signal seen, than the *Regent* and the *Cordelier*, the latter being the largest ship in the French navy, attacked each other as if by mutual consent. The *Cordelier*, it is said, carried 1200 soldiers. Undoubtedly her commander hoped to carry the English ship by boarding. In the course of the action, when locked in a deadly embrace with their grappling-irons, another English ship threw into the *Cordelier* a quantity of combustibles, or fire-works, as they were called, and set her on fire. In vain the crew of the *Regent* endeavoured to free their ship from her perilous position. The magazine of the *Cordelier* was reached, and she and the *Regent* went up into the air together. In the *Regent*, Sir William Knevet and 700 men were lost, and in the *Cordelier*, Sir Pierce Morgan, her captain, and 900 of her crew are supposed to have perished. After this dreadful catastrophe the action ceased; the French, horror-stricken, hurriedly making their way into Brest. The ships, also, of both parties, had received considerable damage.

Although cannon had been employed on board ships since the time of Edward the Third, this was probably one of the first sea-fights in which they were used by both parties on board all the ships engaged. Even on this occasion the combatants seem to have trusted more to their battle-axes and swords than to their artillery. The French give a different account of this battle. They say that an English ship having discharged a quantity of fire-works into the *Cordelier*, she caught fire, when her Breton commander, finding that the conflagration could not be extinguished, and determined not to perish alone, made up to the English admiral and grappled her, when they blew up into the air together. On this the two fleets separated by mutual consent.

The following year another fleet of forty-two men-of-war, under the command of the Lord High Admiral, sailed for Brest, when the French squadron was found at anchor, protected by batteries on shore, and a line of twenty-four hulks chained together across the harbour's mouth. The admiral, however, making a feint with his boats, drew the enemy down to the shore, when he ran up past the batteries, and ravaged the country round the town. The French had been waiting the arrival of six galleys from the Mediterranean, under Monsieur Pregent.

I cannot refrain from giving the first account I have met with of what may properly be called a cutting-out expedition. While the English fleet were at Brest, Monsieur Pregent arrived on the coast with six galleys and four foists, and, apprehensive of being attacked by the enemy, he entered the Bay of Conquêt, which was the nearest place to Brest. He here placed his squadron between two rocks, on which he mounted cannon and threw up a breastwork. Notwithstanding the advantageous position of this squadron, the Lord High Admiral resolved to attack it. He had two galleys in his fleet. He went on board one of these, and entrusted the other to Lord Rivers. He had, besides, only two large barges and two boats. With these, on the 20th of April, he boldly ventured into the Bay of Conquêt to attack the French galleys. He no sooner came abeam of the galley commanded by Monsieur Pregent, than, ordering his vessel to be lashed alongside, he boarded her sword in hand, followed only by Don Carroz, a Spanish cavalier, and seventeen of his men. He appeared at first to be gaining the day; but, by some accident, his galley swinging loose, he and his followers, deprived of all succour, were so hard-pressed by the enemy that they were driven headlong into the sea. Lord Ferrers, who had during this time been engaging the enemy without success, seeing the admiral's galley fall off, retreated. When, however, Lord Howard was missed, a flag of truce was sent to the French commander, who replied that only one seaman had escaped death, and that the admiral and the rest of his companions had been forced overboard. After this the English fleet returned home. In a short time Monsieur Pregent, flushed with success, ravaged the coast of Sussex; but was driven away by Sir Thomas Howard, who succeeded his brother as Lord High Admiral. In the year 1514, the ever-active Pregent again paid the Sussex coast a visit, and burnt Brighthelmstone, as Brighton was then called. In return for this compliment, Sir John Wallop was sent with a fleet to the coast of Normandy, where he burnt twenty-one towns and villages. In consequence of the energetic and summary way in which he carried out his system of retaliation, those who have imitated him have been said to "wallop" the enemy. To replace the *Regent* destroyed in the terrible way above described, the king built a ship at Erith in 1515, and called her the *Henri Grâce de Dieu*. She was of 1000 tons burden, and manned with 301 mariners, 50 gunners, and 349 soldiers. Up to that period, when ships were to be manned in a hurry, soldiers were sent on board to do the duty of seamen as best they could, and generals were turned into admirals at very short notice. However, it would be more correct to say that the fighting was done chiefly by soldiers, and consequently that military officers went to command them, while the ships were navigated by professional seamen, who had their own sea-officers, though generally of an inferior grade, over them. A vestige of this custom still remains in the Royal Navy. On board every ship, besides the captain and his lieutenants, there is a sailing-master, who has also his mates or assistants, who have especial charge of the navigation of the ship. Formerly the captain and his lieutenants were not of necessity seamen. Now, they are so by profession, though they still retain a remnant of their military character. In time, probably, the last representative of the master-of-the-mariners, as he was called, will disappear from the British navy — it being the duty of the lieutenants to attend to the navigation of the ship, as they do now to the management in every other respect.

One of the wisest acts of Henry the Eighth was making the sea-service a regular profession — though long after his time ships, and even fleets, were commanded by men who had hitherto lived and fought only on shore. About the year 1545 port-holes were generally introduced on board the larger ships. Before that time the guns were fought over the bulwarks, or were alone placed on the forecastle, and the aftercastle, which latter portion of the ship is now called the poop. This word *poop* is evidently derived from the Latin *puppis*, as originally the after-part of a ship was called by the Romans, and thence the name was given to the ship herself, a part being taken for the whole. The ports were, however, placed not more than sixteen inches from the water, so close, indeed, as greatly to peril the ship. It was in consequence of this faulty construction that the *Mary Rose* of sixty guns, one of the largest ships in the British navy, heeling over to a squall while encountering the French at Spithead, was capsized, when her captain, Sir George Carew, and upwards of 500 of his men, perished in the waves. As late as the year 1835, Mr Deane, by means of his ingenious invention, the diving-bell, was enabled to recover several guns, parts of the wreck, and some stone-shot of the *Mary Rose*.

Ships generally carried but few guns. A writer, describing a battle which took place off the Isle of Wight, and which lasted two hours, when upwards of ninety ships were engaged, speaks of 300 shot being fired, to prove how desperate was the contest. I have before me an account of the battle in which the *Mary Rose* was lost, not, as the French say, in consequence of their fire, but because it was attempted to keep her ports open when a considerable sea was running, and a strong breeze had suddenly sprung up. The French king had sent over a large fleet to annoy the English coasts. Henry, hearing of the expedition, hurried down to Portsmouth to hasten the equipment of 100 sail, which he had ordered to be got ready. The French appearing, the English sailed out to Saint Helen's to meet them. A squall came on, and the *Mary Rose* foundering, the *Great Harry* which was attacked by the French row-galleys, bore the brunt of the action. The French quickly retired, though they attempted to make a lodgment on the Isle of Wight, but were compelled to return to their ships. The English are described as using pinances, which are vessels of great length and little beam, moving very rapidly, and fitted both with sails and oars.

We hear, also, that the *Carracon* the ship of the French Admiral, was destroyed by fire before the fleet left their coasts. She is described as appearing like a castle among the other ships of the fleet, and so strong that she had nothing to fear at sea but fire and rocks. It is stated that she had 100 brass cannon on board; but as she was not more than 800 tons burden, they must have been very small ones. Still, it is certain that she was the stoutest ship possessed by the French.

From a French account of one of the attacks made on the English fleet before Portsmouth, we ascertain the character of the galleys employed by the French. We are told that they were worked by oars, and we read that so many galley-slaves were killed. It is said, also, that "the galleys had all the advantage of working that they could desire, to the great damage of the English, who, for want of wind, not being able to stir, lay exposed to the French cannon, and being so much higher and bulkier than their galleys, hardly a shot missed them; while the galleys, with the help of their oars, shifted at pleasure, and thereby avoided the danger of the enemy's artillery." The same writer says that, later in the day, "the violence of the wind, and the swelling of the sea, would deprive us of our galleys." We thus see at once that these galleys, though from their lightness easily manoeuvred in smooth water, were unfit to buffet with the winds and waves. They were probably similar to the galleys I have before described, and which for centuries were in use in the Mediterranean.

Another writer says: "A gale arising, the French galleys were in danger, the English ships bearing down upon them with full sail, a danger from which they escaped purely by the skill and experience of their commanders, and the intrepidity of the *Prior of Capua*, who exposed his galley with undaunted courage, and freed himself from danger with equal address." The title of Prior of Capua sounds oddly enough when applied to a naval commander. From these accounts it would appear that the English ships were more powerful than those of the French, and were better calculated to stand the brunt of battle than to chase a nimble enemy, as the French seem to have been. The larger ships in the British navy were at that time fitted with four masts, like the *Henri Grâce de Dieu*.

Though the yards and sails were unwieldy, the rigging heavy, and the top hamper prodigious, we find that they were tending towards the form they had assumed when Howe, Jervis, and Nelson led our fleets to victory.

They had short stout masts, a vast number of shrouds to support them, and large heavy round tops on which a dozen men or more could stand. The sterns were ornamented with a profusion of heavy carved-work, and they had great lanterns stuck up at the taffrail, as big, almost, as sentry-boxes, while the forecastle still somewhat resembled the building from which it took its name. This vast amount of woodwork, rising high above the surface of the water, was very detrimental to the sailing qualities of ships, and must have caused the loss of many. What sailors call fore-and-aft sails had already been introduced, and we hear constantly of ships beating to windward, and attempting to gain the weather-gage. In those days a great variety of ordnance were employed, to which our ancestors gave the odd-sounding names of cannon, demi-cannon, culverins, demi-culverins, sakers, mynions, falcons, falconets, portpiece-halls, port-piece-chambers, fowler-halls, and curthalls. These guns varied very much in length and in the weight of their shot. When a ship is spoken of as carrying fifty or sixty guns it must be understood that every description of ordnance on board was included, so that a very erroneous idea would be formed, if we pictured a ship of sixty guns of those days as in any way resembling in size a third, or even a fourth-rate at the end of the last century. An old author says: "By the employment of Italian shipwrights, and by encouraging his own people to build strong ships of war to carry great ordnance, Henry established a puissant navy, which, at the end of his reign, consisted of seventy-one vessels, whereof thirty were ships of burden, and contained in all 10,550 tons, and two were galleys, and the rest were small barks and row-barges, from eighty tons down to fifteen tons, which served in rivers and for landing men."

Stone-shot had hitherto been used both at sea and on shore, but about the middle of the century they were superseded by iron shot. About the same period matchlocks were introduced on board ships.

An Act was passed in this reign encouraging merchants to build ships fit for men-of-war, such ships being exempt from certain duties, the owners also receiving from the king, when he required them, twelve shillings per ton a-month.

Henry the Eighth established an Office of Admiralty, with a Navy Office, under certain commissioners; and appointed regular salaries, not only for his admirals and vice-admirals, but for his captains and seamen. This established the system, pursued with various alterations, for the maintenance of the Royal Navy. These regulations and appointments encouraged the English to consider the sea as a means of providing for their children, and from this time forward we have a constant series of eminent officers in the Royal Navy, many of them noblemen of the first distinction. Among the most celebrated in this reign were Sir Edward Howard, his brother Sir Thomas Howard, afterwards Earl of Surrey, Sir William Fitzwilliams, afterwards Earl of Southampton, and John Russell, first Earl of Bedford. The most eminent navigator in the reign of Edward the Sixth was Sebastian Cabot, son of John Cabot, who, under Henry the Seventh, discovered Newfoundland. Nothing was done concerning trade without consulting him; he was at the head of the merchant adventurers, and governor of a company formed to find out a passage by the north to the East Indies. Among the regulations for the government of the fleet destined for the voyage to Cathay were several which show a considerable amount of worldly wisdom and sound so quaint, that I am tempted to quote a few of them. Clause 22 — "Item — not to disclose to any nation the state of our religion, but to pass it over in silence without any declaration of it, seeming to bear with such laws and rites as the place hath where you shall arrive." Item 23 — "Forasmuch as our people and ships may appear unto them strange and wondrous, and theirs also to ours, it is to be considered how they may be used, learning much of their nature and dispositions by some one such person whom you may first either allure or take to be brought on board your ship." Item 24 — "The persons so taken to be well entertained, used, and apparelled, to be set on land to the intent he or she may allure others to draw nigh to show the commodities; and if the person taken may be made drunk with your beer or wine, you shall know the secrets of his heart."

Under the judicious management of Sebastian Cabot, the Russian Company was established, though their charter was not granted till the year 1555. Among other discoverers and navigators Captain Wyndham merits notice, having opened up a trade with the coast of Guinea. Both he and his companion Pintado died, however, of fever, forty only of his crew returning to Plymouth. Captain Richard Chancellor is another able navigator of this reign. He sailed with Sir Hugh Willoughby in the service of the company, at the recommendation of Cabot. He made several voyages to Russia; in the last, he parted with Sir Hugh Willoughby, who, putting into a port to winter, was, with all his crew, frozen to death. His ship was found riding safe at anchor by some Russian fishermen, and from a journal discovered on board it was found that the admiral and most of his fellow-adventurers were alive in January, 1554.

During Henry the Eighth's reign the infamous slave-trade was commenced by Mr William Hawkins of Plymouth, father of the celebrated Sir John Hawkins. He, however, evidently did not consider the traffic in the light in which it is now regarded. In his ship, the *Paul*, of Plymouth, he made three voyages to the Brazils, touching at the coast of Guinea, where he traded in slaves, gold, and elephants' teeth. At that time the English, considering themselves lords paramount at sea, insisted that ships of all other nations should strike their flags in presence of their fleets. Even when William Lord Howard, Mary's high admiral, went with a fleet of twenty-eight men-of-war to await the arrival of King Philip, who soon after appeared in the channel, escorted by one hundred and sixty sail, the Spanish flag flying at his main-top, the English admiral compelled him to lower it, by firing a shot before he would salute the intended consort of the Queen. This determination of the English to maintain the sovereignty of the seas was the cause hereafter of many a desperate naval engagement between themselves and the Dutch, who disputed their right to the honour.

Henry died A.D. 1547. No great improvements were made in navigation during his reign, but the encouragement he gave to shipbuilding, and the establishment of a permanent Royal Navy, contributed much to enable England to attain that supremacy on the ocean which she has ever since maintained.

During the early part of Edward the Sixth's reign the navy of England was employed chiefly in operations against the Scotch, but in 1550 the French formed a plan to capture Jersey and Guernsey, which they surrounded with a large fleet, having 2000 troops on board. The inhabitants held out stoutly, and gained time for Captain (afterwards Sir William) Winter to arrive to their succour. Though he had but a small squadron, so hastily did he attack the French, that he captured and burnt nearly all their ships and killed a thousand men, the rest with difficulty escaping to the mainland.

Mary's reign is a blank, as far as most achievements were concerned, and, had the miserable queen obtained her wishes, the ships of England, and all the English hold dear, would have been handed over to the tender mercies of Philip and the Spaniards.

Chapter Six.

Reign of Elizabeth — from A.D. 1558 to A.D. 1603.

When Elizabeth came to the throne, she, without loss of time, took measures to restore the navy, which had been allowed to fall into decay during the reign of her wretched sister Mary. Timber was stored up for building, numerous pieces of brass cannon cast, and gunpowder, which had hitherto been brought from abroad, was manufactured at home. She raised the wages of seamen, increased the number of naval officers, and augmented their salaries, giving also encouragement to foreigners skilled in shipbuilding to repair to her ports and construct strong ships, both for war and commerce. The fortresses in the Isle of Wight and other parts were increased, and scarcely had she governed four days when Vice-Admiral Malyn was ordered to sail, with as many ships as were fit for sea, to protect trade and to defend the channel.

She, of course, took these steps by the advice of Cecil, who likewise directed Sir Thomas Gresham to send over coin from Holland, and to purchase arms and munitions of war. Cecil was thoroughly cognisant of the designs of the Spaniards, and he had soon a proof of their perfidious intentions. A squadron under the command of Sir John Hawkins had been driven into the port of Saint Juan d'Ulloa in the Bay of Mexico, and was suddenly attacked by a Spanish fleet, the commander of which had just before been professing his friendly intentions. Sir John suspected treachery in consequence of observing that the Spaniards were shifting arms from one ship to another, planting and levelling their cannon from their ships towards an island on which some of the English had landed. The master of one of the ships being sent to the Spanish admiral, he was seized; and, causing the trumpet to be sounded, the Spaniards set on the English on all sides. The men on shore being dismayed at the unexpected onset, fled, and endeavoured to recover their ships, but the Spaniards, landing in great numbers, slew most of them without quarter. Several of the English ships were destroyed — the *Minion* and *Judith*, with a small bark of fifty tons, alone escaping. The crews underwent incredible hardships, though they at length found their way to England. The English captured on the island by the Spaniards were afterwards thrown into the Inquisition, where they remained shut up asunder in dungeons for a year and a-half. Three were afterwards burnt; others were condemned to receive two and three hundred blows on horseback with long whips, and to serve in the galleys for many years; and others were confined in monasteries, dressed in the S. Benito or fool's coats. One of them, Job Hartob, after enduring captivity for twenty-three years, escaped, and reached England. So enraged were the nation at this treachery of the Spaniards, that it was with difficulty they could be restrained from breaking the peace with that perfidious nation.

A further cause of dissension arose in consequence of a convoy of vessels, bound from the coast of Biscay for the Low Countries with a large quantity of money on board, being chased by French pirates, having taken shelter in Plymouth, Falmouth, and Southampton. The queen, being informed that the money was on the merchants' accounts, and that the Duke of Alva would certainly seize it to enable him to carry on the war, made bold to borrow the sum. This brought matters to a crisis; reprisals were made by Spain, and the English seized many Spanish and Flemish ships. The English on this, with incredible alacrity, fitted out vessels, and fell upon all merchant-ships belonging to the Spaniards. Spain, it was now known, was preparing a formidable force for the invasion of England; but the queen and her ministers, unintimidated by the boasts of the Spaniards, omitted no precautionary measures to defeat Philip's plans. In 1587, a fleet under Sir Francis Drake was despatched to Cadiz. The admiral here forced six galleys, placed for the guardianship of the port, to shelter themselves under the cannon of the castle; and then, having burnt upwards of a hundred ships laden with ammunition and provisions, he sailed for Cape Saint Vincent, where he surprised some forts, and destroyed all the fishing craft he could fall in with. From thence, appearing off the mouth of the Tagus, he challenged the Spanish admiral, Santa Cruz, to come out and fight; but the Spaniard, obeying his master's orders, allowed Drake to burn and destroy every vessel he could find, rather than hazard an engagement. The King of Spain, hoping to frighten the English, published in every country in Europe a full account of the armada he was preparing for the subjugation, as he hoped, of England. For three years had Philip been making the most mighty efforts to fit out a fleet with which he hoped to humble the pride of the queen of that "tight little island," who had dared to refuse his hand, and to enslave her heretical subjects. The Most Happy Armada, for so he had styled it, consisted of 134 sail of towering ships, of the total burden of 57,868 tons; on board of it wore 19,295 soldiers,

8450 sailors, 2088 slaves, and 2830 pieces of cannon. In addition to the foregoing, there were galleys, galliasses, and galleons stored with 22,000 pounds of great shot, 40,000 quintals, or hundredweights of powder, 1000 quintals of lead for bullets, 10,000 quintals of match, 7000 muskets and calivers, 1000 partisans and halberds, besides double-cannon and field-pieces for a camp on disembarking, and a great many mules, horses, and asses, with six months' provisions of all sorts. To this may be added a large band of monks, with racks, thumbscrews, chains, whips, butchering knives, and other implements of torture, with which it was proposed to convert the English from the error of their ways, and to bring them to the true faith as expounded by the pope and his pupil Philip.

The larger of these ships measured from 1000 to 1200 tons, they carried 50 guns, about 180 mariners, and 300 soldiers. A still larger number measuring from 600 to 800 tons, and carrying from 30 to 40 guns, with crews of about 100 seamen, and 300 soldiers. There was a fleet of patches and zabras, a considerable number of which measured no more than 60 tons, and carried 8 guns and 30 seamen. The galliasses must, however, have been ships of great bulk, as they carried 50 guns, and crews of about 120 men, with a still larger number of soldiers, besides which they each had about 300 slaves for working their oars. The galleys also carried 50 guns and about 230 slaves. This fleet was divided into ten squadrons, each commanded by an experienced officer. The patches are more commonly called carvels. Besides the Dominicans, Franciscans, Flagellants, and Jesuits, there were on board many hundred persons of the best families of Spain; some maintained by the king, with their servants, and those belonging to the duke's court.

This vast armada was followed by a fleet of tenders, with a prodigious quantity of arms on board, intended to put into the hands of those whom it was expected would rise on their reaching the shores of our own land. The command of this mighty squadron, generally known as the Spanish Armada, was given to the Duke of Medina Sidonia, and under him was Don Martinez de Recaldo, an experienced admiral, who managed the affairs of the fleet. The reports of the enormous preparations made by the Spaniards for the destruction of everything they held dear naturally caused the greatest anxiety, if not consternation, among the English, but the nation was true to itself. The queen and her ministers, in no way daunted at the mighty preparations for their enslavement, vigorously prepared for resistance, taking all the measures wisdom could dictate and their means would allow for repelling the invaders. The country flew to arms; every county raised a body of militia; the sea-ports were fortified, and a system of signals arranged so that troops could be brought to the point where they were required with the greatest possible speed. Orders were also given that, should the enemy land, the whole country round should be laid waste, so that the Spaniards might find no food except what they brought with them. The regular army was disposed, a part along the southern coast, another near Torbay, under the command of the Earl of Leicester, while a third, under the leading of Lord Hunsdon, was destined to guard the queen's person. The English Government, not misled by the assurances of the Spanish minister that his master's wish was to remain at peace, took care to keep themselves well informed of the proceedings of the Spaniards, and of the time the Armada was likely to be ready to put to sea.

Offers had been made by Philip to conclude a treaty, and a meeting was held between his envoys and the English commissioners in April near Ostend. The Spaniards, however, purposely squandered away the time, hoping to stop the preparations of the English while their own were going forward, and at length fixed on Brouckburg in Flanders as the place for concluding a treaty of peace. Before the time agreed on had arrived, the Spanish Armada had sailed from the Tagus. The pope having blessed the fleet which was to be engaged in the pious office of subjugating the heretics of England, it was named the Great, Noble, and Invincible Armada, the terror of Europe.

The English fleet was placed under the command of Lord Howard of Effingham, who had, however, only seventeen ships of war actually belonging to the queen. The largest of these, the *Triumph*, was of 1100 tons, carried 500 men, and was commanded by Sir Martin Frobisher. The next in size was the *White Bear*, also with a crew of 500 men, commanded by Lord Edmund Sheffield. The third in size was the *Ark*, the admiral's flag-ship, of 800 tons, commanded by Raleigh. Of the same size was the *Victory*, carrying the flag of Sir John Hawkins, the rear-admiral, with a crew of 400 men. There were two others of 600 tons, the *Elizabeth Bonaventure* and the *Hope*. There were six of 500 tons, two of 400 tons, another of 360 tons, while the rest ranged from 30 to 120 tons. To these were joined twelve hired ships and six tenders. The city of London provided sixteen ships, twice the number demanded, with four store-ships; the city of Bristol, three; Barnstaple, three; Exeter, two, and a tender and stout pinance; Plymouth, seven stout ships, equal to the men-of-war. Sixteen ship were under Lord Henry Seymour. The nobility and gentry and commons of England furnished forty-three ships; the merchant adventurers, ten; to which may be added a fly-boat and Sir W. Winter's pinnace, making in all 143 ships.

Of these ships, thirty-two were under the command of Sir Francis Drake, and several of them were of 400 tons burden; but the greater number were not of more than 200 tons. The largest London ship was only of 300 tons, but the greater number were above 100 tons, and the smallest of 60 tons. Lord Henry Seymour's ships were mostly under 150 tons, the largest being only 160. Altogether the number of their crews did not amount to more than 15,000 men, but they were one and all gallant tars, resolved to fight and conquer, and fearless of danger. Sir Francis Drake, with fifty sail, had been stationed at Plymouth, and here the Lord High Admiral, with a large part of his fleet, joined him on the 23rd May, when Sir Francis was made his vice-admiral. Hence, with about ninety ships, the fleet sailed up and down between Ushant and Scilly, waiting for the arrival of the Armada, which had sailed, as has been said, on the 1st June. A tremendous storm, which compelled the English to run into harbour, had, however, dispersed the Spaniards, and driven them back with some damage into port. Shortly afterwards a report reached England, circulated probably by the Spaniards themselves, that the whole of their fleet had been weather-beaten, and that they would be unable to proceed to sea till the next year. This was actually believed by the English Government, who ordered the Lord High Admiral to send back four of his largest ships into port; but Lord Howard, alleging how dangerous it was to be too credulous, retained the ships, observing that he would rather keep them at his own charge than expose the nation to so great a hazard.

The wind coming from the north, on the 8th of June Lord Howard sailed towards Spain, looking out for the Armada; but the wind changing to the south, and he seeing that it would be favourable to the Spaniards, returned towards England, lest they might slip by and reach the coast before him. On the 12th he arrived at Plymouth, where the whole fleet was assembled, waiting for the enemy, and on the 19th of June —

"'Twas about the lovely close of a warm summer's day.
There came a gallant merchant-ship, full sail to Plymouth Bay.
Her crew hath seen Castile's black fleet, beyond Aurigny's isle,
At earliest twilight, on the wave, lie heaving many a mile;
At sunrise she escaped their van, by God's especial grace,
And the tall Pinta, till at noon, had held her close in chase."

This tall ship was commanded by Captain Thomas Fleming, who had been stationed on the look-out to the eastward. The wind blowing almost directly into the sound, it was scarcely possible for the English fleet to put to sea; at length, however, by dint of warping, the admiral's ship and six more got out of the haven, and by daylight, on the 20th, sixty others joined him; with these he sailed, and when off the Eddystone caught sight of the enemy to the westward. Notice of the appearance of the Armada was spread far and wide throughout the land.

"Night sank upon the dusky beach, and on the purple sea;
Such night in England ne'er had been, nor ne'er again shall be.
From Eddystone to Berwick bounds, from Lynn to Milford Bay,
That time of slumber was as bright and busy as the day;
For swift to east and swift to west the ghastly war-flames spread,
High on Saint Michael's Mount it shone, it shone on Beachy Head.
Far on the deep the Spaniards saw, along each southern shore,
Cape beyond cape in endless range, those twinkling spots of fire."

Onward came the Armada in perfect order, forming a crescent, the horns of which were seven miles apart, the concave part to the rear. Formidable, indeed, from their size and number, did they appear, like so many floating castles, such as had never in the world's history sailed over the surface of the deep. The English captains were eager for the attack, but Lord Howard wisely checked their ardour, pointing out the enormous size of the enemy's ships, which also being full of troops, they could hope to do nothing with by boarding. Had, indeed, the Spaniards ventured to attack the English on that day, it would have been difficult to escape from them. Having wisely waited till the following morning, Sunday, the 21st of June, the admiral was joined by the rest of the fleet, which had got out of the sound, and had, moreover, the wind in its favour. The battle commenced at nine o'clock in the morning, when Lord Howard attacked a Spanish ship commanded by Don Alfonso de Lara. Lord Howard pressed in upon her, tore her hull with his broadside, and brought her to the verge of sinking. Drake, Hawkins, and Frobisher attacked, also, the rearmost of the Spanish ships, commanded by Recaldo, the vice-admiral, ship engaging ship, till the Spaniards were so disabled that they took to flight, and were received into the main body. The British seamen, elated by their success, pressed on more and more boldly, till, darkness coming on, the Lord High Admiral, by signal, ordered them to desist. About midnight the English saw a large ship in the centre of the Spanish fleet blow up. As it proved afterwards, she had on board a large amount of treasure, which was moved before she was deserted to another ship, commanded by Don Pedro Vargas. It coming on to blow hard at night, this ship sprang her foremast, and falling astern, was attacked and captured by Sir Francis Drake. Besides the treasure, several persons of distinction were found on board, the first Spanish prisoners made on this occasion. The ship was sent into Dartmouth, where the plunder of the vessel was divided among the sailors.

A ship which had been destroyed was fallen in with the next day, having fifty men on board cruelly burnt, and vast numbers dead. In the evening Sir Francis Drake was induced to sail in pursuit of several ships he saw in the south-west, but which proved to be German merchant-vessels; and it was evening of the next day before he could rejoin the fleet. Next morning, the two fleets having manoeuvred for some time to gain the weather-gage, about noon the Spaniards at length bore down on a number of the London vessels; but the Lord High Admiral sending a reinforcement, rescued his ships, and nearly took the vice-admiral. So high were the sides of the Spanish ships that their shot generally flew over the heads of the English, and did little damage; while scarcely a shot from the ships of the latter missed its aim. After the fleets had engaged for some time, the wind shifted to the south-south-west. On this Lord Howard led his fleet to the attack of the Armada. One of his ships, the *Triumph*, pushing too far, was surrounded by the Spaniards; but the admiral, with six other vessels, bore down to her assistance, having given orders to his captains not to fire a gun till within musket-shot. The *Triumph* was rescued, and the Spaniards driven back, miserably shattered.

About this period one William Cox, captain of a little pinnace called the *Violet*, belonging to Sir William Winter, behaved valiantly against the enemy, but his gallant little craft was sunk, and he was killed by a great piece of ordnance. As an old author writes on this occasion: "Also the *May Flower* of London, a name known to fame, performed an honourable part. Never, indeed, was seen so vehement a fight;

either side endeavouring to bring about the destruction of the other. For albeit the musqueteers and arquebusiers were in either fleet many in number, yet could they not be discerned or heard by reason of the roar of the greater ordnance that followed so thick one upon another, and played so well that day on either side that they were thought to be equal in number to common arquebusiers in a hot skirmish. The battle was not only long, but also near at hand — within half a musket-shot — and that to the great advantage of the Englishmen, who, with their ships being, as was aforesaid, excellent of sail and of steerage, yet less a great deal than the Spanish ships, and therefore more light and nimble, fought not according to their manner otherwise, to board them, but keeping themselves aloof at a reasonable distance, continually beat upon the hull and tackling of the enemy's ships, which, being a good deal higher, could not so easily beat the English ships with their ordnance. Thus in the space of one day, with the loss only of one small ship and less than a hundred men on the part of the English, was the so-called Invincible Armada utterly beaten and nearly destroyed — though to the God of battles must truly be ascribed the victory, for the power of the elements more than man's strength, caused the destruction of the larger number of the Spanish ships."

ENGLISH ATTACKING SPANISH ARMADA.—p. 91.

At evening the engagement ceased, by which time several of the enemy's ships had been taken, among them a Venetian ship of large size and force. The next day, for want of ammunition, the English were unable to renew the attack; but the Spaniards, not knowing this, did not attempt to molest them. It had been intended, on the night of the 24th, by Lord Howard, to attack the Armada in the dead of the night, but the wind failing he was disappointed in his object. On the 25th, a vast galleon, dropping behind, was captured by Sir John Hawkins after a desperate resistance. Several galliasses, sent by the Spanish admiral to the rescue of the galleon, were nearly taken. The persevering English, in their small vessels, continued their assaults on the vast ships of the enemy, never failing to inflict considerable damage on them. In the meantime, more powder and shot were brought on board to enable them to carry on their assaults. On the following day the admiral determined, however, to allow the Armada to proceed towards the Straits of Calais, where another fleet, under Lord Henry Seymour and Captain Winter, lay in wait for them. Thus the Armada sailed forward till the English saw them anchor before Calais, on the 27th of July. Here, being joined by the before-mentioned squadron, the Lord High Admiral found himself in command of nearly 150 stout ships, and, bearing down on the enemy, anchored at a short distance from them. The Spanish admiral had anchored in the hopes of being joined by the Duke of Parma, but the fleets of Holland and Zealand blockaded him in the ports of Dunkirk and Niewport, and he dared not sail out. Seeing that the Spanish ships lay very close together, Lord Howard planned a new method for their destruction. Eight of the least valuable vessels being fitted out as fire-ships, and having their guns loaded, were conducted towards the Spaniards by Captains Young and Prowse, who, in the most undaunted manner, firing the trains as they got close to the Spaniards, retired. As the burning ships bore down upon them, the Spaniards, struck with dismay, cut their cables, and put to sea. The largest galliasse in the fleet ran on shore, and was captured by the boats of the squadron, after all her fighting men had been killed — the slaves at the oars alone escaping. Several thus ran on the shoals on the coast of Flanders.

The greater number were attacked fiercely by the English, who disabled many of their ships. The Earl of Cumberland sent a large galleon to the bottom, another was sunk by the Lord High Admiral, and two other vessels by Drake and Hawkins. Another large galleon, the *Saint Matthew*, was captured by the Dutch, as was the *Saint Philip*, after in vain endeavouring to escape, having been driven by the English towards Ostend.

One of the most gallant of the English commanders was Captain Robert Cross, who, in a small vessel, sunk three of the enemy; while the Spaniards fled whenever they were attacked — indeed, the whole engagement this day was more a pursuit than a battle. On the 31st of July, the Spaniards, who had attempted to regain Calais Roads, were driven towards the coast of Zealand, when, the wind favouring them just as they were almost on the shoals, their admiral came to the resolution of returning home round the northern end of the British Isles, and making all sail, they steered the course proposed, throwing overboard their horses and mules, and everything that could impede their progress. Lord Howard, leaving Lord Henry Seymour with a squadron to assist the Dutch in blockading the Duke of Parma, sent Admiral Winter with another into the narrow seas to guard the coast, while he himself pursued the Spaniards. Many more were lost in their hurried flight; some were wrecked on the coast of Scotland, and others on the Shetland and Orkney Islands. Those who landed in Scotland were brought to Edinburgh, to the number of 500, where they were mercifully treated; but nearly thirty ships were cast away on the Irish coast, where nearly all their crews, to the number of several thousands, who escaped drowning, were put to death by the inhabitants. About fifty-four ships alone of this mighty Armada returned to Spain, and of those who had embarked upwards of 20,000 men had perished. Not a family in Spain but had lost a relative, though King Philip, in a vain endeavour to conceal his rage and disappointment, forbade any persons to wear mourning.

The encouragement given to maritime adventure raised up a host of gallant seamen and explorers, whose names became renowned for their exploits, and who carried the flag of England into all quarters of the globe. Perhaps of these the most celebrated was Sir Francis Drake, who, having performed numerous daring exploits in the West Indies, sailed round the world, and returned to England, his ship laden with the booty he had taken from the Spaniards; good Sir Humphrey Gilbert, who, after making many discoveries, sank with all his crew off the coast of Newfoundland; Sir Walter Raleigh, Sir Richard Grenville, Sir John Hawkins, and a host of others.

Among other expeditions was one intended for the South Seas, under the command of the Earl of Cumberland, who, at his own charge, fitted out three ships and a pinnace — namely, the *Red Dragon*, of 160 tons and 130 men; the *Clifford*, of 30 tons and 70 men; and the *Rose* and the *Dorothy*. Having touched on the African coast, they crossed over to South America, where they took two Portuguese ships, one of which had forty-five negroes on board, while the only riches in the other, besides slaves and friars, were beads and other spiritual trinkets, and the furniture designed for a new monastery. Several other prizes were made, when, without attempting to reach the Pacific, they returned to England. While numerous English vessels were cruising on the coasts of Old Spain, and destroying its trade and navigation, Thomas Cavendish was despatched with a small squadron to do the like on the coast of New Spain. He carried out his instructions, crossing the South Seas to the Philippines, and afterwards visiting China, having taken on his way many of the ships of the enemy.

To Sir John Hawkins the navy is indebted for the institution of that noble fund the Chest at Chatham, to which, also, Sir Francis Drake contributed considerably. Elizabeth, determined to retaliate on the Spaniards, fitted out a fleet in the following spring of 146 sail, which destroyed Corunna and Vigo, as well as the Castle of Cascacs at the mouth of the Tagus, and captured sixty large ships. In 1590 the queen allotted 8790 pounds a-year for the repairs of the Royal Navy; a sum which would go but a short way at the present day in building a single ship.

About this time the telescope was invented by Janssen, a spectacle-maker of Middleburgh, in Zealand. Hearing of it, Galileo immediately constructed his first *very* imperfect instrument, which magnified only three times. Further experiments enabled him to construct another with a power of eight, and ultimately, sparing neither labour nor expense, he formed one which bore a magnifying power of more than thirty times. With this instrument, he commenced that survey of the heavenly bodies which rendered his name famous as the first of astronomers. In the reign of Charles the Second, in 1671, Sir Isaac Newton constructed his first reflecting telescope, a small ill-made instrument, nine inches only in length — valuable as it was, a pigmy in power compared to Lord Rosse's six-feet reflector of sixty feet in length. Torricelli, the pupil of Galileo, invented the barometer.

In 1591 the first voyage to the East Indies was undertaken by Captain Lancaster, in three ships. One was sent back with invalids, another was lost with all on board, and the crew of the captain's ship mutinied while he was on shore on an uninhabited island, and ran off with her, leaving him and his companions for three years, till they were rescued.

Among the brave admirals of this period, one of the most gallant was Sir Richard Grenville, who, after serving his country for many years, sailed in the *Revenge* as Vice-Admiral to Lord Admiral Howard, in 1591, in search of the Spanish West India merchant-fleet, with a squadron of six men-of-war, six victuallers, and a few pinnaces. The English squadron was at anchor near the island of Flores, when the admiral received intelligence of the approaching Spanish fleet. He was in no condition to oppose the Spaniards, for, besides being greatly inferior in numbers, nearly half the men were disabled by the scurvy, a large proportion of whom were on shore. The admiral immediately weighed and put to sea, and the rest of his squadron followed his example. Sir Richard Grenville, however, remaining to receive the sick men, was the last to weigh. The admiral and the rest of the fleet with difficulty recovered the wind, but Sir Richard, not being able to do this, was advised by his master to set his mainsail and coast about, trusting to the sailing of his ship. As the Spanish squadron was already on his weather-gage, Sir Richard utterly refused to fly from the enemy, declaring that he would rather die than dishonour Her Majesty's ship, persuading his company that he would pass through the two squadrons in spite of them. Standing for the Spaniards, he compelled several of them to spring their luff, who thus fell under the lee of the *Revenge*. Meanwhile, as he was engaging those nearest to him, an enormous Spanish ship, the great *San Philip*, of 1500 tons, being to windward, and bearing down upon him, becalmed his sails, so that his ship could neither make way nor feel the helm. This enormous ship now laid the *Revenge* aboard; while she was thus becalmed, the ships under her lee luffing up, also laid her aboard, one of them the Spanish admiral's ship, mighty and puissant, two on her larboard, and two on her starboard side. The fight, which began at three o'clock in the afternoon, continued very terrible all that evening. The great *San Philip*, however, having received the broadside of the *Revenge*, discharged with cross-bar shot, shifted herself with all diligence from her sides, utterly misliking her first entertainment. The Spanish ships were filled with companies of soldiers, in some 200, in others 800, while the *Revenge* had no soldiers, besides the mariners, but the officers' servants and a few volunteers. After a long interchange of broadsides, and small shot, the Spaniards attempted to board the *Revenge*, hoping by the multitudes of their armed soldiers and musqueteers to force her, but were repulsed again and again, and driven back into their own ships or into the sea. In the beginning of the fight a victualler, the *George Noble*, of London, after receiving some shot, fell under the lee of the Revenge, and asked Sir Richard what he commanded him to do. Sir Richard bade him save himself, and leave him to his fortune. After the fight had continued without intermission while the day lasted and some hours of the night, many of the English were slain and wounded, the great galleon had been sunk, while terrific slaughter had been made on board the other Spanish ships. About midnight Sir Richard was struck by a musket-ball; while the surgeon was dressing his wound, he was again shot in the head, the surgeon being killed at the same moment.

The first ships which had attacked the *Revenge* having been beaten off, others took their places, so that she had never less than two mighty galleons by her sides, and before morning she had fifteen other ships assailing her; and so ill did they approve of their entertainment that by break of day they were far more willing to hearken to a composition than again to attack her. But as the day increased, so did the gallant crew decrease; no friends appeared in sight, only enemies, saving only one small ship called the *Pilgrim*, commanded by Jacob Widdon. He deserves to be handed down to fame, for he hovered near all night in the hopes of helping the admiral, but in the morning, bearing away, was hunted like a hare among many ravenous hounds; but, happily, he escaped.

By this time all the powder of the *Revenge* except the last barrel was spent, her pikes broken, forty of her best men slain, and the most part of the rest hurt. At the commencement she had had but a hundred free from sickness, and ninety lay in the hold upon the ballast. By this hundred was sustained all the volleys and boardings of fifteen ships of war. Sir Richard finding himself helpless, and convinced that his ship must fall a prey to the enemy who now circled round him, proposed to the master-gunner, whom he knew to be a most resolute man, to expend their last barrel of powder by blowing up the ship and sinking her, that thereby the Spaniards might lose the glory of a victory. The master-gunner readily consented, and so did divers others, but the captain and master were of another opinion, alleging that the Spaniards would be ready for a compromise, and that there were many valiant men yet living who might do their country acceptable service hereafter — besides which, as the ship had already six-feet of water in the hold, and three shot-holes under water, which were so weakly stopped that by the first working of the ship she must needs sink, she would never get into port. Sir Richard refusing to hearken to these reasons, the captain went on board the ship of the Spanish admiral, Don Alfonso Bacan, who promised that the lives of all should be preserved, that the ship's company should be sent to England, the officers to pay a reasonable ransom, and in the meantime to be free from the galleys or imprisonment.

From the report which the admiral received, no one showed any inclination to return on board the *Revenge*, lest Sir Richard should blow himself and them up together. On this news being returned, the greater part of the crew, the master-gunner excepted, drew back from Sir Richard, it being no hard matter to dissuade men from death to life. The master-gunner finding himself and Sir Richard thus prevented and mastered by the greater number, would have slain himself with the sword, had he not by force been withheld, and locked into his cabin. The Spanish admiral then sent many boats on board the *Revenge*, the English crew, fearing Sir Richard would still carry out his intention, stealing away on board the Spanish ships. Sir Richard, thus overmatched, was sent unto by Don Alfonso Bacan to remove out of the *Revenge*, the ship being marvellous unsavoury, filled with bodies of dead and wounded men, like a slaughter-house. Sir Richard answered that he might do with his body as he list, for he esteemed it not. As he was carried out of the ship he swooned; on reviving again, he desired the ship's company to pray for him.

Don Alfonso used Sir Richard with all humanity, and left nothing unattempted that tended to his recovery, highly commending his valour and worthiness, and greatly bewailing the danger wherein he was, while he admired the resolution which had enabled the English admiral to endure the fire of so many huge ships, and to resist the assaults of so many soldiers. During the fight two Spanish captains and no less than a thousand men were either killed or drowned, while two large ships were sunk by her side, another sunk in the harbour, and a fourth ran herself on shore to save her crew. Greatly to the regret of the Spanish admiral, the gallant Sir Richard died three days after the action; but whether he was buried at sea or on shore is unknown. His last memorable words were: "Here die I, Richard Grenville, with a joyful and quiet mind, for that I have ended my life as a true soldier ought to do, fighting for his country, queen, religion, and honour, my soul willingly departing from this body, leaving behind a lasting fame of having behaved as every valiant soldier is in duty bound to do."

DEATH OF GRENVILLE.

A storm coming on soon afterwards, the *Revenge*, as had been expected, went to the bottom, while fifteen Spanish men-of-war were cast away, as were many of the merchantmen; so that of the whole fleet, which originally amounted to upwards of a hundred, seventy were lost. While the English sailors were scattered among the Spanish fleet, they received a visit from a traitor, one of the Earl of Desmond's family, who endeavoured to persuade them to serve the King of Spain, but in most cases without success. In 1592 an expedition was fitted out by Sir Walter Raleigh, consisting of several queen's ships and some of his own, with which he intended to attack Carthagena and other places in the West Indies; but as he was about to sail, he was superseded in the command by Sir Martin Frobisher, the queen wishing to retain him in England. Sir Martin was directed to proceed only to the coast of Spain, where he captured a large Portuguese carrack, which, to escape the English, ran on shore, and was burned by her people after the goods had been landed; but the English following made themselves masters of a large part of the booty and of the town of Santa Cruz. After waiting patiently for some weeks, another still larger carrack, called the *Madre de Dios* hove in sight. Though the Portuguese fought bravely to defend her, she was captured in the space of an hour and a-half. On going on board, the English, after hunting about for plunder, each man with a lighted candle in his hand, a cabin was entered in which there was a quantity of powder. The carrack was set on fire, and had it not been for the courage of Captain Norton, both the plundered and the plunderers would have been blown together into the air. The carrack, which was brought home in safety, was larger than any man-of-war or merchantman belonging to England. She was of 1600 tons burden, and measuring from the beak-head to the stern, on which was erected a large lantern, she was 165 feet in length. Her greatest beam was 46 feet 10 inches. On leaving Cochin China she had drawn 31 feet of water, but on her arrival at Dartmouth she drew only 26. She had seven decks — one main or sleeping, three close decks, one forecastle, and a spar deck of two floors. The length of her keel was 100 feet, and of the main-mast 121 feet; the main-yard was 106 feet long. She carried between 600 and 700 persons, and considering the length of the voyage, the large amount of provisions can be calculated. She carried fully 900 tons of cargo, consisting of jewels, spices, drugs, silks, calicoes, quilts, carpets, and colours, as also elephants' teeth, porcelain vessels and china, cocoa-nuts, hides, ebony, bedsteads of the same, cloths made from the rinds of trees, probably of the paper-mulberry tree; the whole valued at not less than 150,000 pounds sterling. This shows that a merchant-vessel of those days was not much less in size than an East Indiaman of late years.

On the death of Elizabeth, the navy consisted of forty-two ships — two only, however, of a thousand tons each, though there were several of 800 and 900 tons; but the greater number were much under that size, being of about 400 tons and less. The larger ships carried 340 mariners, 40 gunners, and 120 soldiers.

A sketch of the history of privateering, which, during the reign of Elizabeth, grew into vast proportions, must not be omitted. The fearful atrocities committed by the Spaniards on the inhabitants of the Low Countries naturally created the utmost horror in the breasts of the Protestants of England against them. Large numbers of the Dutch and Flemish escaping to England from their persecutors, and spreading everywhere the account of the barbarities their countrymen had endured, further increased this feeling, till it extended over the length and breadth of the land, but especially among the people of the seaports, where many of the fugitives took up their abodes. When, therefore, an English shipowner, Clark by name, proposed fitting out a squadron of three ships to cruise against the merchant-vessels of that nation, who, in their bigoted zeal, had vowed to stamp out the Protestant faith, not only in the countries subject to their rule, but in England herself, there was no lack of volunteers. Those who were not influenced by religious feelings, were so by the hope of filling their pockets with Spanish gold. When Clark's squadron, after a cruise of six weeks, returned into Newhaven with eighteen prizes, their cargoes valued at 50,000 pounds, applications from all quarters were made to the queen for letters of marque which would enable ships legally to carry on war against the enemy.

At the period of Elizabeth's accession, owing to the treachery as much as to the supineness of her predecessor, of the Royal Navy which had been created by Henry the Eighth, only twenty-three vessels of war, few of them of more than 600 tons burden, remained. There was one only of 800, one of 700, a few being above 200, while the remainder were sloops or other small craft. The Government had therefore to depend chiefly on private ships in the war with France, and the expected struggle of far greater magnitude with Spain. Numerous English subjects had also suffered from the Spanish Inquisition, and Englishmen of rank and wealth considered that they were justified in retaliating on the authors of the cruelties practised on their own countrymen. From every port and river vessels fitted out as traders went forth heavily armed to plunder on the high seas any of the ships of the common enemy of mankind with which they could fall in. At first the bold privateersmen confined themselves to the narrow seas, pouncing down upon any Spanish ship which approached their shores, either driven in thither by the wind, or compelled to seek shelter by stress of weather. Many a trader from Antwerp to Cadiz mysteriously disappeared, or, arriving without her cargo, reported that she had been set upon by a powerful craft, when, boats coming out from the English shore, she had been quickly unladen, her crew glad to escape with their lives. The Scilly Islands especially afforded shelter to a squadron of vessels under Sir Thomas Seymour, who, sailing forth into the chops of the channel, laid wait for any richly-laden craft he might happen to espy. Among other men of rank who thus distinguished themselves were the sons of Lord Chobham. Influenced by that hatred of Roman abominations which had long been the characteristic of their family, Thomas Chobham, the most daring of the brothers, had established himself in a strongly-fortified port in the south of Ireland, from whence, sailing forth with his stout ships, he attacked the Spaniards on their own coasts. Coming in sight of a large ship in the channel, laden with a cargo valued at 80,000 ducats, and having on board forty prisoners doomed to serve in the galleys, he chased her into the Bay of Biscay, where, at length coming up with her, he compelled her to strike, when he released the prisoners, and transferred the cargo to his own ship. The Spaniards declare that he sewed up all the survivors of the crew in their own sails and hove them overboard; but as the story rests on no better authority than that of the Spaniards themselves, we may be excused from giving it credence. The stories of the cruelties practised by the Spaniards on their prisoners are too well authenticated to be doubted. The men who could be guilty of one-tenth part of the horrors they compelled their fellow-subjects in the Netherlands to endure, or those inflicted on the hapless Indians of America, were capable of any conceivable cruelty.

Petitions upon petitions poured in on the queen from those whose fathers, brothers, husbands, and sons had been put to death, or were still groaning in the Spanish Inquisition, or in other prisons, both in the old and new worlds. Dorothy Seely, whose husband was among them, entreats that she and the friends of such of Her Majesty's subjects "as be there imprisoned, inflicted, and tormented beyond all reason, may be allowed to fit out certain ships for the sea at their own proper charges, and to capture such inquisitors or other papistical subjects of the King of Spain as they can take by sea or land, and to retain them in prison in England with such torment and diet as Her Majesty's subjects had suffered in Spain."

To strengthen this petition, it is stated "that not long since the Spanish Inquisition executed sixty persons of Saint Malo, in France, whereupon the Frenchmen, having armed and manned their pinnaces, lay in wait for the Spaniards, and took a hundred and beheaded them, sending the Spanish ships to the shore with the heads, leaving in each ship only one man to relate the cause of the revenge — since which time the Spanish Inquisition has never meddled with those of Saint Malo."

Froude tells us that one of the French rovers, commanded by Jacques Leclerc, called by the Spaniards Pié de Palo — "timber leg" — sailed from Havre, and captured a Portuguese vessel worth 40,000 ducats, as well as a Biscayan ship laden with iron and wool, and afterwards chased another papist ship into Falmouth, where he fired into her and drove her on shore. The captain of the Spaniard appealed for protection to the governor of Pendennis, but the governor replied that the privateer was properly commissioned, and that without special orders from the queen he could not interfere. Pié de Palo then took possession of her as a prize, and afterwards anchored under shelter of Pendennis, waiting for further good fortune. As it was the depth of winter, and the weather being unsettled, five Portuguese ships, a few days later, were driven in for shelter. Ascertaining the insecurity of their position, they attempted to escape to sea again, but Pié de Palo dashed after them and seized two of the five, which he brought back as prizes. Philip complained to the English Government of the robberies committed on his subjects, and attempts were made to put a stop to these proceedings. A few of the rovers were captured, but were very quickly set at liberty again, and the privateers swarmed everywhere in still increasing numbers. In truth, Cecil, who knew perfectly well what were the ultimate aims of Philip, had no wish to damp the ardour and enterprise of his countrymen.

Not content with the booty they obtained in the narrow seas, the privateers, often in large fleets, boldly traversed the ocean in search of Spanish argosies in the West Indies and on the Spanish main. Drake, Hawkins, and Cavendish were among the foremost in these enterprises. Whatever may be thought of their proceedings at the present day, their example tended to foster that courage, perseverance, and indifference to danger characteristic of British seamen.

The King of Spain having granted letters of reprisals to his subjects, especially to cruise in the Levant and the Mediterranean, the Turkey merchants fitted out five stout ships with letters of marque, to provide for their defence — the *Royal Merchant*, the *Toby*, the *Edward Bonadventure*, the *William*, and the *John*. While up the Levant they were informed that the Spaniards had fitted out two fleets, one of twenty and another of thirty galleys, to intercept them. On this, Mr Williamson, captain of the *Royal Merchant*, was chosen admiral, and the commander of the *Toby*, vice-admiral. As they were sailing between Sicily and the African coast, they descried seven galleys and two frigates under Sicilian and Maltese colours, in the service of Spain, the admiral of which ordered the pursers of the English ships to repair on board his galley. One alone, Mr Rowet, accompanied the messenger. He was received in a haughty manner by the Spanish admiral, who insisted on the surrender of the English ships. On Mr Rowet's return, the Spaniard signified his resolution by firing at the English, which was immediately returned, when the engagement began. The five English merchant-vessels, though heavily laden, maintained an obstinate fight for five hours, and so shattered were the Spanish ships-of-war, that the admiral first, and then two others, were obliged to haul off, scarcely able to keep above water. The remainder not having men enough to man their guns, soon after followed his example. The English lost but two men in this engagement, but their cargoes were too valuable to run any risk by pursuing the enemy; they therefore made the best of their way to England, where they arrived in safety, having, by favour of a thick fog and a brisk easterly wind, escaped the other Spanish squadron, which had waited for them off the Straits of Gibraltar.

The instructions in the articles of war drawn up by the Lord High Admiral, to be observed by the captains and crews of the ships of the Royal Navy, prove that it was expected that the seamen of those days should be pious and well-conducted men. They were to be openly read at service time, twice every week.

"Imprimis, That you take special care to serve God by using common prayers twice every day, except urgent cause enforce the contrary; and that no man, soldier, or other mariner do dispute of matters of religion, unless it be to be resolved of some doubts, and in such case that he confer with the ministers."

"Second, Item, you shall forbid swearing, brawling, and dicing, and such-like disorders as may breed contention and disorders in your ships."

"Five, All persons, whatsoever, within your ship shall come to the ordinary services of the ship without contradiction."

"Sixth, You shall give special charge for avoiding the danger of fire, and that no candle be carried in your ship without a lantern, which, if any person shall disobey, you shall severely punish. And if any chance of fire or other dangers (which God forbid) shall happen to any ship near unto you, then you shall, by your boats and all other your best means, seek to help and relieve her."

"Eighth, You shall give order that your ship may be kept clean daily and sometimes washed, which, with God's favour, shall preserve from sickness, and avoid many other inconveniences."

"Fifteenth, Every captain and master of the fleet shall have a special regard that no contention be found betwixt the mariners and the soldiers."

"Nineteenth, No captain or master shall suffer any spoil to be made aboard any ship or barque that shall be taken by them or any of their companies, because the rest of the company have interest in everything that shall be taken."

"Twenty-second, The watch shall be set every night by eight of the o'clock, either by trumpet or drum, and singing the Lord's Prayer, some of the Psalms of David, or clearing of the glass."

"Twenty-sixth, No person shall depart out of the ship wherein he is placed into another without special leave of his captain."

"Twenty-eighth, No person whatsoever shall dare to strike any captain, lieutenant, master, or other officer, upon pain of death; and furthermore, whatsoever he be that shall strike any inferior person, he shall receive punishment according to the offence given, be it by death or otherwise."

Most of these articles are still in force; but the first, excellent as they are, have unhappily too often been set at nought by officers and men.

Chapter Seven.

James the First — from A.D. 1567 to A.D. 1625.

As James the First was totally unacquainted with nautical affairs, having possessed no fleet when King of Scotland, disputes constantly arose respecting the honour of the flag, which the English claimed, and this induced the famous Hugo Grotius to write a treatise, in which he endeavoured to prove the futility of their title to the dominion of the sea. England, however, still maintained her right to be saluted by the ships of all other nations, and the learned Selden supported the English, asserting that they had a hereditary and uninterrupted right to the sovereignty of the seas, conveyed to them by their ancestors in trust for their latest posterity. During this period numerous colonies were settled, and the commerce of England extended in all directions by her brave navigators. The navy was not neglected, twenty ships being added by the king, and 50,000 pounds voted for the maintenance of the fleet. In the year 1610 the largest ship of war yet constructed in England was built by order of the king, and called the *Prince*. Her keel was 114 feet, her cross-beam was 44 feet in length. She carried sixty-four pieces of great ordnance, and she was of the burden of 1400 tons. She was double built, and adorned most sumptuously within and without with all manner of curious carving, painting, and rich gilding, being in all respects the greatest and goodliest ship that ever was built in England. Raleigh's remarks to Prince Henry on the subject are worthy of note, though it appears his advice was not followed. He recommended that the intended vessel should be of smaller size than the *Victory*, in order that the timber of the old ship might serve for the new. "If she be bigger," he remarks, "she will be of less use, go very deep to water, and be of mighty charge (our channels decaying every year), less nimble, less manageable, and seldom to be used. A well-conditioned ship should be, in the first instance, strongly built; secondly, swift in sail; thirdly, stout sided; fourthly, her ports ought to be so laid that she may carry out her guns in all weathers; fifthly, she ought to hull well; sixthly, she should stay well when boarding or turning on a wind if required." He then continues: "It is to be noted that all ships sharp before, not having a long floor, will fall rough into the sea from the billow, and take in water over head and ears; and the same quality of all narrow-quartered ships to sink after the tail. The high charging of ships is that which brings many ill qualities upon them. It makes them extremely lee-ward, makes them sink deep into the seas, makes them labour in foul weather, and ofttimes overset. Safety is more to be respected than show or niceness for ease. In sea-journeys both cannot well stand to-gether, and, therefore, the most necessary is to be chosen. Two decks and a-half is enough, and no building at all above that but a low mas-ter's cabin. Our masters and mariners will say that the ships will bear more well enough; and true it is, if none but old mariners served in them. But men of better sort, unused to such a life, cannot so well endure the rolling and tumbling from side to side, where the seas are never so little grown, which comes by high charging. Besides, those high cabin-works aloft are very dangerous, in that they may tear men with their splinters. Above all other things, have care that the great guns are four feet clear above water when all loading is in, or else those best pieces are idle at sea; for if the ports lie lower and be open, it is dangerous; and by that default was a goodly ship and many gal-lant gentlemen lost in the days of Henry the Eighth, before the Isle of Wight, in a ship called the *Mary Rose*."

These remarks show how attentively Raleigh had studied the subject of shipbuilding and, undoubtedly, during his time great improve-ments were made in the construction of ships of the Royal Navy. A large East India ship of 1200 tons was also built at Woolwich, and was the first trading ship of that size launched in the kingdom. The king called her the *Trade's Increase*.

In 1622 the first established contract for victualling the Royal Navy was made, and every man's allowance settled. It appears not to have differed greatly from that served out at the present day, except that on Friday fish, butter, and cheese were served out; showing that the Romish custom of what is called fasting on Friday had not been abol-ished. The king also gave annually 30,000 pounds worth of timber from the royal forests for the use of the navy.

The Dutch and other nations had, up to this time, been in the habit of fishing in English waters, but, though the pusillanimous king would not, of his own accord, have interfered for fear of giving offence, so great an outcry was raised by the people, that he was compelled to issue a proclamation prohibiting any foreigners from fishing on the British coast. Though in terms it appeared general, it was in reality levelled only at the Dutch. They yielded, and obtained by treaty per-mission to fish, on payment of certain dues. The nation at large gaining a voice in the management of public affairs, discovered also that vast abuses existed in the administration of the navy, as the large sums granted by Parliament were squandered, the brave commanders were unemployed, and cowardice trusted with the highest offices; and that frauds, corruption, neglect and misdemeanours were frequent and open. Numberless petitions were sent to the sovereign, and a committee of inquiry was appointed; the alleged offences were strictly examined into, some of the culprits were discharged, others fined, and way made for better officers. The Royal Navy being thus placed on a more respectable footing, the spirit of enterprise was encouraged among private persons, and trade once more flourished.

STERN OF MAN-OF-WAR OF OLDEN DAYS.

Considerable progress was made by the East India Company, and, in 1610, Sir Henry Middleton sailed with a larger fleet than had ever before been despatched to that part of the world. On landing at Mocha, Sir Henry was treacherously attacked during an entertainment to which he had been invited, when many of his people were killed, and he and the rest made prisoners. After remaining six months in prison, he and some of his people escaped and regained their ships; then, returning to the town, he threatened to reduce it to ashes unless the remainder of the English were released and a heavy ransom paid him. On this the English were set at liberty, and the sum was paid. He afterwards encountered a large fleet of Portuguese, who, attempting to impede his progress, he sank some and captured others. Several Portuguese ships were captured, and seventeen Arab vessels also fell into the hands of the English. On his voyage home, seized with a mortal illness, he died, honoured and lamented.

About the same time Captain Hudson, who had already performed three voyages to the north, again sailed in search of a north-west passage; but his mate, Ibbott, fearing the dangers they would have to encounter, formed a conspiracy. Hudson, and those who adhered to him, were set on shore, and perished miserably.

In 1611 the East India Company sent out another fleet under Captain Hippin, and the following year a second under Captain Saris, who reached Japan. By judicious conduct, and the due administration of bribes to many persons nearest the emperor, he succeeded in establishing a trade for the English with Japan, returning home with a very profitable cargo.

In the year 1611 the Muscovy Company despatched two vessels to commence the whale fishery. On board these vessels went three Biscayans who were accustomed to the business. Having set sail late, they had only time to catch one whale, but from it were made seven tons of oil. The rest of the crew having observed the manner in which the Biscayans performed the work, became thorough masters of the operation. Though this commencement was but small, it led to great results, and from henceforward there was no want of people ready to enter into the undertaking.

In consequence of the account given by those who were wrecked in the *Sea Venture* on the Bermudas, a colony was sent out, and the hitherto desolate islands were peopled by English settlers.

One of the most gallant exploits of this period was performed by Captain Best, who sailed in command of a fleet sent out by the East India Company. After remaining for some time at Surat, he caught sight of a vast fleet of Portuguese, numbering no less than 240 vessels. Having beaten off a number of them that attacked him, he continued his course. They, however, having repaired damages, the whole fleet came in search of him. As they bore down under a cloud of sail, threatening his destruction, he was advised by one of the Sultan's principal officers to fly. Best replied that he would advise that to the Portuguese, and, weighing anchor, stood out to meet the enemy. The shore was crowded with natives eager to witness the engagement. It ended, after four hours, as the other had done. The Portuguese, after receiving immense damage, sailed away as fast as they could, and Captain Best returned and anchored in the harbour, amid the shouts of the people. The account of the engagement was everywhere told among the natives, and the courage of the English magnified to the highest. After touching at Achin, and renewing his friendship with the people, in the succeeding year, he arrived in England, rich in his lading, more in honour.

In the year 1613 the Muscovy Company sent out seven stout ships to catch whales. They were followed by several Dutch, Flemish, and French ships, and half-a-dozen English interlopers. The Company's ships gathering into a body, ordered the others, in the name of the King of England, to depart from the coast, the fishery of which he had appropriated to his own subjects. The Dutch sending a taunting answer, the English replied with their cannon, compelling their rivals to take their departure, and the English private ships to fish for them. With this help, they made a good return.

In 1614 the celebrated pirate Sir Andrew Barton, with two ships, laid the coasts of England and Scotland under contribution. Two ships of war, under the command of Sir William Monson and Sir Francis Howard, were sent out to effect their capture. One of them was taken off Sinclair Castle, the seat of the Earl of Caithness. Sir Andrew for long managed to keep at a distance from his pursuers, having friends in various places, especially in Ireland, who gave him assistance. Among others was a certain Mr Cormat, who treacherously betrayed the Scotch pirate into the hands of Sir William Monson. His ship was captured, and he, with two or three of his officers, executed.

Considerable progress at this period was made in the science of navigation. In the year 1624 Mr Gunter, professor of astronomy at Gresham College, Cambridge, published his scale of logarithms, sines, etcetera, and invented the scale which has since gone by his name.

No darker stain rests on the memory of James than that of his judicial murder of Sir Walter Raleigh. Influenced by his evil councillors, the pusillanimous king offered up the gallant seaman as a sacrifice to the revengeful Spaniards, or rather to their ambassador, Gondomar. Cheerful to the last, the noble Raleigh bade farewell to all around him; then, taking the axe, he felt along upon the edge, and smiling, said to the sheriff, "This is a sharp medicine, but it is a physician for all diseases." On being asked which way he would lay himself, he placed his head on the block, observing, "So that the heart be right, it is no matter which way the head lieth."

Some lines written on Sir Walter's death thus finish: —

> "I saw in every stander-by
> Pale death; life only in thine eye.
> The legacy thou gavest us then
> We'll sue for when thou diest again.
> Farewell! truth shall this story say,
> We died, thou only livedst that day."

Such was the end of the great Sir Walter Raleigh, once so highly in favour with Queen Elizabeth, and, next to Drake, the great scourge and terror of the Spaniards.

The Algerines were then, as they were for many years afterwards, the pests of the ocean. Their chief cruising ground was in the Straits of Gibraltar. Numerous English merchantmen fell into their clutches. The same determined spirit, however, which has since been exhibited by British seamen, existed in those days, and induced, on several occasions, the captives to make gallant efforts to effect their escape. Among these instances two are especially worthy of note.

The *Jacob*, of Bristol, was entering the straits when she was pounced upon by an Algerine and captured. The pirates took all the crew out of her with the exception of four, and sent thirteen of their own people on board to bring her to Algiers. Four of the captives, knowing the terrible slavery to which they would be subjected should they reach Algiers, resolved to attempt the recapture of their vessel. Happily for them, on the fifth night after they had been taken, a heavy gale sprang up. While the Algerine captain was assisting his followers to shorten sail, two of the English, who had been liberated that they might lend a hand, coming suddenly upon him hove him overboard. Having got hold of a rope which was towing astern, he had almost regained the deck, when one of the Englishmen drove him back with the pump-handle, the act being, fortunately, unobserved during the darkness and confusion by the rest of the pirates. This done, they made their way into the master's cabin, where they found two cutlasses, with which suddenly attacking the pirates, they drove them from one part of the ship to the other, killed two, and made a third leap overboard. The other nine they drove between decks, when they forced the hatches down upon them. Making use of two or three of the Algerines at a time, as they required them for making or shortening sail, they carried the ship triumphantly into Saint Luca, in Spain, where the Algerines were sold for slaves. At the same time the *Nicholas*, of Plymouth, of 40 tons burden, commanded by John Rawlins, and the *Bonaventure* of 70 tons, were bound out together up the straits. On the 18th of November they came in sight of Gibraltar, when they discovered five ships, which they soon perceived to be pirates, making all sail towards them. In vain they attempted to reach Gibraltar; the Algerines coming up with the *Bonaventure*, she was captured by their admiral, while the vice-admiral soon afterwards compelled Rawlins to strike. The same day the admiral put on shore twelve of the *Bonaventure's* crew, with some other English captives before taken, but the vice-admiral ordered Rawlins and five of his men to be brought on board his vessel, leaving three men and a boy, with thirteen Algerines, on board the prize. The following night, during a storm, the *Nicholas* was lost sight of. On the 22nd the vice-admiral, with Rawlins on board, arrived at Algiers. A few days afterwards the *Nicholas* arrived, when the prisoners were carried to the pacha, who, having chosen one of them for himself, the rest were afterwards sent to the market to be sold. Rawlins was bought by the captain, who took him at a low price because he had a lame hand, but perceiving that this rendered him unfit for work, sold him again, with two more of his men, to an English renegado, John Goodhall, who, with his partners, had bought the *Exchange*, of Bristol, a ship formerly taken by the pirates, which at that time lay unrigged inside the mole, and for which they wanted some skilful seamen. On the 7th of January, 1622, the ship, being fitted, was hauled out of the mole. She carried twelve cast guns, with a crew of sixty-three Algerines, nine Englishmen, one Frenchmen, and four Hollanders, all freemen; and for gunners, she had two soldiers, one an

English and the other a Dutch renegado. Rawlins, from the first going on board, resolved to attempt regaining his liberty. For this purpose he furnished himself with ropes and pieces of iron, and iron crowbars to secure the scuttles, gratings, and cabins, and when, having gained over the other Europeans, he hoped, by being masters of the gun-room, ordnance, and powder, either to blow up their captors or to kill them as they came out of their cabins. He first made known his design to the English, and by degrees won over the four Hollanders, who offered to join them and gain the assistance of the Dutch renegadoes, while the English undertook to obtain the assistance of the renegado of their own nation. During this time Rawlins, who was acting as sailing-master, persuaded the Algerine captain to steer to the northward, though he knew very well that they had already passed the straits. On the 16th of February they took an English barque from Torbay, laden with salt. With the exception of the mate and two men, the crew were removed from the prize, and ten Algerines, with the Dutch and one English renegado, who were all in the plot, were sent on board instead. Before they left the *Exchange*, Rawlins assured them that he would make his attempt that night or the next, and give them a signal by which they might know when he was about it, advising them to acquaint the English in the barque with their design, and to steer towards the English coast. Next morning the Algerine captain got very much out of humour in consequence of not seeing the prize; and Rawlins, fearing that he might return to Algiers, thought it high time to put his plan into execution. He had already made the master and crew of the Torbay vessel acquainted with it; he now told the Algerine captain that there was a great deal of water below, and that it did not come to the pumps because the ship was too far by the head. For the purpose of remedying this an order was issued to bring four guns astern; two of them were accordingly placed with their mouths directly before the binnacle. Rawlins had already provided himself with sufficient powder, which he obtained from the gunner, to prime the pieces. He now assured the captain that in order to right the ship all hands must work at the pumps. While this was doing, two matches were brought, one between two spoons, and the other in a can, and immediately one of the guns being discharged, the binnacle was shattered to pieces. On this signal, all the English collected together, and having seized such arms as they could lay hold of quickly cleared the hold, while another party made themselves masters of the magazine and arms. The pirates, who were on the poop, now attacked the English, who, being by this time all armed, compelled them to cry for quarter. They were ordered to come down one by one. So enraged were the English that several of the pirates were killed, while others leaped into the sea. Thus of forty-five Algerines who were on board, the captain and five more alone were saved. With these the gallant Rawlins and his men arrived at Plymouth on the 15th of February, 1622. The Torbay barque reached Penzance, in Cornwall, having all along persuaded the Algerines that they were going to Algiers, till they came in sight of England. When the pirates were below trimming the salt, they nailed the hatches down upon them. Having come to an anchor, they carried their captives to Exeter.

Chapter Eight.

Charles the First to Termination of Commonwealth — A.D. 1625 to A.D. 1660.

The unhappy Charles ascended the throne under disadvantageous circumstances. His father had left him a heavy debt; the Duke of Buckingham, his chief minister, was universally hated, and England had greatly sunk in the estimation of foreign nations. James had agreed to furnish the King of France with some ships of war to assist him against the King of Spain or his allies in Italy. In pursuance of this agreement, Captain John Pennington was despatched in the *Vanguard*, having under him six hired merchant-vessels. The King of France, however, being hotly engaged in a war with his Protestant subjects, intended to make use of the ships for the reduction of Rochelle. Pennington, on discovering this, immediately wrote to the Duke of Buckingham declining so odious a service, and requesting leave to return to England. Buckingham, in reply, having obtained an order from Charles, commanded him to employ his ships in such service as the King of France should direct. The latter, at the same time, sent a letter to the English captain, requiring him to take on board a number of French soldiers, with his admiral, the Duke of Montmorency, and repair before Rochelle. This Captain Pennington, with true English spirit, refused to do; on which the French officer who had brought the letter returned on board the *Vanguard* to protest against him as a rebel to his king and country. Not content with having once done this, he returned again and enforced his request by threats and menaces, at which the seamen were so enraged, that they weighed anchor and set sail, crying out they would rather be hanged at home than be slaves to the French, and fight against their own religion. The *Vanguard* accordingly returned to the Downs. On his arrival, the captain sending an express to court with advice of his proceedings, immediately received a positive order, under the king's sign-manual, to return and deliver up the ships into the hands of a French officer at Dieppe. Having complied with this order, he quitted the command, and he and all the officers and seamen, both of the *Vanguard* and merchant-vessels, left their ships and returned to England.

The whole nation burned with indignation when they heard that Captain Pennington's ships had been delivered up to the French and employed against Rochelle, and demanded their immediate restitution. The French king excused himself on the pretence that his subjects, by whom they were manned, would not now quit them; on which, to appease the people, the Duke of Buckingham issued commissions of reprisal. The *Saint Peter*, of Havre-de-Grâce, and other French vessels were on this captured. Hearing of this proceeding, the French king not only absolutely refused to restore the seven ships, but seized on all the English merchants' property throughout his dominions. To carry on the war with Spain a powerful fleet of eighty English and Dutch ships was fitted out under the command of Cecil, afterwards created Viscount Wimbleton. Ten regiments were embarked on board the fleet, under the Earls of Essex and Denbigh. They proceeded to Cadiz, when the troops, having broken into the wine-stores, became so excessively intoxicated, that had the enemy set on them they must have been put to the sword. The officers hastened, therefore, their re-embarkation, and the expedition returned without having effected anything.

In 1627 three expeditions were undertaken, professedly to assist the people of Rochelle, but, being badly managed, possibly through treachery, they all failed. It was while fitting out one of these fleets that the Duke of Buckingham, then Lord High Admiral, was murdered by Felton.

A severe action was fought near Ormuz, in the Gulf of Persia, between four English ships, under the command of Captain John Weddell, and four Dutch ships, with eight Portuguese galleons and thirty-two frigates. On hearing of the approach of the enemy, the English captain told his Dutch allies that he had resolved, for the glory of God, the honour of his nation, the profit of the worthy employers, and the safeguard of their lives, ships, and goods, to fight it out as long as a man was living in his ship to bear a sword. To whom the Dutchmen answered that they were of a like resolution, and would stick as close to the English as the shirts to their backs; and so in friendly manner each took leave for that night. The Dutch the next morning were the first to get into action. Friends and foes were now within musket-shot of each other, when it fell a calm, and the ships of the allies could not work but as the tide set them. When the Portuguese were aboard and aboard, they had a great advantage with their frigates, which often towed them clear one of another. Thus they lay four or five hours pelting and beating one another with their ordnance, while the Portuguese frigates plied the English and Dutch with their small shot as fast as they could, the *Royal James* being forced to keep the barge ahead to pull the ship's head to and fro. Thus they fought on till night, several men being killed, the Dutch having also lost their chief commander. For several days the fight lasted. On one occasion the *James* singled out a Portuguese lying by her side with foresail and fore-topsail aback, so near that a man might quoit a biscuit into her, and fired not less than five hundred shots before she got clear. Thus the small squadron kept the enemy at bay, till scarcely enough powder and shot remained on board the *Royal James* for another day's fight. The English lost 29 officers and men, and the Dutch about the same number. The Portuguese, whose fleet carried 232 guns and 2100 men, had 481 killed.

Another fight in the same locality, in the year 1625, between three English East India ships, the *Lion*, *Dolphin*, and *Palsgrave*, and eighteen or twenty Portuguese frigates, under the command of Don Rufero, ended more disastrously. The *Lion*, being boarded by both the admiral and vice-admiral, was dreadfully shattered, and torn in pieces in the stem, in consequence of the poop blowing up with fifty or sixty of the enemy on it. The Portuguese then left her, expecting that she would sink or burn down to the water's edge, and pursued the *Palsgrave* and *Dolphin*, which, however, effected their escape. The brave crew of the *Lion*, having put out the fire, succeeded in patching her up sufficiently to reach Ormuz, where they received every assistance they required from the Sultan. They were in hopes of being relieved by other English ships, when Rufero with his frigates came rowing towards them. The *Lion* lay in such a position that she could only bring her chase-pieces to bear upon the enemy. So well were they served that they sank two of the Portuguese frigates before they could board her, and two more after they were by her side. So closely were the English then pressed by Rufero that, unable to open a port in the ship, they were forced to shoot away ports and all. In addition to this, the Portuguese so completely surrounded her by fire-works, that all her masts and sails caught fire, as well as her upper-deck, which in half-an-hour fell down on their heads, and drove them from their guns. On seeing death on either side, some leaped overboard, and put themselves on the mercy of the enemy, while the rest set fire to the powder-room, and blew up the ship. Those who were received on board the frigates were carried into Ormuz Island, and the next morning Rufero gave orders to cut off all their heads, with the exception of one Thomas Winterbrune, whom he sent with a letter to the merchants at Gambroon. The rest, twenty-six persons, were immediately beheaded. This will give us some idea of the mode of proceeding between belligerents in those days. The object of the Portuguese was to prevent the English and Dutch from interfering with their trade, and they hoped by such horrible cruelty to intimidate others from coming out, or else were actuated by a spirit of barbarous revenge. In 1626 the wages of seamen in the Royal Navy were increased to twenty shillings a-month, and of ordinary seamen to fourteen shillings, besides an allowance to a chaplain of fourpence, to a barber twopence, and to the Chest at Chatham of sixpence per month. A clerk and a keeper of all the king's stores and storehouses at Chatham, Portsmouth, Deptford, etcetera, were also appointed.

An arbitrary tax having been imposed in the year 1634, by the name of ship-money, which compelled all the seaport towns to furnish a fleet to prevent the Dutch fishing on the coast of Britain; it was now extended throughout the whole kingdom. The fleet was to consist of 44 ships, carrying 8000 men, and to be armed and fitted for war; but, as will be remembered, the unhappy king raised the money, but spent it on other objects.

In 1637 was laid the keel of the *Royal Sovereign*, of 128 feet, the first three-decked ship built for the Royal Navy. From the fore-end of the beak-head to the after-end of the stern she measured 232 feet, and she had a beam of 48 feet, while from the bottom of the keel to the top of the stern-lantern she measured 76 feet. She carried 30 guns on her lower-deck, 30 on the middle-deck, 26 on the main-deck, 14 on the quarter-deck, 12 on the forecastle, and had 10 stern and bow-chasers. She was of 1637 tons burden; she carried eleven anchors, the largest weighing 4400 pounds; she had five stern-lanterns, the centre so large as to contain ten persons upright. She was built by Peter Pett, under the inspection of Phineas Pett.

The French, at the same time, began to establish a regular marine, having fifty ships and twenty galleys in their navy. And now, for the first time, was showed their superiority over the Spaniards, on which Cardinal Richelieu ordered the following motto to be placed on the stern of the largest: "Even on the main, our Gallic lilies triumph over Spain."

A fund was now established by the king for the relief of maimed and shipwrecked or otherwise distressed sailors in the merchant-service, and for the widows and children of such as should be killed or lost at sea. To form it, sixpence per month was deducted from the pay of sea-officers, and fourpence from all sailors' wages from the port of London. This fund was placed under the management of the Corporation of the Trinity House.

In 1640 the first frigate, the *Constant Hardwick*, was built, under the direction of Peter Pett. The king added ten more ships to the Royal Navy, which, at the commencement of the Civil War, consisted of eighty-two sail.

The Commonwealth.

We now come to that period when one of the greatest men who ever ruled England was to raise her to the highest position among the nations of Europe.

Numerous engagements had taken place between the ships adhering to the king, chiefly under the command of Prince Rupert, and those of the Parliament, under Warwick, Dean, Popham, and Blake. Blake having finally dispersed Prince Rupert's ships, was appointed commander-in-chief of the British fleet. He was at first employed in reducing the Scilly Islands and various places in the West Indies and America, which still held out for the king. On war breaking out with the Dutch, he was summoned home to take command of the fleet sent against them. The Dutch had long been jealous of the commercial progress made by the English, who everywhere interfered with their trade, and they only now sought for an opportunity to break with their ancient allies. It was not long wanting. England claiming the sovereignty of the seas, insisted that the ships of other nations should strike their flags whenever they met them. On the 14th May, Captain Young, the commander of an English man-of-war, fell in with a Dutch squadron off the back of the Isle of Wight. The Dutchman refused to strike his flag, on which Captain Young, without further ado, fired a broadside upon the Dutch commander's ship, which induced her to haul down her flag. This was the commencement of hostilities, which were long carried on between the two nations — the Dutch, notwithstanding the gallantry of Van Tromp, De Witt, De Ruyter, and other admirals, being in most cases defeated by Blake, Penn, and other naval commanders.

Soon after this Admiral Van Tromp put to sea with a fleet of upwards of forty sail, under pretence of protecting the Dutch trade. He was met coming into the Downs by a squadron, when he stated that he was compelled to put in by stress of weather. The English commander immediately sent notice to Blake, who was lying off Dover. Blake at once sailed in search of Van Tromp, and on approaching, fired to put the Dutchman in mind that it was his duty to strike his flag. Blake commenced the action with but fifteen ships, and with them, for four hours, fought the Dutchmen till, late at night, he was joined by the rest of his fleet. By this time two Dutch ships had been taken and one disabled, the English having lost none, when Van Tromp bore away and escaped.

In the Mediterranean, Commodore Bodley, in command of four English ships, fought a gallant action against eight Dutch ships, commanded by Admiral Van Galen. The Dutchman laid the English commodore's ships aboard, but having been thrice set on fire, he sheered off with much loss. The second ship, which then took her place, was also beaten off, having lost her main-mast. Two others next attacked the commodore, but were defeated; though the English lost a hundred men, killed and wounded. The *Phoenix*, an English ship, had meantime boarded one of the commodore's assailants and carried her, but was in turn boarded and captured by another Dutch ship, and taken into Leghorn Roads. Here Captain Van Tromp took command of the *Phoenix*. The Dutchmen, thinking themselves secure, spent their time in mirth and jollity on shore, when Captain Owen Cox, now serving in Commodore Platten's squadron, hearing of what was going forward, manned three boats with thirty men in each. In addition to their weapons, each man was provided with a bag of meal to throw in the eyes of the Dutchmen. Captain Cox pulled in during the night, and got alongside the frigate at daylight. The boats' crews had each their appointed work; one had to cut the cables, the second had to go aloft and loose the sails, while the third closed the hatches and kept the crew in subjection. Van Tromp was below, but hearing the alarm, he rushed out of his cabin, and discharged his pistols at the English, who were by that time masters of the frigate. Finding that his ship was captured, he leaped out of the cabin window, and swam safely to a Dutch ship astern. The *Phoenix* was carried off in triumph, and reached Naples in safety. Of course, the Grand Duke of Tuscany remonstrated, and ordered Commodore Flatten either to restore the *Phoenix* or to quit Leghorn; he was determined not to do the former, and sending to Commodore Bodley, who was lying at Elba with his small squadron, it was arranged he should come off the port, and draw the Dutch away. This he did. Commodore Van Galen's squadron, at the time lying off the port to intercept him, consisted of sixteen sail; while, besides the *Alfred*, of 52 guns, he had only the *Bonaventure*, of 44 guns, the *Sampson*, of 36, the *Levant Merchant*, of 28, the *Pilgrim* and *Mary*, of 30 guns. He contrived, however, to let Commodore Bodley know his position, who attempted to draw the Dutch off, and clear the way for his squadron. Van Galen, after chasing for some time, perceiving Platten's squadron, returned to attack it. During the action which ensued, the *Bonaventure* blew up, while Van Galen lost a leg from a shot, of which wound he died. Commodore Bodley's squadron having now joined, the action became general. Captain Cornelius Van Tromp, who attacked the *Sampson*, was beaten off, but she was directly afterwards destroyed by a fire-ship. The *Alfred*, the *Levant Merchant*, and *Pilgrim* were all overpowered and taken, and the *Mary* alone effected her escaped, and joined the squadron of Commodore Bodley.

Another desperate action soon afterwards took place between the Dutch and the English in the channel, the English having 105 ships, and the Dutch 104. The action had lasted about an hour when Admiral Dean, the second in command, was cut in two by a cannon-shot. Monk, the commander-in-chief, seeing him fall, threw a cloak over his body to conceal it from the seamen. The ship of Van Kelson, the Dutch rear-admiral, was blown up after this. From eleven in the morning till six in the evening the battle raged, when the Dutch endeavoured to escape. Blake joined the English fleet during the night, and pursued them. About noon the battle was renewed, and for four hours continued to rage. Van Tromp grappled Admiral Penn's ship, the *James*, and attempted to board, but was repulsed, and was boarded in return. The English having driven the Dutchmen below, Van Tromp ordered the deck to be blown up, when numbers of the boarders were killed, though he escaped. His ship was again boarded by the crews of the *James* and of another ship, and he would have been captured had not De Witt and De Ruyter bore down and saved him. The battle was decisive; eleven Dutch ships were taken and thirteen hundred prisoners, while seven were sunk, two were blown up, thus making twenty ships taken and destroyed.

Grand naval engagements were carried on in those days with very little order or regularity, each ship singling out an antagonist, and attacking her as opportunities offered. Even then, however, some of the more sagacious naval commanders discerned that this was not the wisest plan for gaining a victory. Sir William Monson, one of the most skilful admirals of the period, observes, that the most famous naval battles of late years were those of Lepanto against the Turks, in 1577, of the Spaniards against the French, 1580, and the English against the Spanish Armada, in 1588. After making various remarks, he continues: "The greatest advantage in a sea-fight is to get the wind of one another; for he that has the wind is out of danger of being boarded, and has the advantage where to board and how to attempt the enemy. The wind being thus gotten, the general is to give no other directions than to every admiral of a squadron to draw together their squadron and every one to undertake his opposite squadron, or where he should do it to his greatest advantage, but to be sure to take a good distance of one another, and to relieve that squadron that should be overcharged or distressed. Let them give warning to their ships not to venture so far as to bring them to leeward of the enemy, for it would be in the power of the enemy to board them, and they not to avoid it."

The strict ordering of battles by ships was before the invention of the bowline, for then there was no sailing but before the wind, nor any fighting but by boarding; whereas now a ship will sail within six points of thirty-two, and by the advantage of wind, may rout any force that is placed in that form of battle — namely, that of the Spanish Armada, to which he is referring. The Admiralty, however, did not appear to agree with Sir William Monson, for the following instructions were issued: — "You are to take notice, that in case of joining battle you are to leave it to the vice-admiral to assail the enemy's admiral, and to match yours as equally as you can to succour the rest of the fleet, as cause shall require, not wasting your powder nor shooting afar off, nor till you come side by side."

The more sagacious commanders saw, that in order to ensure victory, something beyond a vast host of ships fighting without order was necessary, and perceived that the fleet which fought in line was in most cases victorious. The fiercest action of this period was fought on the 9th and 10th of August, when the English fleet, under Monk, came in sight of the Dutch, commanded by Admiral Van Tromp, who had with him many other celebrated officers, and nearly a hundred ships of war. Monk had about the same number of ships, which he drew up in line. The English manoeuvred to gain the wind, but Van Tromp, who had it at the first, kept it with advantage, and drew up his own fleet in a line parallel to that of the English, when, bearing down upon them, he began the battle with so great a fury, that many ships were soon seen dismasted, others sunk, and others on fire. A spectator, who was on board a vessel at a distance, describes the scene: "The two fleets were now enveloped in a cloud of smoke so dense that it was impossible to form a judgment of the fierceness of the battle otherwise than by the horrible noise of the cannon with which the air resounded, and by the mountains of fire which every now and then were seen rising out of the smoke, with a crash that gave sufficient notice that whole ships were blowing up. The battle lasted for eight hours, and was the most hard fought of any that had happened throughout the war. The Dutch fire-ships were managed with great dexterity, and many of the large vessels in the English fleet were in the utmost danger. The *Triumph* was so effectually fired, that most of her crew threw themselves into the sea, though others remaining behind put out the fire. Admiral Lawson engaged Admiral Ruyter, killed and wounded above half his men, and so disabled his ship, that she was towed out of the fleet. About noon Van Tromp was shot through the body by a musket-ball as he was giving his orders. This greatly discouraged the Dutch, so that they began to beat to windward, and to engage only in retreating, having but one flag still flying. As the smoke cleared off, the two fleets were seen in a condition which showed the horrible fury of the conflict in which they had been engaged. The whole sea was covered with dead bodies, with fragments, and with hulls of wrecks, still smoking or burning. Throughout the remainder of the two fleets were seen only dismasted vessels, and sails perforated through and through by cannon-balls. The English pursued them, but being afraid of the shoals, they came to an anchor six leagues off the Texel." The loss of the Dutch amounted to 6200 men, including Admiral Van Tromp and Evertzen, with many other persons of distinction, with twenty-six ships of war sunk or burnt. On the side of the English, 7 captains and 500 men were killed, and 5 captains and 800 men wounded, besides which three of their ships were destroyed. Among the English ships were several merchantmen, and in order to take off the thoughts of their captains from their owners' vessels and cargoes, Monk sent them to each other's ships, a scheme which answered perfectly well, no ships in the fleet having behaved better. He also, it was said, to save time, issued orders at the commencement of the fight, that no quarter should be given or taken. This, however, was not so strictly observed, but that 1200 Dutchmen were saved from the sinking ships. On this occasion the Dutch set the example of fighting in line, though in their case, owing to the desperate valour of the English, the plan did not succeed as well as it did on many other subsequent occasions. Not without difficulty did the English ships get back to England. This victory compelled the Dutch to sue for peace.

It was at this time that the following song is supposed to have been written, showing the spirit which animated the nation. It is probably, as will be seen, the original of "Ye Mariners of England."

> *"When gallants are carousing*
> *In taverns on a row,*
> *Then we sweep o'er the deep*
> *When the stormy winds do blow."*

"Jack," however, was to have his consolation, for at the end, as we read —

> *"When we return in safety,*
> *With wages for our pains;*
> *The tapster and the vintner*
> *Will help to share our gains.*
> *We'll call for liquor roundly,*
> *And pay before we go;*
> *Then we roar on the shore*
> *When the stormy winds do blow," etcetera.*

The gallant Blake's latest achievement was the capture of numerous Spanish galleons, after a desperate battle off Teneriffe. He, however, did not live to receive the fresh honours Parliament was ready to bestow on him, as he died on the 17th of August, on board the *George*, just as she was entering Plymouth Sound. As Clarendon says of him: "He was the first to infuse that proportion of courage into seamen, by making them see by experience what mighty things they could do if they were resolved, and taught them to fight in fire as well as upon water; and although he had been very well imitated and followed, he was the first to give an example of that kind of naval courage which leads to bold and resolute deeds."

The first duty of the English fleet after the restoration had been determined on was to bring over Charles the Second, who landed in Kent on the 23rd May, 1660.

Chapter Nine.

Charles the Second and James the Second — from A.D. 1660 to A.D. 1689.

The object of Roman Catholic France was to keep Protestant England embroiled with Holland, and in the profligate Charles the Second, a willing instrument was found for carrying out her designs. War was declared, and the Duke of York took command of a fleet consisting of 109 men-of-war, and 28 fire-ships and ketches, with 21,000 seamen and soldiers on board. The Duke having blockaded the Texel, was compelled at length for want of provisions to return to England, and immediately the Dutch fleet sailed out under the command of Baron Opdam, Evertzen, and Cornelius Van Tromp. Directly afterwards nine merchant-ships of the English Hamburgh Company and a frigate of 34 guns fell into their hands. Opdam at all risks was ordered to attack the English, which he did, contrary to his own opinion, while his opponents had the advantage of the wind. At first the battle appeared tolerably equal, but the Earl of Sandwich, with the Blue Squadron, piercing into the centre of the Dutch fleet, divided it into two parts, and began that confusion which ended in its total defeat. The Duke of York, who was in the *Royal Charles*, a ship of 80 guns, was in close fight with Admiral Opdam in the *Endracht*, of 84 guns. The contest was severe, the Earl of Falmouth, Lord Muskerry, and Mr Boyle, second son of the Earl of Burlington, standing near the duke, were killed by a chain-shot. In the heat of the action the Dutch admiral's ship blew up, and of five hundred of his gallant men, among whom were a great number of volunteers of the best families in Holland, only five were saved. A fire-ship falling foul of four Dutch ships, the whole were burnt. Shortly afterwards three others suffered the same fate. The whole Dutch fleet seemed now to be but one blaze, and the cries of so many miserable wretches who were perishing either by fire or water was more frightful than the noise of the cannon. The English gave their vanquished enemy all the assistance they could, while with continued fury they assailed the rest. The English lost but one ship, while they took eighteen of the largest Dutch ships, sunk or burnt about fourteen more, killed four thousand men, and took two thousand prisoners, who were brought into Colchester. Among them were sixteen captains. As the bards of old stirred up the warriors of their tribe to deeds of valour, so the naval poets of those days wrote songs to animate the spirits of British tars. The following lines are said to have been written on the eve of the battle by Lord Buckhurst, afterwards Earl of Dorset: —

I.
To all you ladies now on land
We men at sea indite,
But first would have you understand
How hard it is to write;
The muses now, and Neptune too,
We must implore to write to you.
With a fa, la, la, la, la.

II.
For tho' the muses should prove kind,
And fill our empty brain;
Yet if rough Neptune rouse the wind
To wave the azure main,
Our paper, pen and ink, and we
Roll up and down our ships at sea.
With a fa, la, etcetera.

III.
Then if we write not by each post,
Think not we are unkind,
Nor yet conclude our ships are lost
By Dutchmen or by wind,
Ours tears we'll send a speedier way —
The tide shall bring them twice a-day.
With a fa, la, etcetera.

IV.
The king, with wonder and surprise,
Will swear the seas grow bold,
Because the tides will higher rise
Than e'er they used of old,
But let him know it is our tears
Bring floods of grief to Whitehall stairs
With a fa, la, etcetera.

V.
Let wind and weather do its worst,
Be you to us but kind,
Let Dutchmen vapour, Spaniards curse,
No sorrow shall we find;
'Tis then no matter how things go,
Or who's our friend, or who's our foe.
With a fa, la, etcetera.

VI.
And now we've told you all our loves,
And likewise all our fears,
In hopes this declaration moves
Some pity from your tears;
Let's hear of no inconstancy,
We have too much of that at sea.
With a fa, la, etcetera.

Notwithstanding this defeat, the Dutch in a short time were again ready for battle. The fight lasted without interruption from three in the morning till seven in the evening. The remains of the Dutch fleet made sail for the Texel, but were not pursued by the duke. "After the fight," says Burnet, "a council of war was called to concert the method of action when they should come up with the enemy. In that council, Penn, who commanded under the duke, happened to say that they must prepare for better work the next engagement. He knew well the courage of the Dutch was never so high as when they were desperate. The Earl of Montague, who was then a volunteer, and one of the duke's corps, told him it was very visible that remark made an impression upon him; and all the duke's domestics said, 'He had got near enough — why should he venture a second time.' The duchess had also given a strict charge to all the duke's servants to do all they could to hinder him to engage too far. When matters were settled they went to sleep, and the duke ordered a call to be given him when they should get up with the Dutch fleet. It is not known what passed between the duke and Brouncker, who was of his bed-chamber, and then in waiting, but he came to Penn as from the duke and said, 'The duke orders the sail to be slackened.' Penn was struck with the order, but did not go about to argue the matter with the duke himself as he ought to have done, but obeyed it. When the duke had slept, he upon his waking went out upon the quarter-deck, and seemed amazed to see the sails slackened, and that thereby all hopes of overtaking the

Dutch was lost." It was not the only occasion on which James the Second showed the white feather.

Of the unfortunate Dutch officers who escaped, three were publicly shot at the Helder, four were ordered to have their swords broken over their heads by the common hangman, and the master of the vice-admiral to stand upon a scaffold with a halter about his neck under the gallows, while the others were executed, and he was afterwards sent into perpetual banishment. Two more were degraded and rendered incapable of serving the States more.

Before long the Dutch had their revenge. Charles being easily persuaded to lay up his ships and pocket the money voted for their maintenance, the Dutch, prompted by the French, who promised their assistance, rapidly fitted out a fleet under Admiral Van Ghendt. To deceive the English, he sailed for the Firth of Forth, which he entered, and after firing away to little purpose for some time, took his departure, and joined De Ruyter, who with seventy sail of ships appeared in the mouth of the Thames on the 7th of June, 1667. A squadron was immediately despatched up the river, when the fort of Sheerness was burnt and plundered, though bravely defended by Sir Edward Spragg. Monk, Duke of Albemarle, hastening down with some land forces, sank several vessels in the entrance of the Medway, and laid a strong chain across it; but the Dutch, with the high tide and strong easterly wind, broke their way through and burnt the *Matthias*, the *Unity*, and the *Charles the Fifth*, which had been taken from them. The next day they proceeded with six men-of-war and five fire-ships as far as Upnor Castle, but met with so warm a reception, that they advanced no farther. On their return they burnt the *Royal Oak*, and damaged the *Loyal London* and the *Great James*. They also carried off with them the hull of the *Royal Charles*, which the English twice set on fire, but which they as often quenched. Captain Douglas, when the enemy had set her on fire, having received no command to retire, said it should never be told that a Douglas had quitted his post without orders, and resolutely continuing on board, was burnt with his ship, falling a glorious sacrifice to discipline, and showing an example of no common bravery.

While the Dutch were in the Thames, a large number of their merchantmen, however, fell into the hands of the English, amply recompensing the latter for the loss they had sustained. The gallant action of Captain Dawes, commanding the *Elizabeth* frigate, must be mentioned. Falling in with fifteen sail of Rotterdam men-of-war, he fought their rear-admiral, of 64 and five others of 48 and 50 guns, and presently fought the admiral, of 70 guns, and two of his seconds, yet got clear of them all. Shortly afterwards he engaged two Danish men-of-war, of 40 guns each, in which action, after four hours' fight, he was struck by a cannon-ball, crying with his last breath, "For God's sake! don't yield the frigate to those fellows." Soon after, his lieutenant being desperately wounded, and the master who succeeded him slain, the gunner took their places, and so plied the two Danes, that they were glad to sheer off. The English anchored within a mile of them during the night to repair damages. The next morning they expected the Danes again, but though they were to windward and had the advantage of the current, yet they would not venture — upon which the English, after having saluted them with a shot of defiance, bore away for England.

A squadron under Sir Edward Spragg was sent out to punish the Algerines for their piracies. He drove many of their ships on shore and burnt seven, each carrying thirty-four guns. In the same year, 1670, the captain and first lieutenant of the *Sapphire* were condemned to be shot for cowardice, having run from four sail which they supposed to be Turkish men-of-war, and also for getting the ship on shore, by which she was lost, contrary to the opinion of the master and crew, who offered to defend her. The sentence was executed on board the *Dragon* at Deptford.

The peace of Breda terminated for a time the contest with the Dutch. War was, however, soon again to break out. The statesmen Clifford, Ashley, Buckingham, Arlington, and Lauderdale, the initial letters of whose titles gave the name of the Cabal to their ministry, now formed a scheme for rendering the king absolute; Charles, acting under the influence of the King of France, who agreed to assist England in humbling the States-General. Every slight offence committed by the Dutch was magnified into a sufficient reason for engaging in a fresh war with the States, till it at last broke out with great violence. The English had formed an alliance with the French, when their united fleets, under the command of Prince Rupert — the English having sixty men-of-war and frigates and the French thirty — encountered the Dutch under De Ruyter, who had about seventy ships. De Ruyter bearing down with his fleet in three squadrons prepared to attack the Prince himself, while Tromp engaged Spragg and the Blue Squadron, the English admiral having, contrary to the express orders of Prince

Rupert, laid his fore-topsail to the mast in order to stay for him. The French admiral had received orders to keep aloof, which he in part obeyed, while owing to Spragg's too daring conduct Prince Rupert found himself separated from a large portion of his fleet. The fiercest engagement was that between Tromp, in the *Golden Lion*, and Spragg, in the *Royal Prince*. For long they fought ship to ship, till the *Royal Prince* was so disabled, that Sir Edward Spragg was forced to go on board the *Saint George*, and Tromp quitted his *Golden Lion* to hoist his flag on board the *Comat*, when the battle was renewed with incredible fury. The aim of the Dutch admiral was to take or sink the *Royal Prince*, but the Earl of Ossory and Sir John Kempthorne, together with Spragg himself, so effectually protected the disabled vessel, that none of the enemy's fire-ships could come near her, though this was often attempted. At last the *Saint George*, being terribly torn and in a manner disabled, Sir Edward Spragg designed to go on board a third ship, but before he was got six boats' length a shot, which passed through the *Saint George*, struck his boat, and, though her crew immediately rowed back, yet before they could get within reach of the ropes the boat sank, and Sir Edward was drowned. The fight continued till sunset, when darkness and smoke obliged them on all sides to desist, the English having all this time maintained the fight alone against the whole Dutch fleet, while the French continued to look on at a distance.

The English could not claim this action as a victory, for though the Dutch carried off no trophies, they had decidedly the best of it. The English officers, however, behaved with the greatest gallantry, and had they not been so shamefully deserted by their pretended allies, would have won the day. Prince Rupert highly praised the conduct of the Earl of Ossory for the way in which he bore down to the rescue of the *Royal Prince*. Sir John Chichely and Sir John Kempenthorne, as did many others, behaved with conspicuous courage, while several commanders of distinction lost their lives. The conduct of the gunner of the *Royal Prince*, Richard Leake — whose son became the famous Sir John Leake — is worthy of mention. Before Sir Edward Spragg quitted the ship, she had lost all her masts, the larger number of her upper deck guns were disabled, and 400 of her crew, out of 750, were killed or wounded. While in this disabled condition, a large Dutchman, with two fire-ships, bore down on her for the purpose of effecting her capture or destruction. The lieutenant who had been left in command, believing that it was hopeless to resist, was on the point of striking, when the gallant Leake, calling on the crew to support him, took the command, and so ably fought the remaining guns that both the fire-ships were sunk, his large assailant compelled to sheer off, and the ship preserved from capture.

The nation, discovering that England had become the mere tool of France, loudly cried out for peace with Holland, which was signed in London on the 9th of February, 1674. By this treaty it was agreed on the part of the Dutch that their ships, whether separate or in fleets, should be obliged, as a matter of right, to strike their sails to any fleet or single ship carrying the King of England's flag.

Very considerable improvements were carried out in the naval service during Charles the Second's reign by the influence of the Duke of York. In 1662 a judge-advocate, John Fowler, was first appointed to the fleet. In 1663 an established number of seamen was fixed to each ship of war according to her rate, and servants were at this time first allowed to the captains and officers. Under this rating it was usual for officers to take a certain number of young gentlemen to sea, who, in consequence, gained the name of midshipmen. They are often spoken of as captains' servants or cabin-boys, signifying that they were berthed and messed in the cabin — not that they had of necessity me-nial duties to perform. An allowance of table-money was first estab-lished to the flag-officers; a Surgeon-General to the fleet was also first appointed by warrant from the Lord High Admiral.

In 1666, in addition to the complement of men borne on board a ship bearing the flag of an admiral, fifty men were allowed; to a Vice-Admiral, twenty; and to a Rear-Admiral, ten.

We have the first instance in this year of gratuities being allowed to captains in the navy who were wounded in battle.

From the instances already given, it will be seen that the naval officers of those days possessed a dashing, dauntless courage which no dan-gers could subdue. The following is one among many others. The *Tiger* frigate, commanded by Captain Harman, was lying in the Port of Cadiz at the same time that a Dutch squadron was there. De Witt, the captain of one of the Dutch frigates, was particularly friendly with Captain Harman; this made the Spaniards insinuate that he dared not fight the English frigate. Evertzen, the Dutch admiral, on hearing this report, told De Witt that he must challenge the English captain to go to sea and fight him, to support the honour of his nation, and that he would assist him with sixty seamen and seventy soldiers. Captain

Harman readily accepted his proposal, and on a day fixed both ships stood to sea, and began to engage within pistol-shot of each other. In a short time the Dutch ship's main-mast was shot away. Captain Harman, availing himself of the confusion into which this disaster had thrown the enemy, boarded and compelled her to surrender, with the loss of 140 men. The English had only nine killed and fifteen wounded.

Since the increase of the navy, the Cinque Ports being of less consequence than formerly, the king granted them a new charter confirming their ancient privileges, with the addition of some regulations more suitable to modern times.

As an encouragement for seamen to enter into the navy, a bounty was given to all who entered on board first and second-rates of six weeks' pay, and on board of third-rates one month's pay.

In 1673 an order was issued to all commanders of His Majesty's ships of war that in future they were not to require French ships to strike the flag or topsail, or salute, neither were they to salute those of the French king.

In 1673 the oaths of allegiance and supremacy were first administered to the officers in His Majesty's navy. The king granted half-pay to several captains in the navy, according to the rates they commanded, as a gratuity for their bravery during the war.

The regulating and allotting of cabins to each particular officer was first established.

For some years merchant-ships had been sheathed with lead, and the experiment was now tried on the *Harwich* and *Kingfisher* ships of war, as also on several other ships ordered for foreign service. The practice was, however, in a few years discontinued.

The Royal Navy was now becoming far larger than it had ever before been. In 1675 the Parliament granted 300,000 pounds for the building of twenty large ships of war, one first-rate of 1400 tons, eight second-rates of 1100 tons, and eleven third-rates of 700 tons. At the same time the tonnage and poundage money was applied to the benefit of the Royal Navy. The Newfoundland fishery had begun to assume considerable importance, it being considered especially useful as a nursery to furnish seamen for the Royal Navy. Thus in the year 1676, 102 ships were employed, each ship carrying 20 guns, 18 boats, and 5 men to each boat, making in all 9180 men.

The corsairs which sailed forth from the States of Tunis, Tripoli, and Algiers, continuing their depredations on English merchant-ships, Sir John Narborough was in 1675 despatched with a powerful squadron to teach them better behaviour. On arriving off Tripoli Sir John sent Lieutenant Cloudesly Shovel, of whom we now first hear, to open negotiations with the Dey. That Oriental potentate, despising Mr Shovel for his youthful appearance, sent him back with a disrespectful answer. He had, however, made a note of everything he saw, and on returning on board he assured the commodore of the practicability of burning the piratical fleet. The night being extremely dark, the commodore despatched Lieutenant Shovel with all the boats of the fleet to destroy the ships in the mole. Lieutenant Shovel first seized the guard-boat, then entered the mole, and burnt four large armed ships, without losing a man. The Dey, terrified by these unexpected proceedings of the English, sued for peace; but, according to time-honoured eastern custom, delayed the fulfilment of his engagements, on which Sir John sailing in, cannonaded the town, landed a party of men, burnt some stores, and finally brought him to terms. One of the pirate ships carried 50 guns, one 30, one 24, and another 20 guns. These powerful rovers were indeed a match for any ordinary merchant-vessel, and often contended desperately with men-of-war. In 1677 the 26-gun ship *Guernsey*, Captain James Harman, fell in with one of them, an Algerine called the *White Horse*, carrying 50 guns, and 500 men, while the crew of the *Guernsey* numbered only 110. A fierce action ensued, when at length the Algerine, taking advantage of the *Guernsey's* disabled state, sheered off, these pirates always fighting for booty rather than for honour. The gallant Captain Harman received three musket-balls in his body, and a severe contusion from a cannon-shot. He still fought his ship till he sank from exhaustion, when Lieutenant John Harris took command. The *Guernsey* in the action lost nine killed and many wounded, besides the captain, who three days afterwards expired.

A still more successful action was fought between the 40-gun ship *Adventure*, Captain William Booth, and an Algerine ship of war called the *Golden Horse*, of 46 guns, commanded by Morat Rais, a notorious Dutch renegado, who had a crew of 508 Moors and 90 Christian slaves. During the action a stranger hove in sight under Turkish colours; but night coming on, the Algerine drew off, when Captain

Booth, having a fire-ship in company, gave orders to burn her or the new-comer. Fortunately, the fire-ship failed to reach either one or other, and in the morning the stranger hoisted English colours, and proved to be the 40-gun ship *Nonsuch*. The *Golden Horse* being dismasted, and 109 of her crew killed and 120 wounded, and having six-feet of water in the hold, surrendered.

In the same year a 42-gun ship, Captain Morgan Kempthorne, beat off seven Algerine corsairs, after they had made several desperate attempts to board her. Unhappily the Captain and eight of his crew were killed, and 38 wounded.

Many other similar gallant actions were fought with the Algerines and Sallee rovers, who, however, notwithstanding their frequent defeats, continued their depredations on the commerce of England and other European countries. Tangiers had been in possession of the English about twenty years, but, to save the expense of keeping it up, a fleet under Lord Dartmouth was sent out to destroy all the works, and to bring home the garrison. The destruction of the mole, which was admirably built, caused much labour, it being necessary to blow it up by piecemeal. Its ruins, as well as the rubbish of the town, were thrown into the harbour to prevent its again becoming a port.

The navy had long been held in high estimation by the English, who were always ready to grant any sum required for its improvement. It is stated that between the years 1660 and 1670 never less than 5000 pounds a-year was granted for its support. On the death of Charles the Royal Navy amounted to 113 sail.

James the Second.

James, on his accession, assigned a stated sum of 400,000 pounds a-year, to be paid quarterly from the treasury, for the service of the navy. Four additional commissioners were also appointed for the better regulating of the docks and naval storehouses, and for the more speedy repairs of ships of war. During this time a plan was proposed and patent granted for making salt water fresh by distillation. All captains and officers received orders to despatch perfect copies of their journals to the Secretary of the Admiralty. An increased allowance of table-money was granted in lieu of several perquisites and advantages they had before enjoyed.

The larger number of the officers and men of the navy were sound Protestants, who regarded the proceedings of James with jealous eyes; and thus, notwithstanding his magnificent fleet, Lord Dartmouth could only muster 17 sail of the line, chiefly third and fourth-rates, 3 frigates, 13 fire-ships, and 3 yachts to oppose the landing of the Prince of Orange.

On the 12th of December, 1688, James the Second finished his short reign by abdicating the throne, at which time the navy consisted of 173 sail, showing that he must have either built or purchased sixty ships.

Chapter Ten.

A View of Naval affairs in Charles the Second's Reign. — A.D. 1660 to A.D. 1689.

When great guns or cannon came into use, the old style of fighting at sea was completely changed. We hear of them as early as the thirteenth century, employed in a naval engagement between the King of Tunis and the Moorish King of Seville. They were first used on shore by the English at the battle of Crescy, fought in 1346, and at sea by the Venetians about the year 1380. In the reigns of Richard the Third and Henry the Seventh they were first employed by the English at sea. They were not then, however, as now, pointed through port-holes, but were mounted so as to fire over the bulwarks of the vessel. In those days, therefore, ships of war could have had but one armed deck, and were probably urged by oars as well as by sails. Port-holes were invented by Descharves, a French builder at Brest, and the first English ship in which they were formed was the *Henry Grâce de Dieu*, built at Erith in 1515. She was said to have been of no less than 1000 tons burden, but as we are ignorant of the mode in which ships were measured for tonnage in those days, we cannot tell her actual burden. She must, however, have been a large vessel, for she had two whole decks, besides what we now call a forecastle and poop. She mounted altogether eighty pieces, composed of every calibre in use; but of these not more than fifty-four, according to the print before us, were pointed through broadside ports. The rest were either mounted as bow or stern chasers, or as "murdering pieces," as they were called, which pointed down on the deck; their object apparently being, should a ship be boarded, to fire on the enemy. The calibre of great guns was not in those days designated by the weight of the shot they discharged. This was probably from the reason that the balls were not all made of the same materials. At first they were of stone; then those of iron were introduced; and sometimes they were formed of lead; and, at an early period, hollow iron shot, filled with combustible matter, were brought into use. Thus the weight of shot fluctuated too much to serve for the classification of the gun from which it was fired. Ships' guns in those days were known as cannon, cannon royal, cannon serpentine, bastard cannon, demi-cannon, and cannon petro.

The *Sovereign of the Seas* was built at Woolwich Dockyard, in 1637, by Mr Phineas Pett, and Mr Thomas Haywood was the designer of her decorations. She measured, probably, about 1500 tons. He describes her as having three flush-decks and a forecastle, one half-deck, a quarter-deck, and a round house. Her lower tier had 30 ports which were furnished with demi-cannon and whole cannon throughout; her middle tier had also 30 ports of demi-culverins and whole culverins; her third tier had 36 ports for other ordnance; her forecastle had 12 ports; and her half-deck 13 ports. She had 13 or 14 ports more within-board for murdering pieces, besides a great many loop-holes out of the cabins for musket-shot. She carried, moreover, 10 pieces of chase ordnance forward and 10 right aft. This first-rate of the seventeenth century would thus have had 126 guns; in reality, however, these ports right forward and right aft, as well as those on the forecastle, had no guns, and thus she actually carried only 100.

About the middle of the seventeenth century the ships of the British Navy ceased to carry guns of a similar calibre on the same deck. At the same time the cumbrous forecastles and aftercastles, which must have been equally inconvenient both in action and in a sea way, were removed. The murdering pieces were likewise got rid of, and at the same time, an English ship of war could fire from her broadside half the number of guns she carried.

In 1546 Henry the Eighth possessed fifty-eight ships, which were classed according to their quality; thus there were shyppes, galliasses, pinnaces, and row-barges. The galliasse was somewhat like the lugger or felucca of modern days. She probably was a long, low, and sharp-built vessel, propelled by oars as well as sails — the latter not fixed to a standing yard, but hoisted like a boat's sail when required. The pinnace was a small kind of galliasse.

In 1612 we find a list in which the vessels of the Royal Navy were classed as ships-royal, which measured from 800 to 1200 tons, middling ships from 600 to 800 tons, small ships from 350 tons, and pinnaces from 80 to 250 tons, divided into rates. They were six in number, and each rate consisted of two classes, to which different complements of men were assigned. We are not told what were the armaments of the classes. The division into rates was adopted to regulate the pay of the officers and seamen, as is the case at the present day.

In 1651-2, we find a list of all ships, frigates, and other vessels belonging to the States' Navy classified by the guns they carried. Of these there were twenty-three classes comprised within the second-rates, exclusive of two unrated classes — namely, hulks and shallops or row-barges. The former were used either to lodge the officers and crews of vessels undergoing repair, or were fitted with shears to erect or remove masts. In the course of a few years after this, sloops, bombs, fire-ships, and yachts are spoken of as among the unrated classes; but in the sixth-rate were comprised vessels mounting only two guns. Towards the end of the century such small craft were classed by themselves as sloops.

In 1675 fire-ships first appear in a list of the navy. They were much used at that time for the purpose of setting fire to the enemy's vessels. Mr Pepys, who is the chief authority on naval affairs at this period, says that the Dutch, in the year 1660, made a present of a yacht, called *Maria*, to Charles the Second, remarking, "until which time we had not heard of such a name in England."

About the year 1650 a difference was made between the number of guns and men carried by ships in war time and in peace time, and in war and peace abroad. This difference, it is evident, arose from the inability of a ship to carry a sufficient amount of provisions for her crew when sent on a long voyage. When such was the case it was necessary to reduce both the number of men and guns, in order to allow room for a sufficient supply of provisions. As far as we can judge, a first-rate of the latter end of the seventeenth century mounted her guns on three whole decks, a quarter-deck, forecastle, and poop; a second-rate mounted hers on three whole decks and a quarter-deck; a third-rate on two whole decks, a quarter-deck, forecastle, and poop; a fourth-rate on two whole decks and a quarter-deck; a fifth-rate on her first gun-deck, with a few guns on her quarter-deck; a sixth-rate on a single-deck, with or without any on her quarter-deck.

There were at that period three-deckers of sixty-four guns, and two-deckers of only thirty guns. With regard to the guns themselves, the demi-cannon was probably a 32-pounder, the cannon petro a 24-pounder, and the basilisk a 12-pounder; the whole culverin an 18-pounder, and the demi-culverin a 9-pounder; the saker a 6-pounder, and the mignon a 4-pounder. The smaller guns were called swivels, and were mounted on upright timbers, having a pivot on which the gun traversed. Guns at sea were formerly known by the names of beasts and birds of prey, till about the year 1685 they were designated by the weight of the shot they carried.

In 1688 we find mention made of bombs, which were vessels carrying six or eight light guns, and one or two heavy mortars for the purpose of throwing shells into a town. It is said that they were invented by Reynaud, a Frenchman, and that they were first employed at the bombardment of Algiers in 1681.

In the year 1714 we find the navy divided into ten classes, ships carrying 100, 90, 80, 70, 60, 50, 40, 30, 20, and 10 guns. The first-rate descended no lower than to ships carrying 100 guns; the second no lower than to those of 90 guns; the third admitted all classes below and above 60; the fourth between 60 and 50; the fifth between 50 and 30; the sixth comprised all vessels below 50, except sloops, bombs, etcetera.

By the end of the reign of George the First, ships no longer carried guns on their poops.

The English style of naming the decks of a ship differs from that of other nations, and though perfectly understood by her crew, is calculated to puzzle a landsman. In a one-decked ship the deck on which the guns are carried is called the main-deck, while the deck below it, to which there are no ports, the lower or gun-deck. Hence the term gun-room, occupied by lieutenants or gun-room officers; indeed, the lowest deck of every ship is called the gun-deck. The quarter of a ship is that part of the side which lies towards the stern, and hence that part of the deck is called the quarter-deck, in reference to that portion of the ship's length over which it originally extended. The elevation above it is known as the poop, and the raised deck over the fore-part of the ship is known as the top-gallant forecastle. In early days, as we have seen in the case of the *Great Harry* and other ships, and even in later days, both at the fore and after-part of the ship there were elevated structures, very properly called castles. In time these were done away with, but short decks elevated above the main or chief deck were still retained, as it was found inconvenient for the seamen when working the ship to descend from one of these elevated decks and then to be compelled to mount the other to get either fore or aft. They were connected by a grating or gangway of sufficient width to allow the crew to pass backwards and forwards. This gangway was still further widened; it being strengthened by beams running across the ship, allowed guns to be carried on it. The after-part had long been called the quarter-deck, and the fore-part the forecastle, while the intermediate part was now known as the gangway. This name was also applied to the space left in the bulwarks for entering or leaving the ship. These portions of the decks now assumed the appearance of an entire even deck running fore and aft, but it still retained the names originally bestowed on it, and its imaginary divisions. The centre part of the ship, where the gangway is placed, is also commonly called the waist, because originally there was no deck. The deck immediately below this once-divided deck is always called the main-deck. In a three-decker the next is called the middle-deck, and the lowest deck on which guns are carried the lower-deck. Below this again is one still lower-deck called the orlop-deck. A two-decked ship has no middle-deck, but possesses only a main and lower-deck, besides the before-mentioned quarter-deck, gangway, and forecastle. The deck on which a frigate's single battery is carried is always called her main-deck, because the sailors are wont to denominate the upper-deck of every ship carrying guns the main-deck. In a sloop-ship or corvette the only deck, without any one above it on which guns are carried, is thus in-variably called the main-deck, and, as has before been said, the one beneath it on which the officers and crew live, and which has no guns, the gun-deck. Ships which have their only gun-deck running fore and aft for the same height all along are called flush-decked ships. When the after-part of the deck is raised they are known as being deep-waisted, as is the case with many merchantmen. The highest deck of many men-of-war of all rates is often perfectly level, but others have a short raised deck, extending from just before the mizen-mast to the stern, which is called the poop, and in many instances serves as a cover to the captain's cabin. When the admiral is on board he occupies the after-cabins on the upper-deck. In small men-of-war no cabins are placed under the poop, nor are they ever under the topgallant forecas-tle. On board merchantmen, however, where the poop is of sufficient elevation and extent to allow of it, the best cabins are always placed under it, while the crew are almost invariably berthed under the top-gallant forecastle. Of course, speaking of men-of-war, we are referring to ships as they were till the invention of low-sided armour-plated craft, which necessitated a great, if not an entire, change of terms, and the introduction of a considerable number of new ones.

Line of battle ships, as their name implies, were such as were capable from their size, strength, and the number of their guns, of entering into the line of battle and contending with the largest ships of the en-emy. We first hear of ships appearing in that character in 1691, form-ing the British Channel Fleet under Admiral Russell. As far back, however, as the year 1614, in a list of the ships of the navy, the line of battle ships are separated from the others. They included all ships from the first-rate to the fourth-rate. A fleet was now attended by smaller, swift vessels, whose duty it was to look out for the enemy, and to perform other detached services. These vessels were comprised in the fifth and sixth-rates, and from an early period were denominated frigates. In early days a large number of fast-sailing or fast-rowing vessels, whether intended for war or for carrying merchandise, were called frigates. The word friggot or frigat, as it was often written, derives its origin from a class of long, sharp vessels used in the Mediterranean, and impelled either by sails or oars, which had a deck, the topside of which was higher than that of the galley. It in general had openings like port-holes, through which the oars passed. An Italian describes the fregata as a little vessel with oars, but whence that name is derived is uncertain. A species of swift-flying sea-gull is called by the French a frégate. We have also the frigate-bird; but the name is generally supposed to be derived from the ship, which, however, may not really be the case. It is very clear that its principal quality was the power of moving rapidly either with sails or oars. The French transferred the frégate of the Mediterranean to the northern shore of their country, and constructed it with bluffer bows and of a large size, to contend with the heavy seas of a northern region. English merchant-ships of the early part of the sixteenth century are frequently spoken of as frigates, and in the latter part of the century were often, as we have seen, hired by the sovereign to serve as ships of war. As we know from the accounts we have already given of the early voyages, some of their ships were denominated frigates. Thus, one of the ships serving with Sir Francis Drake is called the frigate *Elizabeth Fownes*, of 80 guns and 50 men. The Duke of Northumberland, then Sir Robert Dudley, towards the close of the sixteenth century, designed a ship to measure 160 feet in length and 24 in breadth, and constructed to carry a tier of guns on a single whole deck, besides other guns on two short decks, resembling the poop and top-gallant forecastlc of a modern ship. He named his vessel a fregata, and her guns were placed exactly as those of a modern frigate.

He designed at the same time seven distinct classes of ships of war, which he named the *Galleon, Ranibargo, Galizabra, Frigata, Gallerone, Gallerata*, and *Passavolante*. His designs not being accepted, he, in the year 1594, built a vessel for himself at Southampton, which measured

300 tons and mounted 30 guns — of course, of small calibre. In her he made a voyage to India.

Charles the First possessed two frigates, the *Swan* and *Nicodemus*, each of 60 tons, 10 men, and 3 guns. They probably were only used as yachts. The Duke of Buckingham, who was Lord High Admiral from 1619 to 1636, ordered some frigates to be built from the model of two called the *Providence* and *Expedition*, captured from the Dunkirkers, mounting, it is supposed, from 20 to 30 guns, the greater number of which were on a single-deck. In consequence of seeing a French frigate in the Thames, Mr Peter Pett took her as his model for building the *Constant Warwick* in 1649, which was, as he says, the first frigate built in England. She was intended as a privateer for the Earl of Warwick, who afterwards sold her to the king. She measured somewhat under 400 tons, and mounted 60 guns, consisting of 18 light demi-culverins or short 9-pounders on the main-deck, 6 light sakers on the quarter-deck, and 2 mignons on the after-raised deck, which we should now call the poop.

In those days, and for many years afterwards, the English were addicted to crowding their vessels with guns, and there can be no doubt that many, like the *Mary Rose* and others, were in consequence lost; especially as their lower-deck ports were often not more than three feet above the water. The *Constant Warwick* had afterwards many more guns placed in her, so that she ultimately rated as a 46-gun ship, when, from being an incomparable sailer, she became a slug. Mr Pepys remarks on this subject, in 1663 and 1664: "The Dutch and French built ships of two decks, which carried from 60 to 70 guns, and so contrived that they carried their lower guns four feet from the water, and could stow four months' provisions — whereas our frigates from the Dunkirk build, which were narrower and sharper, carried their guns but little more than three feet from the water and but ten weeks provisions."

Attempts were made to counteract this great defect, but without much success. For several years afterwards Mr Pepys still complained that frigates were unable to stow a sufficient quantity of provisions, or to carry their guns high enough out of the water to make them safe.

Up to the early part of the eighteenth century it was a general complaint that ships of war had more guns placed on board than they could carry — in consequence, that their lower batteries could not be opened when there was any sea on, and that they sailed and worked heavily. It is wonderful, indeed, how British seamen managed to keep them afloat, as it is worthy of note that those which fell into the hands of the enemy were nearly always lost under charge of their new masters. The English, it was said, employed the best materials and workmanship on their vessels, but the French greatly surpassed them in their models. The English were the first to abandon the flat form of the stern under the counter, and to introduce the curved instead, by which greater strength and lightness as well as beauty was obtained.

In 1748 a ship of 585 tons, to carry 28 guns, 9-pounders on the main-deck and 3-pounders on the quarter-deck, was built; and in 1757 five other vessels, also called frigates, to carry 28 guns, were constructed of fir instead of oak, of the same size; but one of them was captured by the French, and the others in about nine years were broken up as unserviceable.

The first ship which, according to our present ideas, could properly be considered a frigate, was the *Southampton*, built at Rotherhithe in the year 1757 by Mr Robert Inwood, according to a draft of Sir Thomas Slade, one of the surveyors of the navy. She measured 671 tons, and mounted 26 12-pounders on the main-deck, 4 6-pounders on the quarter-deck, and 2 6-pounders on the forecastle. She thus carried all her guns on a single whole deck, a quarter-deck and forecastle, the characteristic of the true frigate. She was considered a prime sailer and first-rate sea-boat, and lasted for fifty-six years, and possibly would have lasted longer had she not gone to pieces on the rocks.

Shortly after this several 36-gun frigates were built. Each was about fifty tons larger than the *Southampton*, and carried four guns more, which were placed on the quarter-deck.

Several French 36-gun frigates captured by the English were found to be considerably larger. One, the *Dana*, was of 941 tons; and three French 32-gun frigates averaged about 700 tons, though armed like the *Southampton*.

About 1779 five frigates of 38 guns, and averaging 946 tons, were launched. They were the *Minerva*, built at Woolwich, the *Arethusa*, *Latona*, *Phaeton*, and *Thetis*. They were first armed with 28 18-pounders on the main-deck and 10 6-pounders, 8 18-pound carronades and 14 swivels on the quarter-deck and forecastle, and with a complement of 270 men. Shortly afterwards the complement was increased to 280 men, 9-pounders were placed on board instead of the sixes, the swivels were omitted, and carronades substituted.

About the same time frigates of 880 tons, to carry 36 guns, 18 and 9-pounders, were built.

Formerly, as has been seen, a number of small vessels were classed as frigates. About the year 1775 they were placed in a different rate, and those carrying 20 guns had now the name of 20-gun post-ships given to them, signifying that they were commanded by post-captains. Afterwards vessels still called frigates, carrying 24 guns, were also ranked as post-ships. The French called vessels of this size corvettes, from the Italian word corvettore, to leap or bound, from which we have derived the word curvet. The French afterwards applied the name to ships of 24 guns. In order to mount all these guns on a single tier, it was necessary to increase the dimensions of the ship, and thus she could carry heavier metal than those ships mounting their guns on a quarter-deck and forecastle. The English, following their example, afterwards called all ships carrying 24, 22, and 20 guns post-ships, and those carrying 18, 16, and 14, or any less number, ship-sloops, to which the general term of corvette was afterwards applied. The English did not apply the term corvette to brigs, but designated such two-masted vessels as brigs-of-war, though they are sometimes spoken of as brig-sloops.

It will thus be understood that a ship that mounts 24 guns at least on a single-deck, and other guns on a quarter-deck and forecastle, is properly called a frigate. When, however, the waist is decked over and has raised bulwarks with ports in them filled with guns, the vessel becomes a two-decked ship.

It is necessary to explain the term "flush." In sea language it means level, a flush-deck is consequently a level deck extending fore and aft. Such are all the decks of a man-of-war, except of the upper ones. Many merchantmen are also built in the same way, but others rise abruptly a foot, or two or three feet, towards the stern, the higher part of the deck becoming the quarter-deck. Ships thus built are spoken of as deep-waisted, because the centre part is deeper or lower than the after-part. The bulwarks in the same way sink in proportion at the break of the quarter-deck. Up to the present day many of the largest ships-of-war are flush-decked, as are all brigs-of-war and many corvettes, but a frigate, which must have a quarter-deck and forecastle, cannot properly be said to be flush-decked, although, in fact, the gratings or gangway at the waist give her the appearance of being so to the unsophisticated eye.

Our knowledge of the state of the navy during the reigns of Charles the Second and his brother is derived chiefly from Mr Samuel Pepys, who was clerk of the Acts, through the interest of his relative the Earl of Sandwich, and was ultimately clerk of the treasurer to the commissioners of the affairs of Tangier, and surveyor-general of the victualling department. He spared no pains to check the rapacity of contractors by whom the naval stores were then supplied; he studied order and economy in the dockyards, advocated the promotion of old-established officers in the navy, and resisted to the utmost the infamous system of selling places, then most unblushingly practised. During the Dutch war the care of the navy in a great measure rested upon him alone, and by his zeal and industry he gained the esteem of the Duke of York, with whom, as Lord High Admiral, he was in constant intercourse. Thus from his diary we can gain a pretty accurate knowledge of the customs of the times in the naval service, and the way the affairs of the navy were managed.

In an entry of the 4th of June, 1661, he describes a dinner, where the discourse was on the subject of young noblemen and gentlemen who thought of going to sea, the naval service being considered as noble as that of the land. Lord Crewe remarked that "in Queen Elizabeth's time one young nobleman would wait with a trencher at the back of another till he come of age himself;" and he mentioned the Earl of Kent, who was waiting on Lord Bedford at table when a letter came to that lord announcing that the earldom had fallen to his servant the young lord; at which he rose from table and made him sit down in his place, taking a lower for himself.

It was undoubtedly in this way that many lads of family went to sea to serve as cabin-boys to captains of distinction, and at the same time to learn seamanship and navigation.

He gives an amusing account of the sale of two ships at an auction by an inch of candle. The auctioneer put them up when the candle was first lighted, and bidding went on till it was burnt down. He describes "how they do invite one another, and at last how they all do cry, and we have much to do to tell who did cry last. The ships were the *Indian*, sold for 1300 pounds, and the *Half-Moone*, sold for 830 pounds." Of course, the ships were knocked down to the person who made the last bidding before the candle was burnt out.

It is no wonder that naval affairs went wrong in those days, when money was wanting to pay both officers and seamen, and to supply stores and provisions; indeed, what should have been devoted to the purpose was fearfully misappropriated. On the 14th of August, 1661, he says: "This morning Sir W. Batten and Sir W. Penn and I waited upon the Duke of York in his chamber, to give him an account of the condition of the navy for lack of money, and how our own very bills are offered upon the exchange to be sold at 20 in the 100 loss. He is much troubled at it, and will speak to the king and council of it this morning."

The debts of the navy at that time amounted to near 374,000 pounds. He tells us that he was "writing a little treatise to present to the duke, about our privileges in the seas, as to other nations striking their flags to us." The English had long claimed the right to have this honour paid to their flag, though the people of other countries were naturally inclined to dispute it, and if not the cause was the pretext of our wars with the Dutch.

On the 25th of January he met Sir Richard Brown, and discussed with him Sir N. Crisp's project for "making a great sluice in the king's lands about Deptford, to be a wet-dock to hold 200 sail of ships. But the ground, it seems, was long since given by the king to Sir Richard."

On the 14th of March the German Dr Knuffler "came to discourse about his engine to blow up ships. We doubted not the matter of fact, it being tried in Cromwell's time, but the safety of carrying them in ships; but he do tell us that when he comes to tell the king his secret (for none but the kings successively and their heirs must know it), it will appear to be of no danger at all. We concluded nothing, but shall discourse with the Duke of York tomorrow about it."

Chaplains were appointed in those days to ships, though several instances are given which prove that they were not men likely to advance the interests of religion. After visiting the yard, he went on board the *Swallow* in the dock, "where our navy chaplain preached a sad sermon, full of nonsense and false Latin; but prayed for the Right Honourable the principall officers."

Again, he speaks of many rogueries practised. Among others, on the 4th of June he went "by water to Woolwich, and there saw an experiment made of Sir R. Ford's Holland's yarne (about which we have lately had so much stir, and I have much concerned myself for our ropemaker, Mr Hughes, who represented it so bad), and we found it to be very bad, and broke sooner than upon a fair trial, five threads of that against four of Riga yarne; and also that some of it had old stuffe that had been tarred, covered over with new hempe, which is such a cheat as hath not been heard of."

The war with the Dutch had not yet commenced, but there was every probability of it soon breaking out, though the English fleet was at that time in a sadly unprepared state. On the 28th of June, 1662, he says: "Great talk there is of a fear of a war with the Dutch, and we have orders to pitch upon 20 ships to be forthwith set out; but I hope it is but a scarecrow to the world to let them see that we can be ready for them; though God knows, the king is not able to set out five ships at this present without great difficulty, we neither having money, credit, nor stores."

With regard to the stores, he says, on the 21st of July: "To Woolwich to the rope-yard, and there looked over several sorts of hemp, and did fall upon my great survey of seeing the working and experiments of the strength and the charge in the dressing of every sort; and I do think have brought it to so great a certainty, as I have done the king some service in it, and do purpose to get it ready against the duke's coming to towne to present to him. I see it is impossible for the king to have things done as cheap as other men."

On the 4th of September he remarks, notwithstanding all their short-comings, that the fleet was in a far better condition than in the days of Queen Elizabeth. "Sir William Compton I heard talk with great pleasure of the difference between the fleet now and in Queen Elizabeth's days; where, in 1588, she had but 36 sail great and small in the world, and ten rounds of powder was their allowance at that time against the Spaniards."

He speaks of yachts as pleasure vessels, a name derived from the Dutch, one of which class of vessels so-called had been presented by them to the late king. "By water to Woolwich; in my way saw the yacht lately built by our virtuosos (my Lord Brunkard and others, with the help of Commissioner Pett also), set out from Greenwich with the little Dutch bezan to try for mastery; and before they got to Woolwich the Dutch beat them half-a-mile (and I hear this afternoon that, in coming home, it got above three miles), which all our people are glad of."

On the 18th of February, 1663, he says that he finds "the true charge of the navy" to be "after the rate of 374,743 pounds a-year."

On the 14th of April Sir George Carteret tells him that Parliament "will call all things in question; and, above all, the expenses of the navy;" "and into the truth of the report of people being forced to sell their bills at 15 per cent, losse in the navy."

On the 23rd of May Sir George says that Parliament intend to report 200,000 pounds per annum as the ordinary charge of the navy.

The importance of having wet-docks in which ships could be fitted out was well understood. He speaks of finding certain creeks at Portsmouth, and mentions Commissioner Pett's design to form a wet-dock in Saint Mary's creek, "which can be done at no great charge, and yet no little one; he thinks, towards 10,000 pounds;" and that the place is likely to be a very fit one when the king has money to do it with.

He mentions a letter of Sir William Petty, "wherein he says that his vessel, which he hath built upon two keels (a model whereof, built for the king, he shewed me), hath this month won a wager of 50 pounds, in sailing between Dublin and Holyhead, with the pacquett-boat, the best ship or vessel the king hath there; and he offers to lay with any vessel in the world. It is about 30 ton in burden, and carries 30 men, with good accommodation (as much more as any ship of her burden), and so any vessel of this figure shall carry more men, with better accommodation by half, than any other ship. This carries also ten guns of about five tons weight. In their coming back from Holyhead they started together, and this vessel came to Dublin by five at night, and the pacquett-boat not before eight the next morning; and when they come they did believe that this vessel had been drowned, or at least behind, not thinking she could have lived in that sea." He concludes, "I only affirm that the perfection of sailing lies in my principle, find it out who can."

By his account we find that machines to perform the same service as torpedoes were thought of in those days. He tells "Dr Allen," with whom he had "some good discourse about physick and chymistry, what Dribble, the German Doctor, do offer of an instrument to sink ships he tells me that which is more strange, that something made of gold, which they call in chymistry *aurum fulminans*, a grain, I think he said, of it, put into a silver spoon and fired, will give a blow like a musquett, and strike a hole through the silver spoon downward, without the least force upward."

He gives an amusing account of a trial about the insurance of a ship, before Lord Chief-Justice Hide. "It was pleasant to see what mad sort of testimonys the seamen did give, and could not be got to speak in order; and then their terms such as the judge could not understand; and to hear how sillily the counsel and judge would speak as to the terms necessary in the matter, would make one laugh; and, above all, a Frenchman, that was forced to speak in French, and took an English oath he did not understand, and had an interpreter sworn to tell us what he said, which was the best testimony of all."

On the 3rd of December, 1663, he gives us the satisfactory intelligence "that the navy (excepting what is due to the yards upon the quarter now going on) is quite out of debt; which is extraordinary good news, and upon the 'Change, to hear how our credit goes as good as any merchant's upon the 'Change is a joyfull thing to consider, which God continue!"

The next day he remarks, "The King of France, they say, is hiring of 60 sail of ships of the Dutch, but it is not said for what design."

On the 22nd of January he went down to Deptford, "and there viewed Sir William Petty's vessel; which hath an odd appearance, but not such as people do make of it."

On the 4th of March he "saw several people trying a new-fashion gun, brought by my Lord Peterborough this morning, to shoot off often, one after another, without trouble or danger." This must have been something of the fashion of a revolver of the present day.

One of the first entries regarding the Dutch war is on the 21st of November, 1644. "This day, for certain, news is come that Teddiman hath brought in eighteen or twenty Dutchmen, merchants, their Bourdeaux fleet, and two men-of-war to Portsmouth. And I had letters this afternoon, that three are brought into the Downes and Dover; so that the warr is begun: God give a good end to it!"

On the 31st of December he says: "My Lord Sandwich at sea with the fleet at Portsmouth, sending some about to cruise for taking of ships, which we have done to a great number."

On the 11th of January, 1665: "This evening, by a letter from Plymouth, I hear that two of our ships, the *Leopard* and another, in the

Straights, are lost by running aground; and that three more had like to have been so, but got off, whereof Captain Allen one; and that a Dutch fleet are gone thither; and if they should meet with our lame ships, God knows what would become of them. This I reckon most sad news; God make us sensible of it!"

The following remarks show the threatening attitude of the Dutch: on the 12th of January, 1665, "Spoke with a Frenchman, who was taken, but released, by a Dutch man-of-war, of 36 guns (with seven more of the king's or greater ships), off the North Foreland, by Margett. Which is a strange attempt, that they should come to our teeth; but, the wind being easterly, the wind that should bring our force from Portsmouth, will carry them away home."

On the 15th he was called in, with Sir William Penn, to see the king, "And there Sir W. Penn spoke pretty well to dissuade the king from letting the Turkish ships go out; saying (in short), the king having resolved to have 130 ships out by the spring, he must have above 20 of them merchantmen. Towards which, he, in the whole river, could find but 12 or 14, and of them the five ships taken up by these merchants were a part, and so could not be spared. That we should need 30,000 sailors to man these 130 ships, and of them, in service, we have not above 16,000; so that we shall need 14,000 more. That these ships will, with their convoys, carry about 2000 men, and those the best men that could be got; it being the men used to the southward that are the best men of warr, though those bred in the north, among the colliers, are good for labour. That it will not be safe for the merchants, nor honourable for the king, to expose these rich ships with his convoy of six ships to go, it not being enough to secure them against the Dutch, who, without doubt, will have a great fleet in the Straights."

At a visit of the Duke of York, he hears, by a letter from Captain Allen, "First, of our own loss of two ships, the *Phoenix* and *Nonsuch*, in the Bay of Gibraltar; then of his and his seven ships with him, in the Bay of Cales, or thereabouts, fighting with the 34 Dutch Smyrna fleet; sinking the *King Solomon*, a ship worth 150,000 pounds, or more, some say 200,000 pounds, and another; and taking of three merchant-ships. Two of our ships were disabled by the Dutch unfortunately falling, against their will, against them — the *Advice*, Captain W. Poole, and *Antelope*, Captain Clerke. The Dutch men-of-war did little service. Captain Allen, before he would fire one gun, come within pistol-shot of the enemy. The Spaniards, at Cales, did stand laughing at the

Dutch, to see them run away and flee to the shore, 34 or thereabouts, against eight Englishmen at most."

"Captain Allen led the way, and himself writes that all the masters of the fleet, old and young, were mistaken, and did carry their ships aground."

"Captain Seale, of the *Milford*, hath done his part very well, in boarding the *King Solomon*, which held out half-an-hour after she was boarded; and his men kept her an hour after they did master her, and then she sank, and drowned about 17 of her men."

He speaks, a few days afterwards, of meeting the owners of the double-bottomed boat the *Experiment*, which again reminds us of the plan, at present adopted, to guard ships against the effects of torpedoes.

On the 17th of April he heard an account of the capture of three privateers, one of which was commanded by Admiral Everson's son. Captain Golding, of the *Diamond*, was killed in the action. "Two of them, one of 32, and the other of 20 odd guns, did stand stoutly up against her, which hath 46, and the *Yarmouth* that hath 52, and as many more men as they. So that they did more than we could expect, not yielding till many of their men were killed. And Everson, when he was brought before the Duke of York, and was observed to be shot through the hat, answered, that he wished it had gone through his head, rather than been taken. One thing more is written; that two of our ships, the other day, appearing upon the coast of Holland, they presently fired their beacons round the country to give them notice. And news is brought the king, that the Dutch Smyrna fleet is seen upon the back of Scotland; and, thereupon, the king hath wrote to the duke, that he do appoint a fleet to go to the northward to try to meet them coming home round; which God send!"

On the 28th he went down the river to visit the victualling ships, "where I find all out of order."

On the 8th of June he writes: "Victory over the Dutch, June 3, 1665. This day they engaged, the Dutch neglecting greatly the opportunity of the wind they had of us, by which they lost the benefit of their fireships. The Earl of Falmouth, Muskerry, and Mr Richard Boyle killed on board the duke's ship, the *Royall Charles*, with one shot, their blood and brains flying in the duke's face, and the head of Mr Boyle striking down the duke, as some say. The Earle of Marlborough, Portland, Rear-Admirall Sansum killed, and Capt. Kerby and Ableson. Sir John

Lawson wounded, hath had some bones taken out, and is likely to be well again. Upon receiving the hurt, he sent to the duke for another to command the *Royal Oake*. The duke sent Jordan out of the *Saint George*, who did brave things in her. Capt. Jer. Smith, of the *Mary*, was second to the duke, and stepped between him and Captain Seaton, of the *Urania* (76 guns and 400 men), who had sworn to board the duke, killed him 200 men, and took the ship himself, losing 99 men, and never an officer saved but himself and lieutenant. His master, indeed, is saved, with his leg cut off; Admiral Opdam blown up, Trump killed, and said by Holmes; all the rest of their admiralls, as they say, but Everson (whom they dare not trust for his affection to the Prince of Orange), are killed, we having taken and sunk, as is believed, about 24 of their best ships, killed and taken 8 or 10,000 men, and lost, we think, not above 700. A greater victory never known in the world. They are all fled. Some 43 got into the Texell, and others elsewhere, and we in pursuit of the rest."

On the 16th he goes down to Whitehall, and hears more about the battle. "Among other things, how my Lord Sandwich, both in his councils and personal service, hath done most honourably and serviceably. Jonas Poole, in the *Vanguard*, did basely, so as to be, or will be, turned out of his ship. Captain Holmes expecting upon Sansum's death to be made rear-admirall to the prince (but Harman is put in), hath delivered up to the duke his commission, which the duke took and tore. Several of our captains have done ill. The great ships are the ships to do the business, they quite deadening the enemy. They run away upon sight of the prince. Captain Smith, of the *Mary*, the duke talks mightily of, and some great thing will be done for him. Strange to hear how the Dutch do relate, as the duke says, that they are the conquerors, and bonfires are made in Dunkirke in their behalf, although a clearer victory can never be expected. Mr Coventry thinks they cannot have lost less than 6000 men, and we not dead above 200, and wounded about 400; in all about 600. Captain Grove, the duke told us this day, hath done the basest thing at Lowestoffe, in hearing of the guns, and could not (as others) be got out, but staid there, for which he will be tried, and is reckoned a prating coxcombe, and of no courage."

The fleet did not escape the plague, which was at that time raging in London. On the 12th of August it appeared at Deptford, on board the *Providence* fire-ship, which was just fitting out to go to sea.

At Sheerness, a yard was in course of being laid out to lay provisions for cleaning and repairing of ships, the most proper place for the purpose.

On the 19th the fleet came home, "to our great grief, with not above five weeks dry and six weeks wet provisions, however, must go out again, and the duke hath ordered the *Soveraigne*, and all other ships ready, to go out to the fleet and strengthen them. This news troubles us all, but cannot be helped."

On the 9th of September, 1665, he meets Sir William Doyly and Evelyn at supper: "And I with them full of discourse of the neglect of our masters, the great officers of state, about all business, and especially that of money, having now some thousands prisoners kept to no purpose, at a great charge, and no money provided almost for the doing of it."

"Captain Cocke reports as a certain truth that all the Dutch fleet, men-of-war and merchant East India ships, are got every one in from Bergen, the 3rd of this month, Sunday last, which will make us all ridiculous."

On the 14th, however, he says: "A letter from my Lord Sandwich at Solebay, of the fleet's meeting with about eighteen more of the Dutch fleet, and his taking of most of them; and the messenger says, that they had taken three after the letter was wrote and sealed, which being twenty-one, and the fourteen took the other day, is forty-five sail, some of which are good and others rich ships."

On the 18th he goes to Gravesend in the bezan yacht, and "by break of day we come to within sight of the fleet, which was a very fine thing to behold, being above 100 ships, great and small, with the flag-ships of each squadron distinguished by their several flags on their main, fore, or mizen-masts. Among others, the *Soveraigne, Charles*, and *Prince*, in the last of which my Lord Sandwich was. And so we come on board, and we find my Lord Sandwich newly up in his night-gown very well."

He attends a council of war on board, "When comes Sir W. Penn, Sir Christopher Mingo, Sir Edward Spragg, Sir Jos. Jordan, Sir Thomas Teddiman, and Sir Roger Omittance." Sir Christopher Mings was one of the bravest admirals of the day. He was the son of a shoemaker, and had worked his way up in the sea-service. He was killed the following year, June, 1666, in action with the Dutch. Pepys describes him as "a very witty, well-spoken fellow, and mighty free to tell his parentage, being a shoemaker's son."

On the 25th of January, 1666, he writes: "It is now certain that the King of France hath publickly declared war against us, and God knows how little fit we are for it."

As an example of the way affairs were managed, he tells us that, viewing the yard at Chatham, he observed, "among other things, a team of four horses coming close by us, drawing a piece of timber that I am confident one man could easily have carried upon his back. I made the horses be taken away, and a man or two to take the timber away with their hands."

Still more abominable was the way in which the wages of the unfortunate seamen were kept back. On the 7th of October, 1665, he writes: "Did business, though not much, at the office, because of the horrible crowd and lamentable moan of the poor seamen that lie starving in the streets for lack of money, which do trouble and perplex me to the heart; and more at noon, when we were to go through them, for then above a whole hundred of them followed us, some cursing, some swearing, and some praying to us." He continues: "Want of money in the navy puts everything out of order; men grown mutinous, and nobody here to mind the business of the navy but myself."

On the 19th of May, 1666: "Mr Deane and I did discourse about his ship *Rupert*, built by him, which succeeds so well as he hath got great honour by it, and I some by recommending him — the king, duke, and everybody saying it is the best ship that ever was built. And, then, he fell to explain to me his manner of casting the draught of water which a ship will draw beforehand, which is a secret the king and all admire in him; and he is the first that hath come to any certainty beforehand of foretelling the draught of water of a ship before she be launched."

On the 4th he describes the fight between the English and Dutch, the news brought by a Mr Daniel, "who was all muffled up, and his face as black as the chimney, and covered with dirt, pitch, and tar, and powder, and muffled with dirty clouts, and his right eye stopped with okum." The English "found the Dutch fleet at anchor, between Dunkirke and Ostend, and made them let slip their anchors; they about ninety and we less than sixty. We fought them and put them to the run, till they met with about sixteen sail of fresh ships, and so bore up again. The fight continued till night, and then again the next morning from five till seven at night. And so, too, yesterday morning they began again, and continued till about four o'clock, they chasing us for the most part of Saturday, and yesterday we flying from them." Prince Rupert's fleet, however, was seen coming, "upon which De Ruyter called a council, and thereupon their fleet divided into two squadrons — forty in one, and about thirty in the other; the bigger to follow the duke, the less to meet the prince. But the prince come up with the generall's fleet, and the Dutch come together again, and bore towards their own coast, and we with them. The duke was forced to come to anchor on Friday, having lost his sails and rigging."

Some days afterwards he continues the description of the fight: "The commanders, officers, and even the common seamen do condemn every part of the late conduct of the Duke of Albemarle; running among them in his retreat, and running the ships on ground; so as nothing can be worse spoken of. That Holmes, Spragg, and Smith do all the business, and the old and wiser commanders nothing."

"We lost more after the prince came than before. The *Prince* was so maimed, as to be forced to be towed home." Among several commanders killed in the action was Sir Christopher Mings.

He describes the affection the seamen entertained for those commanders they esteemed: "About a dozen able, lusty, proper men come to the coach-side with tears in their eyes, and one of them that spoke for the rest begun and said to Sir W. Coventry, 'We are here a dozen of us, that have long known and loved and served our dead commander, Sir Christopher Mings, and have now done the last office of laying him in the ground. We would be glad we had any other to offer after him, and in revenge of him. All we have is our lives; if you will please to get His Royal Highness to give us a fire-ship among us all, here are a dozen of us, out of all which choose you one of us to be commander, and the rest of us, whoever he is, will serve him; and, if possible, do that which shall show our memory of our dead commander, and our revenge.' Sir W. Coventry was herewith much moved, as well as I, who could hardly abstain from weeping."

"Sir Christopher Mings was a very stout man, and a man of great parts, and most excellent tongue among ordinary men; and would have been a most useful man at such a time as this."

He gives a deplorable account of the state of the navy, the neglect of business by Charles and his brother, and the want of money. On the 8th of October, 1665, he writes: "I think of twenty-two ships, we shall make shift to get out seven. (God help us! men being sick, or provisions lacking.) There is nothing but discontent among the officers, and all the old experienced men are slighted."

Speaking of the action with the Dutch, he says: "They do mightily insult of their victory, and they have great reason. Sir William Barkeley was killed before his ship taken; and there he lies dead in a sugar-chest, for everybody to see, with his flag standing up by him. And Sir George Ascue is carried up and down the Hague for people to see."

The abominable system of the press-gang was then in full force, and was carried on with the same cruelty which existed till a much later period: "To the Tower several times, about the business of the pressed men, and late at it till twelve at night shipping of them. But, Lord! how some poor women did cry; and in my life I never did see such natural expression of passion as I did here in some women bewailing themselves, and running to every parcel of men that were brought one after another to look for their husbands, and wept over every vessel that went off, thinking they might be there, and looking after the ship as far as ever they could by moone-light, that it grieved me to the heart to hear them. Besides, to see poor, patient, labouring men and housekeepers leaving poor wives and families, taken up on a sudden by strangers, was very hard, and that without press-money, but forced against all law to be gone. It is a great tyranny."

The next morning he went "to Bridewell to see the pressed men, where there are about 300; but so unruly that I durst not go among them; and they have reason to be so, having been kept these three days prisoners, with little or no victuals, and pressed out and contrary to all course of law, without press-money, and men that are not liable to it."

PRESS-GANG.

"I found one of the vessels loaden with the Bridewell birds in a great mutiny; I think it is much if they do not run the vessel on ground."

He continues: "With regard to the building of ten great ships, none to be under third-rates; but it is impossible to do it, unless we have some money."

Sir W. Penn gives his advice as to the mode of fighting at sea: "We must fight in a line, whereas we fight promiscuously, to our utter and demonstrable ruin; the Dutch fighting otherwise; and we, whenever we beat them. 2. We must not desert ships of our own in distress, as we did, for that makes a captain desperate, and he will fling away his ship when there are no hopes left him of succour. 3rd. That ships when they are a little shattered must not take the liberty to come in of themselves, but refit themselves the best they can, and stay out — many of our ships coming in with very small disableness. He told me that our very commanders, nay, our very flag-officers, do stand in need of exercising among themselves, and discoursing the business of commanding a fleet; he telling me that even one of our flagmen in the fleet did not know which tack lost the wind or kept it in the last engagement. Then in the business of forecastles, which he did oppose, all the world sees now the use of them for shelter of men."

He observes that "we see many women now-a-days in the streets, but no men; men being so afraid of the press." He speaks of purchasing "four or five tons of corke, to send this day to the fleet, being a new device to make barricados with, instead of junke." The importance of protecting men against shot was even then, it will be seen, thought of.

On the 10th he goes "to the office; the yard being very full of women coming to get money for their husbands and friends that are prisoners in Holland; and they lay clamouring and swearing and cursing us, that my wife and I were afraid to send a venison-pasty that we have for supper to-night, to the cook's to be baked."

On the 23rd July Sir W. Coventry talks to him of the "*Loyal London* (which, by the way, he commends to be the best ship in the world, large and small) hath above eight hundred men. The first guns made for her all bursted, but others were made, which answered better."

Speaking of the late battle, he remarks that "the *Resolution* had all brass guns, being the same that Sir John Lawson had in her in the Straights. It is to be observed that the two fleets were even in number to one ship."

Sir W. Coventry "spoke slightingly of the Duke of Albemarle, saying, when De Ruyter come to give him a broadside — 'Now,' says he (chewing of tobacco the while), 'will this fellow come and give me two broadsides, and then he shall run;' but it seems he held him to it two hours, till the duke himself was forced to retreat to refit, and was towed off, and De Ruyter staid for him till he come back again to fight. One in the ship saying to the duke, 'Sir, methinks De Ruyter hath given us more than two broadsides.' 'Well,' says the duke, 'but you shall find him run by-and-by,' and so he did, but after the duke himself had been first made to fall of."

From the accounts he gives of the condition of the navy, it is surprising that our ships were not everywhere beaten. On the 20th of October he writes: "Commissioner Middleton says that the fleet was in such a condition as to discipline, as if the devil had commanded it; so much wickedness of all sorts. Enquiring how it came to pass that so many ships had miscarried this year, he tells me that the pilots do say that they dare not do nor go but as the captains will have them; and if they offer to do otherwise, the captains swear they will run them through. That he heard Captain Digby (my Lord of Bristoll's son, a young fellow that never was but one year, if that, in the fleet) say that he did hope he should not see a tarpawlin have the command of a ship within this twelve months" — tarpaulin being the common name applied to a sailor in those days.

On the 19th: "Nothing but distraction and confusion in the affairs of the navy."

On the 28th he adds: "Captain Guy to dine with me. He cries out of the discipline of the fleet, and confesses really that the true English valour we talk of is almost spent and worn out; few of the commanders doing what they should do, and he much fears we shall therefore be beaten the next year. He assures me we were beaten home the last June fight, and that the whole fleet was ashamed to hear of our bonfires. The *Revenge* having her forecastle blown up with powder to the killing of some men in the river, and the *Dyamond* being overset in the careening at Sheerness, are further marks of the method all the king's work is now done in. The *Foresight* also and another come to disasters in the same place this week in the cleaning."

On the 2nd of November he describes the *Ruby*, French prize, "the only ship of war we have taken from any of our enemies this year. It seems a very good ship, but with galleries quite round the sterne to walk in as a balcone, which will be taken down."

News of the Dutch having been seen off the mouth of the Thames alarms every one; and on the 24th of March, 1667, he writes: "By-and-by to the Duke of Yorke, where we all met, and there was the king also; and all our discourse was about fortifying of the Medway and Harwich; and here they advised with Sir Godfrey Lloyd and Sir Bernard de Gunn, the two great engineers, and had the plates drawn before them; and indeed all their care they now take is to fortify themselves, and are not ashamed of it."

On the 9th of June he writes: "I find an order come for the getting some fire-ships presently to annoy the Dutch, who are in the king's channel, and expected up higher."

The next day: "News brought us that the Dutch are come up as high as the Nore; and more pressing orders for fire-ships. We all went down to Deptford, and pitched upon ships and set men at work, but,

Lord! to see how backwardly things move at this pinch, notwithstanding that by the enemy being now come up as high as almost the Hope."

Anxiety and terror prevailed in the city, and people were removing their goods — the thoughtful Mr Pepys making a girdle to carry 300 pounds in gold about his body. The alarm is further increased when a neighbour comes up from Chatham, and tells him that that afternoon he "saw the *Royal James*, the *Oake*, and *London* burnt by the enemy with their fire-ships; that two or three men-of-war come up with them, and made no more of Upnor Castle's shooting than of a fly; that the Dutch are fitting out the *Royal Charles*."

Ships were to be sunk in the river, about Woolwich, to prevent the Dutch coming up higher.

"The masters of the ships that are lately taken up, do keep from their ships all their stores, or as much as they can, so that we cannot despatch them, having not time to appraise them, nor secure their payment. Only some little money we have, which we are fain to pay the men we have with every night, or they will not work. And, indeed, the hearts as well as the affections of the seamen are turned away; and in the open streets in Wapping, and up and down, the wives have cried publickly, 'This comes of not paying our husbands; and now your work is undone, or done by hands that understand it not.'"

Some of the men, "instead of being at work at Deptford, where they were intended, do come to the office this morning to demand the payment of their tickets; for otherwise they would, they said, do no more work; and are, as I understand from everybody that has to do with them, the most debauched, swearing rogues that ever were in the navy, just like their prophane commander."

"Nothing but carelessness lost the *Royal Charles*, for they might have saved her the very tide that the Dutch came up. The Dutch did take her with a boat of nine men, who found not a man on board her; and presently a man went up and struck her flag, and jacke, and a trumpeter sounded upon her, 'Joan's placket is torn;' they did carry her down at a time, both for tides and wind, when the best pilot in Chatham would not have undertaken it, they heeling her on one side to make her draw little water, and so carried her away safe."

"It is a sad sight to see so many good ships there sunk in the river, while we would be thought to be masters of the sea."

He also examines the chain which had been carried across the river, "and caused the link to be measured, and it was six inches and one-fourth in circumference."

He commends the Dutch "for the care they do take to encourage their men to provide great stores of boats to save them; while we have not credit to find one boat for a ship." The English mode "of preparing of fire-ships," he observes, "do not do the work, for the fire not being strong and quick enough to flame up, so as to take the rigging and sails, lies smothering a great while, half-an-hour before it flames, in which time they can get the fire-ships off safely. But what a shame it is to consider how two of our ship's companies did desert their ships. And one more company did set their ship on fire and leave her; which afterwards a Feversham fisherman came up to, and put out the fire, and carried safe into Feversham, where she now is. It was only want of courage, and a general dismay and abjectness of spirit upon all our men; God Almighty's curse upon all that we have in hand, for never such an opportunity was of destroying so many good ships of theirs as we now had."

To replace the *Royal Charles* carried away, a new ship was launched on the 4th of March, 1668, called the *Charles*; "God send her better luck than the former."

At a Privy Council which he attended, "to discourse about the fitness of entering of men presently for the manning of the fleet, before one ship is in condition to receive them," the king observed, "'If ever you intend to man the fleet without being cheated by the captains and pursers, you may go to bed and resolve never to have it manned.'"

At another council he speaks of "a proposition made to the Duke of York by Captain Von Hemskirke, for 20,000 pounds to discover an art how to make a ship go two feet for one what any ship do now, which the king inclines to try, it costing him nothing to try; and it is referred to us to contract with the man." He afterwards says that the secret was only to make her sail a third faster than any other ship.

On the 25th of March, 1669, a court-martial was held about the loss of the *Defyance*. The sentence was, "That the gunner of the *Defyance* should stand upon the *Charles* three hours with his fault writ upon his breast, and with a halter about his neck, and so be made incapable of any service." The ship was burnt by the gunner allowing a girl to carry a fire into his cabin.

Whatever our shortcomings in regard to naval affairs, it is pleasant to believe that they cannot possibly be so great as in the days of Mr Samuel Pepys.

Chapter Eleven.

William and Mary — from A.D. 1689 to A.D. 1702.

One of the last acts of James was to send a fleet under the command of Lord Dartmouth to intercept that of William of Orange, which it was known was on the point of sailing. On board the Dutch fleet was Admiral Herbert, acting as commander-in-chief, though all the officers were Dutch. It was hoped that he would win over the English fleet. As it proved, both the officers and men of the navy were as ill-affected to James as were those of the army. Thus, as an old writer observes, "that naval force which James had cultivated with so much care, and on which he depended so much, proved of no use — so difficult a thing is it to bring Englishmen to enslave England."

The Dutch fleet consisted of about 50 men-of-war, 25 fire-ships, and near 400 transports and victuallers and other vessels, carrying about 4000 horse and 10,000 foot. Admiral Herbert led the van of the fleet, Vice-Admiral Evertzen brought up the rear, and the prince himself was in the centre, carrying a flag with English colours, and their highnesses' arms surrounded with this motto, "The Protestant Religion and the Liberties of England," and underneath the motto of the House of Nassau, "Je Maintiendrai," "I will maintain."

After being driven back by a storm, the fleet came to an anchor in Torbay on the 4th of November. The prince wished to land that day, it being the one on which he was born and married, and he fancied that it would look auspicious to the army, and animate the soldiers, but the general wish was that he should not land till the following, being Gunpowder Treason day, that their landing on that day might have a good effect on the minds of the English. No sooner had the Dutch fleet got into harbour than a heavy storm sprang up from the westward, which compelled the English fleet to run into Portsmouth, from which they could not again issue till William had won the day. When Lord Dartmouth was able to leave the port he conducted the fleet to the Downs, and there holding council of war, it was resolved — first, to dismiss from their commands all such officers as were known to be papists, and then to send up an address to his highness setting forth their steady affection to the Protestant religion, and their sincere concern for the safety, freedom, and honour of their country.

Not long after this the ships were dispersed, some to the dockyards to be dismantled and laid up, others to be cleaned and repaired, and such as were in the best condition for sea were appointed for necessary services. The first service in which Admiral Herbert was employed was to endeavour to intercept the French fleet which had sailed for Ireland to support the landing of King James. On the 1st of May, 1689, the English admiral discovered the enemy's ships at anchor in Bantry Bay; when the French stood out to sea in a well-formed line of battle to meet him. After a warm engagement of some hours the two fleets separated, when the French, claiming the victory, retired into Bantry Bay, and the English towards Scilly. After waiting for reinforcements in the chops of the channel, none arriving, Admiral Herbert returned to Portsmouth. Notwithstanding his ill-success, the king, in gratitude for the services he had before rendered him, created him Earl of Torrington, while Captains John Ashby, and Cloudesly Shovel were knighted. In 1690 Sir Cloudesly Shovel commanded a squadron of six men-of-war, which escorted the fleet of transports conveying King William's forces to Carrickfergus, in Ireland. The Earl of Torrington, when in command of the combined English and Dutch squadrons in the channel, on the 30th of June, fell in with the French fleet commanded by the Count de Tourville between Cherbourg and the Isle of Wight. The combined fleets amounted to 56 ships only, while the French possessed 78 men-of-war and 22 fire-ships. The Dutch and Blue Squadrons being surrounded by the French, after making a gallant defence, were rescued by the Earl of Torrington. After this, finding that no impression could be made on the French fleet, it was decided in a council of war that it would be wiser to destroy the disabled ships than, by protecting them, hazard an engagement. The *Anne*, of 70 guns, which was dismasted, was forced on shore and destroyed. The enemy also attempted to destroy a Dutch 64 which was driven on shore, but her commander defended her with so much bravery, that he compelled the French to desist, and she, being got off, arrived safe in Holland. The earl then retreated into the Thames, leaving a few frigates to observe and watch the motions of the enemy, who remained masters of the channel. In consequence of his conduct, the earl was brought to a court-martial, but having ably defended himself, he was unanimously acquitted. The king, notwithstanding, to appease the clamours of the nation and the Dutch, took away his commission.

He was succeeded in the command of the fleet by Admiral Russell, who, greatly owing to the energetic proceedings of Queen Mary, while the king was absent in Ireland, had, by May, 1691, a squadron of considerable force, equipped and ready for sea, at his disposal. So elevated were the French at their unusual success, that they had the following inscription engraved on the stern of a new first-rate ship of war named the *Saint Louis*: —

"I, on the ocean, am the mightiest thing, As on the land, is my all-potent king."

English men-of-war were ere long, however, to teach them to sing a different note. A fleet of ninety-nine sail, including the Dutch ships, was got ready by May, 1692. The English fleet was divided into two squadrons, the Red and the Blue. Among the ships we find the names of many which have become famous in naval history. There were six ships of 100 guns each. In the Red Squadron there was the *Britannia*, carrying the flag of Admiral Russell; the *Royal Sovereign*, that of Vice-Admiral Sir Ralph Delaval; the *London*, that of the rear-admiral, Sir Cloudesly Shovel; the *Sandwich*, of 90 guns; the *Swiftsure, Hampton Court, Eagle*, and *Captain*; of 70; the *Ruby, Oxford*, and *Centurion*, of 50. In the Blue Squadron there were the *Victory*, of 100 guns, with the flag of Admiral Sir John Ashby; the *Windsor Castle*, with that of Vice-Admiral Sir George Rooke; the *Neptune*, of 96 guns; the *Albemarle* and *Vanguard*, of 90 guns; the *Royal Oak*, of 74; the *Northumberland, Berwick, Warspight, Monmouth*, and *Edgar*, of 70; the *Lion* and *Dreadnought*, of 60 — names long known in the British Navy. Altogether, the English fleet carried 4504 guns, and 27,725 men. The Dutch fleet carried rather more than half the number of guns, and less than half the number of men. No more powerful fleet had ever yet ploughed the ocean — it was, probably, immeasurably more so than that which encountered the Spanish Armada; while the commanders were as expert and daring as their predecessors, the seamen were infinitely better trained.

The combined fleet sailed from Spithead on the 18th of May, and stood across to the coast of France. The *Chester* and *Charles* galleys, being sent ahead, just at dawn on the 19th, Cape Barfleur bearing south-west by south, distant about seven leagues, made the signal of the French fleet being in sight, by firing some guns. Admiral Russell thereon ordered his fleet to form a line of battle, and directed the rear to attack, so that, should the French stand to the northward, they might the sooner come up and engage. As the sun rose above the ocean on that May morning, soon after four o'clock, the enemy were seen standing southward, forming their line on the same tack as that of the allied squadrons. The French admiral, De Tourville, who had till now supposed that he was about to meet only a portion of the English fleet, nevertheless considering that their hasty retreat would cause a confusion which might prove more hazardous than the battle itself, continued his orders for the engagement, and bore down on the allies. Admiral Russell on seeing this, annulled the signal for the rear to attack, and bore away to join the leeward-most ships, and formed a line ahead in close order of sailing. The French advanced till within musket-shot of the English line, when, hauling up to windward, the *Soleil Royal*, at 11:30 a.m., opened fire upon the *Britannia*. De Tourville's object was to cut through the English line, but in consequence of the light breeze having dwindled to a calm, in bearing up as he did the French admiral lost his advantage. The *Soleil Royal* and the *Britannia* thus lay for an hour and a quarter about three-quarter's musket-shot of each other, the English plying their guns so warmly, that the Frenchman was in that time dreadfully cut up in his rigging, sails, and yards; it being evident, also, that he had lost a great many men, for no effort was being made to repair damages. So actively did the English gunners work their pieces, that it was reckoned that during the whole fight they fired at least three broadsides while the French fired two. Captains Churchill and Aylmer who had come up to assist the admiral, had six of the enemy's largest ships to deal with; while Sir Cloudesly Shovel, who had got to windward, briskly plied the Count de Tourville's squadron. As the day advanced, however, a dense fog came on, so that in a short time not a ship of the enemy could be seen, and the English, for fear of injuring their friends, ceased firing. The ships which had not yet got into action on account of the calm, had their boats ahead, and used their utmost endeavours to tow them into the fight. The English fire-ships had, however, been put to good use, having burnt four of the enemy's ships. The killed and wounded were already numerous; the *Eagle* alone having 70 men killed and 150 wounded. Among the former were Rear-Admiral Carter, and Captain Hastings of the *Sandwich*.

Night coming on, the darkness, increased by the thick fog, put an end to the fight for that day. On the morning of the 10th a portion of the French fleet was discovered, when, the wind springing up, a general chase was ordered. This continued till 4 p.m., when, the wind shifting to the southward, and the ebb ceasing, both fleets anchored and furled sails.

On the 21st the fleet anchored near the Race of Alderney, Cape La Hogue, bearing about south. Twenty-three of the French ships had anchored still nearer the Race, and fifteen others about three leagues to the westward. The flood-tide setting in strong, a number of the French ships were observed to be driving; on this Admiral Russell threw out a signal to Vice-Admiral Delaval to stand inshore and destroy them. On following out his directions, he found the *Soleil Royal* and two others aground, close to the beach. Finding, however, that his ships drew too much water, he sent in three fire-ships, embarking in one of them himself. He succeeded in burning two of the three-deckers, but another fire-ship was sunk by the enemy's shot. The *Saint Albans* and *Ruby* standing in, now attacked a third French ship, when Vice-Admiral Delaval, observing that her crew had deserted their guns, boarded. On finding dead and wounded men alone on her decks, he ordered the latter to be removed, and then set the ship on fire.

One of the fire-ships, commanded by Captain Fowlis, who was conducting her against the *Soleil Royal*, was set on fire by her shot, though he and his crew escaped. Captain Heath, however, succeeded in burning her with another fire-ship, in the most gallant manner. The *Conquirant* was burnt by Captain Greenaway, and the *Admirable* by the boats. The greater number of the enemy's ships had run in for shelter close to the shore. Accordingly, on the 23rd of May, Admiral Russell despatched Vice-Admiral Rooke with a squadron of men-of-war, frigates, and fire-ships, and the boats of the fleet, to destroy those ships. It was found, however, that the small frigates alone could advance near enough to effect anything. The boats, however, gallantly led by Rooke, pulled in at night and destroyed seven of them, and the next morning, again pulling in, burnt eight, with several transports and ammunition vessels. Several of the ships were first boarded, and the French, with their own guns, driven from their platforms and batteries on shore; and this was done in sight of the French and Irish camps, which lay ready to invade England. Altogether, sixteen sail of the line and numerous transports were destroyed. The victory was complete, and the annihilation of the French fleet entirely dissipating the hopes of James, its effect contributed greatly to place William the Third on his throne. Vice-Admiral Rooke, who became one of England's greatest admirals, was knighted for his gallantry on this occasion.

While some of the ships returned to Spithead, a considerable portion were stationed in different parts of the channel to watch the French fleet, and to prevent them making their way either to the eastward or westward.

Among the gallant men who have contributed to the naval glory of England, the name of John Benbow must ever be had in remembrance. His father, Colonel Benbow, was one of those true-hearted cavaliers who fought bravely for their king to the last, and having seen one of his brothers shot by the Parliamentary forces, he made his escape, till an amnesty being granted, he was able to return and live in private in England. His fortune having been expended, he was glad to accept a small office belonging to the Ordnance, in the Tower. On the breaking out of the first Dutch war, the king came to examine the magazines. Charles, whose memory was as quick as his eye, recognised the veteran, who had for twenty years been distinguished by a fine head of grey hair. "My old friend, Colonel Benbow," said he, "what do you here?"

"I have," returned the colonel, "a place of 80 pounds a-year, in which I serve your majesty as cheerfully as if it brought me in 4000 pounds a-year."

"Alas!" said the king, "is that all that could be found for an old friend of Worcester? Colonel Legge, bring this gentleman to me to-morrow, and I will provide for him and his family as it becomes me."

Short as the time was, the colonel did not live to claim the royal promise; for, overcome by the king's unexpected gratitude, sitting down on a bench, he there breathed his last before his majesty was well out of the tower. Whatever might have been the king's intentions, he thought no more of the old cavalier's family, and the colonel's son, John, went to sea in a merchant-vessel, and shortly became owner and commander of a ship, called the *Benbow* frigate. No man was better known or more respected by the merchants upon the Exchange. The following anecdote shows his character, and is in accordance with the spirit of the times in which he lived. In the year 1688 he was, while in command of the *Benbow* frigate, attacked on his passage to Cadiz by a Sallee rover of far superior force, against which he defended himself with the utmost bravery. At last the Moors boarded him, but were quickly beaten out of his ship again with the loss of thirteen men, whose heads Captain Benbow ordered to be taken off, and thrown into a tub of pork pickle. On reaching Cadiz he went on shore, ordering a negro servant to follow him with the Moors' heads in a sack. Scarcely had he landed when the officers of the revenue inquired of the servant what he had in his sack. The captain answered, "Salt provisions for his own use."

"That may be," answered the officers, "but we must insist upon seeing them." Captain Benbow said that he was no stranger there, that he was not accustomed to run goods, and pretended to take it very ill that he was thus suspected. The officers told him that the magistrates were sitting not far off, and if they were satisfied, the servant might carry the provisions where he pleased. The captain consented to the proposal, and away they marched to the custom-house. The magistrates, when he came before them, treated Captain Benbow with great civility, telling him that they were sorry to make a point of such a trifle, but that since he refused to show the contents of his sack to their officers, they were compelled to demand a sight of them.

"I told you," said the captain, sternly, "they were salt provisions for my own use. Cassar, throw them down upon the table; and, gentlemen, if you like them, they are at your service."

The Spaniards were much struck at the sight of the Moors' heads, and no less so at the account the captain gave them of his engagement, and defeat of so large a force of barbarians. They sent an account of the whole matter to the court at Madrid, and the King of Spain was so much pleased with it, that he requested to see the English captain, who made a journey to court, where he was received with much respect, and not only dismissed with a handsome present, but the king was to write a letter on his behalf to King James, who, upon his return, gave him a ship, which was his introduction to the Royal Navy.

He had always been looked upon as a bold, brave, and active commander, and one who, though he maintained strict discipline, took care of, and was therefore cheerfully obeyed by, his seamen. He maintained the same character in the Royal Navy, and was ever beloved and honoured by his ships' companies. As the channel was much infested by French privateers, a large number of which were fitted out at Saint Malo, it had been considered advisable to destroy that town and the vessels within its harbour. Captain Benbow, with a squadron of twelve ships of the line, four bomb-galliots, ten or twelve frigates, and several sloops, having crossed the channel, entered the harbour and came to an anchor within half-a-mile of the town. The ships then opened fire, and continued battering away at the place till four in the morning, when they were compelled to come out to prevent grounding. Two successive days they continued doing the same, firing seventy bombs one day, but with frequent intermissions, inducing the inhabitants to believe that they were about to retire. The captain had, however, prepared a fire-ship, with which it was intended to have reduced the town to ashes. This vessel was a new galliot, of about 300 tons. In the bottom of the hold were placed above a hundred barrels of powder, covered with pitch, tar, resin, brimstone, and faggots. Over this was a row of thick planks or beams, with holes pierced through them in order to communicate the fire from above, and upon them were placed 340 carcases filled with grenadoes, cannon-balls, iron chains, firearms loaded with ball, large pieces of metal wrapped up in tarpaulins, and other combustible matters. This craft was sent in before the wind, and was near the very foot of the wall where it was to be fastened, when a sudden gust of wind drove it upon a rock, where it stuck, near the place where it was intended to have blown up. The engineer, however, had time to set fire to it before he retired. It blew up soon afterwards, but the carcases, which were to have done the greatest execution, being wet, did not take fire; yet the shock was so terrible, that it threw down part of the town wall, shook every house in the town, and overthrew the roofs of above 300 which were nearest. The capstan, weighing above a ton, was thrown over the wall on the top of a house, which it beat down. A similar machine had been used for blowing up the bridge at the siege of Antwerp in 1585.

In 1694 another expedition, under the command of Sir Cloudesly Shovel, was sent to the coast of Flanders, for the purpose of destroying the town of Dunkirk. Previous attacks had been made on the coast of France of a similar character. Mr Meesters, the inventor of some infernal machines, accompanied the expedition. He requested that a captain might be appointed to the command of the smaller craft, and Captain Benbow was accordingly directed to take command of the bomb-galliots and fire-ships. Owing to numerous delays, the French having got notice of the intended attack, had time to make preparations for defeating it, which resulted in the loss of several ships. Dieppe, however, had been bombarded, when 1100 bombs and carcases were thrown into it with such success, that the town was set on fire in several places, and the townsmen and some regiments sent to their assistance had to beat a rapid retreat.

An infernal machine, such as has before been described, was blown up at the pierhead. It made a frightful noise, but did little execution, occasioned, as was supposed, by the pierhead lying too low. The fuzee having gone out, Captain Dunbar, who commanded the vessel, again went on board and set fire to it in the most gallant manner.

Havre-de-Grâce was likewise bombarded, when the town was set in flames. Bad weather coming on, the bomb-vessels were ordered off, the mortars being either melted or the vessels so shattered, that no present use could be made of them. One of them, the *Granado*, was entirely blown to pieces by a bomb, which fell into her. It was it hoped, however, that Sir Cloudesly's expedition would be more successful. Notwithstanding a heavy fire from a French frigate in the roads, from numerous forts, and from five other frigates near the basin, Captain Benbow carried his vessels and boats close up to the town, and came off again in the night without any damage. The next day, the weather being fair, the boats and vessels were again sent in, when the French frigate, after firing her broadside, ran in to the pier. In the afternoon, two infernal machines were blown up at a little distance from the pierhead, but without doing any damage, except to the crew of the boat which towed them in, who were all blown up on board. The French, also, having driven piles outside the pierheads, and sunk four ships, it was found impossible to approach nearer the town, and the undertaking was therefore abandoned. This is one of the many instances which prove that fire-ships, if resolutely met by the enemy against whom they are intended to act, are not capable of effecting much damage.

A remarkable instance of promotion for gallant conduct occurred early in the reign of William and Mary. On the 25th of March, 1689, the 36-gun frigate *Nonsuch*, Captain Roome Coyle, fell in with two French ships, one mounting 30, the other 22 guns, off Guernsey. He without hesitation engaged them, when he and the master being killed, and there being no lieutenant on board, the boatswain, Robert Simcock, took the command. So spiritedly did the brave boatswain continue the action, that both French ships were captured. For his gallant conduct Mr Simcock, on reaching Portsmouth with his prize, was forthwith promoted to the rank of captain, and appointed to command the *Nonsuch*.

Next year a ship called the *Friends' Adventure*, belonging to Exeter, was captured by a French privateer, who took out of her the master and five of his men, leaving on board only the mate, Robert Lyde, of Topsham, twenty-three years of age, and John Wright, a boy of sixteen, with seven Frenchmen, who had orders to navigate the ship to Saint Malo. When off Cape la Hogue, a strong wind springing up, drove them off the French coast. Lyde now began to entertain hopes of recovering the ship, and on the 6th of March he and his companion took the opportunity, while two of the Frenchmen were at the pump, one at the helm, one on the forecastle, and three asleep in the cabin, to attack them. Lyde with an iron crowbar killed one of the men at the pump, and knocked down the other at one blow. Wright at the same moment knocked down the man on the forecastle, and they then secured the man at the helm. One of the Frenchmen hearing a scuffle, and running up from between decks to the assistance of his companions, was wounded by the mate, but the two others coming to his relief seized and had nearly secured the gallant fellow, when the boy, bravely hurrying to his aid, after a sharp struggle, killed one and gave the other quarter. Having thus made themselves masters of the ship, they put the two disabled men into bed, ordering a third to look after them, and secured them between decks. One they kept bound in the steerage, and made use of the remaining man to navigate the vessel, which, on the 9th of March, they brought safely into Topsham, with their five prisoners on board.

About the same time the sloop *Tryal* was captured by a French man-of-war, who put five Frenchmen on board, leaving only the master, Richard Griffiths, afterwards Captain Griffiths, commonly known by the name of "Honour and Glory," and a boy, John Codamon, in the sloop. Griffiths and his boy having formed their design, suddenly set upon the five Frenchmen, and, having wounded three and forced all five down into the hold, carried their vessel with their prisoners safe into Falmouth.

I give these instances to show the stuff out of which the commanders and crews of men-of-war were formed in those days. They show, also, that the authorities who governed the navy appreciated bravery, and were ready to obtain the services of such gallant fellows for the advantage of the country.

We find fire-ships at this period universally sent to sea with fleets. Sir Francis Waller, on board the *Sussex*, was ordered to proceed to Cadiz, and from thence to convoy the merchant-vessels he might find there to Turkey or any ports in Spain or Italy. His fleet consisted of fifteen third-rates, seven fourth-rates, one fifth-rate, six fire-ships, two bomb-vessels, a hospital-ship, and a store-ship in company with several

Dutch ships of war. Having touched at Gibraltar, he again put to sea, and met with gales of wind; and ultimately, in thick weather, he with part of his fleet running to the straits mistook the entrance. The *Sussex*, with 550 men on board, foundered, two Moors only escaping. The admiral's body was afterwards discovered on shore much mangled. Besides this loss, 409 were drowned belonging to various ships which were either driven on shore or foundered. Among them was the *Cambridge*, a ship of 70 guns, and the *Lumley Castle*.

On most occasions the fire-ships, being generally old vessels fit for no other purpose, were the chief sufferers. A Dutch ship of 70 guns ran on shore, but was got off again, as were several other ships; indeed, few escaped without much damage. This was the most violent storm that had ever been known in those seas since the memory of man.

William was now taking measures for retrieving the honour of the British Flag, and appointed Admiral Russell commander-in-chief of the navy, and several other eminent officers to form a new commission of admiralty. He also, finding that the pay of sea-officers was less than that of other countries, directed that the sea pay of flag-officers, commanders, lieutenants, masters, and surgeons should be doubled; as also that all flag-officers and captains of first, second, third, fourth, and fifth-rate ships, and also the masters of first, second, and third-rates, who had served a year in the same post in the ships of those rates, or been in a general engagement, should have half-pay while on shore, to be paid quarterly out of the general estimate of the navy. From this it is evident that they before this time, as also those of other ranks, received no half-pay while on shore. It was also ordered that only such commissioned officers as had been put in by the Admiralty, and warrant officers as had been put in by the Navy Board, should receive the benefit of half-pay; that half-pay officers be expected to assist the Navy Board; that no convoy money be demanded or received under the penalty of forfeiting and losing employment for ever; that the commanders transmit to the Admiralty when and why they came into port.

The French had not abandoned their design of restoring James the Second to the throne. He had abdicated, and in 1696, while most of the British ships were laid up, and the rest were employed in the protection of the trade up the Mediterranean, it was discovered that 500 transports were in Dunkirk ready to take on board an army of 20,000 men, under the escort of fifteen sail of men-of-war, for the invasion of

England. While these preparations were making, and every ship was of consequence, the *Royal Sovereign*, laid up at Chatham to be rebuilt, took fire, and was totally consumed. She was the first great ship that ever was built in England. The great object then was only to exhibit as much splendour and magnificence as possible. In the reign of Charles the Second, however, being taken down a deck lower, she became one of the best men-of-war in the world, and so formidable to her enemies, that none of the most daring among them would willingly lie by her side. She had been in almost all the great engagements that had been fought between England and Holland, and in the last fight between the English and French, when she compelled the *Soleil Royal* to fly for shelter among the rocks. At length, leaky and defective with age, she was laid up at Chatham, in order, as has been said, to be rebuilt.

In the year 1691 the first mention is made of a regular regiment of marines being raised to serve on board ship. In this year one dry and two wet docks were ordered to be constructed at Portsmouth, and orders were given to survey the harbour of Falmouth, and report whether it was capable of being made a proper port for the refitting and docking ships of the Royal Navy.

It was not till the year 1693 that men-of-war on the home service were allowed to carry to sea spare topmasts and sails.

In 1694 the king, by the advice of the excellent Queen Mary, granted the royal palace of Greenwich to be converted into a hospital for decayed seamen in the Royal Navy. Sir Christopher Wren was appointed as architect, and an annual sum of money was granted to complete and extend the buildings. The foundation of the first new building was laid on the 3rd of June, 1696.

In the same year the landmark on the beach at Stoke, near Gosport, called the Kicker, was erected, and the buoy of the horse placed at Spithead, for the better security of ships going into Portsmouth Harbour. Some docks were made at Plymouth, and storehouses, as also residences for the accommodation of the officers of the dockyard, were built.

In 1695 brass box-compasses were invented and allowed to the ships in the Royal Navy. Many ships having been wrecked upon the Eddystone Rock off Plymouth, an application was made to the Trinity House to erect a lighthouse on it, which was begun to be built in 1696, and was finished in three years. Many masters and owners of ships agreed to pay one penny per ton outwards and inwards, to assist in defraying the expense.

In 1696 an Act of Parliament was passed to establish a register for 30,000 seamen, to be in readiness at all times for supplying the Royal Navy. They were to have a bounty of forty shillings yearly. None but such registered seamen were to be preferred to the rank of commissioned or warrant officers in the Royal Navy. They were likewise entitled to a double share in all prizes, and when maimed or superannuated, were admitted into Greenwich Hospital. The widows and children of such registered seamen who might be killed in the service were admissible into that hospital. It was also enacted that sixpence per month should be deducted from the wages of all seamen both in the merchant-service as well as in the Royal Navy, for the support of Greenwich Hospital.

A composition was invented to be laid on the bottoms of ships to preserve them against worms. The experiment was ordered to be tried on his majesty's ship the *Sheerness*.

In 1696 the Parliament voted 2,372,197 pounds for the maintenance of 40,000 seamen and two regiments of marines, the ordinary of the navy, and the charge of the registry of seamen. This was the largest sum by far hitherto voted for the maintenance of the navy.

In 1697 Commissioner Greenhill proposed a plan for rowing of ships in a calm, which was tried on board His Majesty's ship the *Experiment*.

In 1700 the rate of pay of sea-officers was again reduced. It was far less than that of the French; the French admiral having 1500 pounds per annum for his table-money, whereas the English admiral had only 365 pounds, no allowance whatever being made to other admirals, unless commanders-in-chief.

For several years the West Indies and Spanish Main had been infested by the buccaneers, who plundered without distinction the ships of all nations, but particularly those of the Spaniards. Several were taken, among the most notorious of whom was Captain Kidd, who, being brought to England and tried at the Old Bailey, was fully convicted, and executed with several of his companions. The immense property which Kidd had amassed was given for the support of Greenwich Hospital. The Earl of Bellamont, Governor of New England, and others, were accused in Parliament of favouring Kidd, and giving him a commission, but the charges were refuted.

On the 25th of July, 1701, a new *Royal Sovereign*, of 110 guns, was launched at Woolwich. She was the largest ship in the navy, the length of her keel was 146 feet 6 inches, and from the top of the taffrail to the fore-part of the figure-head, 210 feet 7 inches; her extreme breadth being 54 feet 3 and a half inches.

Several actions exhibiting extraordinary courage, performed during the war with France, are worthy of notice. On the 30th of May, 1695, William Thompson, master of a fishing-boat belonging to Poole, in Dorsetshire, with a crew of one man and a boy, observed a French sloop privateer standing towards him. He had but two swivel guns and a few muskets; the privateer had two guns, several small-arms, and sixteen men. Thompson, finding that his small crew were ready to support him, made up his mind to do battle with the Frenchman. As she approached, he began blazing away, and in a short time wounded the captain, and mate, and six men of the privateer, upon which she sheered off. Thompson on this made chase, and so skilfully did he manage his little craft, and with so much determination keep up his fire, that after engaging the privateer for two hours, she struck. On his arrival at Poole with his prize, he was warmly received, and the Lords of the Admiralty, hearing of his gallantry, presented him with a gold chain and a medal of the value of 50 pounds.

Another fishing-vessel, belonging to Whitesand, commanded by a Mr Williams, falling in with some merchant-vessels which had been captured by French privateers, attacked them with so much courage and skill, that he retook the whole. He received the same reward as had Mr Thompson.

Not long afterwards a coasting sloop, the *Sea Adventure*, commanded by Peter Jolliffe, fell in, off Portland, with a French privateer, which was in the act of taking possession of a small fishing-vessel belonging to Weymouth. The privateer endeavoured to escape, when Jolliffe made sail in chase, and coming up, briskly opened his fire, when he compelled her to release her prize. Not content with this success, he continued the fight, and at length drove her on shore in Lulworth Bay. The seafaring population of the village hurrying out, captured the privateer, and made prisoners of her crew.

Just before the close of the war, Captain William Jumper, commanding the *Weymouth*, engaged and sank the *Fougueux*, a French 48-gun ship, and shortly afterwards he fell in with another French 50-gun ship, but in the heat of the engagement, some powder on board the *Weymouth* blew up the poop, and disabled her for further immediate action. Having repaired damages, Captain Jumper again closed with the enemy, but unhappily his bowsprit and three lower-masts fell overboard, when the French ship made sail and escaped. On the 19th of the following August he fell in with a sail to leeward, between the island of Cloune and Saint Martins. He immediately ran down, hoisting the French ensign, and yawing a little to show it. Another French frigate at anchor under the castle, weighed and stood off. The first man-of-war, suspecting the character of the stranger, made sail, but the *Weymouth*, outsailing her, got close under her lee, keeping his French ensign flying to prevent the enemy from firing at his masts till he was near enough. He then hoisted the English ensign and poured in a broadside, and commenced bracing his main-topsail back; when, before he had fired off a second round, the enemy, which proved to be *L'Amore*, of Rochefort, a king's ship, struck her colours. The other ship, seeing the fate of her consort, escaped. The prize was a vessel similar to an English galley. She carried 20 guns on the upper-deck, and 9 on the lower-deck, but 4 on the quarter-deck, and between decks she had small ports for oars.

Chapter Twelve.

Queen Anne — from A.D. 1702 to A.D. 1714.

Anne, daughter of James the Second, married the Prince George of Denmark, and ascended the throne March the 8th, 1702. Although the army was held in more consideration during her reign than the navy, the British seamen managed by their gallant deeds to make the service respected at home and abroad. It was not much to his advantage that the queen appointed her consort, Prince George, to be Lord High Admiral. The acts done in his name were not so narrowly scrutinised as they would otherwise have been, and the commissioners of the Admiralty took good care to shelter themselves under his wing.

Three of the most celebrated admirals in this reign were Sir George Rooke, Sir Cloudesly Shovel, and Admiral Benbow. Sir George, upon the breaking out of war with France, was appointed to the chief command of the fleet. An expedition, which he at once sent against Cadiz, was unsuccessful. Not long afterwards, intelligence was carried to Sir George that a French squadron and a fleet of Spanish galleons was at Vigo. Sir George immediately sailed with the English and Dutch fleets, and appeared before that port. The weather being hazy, the people in the town did not discover them. The passage into the harbour is not more than three-quarters of a mile across. Batteries had been thrown up on either side, and garrisoned with a large body of troops, while a strong boom, composed of ships-yards and topmasts fastened together with three-inch rope, had been carried across it. The top chain at each end was moored to a 70-gun ship, while within the boom were moored five ships, of between 60 and 70 guns each, with their broadsides fronting the entrance to the passage, so that they could fire at any ship which came near the boom, forts, or platform. As it was impossible for the whole fleet to enter, a detachment of fifteen English and ten Dutch men-of-war, with all the fire-ships, followed by the frigates and bomb-vessels, were ordered to enter and attempt the destruction of the enemy's fleet, while the troops were to land and attack the forts in the rear. Vice-Admiral Hopson in the *Torbay* led the van; but when he got within shot of the batteries it fell calm, so that the ships were compelled to come to an anchor. A strong wind, however, soon afterwards springing up, Admiral Hopson cutting his cables clapped on all sail, and, amidst a hot fire from the enemy, bore up directly for the boom, which he at once broke through, receiving broadsides from the two ships at either end. The rest of the squadron and the Dutch following, sailed abreast towards the boom, but being becalmed they all stuck, and were compelled to hack and cut their way through. Again a breeze sprang up, of which the Dutchman made such good use that, having hit the passage, he went in and captured the *Bourbon*. Meantime Admiral Hopson was in extreme danger, for the French fire-ship having fallen on board him, whereby his rigging was set on fire, he expected every moment to be burnt; but it happened that the fire-ship was a merchantman, and laden with snuff, and being fitted up in haste, the snuff in some measure extinguished the fire. The gallant Hopson, however, received considerable damage, for, besides having his fore-topmast shot away, he had 115 men killed and drowned, and 9 wounded, while his sails and his rigging were burnt and scorched. He was, therefore, compelled to leave his ship, and hoist his flag on board the *Monmouth*.

At the same time, Captain Bokenham, in the *Association*, laid his broadside against the town, while Captain Wyvill, in the *Barfleur*, a ship of the like force, was sent to batter the fort on the other side. The firing of the great and small shot of both sides was continued for some time, till the French admiral, seeing the platform and fort in the hands of the English and his fire-ship useless, while the confederate fleet were entering, set fire to his own ship, ordering the rest of the captains under his command to follow his example, which was done in so much confusion, that several men-of-war and galleons were taken by the English and Dutch. The allies and French lost about an equal number of men, but by this victory a vast amount of booty, both of plate and other things, was captured. The Spanish fleet was the richest that ever came from the West Indies to Europe. The silver and gold was computed at 20,000,000 of pieces of eight, of which 14,000,000 only had been taken out of the galleons and secured by the enemy at Lagos, about twenty-five leagues from Vigo, and the rest was either taken or sunk in the galleons. Besides this, there were goods to the value of 20,000 pieces of eight, and a large quantity of plate and goods belonging to private persons. A few years ago only, a company was formed in England for the purpose of dredging for the treasure sunk in the galleons, but the scheme was abandoned on the discovery that much less amount of treasure than here described was really lost, the confederates having captured nearly all of that which had not been landed at Lagos.

By this blow the naval power of France was so deeply wounded, that she never recovered it during the war.

Admiral Benbow had in the meantime been despatched to the West Indies, in command of a small squadron, to prevent the Spanish islands from falling into the power of France. Hearing that Monsieur de Casse, the French admiral, had sailed for Carthagena, he pursued him. On the 19th of August, in the afternoon, he discovered ten sail steering westward along the shore under their topsails. Upon this, he threw out a signal for a line of battle. The frigates being a long time coming up, and the night advancing, Benbow steered alongside the French, having disposed his line of battle in the following manner: — The *Defiance, Pendennis, Windsor, Breda, Greenwich, Ruby,* and *Falmouth.* Though he endeavoured to near them, he intended not to make any attack until the *Defiance* had got abreast of the headmost. He, however, was compelled before long to open his fire; but after two or three broadsides had been exchanged, the *Defiance* and *Windsor* luffed up out of gunshot, leaving the two sternmost ships of the enemy engaged with the admiral, while his own ships in the rear did not come up as he had expected. He afterwards altered his line of battle. The next morning at daybreak, he was near the French ships, but none of his squadron, excepting the *Ruby,* were with him, the rest lying some miles astern. There was but little wind, and though the admiral was within gunshot of the enemy, they did not fire. In the afternoon, a sea-breeze springing up, the enemy got into line and made what sail they could, while the rest of the English ships not coming up, the admiral and *Ruby* plied them with chase-guns, and kept them company all the next night. On the 21st the admiral again exchanged fire with the enemy's fleet, as did the *Ruby,* and he would have followed had not the *Ruby* been in such a condition that he could not leave her. The *Ruby* was so disabled during this and the following day, that the admiral ordered her to return to Port Royal.

The rest of the squadron now came up, and the enemy being but two miles off, the gallant Benbow was at last in hopes of doing something, and continued, therefore, to steer after them, but again, all his ships, with the exception of the *Falmouth,* were astern, and at twelve the enemy began to separate. Early on the morning of the 24th he again came within hail of the sternmost of the French ships. At three, while hotly engaged with them, the admiral's right leg was shattered to pieces by a chain-shot, and he was carried below, but soon after, he ordered his cradle on the quarter-deck, and the fight was continued till daylight, when one of the enemy's ships, of 20 guns, was discovered to be very much disabled. A strong breeze now brought the enemy down upon him, when three of his own ships getting to leeward of the disabled ship, fired their broadsides and stood to the southward. Then came the *Defiance*, which, after exchanging fire with the disabled ship, put her helm a-weather and ran away before the wind, without any regard to the signal of battle. The French seeing the two ships stand to the southward, and finding that they did not attack, immediately bore down upon the admiral, and running between their disabled ship and him, poured in all their shot, by which they brought down his main-topsail yard, and shattered his rigging very much.

Some time after this, his line of battle signal flying all the while, Captain Kirby came on board and told him that he had better desist, that the French were very strong, and that from what was past, he would guess he would make nothing of it. On this he sent for the rest of the captains. They obeyed him, but were most of them of Captain Kirby's opinion. This satisfied the admiral that they were not inclined to fight; when, had they supported him, the whole French fleet might have been captured. On this he returned with his squadron to Jamaica. As soon as he arrived he ordered a court-martial on the captains who had deserted him. One, Captain Hudson, died a few days before his trial came on. Captains Kirby and Wade were condemned to death, and being sent home, were shot immediately on their arrival at Plymouth, in 1703.

The gallant Benbow, in spite of the fearful wound he had received, lingered till the 4th of November, when he yielded up his brave spirit, feeling more the disgrace which his captains had brought upon the English flag than his own sufferings. All the time of his illness he continued to issue his orders, and showed more anxiety for the interests of the nation than for his private affairs. He received a proof of what would have been the result of the action had he been properly supported, in a letter from the brave French Admiral Du Casse. "Sir, — I had little hopes on Monday last but to have supped in your cabin, but it pleased God to order it otherwise. I am thankful for it. As for those cowardly captains who deserted you, hang them up, for by God they deserve it. — Yours, Du Casse."

The opinion of the nautical poets of the time is well shown in one of those sea-songs which have done so much to keep up the spirits of British tars.

"The Death of Benbow."

Come all ye sailors bold,
Lend an ear, lend an ear,
Come all ye sailors bold, lend an ear;
'Tis of our Admiral's fame,
Brave Benbow called by name,
How he fought on the main,
You shall hear, you shall hear.

Brave Benbow he set sail,
For to fight, for to fight;
Brave Benbow he set sail
With a free and pleasant gale,
But his captains they turned tail.
In a fright, in a fright.

Says Kirby unto Wade,
I will run, I will run;
Says Kirby unto Wade, I will run;
I value not disgrace,
Nor the losing of my place,
My en'mies I'll not face
With a gun, with a gun.

'Twas the Ruby and Noah's Ark
Fought the French, fought the French;
'Twas the Ruby and Noah's Ark fought the French;
And there was ten in all;
Poor souls they fought them all,
They valued them not at all,
Nor their noise, nor their noise.

It was our Admiral's lot,
With a chain-shot, with a chain-shot;
It was our Admiral's lot, with a chain-shot
Our Admiral lost his legs;
Fight on, my boys, he begs,
'Tis my lot, 'tis my lot.

While the surgeon dressed his wounds,
Thus he said, thus he said;
While the surgeon dressed his wounds, thus he said,
Let my cradle now, in haste,
On the quarter-deck be placed,
That my enemies I may face,
Till I'm dead, till I'm dead.

And there bold Benbow lay,
Crying out, crying out;
And there bold Benbow lay, crying out,
Let us tack about once more,
We'll drive them to their own shore;
I don't value half-a-score,
Nor their noise, nor their noise.

In 1703 Rear-Admiral Dilkes did good service by pursuing a fleet of forty-three French merchantmen, convoyed by three men-of-war, into a bay between Avranches and Mount Saint Michael. He first sent in his boats, under cover of the ships, when fifteen sail were taken, six burnt, and three sunk; and, on the following morning, the enemy having got into too shoal water for the large ships to approach, he in person led the boats, when two men-of-war were burnt, a third was taken, and seventeen more of the merchant-vessels were burnt, so that only four escaped. For this signal service the queen ordered gold medals to be struck, and presented to the admiral and all his officers.

Parliament this year voted 40,000 men, including 5000 marines, for the sea-service.

On the night between the 26th and 27th of November, one of the most fearful storms ever known in England began to blow. It commenced between eleven and twelve o'clock, from the west-south-west, with a noise which resembled thunder, accompanied by bright flashes of lightning, and continued with almost unrelenting fury till seven the next morning. During these few hours thirteen men-of-war were cast away, and 1509 seamen were drowned. Among the officers who lost their lives were Rear-Admiral Beaumont, when his ship, the *Mary*, was driven on the Goodwin Sands. Of the whole ship's company, Captain Hobson, the purser, and one man, Thomas Atkins, alone were saved. The escape of Atkins was remarkable. When the ship went to pieces, he was tossed by a wave into the *Stirling Castle*, which sank soon after, and he was then thrown by another wave, which washed him from the wreck into one of her boats. Sir Cloudsley Shovel, who was lying in the Downs, saved his ship by cutting away her mainmast, though she narrowly escaped running on the *Galloper*. The wives and families of the seamen who perished on this occasion received the same bounty as would have been granted had they been actually killed in fight in her majesty's service. The House of Commons also resolved to present an address to her majesty, stating, that as they could not see any diminution of her majesty's navy without making provision to repair the same, they besought her immediately to give directions for repairing this loss, and for building such capital ships as her majesty should think fit.

In 1704 Sir George Rooke, who commanded a large squadron in the Mediterranean, on board of which was a body of troops under the Prince of Hesse, resolved to attempt the capture of Gibraltar. On the 17th of July, while the fleet lay in Tetuan Roads, he called a council of war, when, finding that his officers were ready to support him, he gave orders that the fleet should at once proceed to the attack. Entering the Bay of Gibraltar, the ships took up a position to prevent all communication between the rock and the continent, and the Prince of Hesse landed on the isthmus with 1800 marines. His highness having taken post there, summoned the governor, who answered that he would defend the place to the last. At daybreak on the following morning, the 22nd, Sir George ordered the ships under the command of Rear-Admiral Byng and Rear-Admiral Vanderduesen to commence the cannonade, but owing to want of wind they were unable to reach their stations till nearly nightfall. In the meantime, to amuse the enemy, Captain Whitaker was sent in with some boats, who burnt a French privateer of 12 guns at the old mole. On the 23rd, soon after daybreak, the ships having taken up their stations, the admiral gave the signal for commencing the cannonade, when, in five or six hours, 15,000 shot were thrown into the fortress, compelling the enemy to retreat from their guns. Sir George now considering that could the fortifications be captured, the town would yield, sent in Captain Whitaker with all the boats, to endeavour to possess himself of it. Captain Hicks and Captain Jumper, who lay next the mole, were the first to reach the shore with their pinnaces, and before the other boats could come up, the enemy sprang a mine, which blew up the fortifications on the mole, killed 2 lieutenants and about 40 men, and wounded about 60 others. The gallant captains, then advancing, gained possession of the great platform, Captain Whitaker capturing a redoubt half-way between the mole and the town, many of the enemy's guns being also taken. The next day the governor offered to capitulate; when, hostages being exchanged, the Prince of Hesse marched into the town, of which he took possession, the Spaniards composing the garrison being allowed to march out with all the honours of war — though the French were excluded from this part of the capitulation, and were detained as prisoners of war.

CAPTURE OF GIBRALTAR. — p. 196.

The town was found to be extremely strong, with 100 guns mounted, all facing the sea, and with two narrow passes to the land. It was also well supplied with ammunition, but the garrison consisted of less than 150 men. However, it was the opinion that fifty men might have defended the fortifications against thousands, and the attack made by the seamen was brave almost beyond example. Sixty only were killed, including those blown up, and 216 wounded. As this design was contrived by the admiral, so it was executed entirely by the seamen, and to them was the honour due.

Leaving a garrison under the Prince of Hesse, the fleet sailed to Tetuan, in order to take in wood and water. At the end of the year the Spaniards attempted its recapture, but Sir John Leake arriving to its relief, surprised and took three French frigates, a fire-ship, corvette, and storeship laden with warlike stores, the very night before the

Spaniards had intended to storm it. The following month 2000 troops arrived to garrison the place, making it no longer necessary for the ships to remain in the bay.

Notwithstanding the many important services rendered by Sir George Rooke, his political opponents gaining the ascendant, so annoyed him that he resolved to retire, to prevent public business from receiving any disturbance on his account. He passed the remainder of his days as a private gentleman, for the most part at his seat in Kent. He left but a small fortune, so moderate that when he came to make his will, it surprised those who were present. The reason he assigned reflected more honour on him than had he possessed unbounded wealth. His words were: "I do not leave much, but what I leave was honestly gotten — it never cost a sailor a tear, or the nation a farthing." He died on the 24th of January, 1708-9, in the fifty-eighth year of his age, leaving one son, George Rooke, by the daughter of Colonel Luttrell, of Dunster Castle, Somersetshire.

On the resignation of Sir George Rooke, Sir Cloudsley Shovel was appointed Vice-Admiral of England.

In 1704 a sum of 10,000 pounds was voted by Parliament for building a wharf and storehouses in the dockyard at Portsmouth, and 40,000 men for the sea-service, including 8000 marines, proving the value which was attached to this arm. Probably they were trained even then to assist in working the ship, while to them was committed those duties exclusively which have since been so ably performed by our gallant blue-jackets on shore.

On the 1st of December, 1704, Greenwich Hospital was opened for the reception of seamen, and a lieutenant-governor, captain, and two lieutenants, a physician, and surgeon, were appointed by warrant. Numerous other officers were afterwards appointed, as well as two chaplains.

In 1705, the Eddystone Lighthouse, which had been blown down during the great storm, was rebuilt by Act of Parliament, and the contribution from the English shipping, which had before been voluntary, was fixed by its authority. The contest with France, Queen Anne's war, as it was called, resulted in the general destruction of the French power at sea; and after the battle of Malaga, we hear no more of their great fleets. The number of their privateers, however, was *very* much increased, in consequence of which Parliament was urged on by the mercantile interest to put them down. The loss also by the great storm, and the misfortunes met with in the West Indies, indeed, every untoward accident, induced the nation more eagerly to demand an augmentation of the navy. Thus, at the close of 1706, not only were the number but the quality of the men-of-war greatly superior to what they had been in Charles's reign. The economy and discipline of the navy was also much improved. Great encouragement was also given to seamen, by the utmost care being taken in the treatment of the wounded, and exact and speedy payment of prize-money.

A bounty was now given for hemp imported from the plantations, and every encouragement was afforded to British merchants to enable them to carry on their schemes with vigour.

The gallantry of Captain Mordaunt, son of the Earl of Peterborough, in command of the *Resolution*, of 70 guns, in the Mediterranean, deserves to be remembered. He had sailed with his father from Barcelona on the 13th of March, 1706, with an envoy of the King of Spain to the Duke of Savoy on board, and had in company the *Enterprise* and *Milford* frigates. When within about fifteen leagues of Genoa, six French line of battle ships were seen, who immediately gave chase to the English squadron. Lord Peterborough and the Spanish envoy on this went on board the *Enterprise*, and, with the *Milford*, made their escape to Leghorn. The enemy continued the chase of the *Resolution*, when one of their ships came about ten o'clock at night within shot of her, but did not begin to fire till the other ships had come up. The *Resolution* had been much shattered a few days before in a heavy gale of wind, and was at no time a fast sailer. Notwithstanding the great disparity in force, Captain Mordaunt made a brave resistance; but by the advice of his officers he ran the ship ashore under the guns of a Genoese fort, from which, however, he received no manner of protection; and shortly afterwards he was wounded in the thigh, when he was carried on shore. At five the French commodore sent in all the boats of his squadron, but the enemy were repulsed and obliged to retire to their ships. The next morning a French 80-gun ship, brought up under the *Resolution's* stern, with a spring in her cable, and opened a heavy fire upon her. Her officers finding that there was no prospect of saving the ship, with the consent of Captain Mordaunt, set her on fire, and in a short time she was consumed, while they and the crew got safely on shore.

The last act of the gallant Sir Cloudsley Shovel was an attempt to assist the Duke of Savoy and Prince Eugene, who were closely investing Toulon. A large number, however, of the French ships were destroyed before the siege was raised. On his return to England, on the 23rd of October, 1707, a strong gale blowing from the south-south-west, his ship, the *Association*, ran upon the rocks called the Bishop and his Clerks off Scilly, and immediately going to pieces, every soul perished. The *Eagle* and *Romney* shared the same fate; other ships struck, but happily got off. The body of the brave Sir Cloudsley was the next day cast on shore, and was known by a valuable ring which he wore on his finger. Being brought to Plymouth, it was thence conveyed to London and interred in Westminster Abbey, where a magnificent monument was erected by Queen Anne to his memory.

We may judge of the progress of the navy by the sums voted by Parliament for its support, which in this year amounted to 2,300,000 pounds.

In 1708, Commodore Wager, with a small squadron, attacked a fleet of galleons on their way from Porto Bello to Carthagena. The Spanish admiral's ship, the *San Josef*, of 64 guns and 600 men, blew up with a cargo on board of 7,000,000 pounds in gold and silver, only seventeen men being saved. The vice-admiral escaped, but the rear-admiral, of 44 guns, was captured. She had, however, only thirteen chests of eight and fourteen sows of silver. The rest of the galleons were for the most part loaded with cocoa. Two of Commodore Wager's captains, who had disobeyed his orders, were tried by a court-martial, and dismissed from the command of their ships.

About the same time Captain Purvis, while chasing a French ship, got his vessel on a ledge of rocks, where she was bilged. He, and some of his men, however, reached a small Key within shot of the French ship, which mounted 14 guns and had on board 60 men. She kept up a brisk fire upon the Key until Captain Purvis with his own boats and a canoe had boarded her, when her commander called for quarter and surrendered on condition that he and his crew should be set on shore. Captain Purvis got the French ship off and returned in her to Jamaica.

Another gallant exploit was performed by Captain Colby, commanding a privateer. Being on a cruise on the Spanish main, he fell in with fourteen sail of brigantines and sloops, laden with valuable goods taken out of the galleons at Porto Bello. They were bound to Panama, under convoy of a guard sloop, which he bravely fought and took, with six of her convoy.

An Act of Parliament was passed this year, by which the forfeited and unclaimed shares of prize-money were to be paid into Greenwich Hospital.

The Prince George of Denmark dying, the Earl of Pembroke was appointed Lord High Admiral of Great Britain in his stead.

England was, as before, determined to assert her supposed sovereignty of the narrow seas, and to compel other nations to acknowledge her claims. While cruising in the chops of the channel the *Winchester*, Captain Hughes, chased a strange sail, on coming up with which he discovered her to be a large Dutch privateer. The commander, on being required to pay the usual compliment to the British flag, not only refused, but discharged a broadside into the *Winchester*. An obstinate fight ensued, in which the Dutch commander and forty of his men were killed. The Dutch and English were at this time, it will be remembered, at peace; but we hear of no complaint being made of the proceeding.

On the retirement of the Earl of Pembroke, the queen, in November, 1709, issued a warrant for the executing of the office of Lord High Admiral by commission. The next year an Act was passed for the purchase of lands in order to fortify and better secure the royal docks at Portsmouth, Chatham, Harwich, Plymouth, and Milford Haven.

By another Act, any seaman in the merchant-service, who had been disabled in defending or taking enemy's ships was deemed qualified to be admitted into Greenwich Hospital.

A fleet, under Sir Hovenden Walker, whose flag-ship was the *Edgar*, was sent out to attack Quebec, and to recover from the French Placentia, in the island of Newfoundland. Having arrived too late in the season he was compelled to return. While he and most of the officers were on shore, on the 15th of October, the *Edgar* blew up at Spithead, when every soul perished.

There lay at that time in the Downs two privateers, the *Duke*, of 30 guns and 170 men, commanded by Captain Wood Rogers, and the *Duchess*, of 26 guns and 150 men, commanded by Captain Stephen Courtnay, having been fitted out by some Bristol merchants to cruise against the Spaniards in the South Seas. They had just returned from thence, having captured a Spanish ship with two millions of pieces of eight on board. On their voyage they had touched at the island of Juan Fernandez, which they reached on the 31st of January, 1708-9. Two of the officers with six armed men had gone on shore, but not quickly returning, the pinnace was sent well manned to bring them off. Towards evening they both came back bringing with them a man clothed in goat-skins, who appeared wilder than the goats themselves. He seemed very much rejoiced at getting on board, but at first could not speak plainly, only dropping a few words of English by times, and without much connection. However, in two or three days he began to talk, when he stated that, having been four years and as many months upon the island without any human creature with whom to converse, he had forgotten the use of his tongue. He had been so long inured to water and such insipid food as he could pick up, that it was some time before he could reconcile himself to the ship's victuals, or to the taking of a dram. He stated that he was a native of Largo, in Fifeshire, that his name was Alexander Selkirk, and that he had belonged to a ship called the *Cinque Ports*, commanded by one Stradling, who, upon some difference, set him on shore here, leaving him a firelock with some powder and ball, a knife, a hatchet, a kettle, some mathematical instruments, a Bible, and two or three other useful books, with a small quantity of tobacco, a bed, bedding, etcetera. At first his loneliness weighed heavily on his spirits, but in time he became inured to it, and got the better of his melancholy. He had erected two huts, one of which served him for a kitchen, the other for a dining-room and bed-chamber. They were made of pimento wood, which supplied him also with fire and candle, burning very clear, and yielding a most refreshing fragrant smell. The roof of his hut was of long grass, and it was lined with the skins of goats, nearly five hundred of which he had killed during his residence on the island, besides having caught above five hundred more, which he marked on the ears, and then set at liberty. When his ammunition was exhausted he caught them by running, and so active was he, that the swiftest goat upon the island was scarcely a match for him. While the ships remained, Mr Selkirk often accompanied the men to hunt the goats with the dogs, whom he always distanced, and frequently tired out. At first, for want of salt, he was unable to relish his food, which consisted of goats' flesh and crawfish, but in time he took to seasoning it with pimento fruit, which is not unlike the black pepper of Jamaica. At first the rats plagued him very much, growing so bold as to gnaw his feet and clothes while he slept. However, he managed to tame some cats which had been left on shore, and these soon kept the rats at a distance. He also made pets of a few kids, and used to divert himself by dancing among them, and teaching them a thousand tricks. When his clothes were worn out, he made a fresh suit of goat-skins joined together with thongs which he had cut with his knife, and which he ran through holes made with a nail instead of a needle. He had a piece of linen remaining, of which he made a shirt to wear next his skin. In a month's time he had no shoes left, and his feet having been so long bare were now become quite callous, and it was some time after he had been on board that he could wear a shoe.

Alexander Selkirk subsequently entered the Royal Navy and became a lieutenant. A monument to his memory was erected on the island of Juan Fernandez by the captain and officers of a British ship of war which touched there a few years ago. On Selkirk's adventures Daniel Defoe founded his immortal story of "Robinson Crusoe."

For some time before the end of Queen Anne's reign no general action worthy of particular mention was fought, although in several engagements between single ships or small squadrons the seamen of England maintained the honour of the British flag. At length, in 1713, the peace of Utrecht put an end to the war. During it the French had been deprived of all pretensions to the dominion of the sea. England had gained and retained possession of Gibraltar, Minorca, Hudson's Bay, the whole of Nova Scotia, the island of Saint Christopher, and also the chief part of Newfoundland; her fleets had literally swept the Mediterranean of all foes, scarcely a French ship daring to navigate its waters, and even the Algerines and other piratical states of Barbary, instead of paying court to the French, now yielded to us, and acknowledged the superiority of the British flag.

Chapter Thirteen.

George the First and Second — from A.D. 1714 to A.D. 1760.

Happily, England being at peace with France when George the First came to the throne, and the Dutch being our firm allies, the history of that period is barren of naval engagements. We possessed, however, numerous skilful commanders, and the navy was in as efficient a state as at any previous period. Sir George Byng, afterwards Viscount Torrington, commanded the fleets of England during the greater part of this reign. The principal officers who served under him were Sir John Leake, Sir John Jennings, Sir James Wishart, Admiral Baker, the Marquis of Carmarthen, Sir William Jumper, and Admiral Aylmer.

On the meeting of Parliament in 1715, 10,000 seamen, at 4 pounds a man per month, were voted for the navy. It also granted 35,574 pounds for the half-pay of sea-officers; and the piratical States of Barbary again becoming troublesome, Admiral Baker cruised against them, and destroyed most of their vessels.

In 1716 Captain Delgarno, an active officer in command of the *Hind*, 20 guns, came up with one of their best men-of-war, mounting 24 guns; when, after a most obstinate and bloody battle, he compelled her to strike, and soon after she sank, all her crew, with the exception of thirty-eight, perishing.

The West Indies being at this time overrun with a desperate set of pirates, a proclamation was issued offering a pardon to all who would surrender themselves within a twelvemonth. After the expiration of that time a reward was offered to any of his majesty's officers, by sea or land, who should take a pirate, after he had been legally convicted: for a captain, 100 pounds; for any other officer down to a gunner, 40 pounds; an inferior officer, 30 pounds. Any private man delivering up a captain or commodore was entitled to 200 pounds.

In 1718 the Spaniards sent a fleet and army to attack the possessions of the King of Naples, on the island of Sicily. This giving offence to the English, Sir George Byng was appointed to the command in the Mediterranean, with directions to protect the Neapolitans. Soon after Sir George arrived off Messina he discovered a Spanish fleet amounting to twenty-seven sail, besides fire-ships, bomb-vessels, and galleys. On seeing the English, the Spaniards stood away, and the admiral chased them, and finally, after a running fight, captured the Spanish admiral, Chacon, with five ships of the line, one frigate of 44 guns, and one of 36. Captain Walton in the *Canterbury*, with five more ships, had been sent in pursuit of another part of the Spanish fleet. On the 22nd August Sir George received the following pithy despatch from him: —

"We have taken and destroyed all the Spanish ships and vessels which were upon the coast, the number as per margin. — I am, yours, etcetera, G. Walton."

In 1722, the navy being on a peace establishment, 7000 seamen alone were voted at the usual rate of 4 pounds a man per month.

Notwithstanding the proclamation which had been issued for the apprehension of pirates, those daring sea-robbers continued their depredations, and became especially formidable on the coast of Africa, as well as in the West Indies. The most notorious of them was one Roberts, an able seaman, of undaunted courage, and capable of command. His force consisted of three stout ships; his own carried 40 guns and 152 men; another 32 guns and 132 men, and a third 24 guns and 90 men. In April, 1722, Captain Ogle, commanding the *Swallow*, being on a cruise off Cape Lopez, received intelligence that Roberts was lying with his three ships in an adjoining bay. Upon this, he disguised his ship to look like a merchant-vessel, and stood in, when one of the pirates slipped her cable and gave chase. Captain Ogle decoyed him off the land till he had reached such a distance as to prevent his associates hearing the report of the guns. He then shortened sailed, tacked, and brought the pirate to action, which continued an hour and a-half, when, her commander being killed, she struck. Captain Ogle then steered in for the bay, with the pirate's colours hoisted over the king's. This stratagem succeeded, for the pirates, seeing the black flag uppermost, concluded that the king's ship had been taken, and stood out to sea to meet and congratulate their consort on his victory. Their joy was of short duration, for no sooner did they come alongside the *Swallow* than Captain Ogle, throwing off the deception, opened his broadsides upon them. The action lasted two hours, when, Captain Roberts being killed, with a large number of his men, both ships struck. Captain Ogle carried his prizes into Cape Coast Castle, where the prisoners, to the amount of 160, were brought to trial; 74 of them were capitally convicted, 52 of whom were executed and hung in chains along the coast.

In 1725 the South Sea Company commenced a whale-fishery, in which they employed twelve ships, and were sometimes very successful.

In 1726 an expedition was sent to the Spanish West Indies, under Rear-Admiral Hosier, for the purpose of blocking up the galleons or seizing them should they venture out. On the first arrival of the squadron its appearance struck terror along the whole coast, and several Spanish ships were captured. Conceiving that it was his duty to blockade Porto Bello, the brave Hosier remained before it, suffering no ships to go in or come out without strict examination; but, after remaining for six months, fever made such havoc among his seamen, while the ships were so eaten with worms, that he was compelled to return to Jamaica. In two months, however, he was again at sea, and standing over to Carthagena, continued to cruise in those seas. It is said that he lost his crews twice over. Thus the gallant Hosier, mourning for his men, and suffering himself from the deadly effects of the climate, still kept at his post in performance of his duty till, on the 23rd of August, 1727, he breathed his last.

In 1727 a fleet was despatched, under Sir John Norris, into the Baltic, where he was joined by a Danish squadron, to keep a watch on the proceedings of the Empress Catherine, but her death put a stop to the war.

The last naval expedition in this year was one for the purpose of relieving Gibraltar. Sir Charles Wager and Rear-Admiral Hopson on arriving there soon compelled the Spaniards to raise the siege.

George the First ended his reign on the 11th of June, 1727.

George the Second.

Soon after the accession of George the Second in 1727, a peace was concluded with Spain, which lasted twelve years.

Parliament voted a sum of 780,000 pounds to pay the wages of 15,000 seamen.

On the 16th of April, by an order in council, twenty of the oldest surgeons in the Royal Navy were to be allowed two shillings and sixpence per day, half-pay, and the twenty next in seniority two shillings per day.

Notwithstanding the treaty with Spain, the Spaniards continued to annoy the British trade, and to treat British subjects with the greatest insolence and inhumanity. As an instance, Robert Jenkins, master of the *Rebecca* brig, of Glasgow, was boarded by a Guarda Costa. The Spaniards treated the crew with the greatest barbarity, and cut off one of the master's ears, which the captain of the Guarda Costa, giving to Jenkins, insolently told him to carry that present home to the king his master, whom, if he were present, he would serve in the same manner. Some years afterwards, when Jenkins was examined at the bar of the House of Commons, being asked what he thought when he found himself in the hands of such barbarians, he replied with great coolness, "I recommended my soul to God, and my cause to my country."

Four 20-gun ships and two sloops of war were sent out, therefore, to the West Indies to cruise for the protection of British trade.

In 1731 an account of the reflecting or Hadley's quadrant appeared in a paper given by a member of the Royal Society. After Dr Hadley's death, however, among his papers a description was found of an instrument not much dissimilar to Hadley's, written by Sir Isaac Newton, who may, therefore, be considered the first inventor of the reflecting quadrant.

In 1732 the king granted a commission to the Lords Commissioners of the Admiralty to erect a corporation to relieve the poor widows of sea-officers. The terms of admission to the institution were that each member, who must be an officer in the navy, was to allow threepence in the pound per annum out of his pay. Soon after the establishment of this fund, Lieutenant George Crow generously resigned his half-pay for the use of this charity, stating that he had a competency to live on. The king gave 10,000 pounds for the support of the charity.

The Sallee rovers still continued very daring and troublesome to our trade, and in 1734 a small squadron was sent out, under Captain James Cornwall in the *Greyhound*, to block up the ports of Morocco, and capture the vessels of the barbarians. Two large corsairs were taken and destroyed, and 140 British subjects released by the Emperor of Morocco, who concluded a treaty with Great Britain.

That year his majesty issued his royal proclamation recalling all British seamen from the service of foreign powers, and offering a bounty of twenty shillings to every able-bodied seaman, and fifteen shillings to every able-bodied landsman who should enter the navy.

In the following year 30,000 men were voted for the sea-service.

An Act of Parliament was passed this year appropriating the rents of the estates of the Earl of Derwentwater and Charles Ratcliff to the completion of the royal hospital at Greenwich. By this Act all seamen in the merchant-service who may happen to be maimed, not only in fighting against pirates, but also in fighting against any enemy whatever, should be admitted into, and provided for, in that hospital.

In 1739, Spain still obstinately refusing to make any compensation for the injuries inflicted on English merchant-vessels by guarda costas, Great Britain prepared for war. Numerous ships were put in commission, and letters of marque and reprisal were issued by the Admiralty against Spain. For some time previously the opponents of the English ministry were continually taunting them with their want of courage. Among others, Admiral Vernon, who was then in Parliament, boasted that with six ships he would undertake to capture the Spanish settlement of Porto Bello. The whole nation fully believing him, a squadron was at once placed under his command, when, after remaining for a few days at Port Royal, Jamaica, he sailed on the 5th of November, with six ships of war. Light winds prevented him reaching Porto Bello till the 20th, when, on the following day, Commodore Brown, who led in the *Hampton Court*, got close to the *Iron Castle*, where, being becalmed by the high land to windward, she was exposed for some time to a smart fire from the enemy, without being able to return it. As soon, however, as she could do so, she began firing her broadside with such rapidity that she is said, in twenty-five minutes, to have expended four hundred shot. She was soon supported by the *Burford*, *Norwich*, and *Warwick*; these ships opened a tremendous fire, and did great execution, the small-arms from their tops compelling the Spaniards to desert their guns. As the boats with seamen and marines passed the admiral, he ordered them to land immediately under the walls, though there was no breach made, nor had the scaling-ladders arrived. As a substitute for them, however, one man placed himself close to the wall under an embrasure, while another climbed upon his shoulders. Thus the sailors became masters of the fort, and drew up the soldiers. The Spaniards, panic-stricken, tied, and the seamen, no longer obedient to the commands of their officers, plundered the town, and committed great outrages on the inhabitants. The governor soon after this hoisted the white flag and surrendered at discretion. Two ships of 20 guns each and other vessels were taken in the harbour, as also ten thousand dollars intended for the payment of the

178

garrison, which the admiral ordered to be distributed among the British forces for their encouragement.

The squadron's loss amounted to scarcely twenty men, while a large number of great guns, powder, and shot were captured. To prevent the place from being longer an asylum for the enemy's guarda costas, Admiral Vernon directed the whole of the fortifications to be dismantled and blown up. The news of this success caused unbounded satisfaction at home.

In 1740 two Acts were passed, one for the better supply of seamen to serve in the Royal Navy, one allowing English merchant-vessels to be navigated by foreign sailors, not exceeding three-fourths of the crew, such foreign seamen serving for two years to be considered natural-born subjects. Another was to prevent impressment of seamen of the age of fifty or upwards, and all such as have not attained the full age of eighteen; also all foreigners serving in merchant-vessels, sea-apprentices for the first three years, and persons of any age for the first two years of their being at sea. A new board was also appointed to superintend the business of the Sick and Hurt Office. The charge of the prisoners of war was also intrusted to this board.

Anson, one of the most celebrated of British admirals, entered the navy in 1712, as a volunteer on board the *Ruby*, Captain Chamberlain, with whom he continued for several years, till, in 1718, he was appointed second lieutenant of the *Montague*. After commanding the *Weasel* sloop, he was promoted to the rank of post-captain in 1724. After commanding numerous ships, and conducting himself with much ability and discretion, he was selected to command that expedition to the South Seas which made his name famous. In 1740 he sailed from Spithead on the 18th of September, with a squadron of five ships, the *Centurion*, of 60 guns; the *Gloucester*, of 50, Captain Norris; the *Sovereign*, of 50, Captain Legge; the *Pearl*, of 40 guns, Captain Mitchell; the *Wager*, 28, Captain Kidd; the *Tryal*, 8 guns, Captain Murray; and two victuallers, the *Anna* and *Industry* pinks. On board the *Wager* sailed the Honourable John Byron, then a midshipman. The *Wager* must serve as an example for the rest of the ships. She was an old Indiaman, bought into the service, and now fitted out as a man-of-war, but also deeply laden with stores and merchandise of all sorts. Her crew consisted of men pressed from long voyages, while her land forces were a wretched detachment of infirm and decrepit invalids from Chelsea Hospital, desponding under the prospect of a long voyage. Her commander, Captain Kidd, before his death, predicted that misfortunes would overtake her. The *Centurion*, however, under the judicious management of Commodore Anson, performed a successful voyage, and had the good fortune to capture a rich Spanish galleon.

In consequence of the way ships had suffered from the attacks of worms on former occasions, those now destined for the West Indies were sheathed by a new process.

On the 25th of February Admiral Vernon again sailed on an expedition against Carthagena, but finding his force inadequate to reduce it, after refitting at Porto Bello, he proceeded to the river Chagres, an accurate chart of which he had obtained from the pirate Lowther, who, by doing this piece of service, had his majesty's pardon granted him. The castle of San Lorenzo was quickly captured, and a large amount of merchandise and plate found in the place. After blowing up the fortifications, and destroying two guarda costas, he returned to Jamaica. He next, being joined by Sir Challoner Ogle with a large body of troops, attacked Carthagena; forcing a beam which had been laid across the harbour, the fleet entered and blew up a considerable number of forts, great gallantry being shown by the commanders of the ships of war and their crews. The British troops, however, were repulsed with great slaughter in their attempts to storm Fort Saint Lazare. In consequence of sickness, it became at length necessary to raise the siege, and the admiral returned to Jamaica. The establishment of a settlement on the island of Rattan and an attack on Cuba were designed by Admiral Vernon, but this and other plans were thwarted by the commander of the land forces, General Wentworth — showing the inconvenience which, in nearly all instances, arises from a division of command. Probably, had the whole power been vested with Admiral Vernon, his plans would have succeeded. Soon after his arrival in England, in consequence of a disagreement with the Admiralty, he was deprived of his command in 1746, after which he did not again go to sea. Probably in consequence of observing the ill effects of undiluted spirits among his crews in the West Indies, he was the first to order a sailor's allowance of rum to be mixed with water, to which the name of grog has since been given.

During this war the English merchants lost a number of their vessels in the British Channel and the German Ocean, the prizes being carried into Vigo, Bilboa, and San Sebastian, where the poor sailors suffered inexpressible hardships, being driven barefooted a hundred or two hundred miles up the country, lodged in damp dungeons, and fed only on bread and water. On hearing of this treatment, the British Government allowed to every prisoner sixpence a-day, which was regularly paid to them. On the other hand, the English ships of war and privateers took several valuable prizes from the Spaniards, and destroyed many of their privateers; while the masters of the merchant-ships bravely defended themselves, and were never taken but by a superior force. One of these actions is worthy of being recorded. On the 27th of December, the *Pulteney* privateer, a large brigantine, mounting 16 carriage-guns and 26 swivels, with 42 men, commanded by Captain James Purcell, was standing into the Bay of Gibraltar after a cruise, when she was seen from Old Gibraltar, from whence 2 large Spanish xebeques, each carrying 120 men, 12 carriage-guns, and a great number of patereroes and musquetoons, were sent out to take her. They soon came up with her, a little to the eastward of Europa Point, and almost within reach of the guns of Gibraltar. In the bay lay an 80-gun ship, but without her topmasts, so that the only way of assisting the privateer was to send a reinforcement of men, which might easily have reached her before the xebeques, but the commander of the ship of war, alleging that so small a vessel could not escape, declined to do so. The gallant Captain Purcell, however, was of a different opinion, and resolved to defend his vessel to the last, being supported by his officers and men. After the Spaniards had fired a few single guns, they came near and hailed the vessel by her name, the captain entreating the English to strike and preserve their lives. These threats were returned by the *Pulteney's* guns. The Spaniards then attempted to board, but were resolutely beaten off. They twice more renewed the attempt; Captain Purcell having prudently reserved half his broadside, they had not the courage to board him. For an hour and three-quarters the engagement continued, till the Spaniards, unable to stand the pounding they were receiving, made off with their oars towards Malaga, having lost above a hundred of their men — the *Pulteney* having had but one man killed and five more badly wounded, though it is remarkable that every man on board was shot through the clothes, the sails and rigging were cut to pieces, and some 9-pounders went through the hull and masts of the privateer. The governor, officers, and principal inhabitants of Gibraltar, who were witnesses of the action, to show Captain Purcell the high estimation in which they held his character, presented him with a piece of plate with a suitable inscription, and gave a handsome reward to the sailors for their bravery.

In 1742 the *Tiger*, of 50 guns, Captain Herbert, was lost on a cayo near the island of Tortuga, when the crew got on shore and saved most of their stores. They then mounted twenty of the ship's guns for their protection, thus saving themselves from being made prisoners by the Spaniards, who had sent a ship, *El Fuerte*, of 60 guns, for that purpose. In the attempt, however, she also got on shore and was lost. On this cayo Captain Herbert remained nearly two months. At length, a sloop and schooner appeared off the spot; Captain Herbert, pulling off in his boats, boarded and took them, and returned in them with his ship's company safe to Jamaica.

In 1744, the French fleet having united with that of Spain, war was declared against France. Admiral Matthews was at this time commander-in-chief in the Mediterranean. In an action which ensued soon afterwards, Admiral Matthews accused his second in command, Admiral Lestock, of not doing his duty, and sent him to England, but was himself recalled to undergo a court-martial, the issue of which was that he was dismissed and rendered for ever incapable of serving his majesty. Several other officers were also tried on various charges, some of whom were cashiered. The sentence of several of them was considered extremely hard, and many circumstances appearing in their favour, his majesty was pleased to restore them to their former rank. Courts-martial, indeed, appear to have taken place very frequently. Discipline was often lax, and that high tone which afterwards prevailed in the navy was apparently greatly wanting.

An action, which, had the English been successful, would have saved the lives and fortunes of many of the leading Jacobites, took place in 1745. On the 9th July of that year the *Lion*, a 60-gun ship of 400 men, commanded by Captain Piercy Brett, being on a cruise, fell in with the *Elizabeth*, a French ship of war, of 64 guns and 600 men, and a small frigate, the latter having on board Prince Charles, son of the old Pretender, and several officers of distinction who were accompanying him in order to support his cause in Scotland. At five o'clock in the evening the *Lion* got within pistol-shot of the *Elizabeth*, when a most obstinate battle began, and continued with great fury till ten, at which time the *Lion* had lost her mizen-mast, all her other masts and yards being so much wounded, and rigging and sails cut to pieces, that she became unmanageable. The *Elizabeth* not being so much crippled in her rigging, her commander availed himself of the opportunity, to set what sail he could, and got off. The *Lion* had 45 men killed and 107 wounded. Among the latter were Captain Brett, with all his lieutenants and the master. The *Elizabeth* had her captain and 64 men killed, and 144 wounded. She was so much damaged that it was with difficulty she reached Brest. The frigate pursuing her course landed Prince Charles at Lochaber on the 27th day of July.

In order to prevent succours being sent to the rebels from France, Admiral Vernon proceeded with a strong squadron to the Downs, and Rear-Admiral Byng was sent with some ships to the coast of Scotland.

English ship-owners and merchants had sent many large privateers of considerable force to sea, and they were especially fortunate this year. The *Prince Frederick*, of 28 guns and 250 men, commanded by Captain James Talbot, fell in off the western islands with two large French ships with valuable cargoes, which had just returned from the South Seas. After an obstinate engagement they captured the *Marquis D'Autin*, of 400 tons, 24 guns, and 68 men; and the *Lewis Erasmus*, of 500 tons, 28 guns, and 66 men. The privateers and their prizes having been convoyed to Bristol by three men-of-war, the treasure and plate taken out of them were put into forty-five waggons and carried to London, when, upon a division of the prize-money, each sailor's share amounted to 850 pounds. The captains and crews of the privateers behaved with great generosity to their prisoners, allowing them to keep their valuable effects, and when the common men were landed, they distributed to each twenty guineas. The proprietors, whose share amounted to 700,000 pounds, made a voluntary tender of it to the Government to assist in putting down the Jacobite rebellion.

Another privateer took a Spanish ship worth 400,000 pounds; and another, one of 50,000 pounds; but a fourth, the *Surprise*, commanded by Captain Redmond, was less fortunate, for having taken a French East India ship, after an action of six hours, with a cargo valued at 150,000 pounds, the prize, from the number of shot in her hull, sank the next day with all her wealth on board.

There are many instances of captains of privateers being at once given commands in the Royal Navy. Captain Rous in the *Shirley* galley, and ten more stout privateers, having escorted a body of troops from Boston to assist in the reduction of Louisbourg, as a reward, his majesty directed that the privateer, which carried 24 guns, should be purchased into the navy as a post-ship, and Captain Rous appointed to command her.

Fortunes were very frequently rapidly made, not only by commanders of privateers, but by captains of men-of-war. Among these fortunate men was Captain Frankland, afterwards Admiral Thomas Frankland. When in command of the *Rose*, of 20 guns and 125 men, being on a cruise off the coast of South Carolina, he fell in with *La Concepcion*, of 20 guns and 326 men, from Carthagena bound to Havannah; and after a severe and obstinate battle captured her, she having 116 killed and 40 wounded, while he had only 5 men killed and 13 wounded. Her cargo consisted of 800 serons of cocoa, 68 chests of silver, gold and silver coin to a large amount, plate, a curious two-wheeled chase, the wheels, axles, etcetera, all of silver, diamonds, pearls, precious stones, and gold. So great was the quantity of money that the shares were delivered by weight, to save the trouble of counting it; and when the cargo was taken out of the ship, and she was put up for sale, the French captain, upon the promise of reward from Captain Frankland, discovered to him 30,000 pistoles which were concealed in a place that no one would ever have thought of looking for them. Captain Frankland presented the French captain with a thousand pistoles, with which he was far from contented.

The captain also made another fortunate discovery by means of a young French boy whom he had taken into his service. The boy complained to him that one of the sailors had taken from him a stick which was in appearance of no value. Captain Frankland recovered it for the boy, and on returning it gave him a tap on the shoulder, when, hearing something rattle, he took off the head, and found jewels (according to the Frenchman's account) worth 20,000 pistoles. When the captain surrendered, he had given this stick to the boy in the hopes of saving it, not imagining such a trifle would be ever noticed.

That year 531 prizes were taken from the Spaniards and French, but the English lost very nearly as many, though their vessels were smaller and of much less value.

Mr William Brown, master of the *Shoreham*, having been placed by Captain Osborne in command of a small privateer of 2 guns and 12 swivels, captured a Spanish privateer of 10 guns and 18 swivels; and shortly afterwards another of 5 guns and 32 men; and was for his gallantry promoted by the Lords of the Admiralty to the command of a sloop of war.

Among the gallant deeds performed at this time, an action fought by the *Fame*, a privateer belonging to Liverpool, and commanded by

Captain Fortunatus Wright, deserves to be recorded. While on a cruise in the Levant, she encountered sixteen French ships, one of them mounting 20 guns, with 150 men, fitted out expressly for the purpose of taking her. They engaged her furiously for three hours off the island of Cyprus, when the large ship was run ashore and her crew fled up the country. The *Fame's* crew then boarded and brought her off.

By an Act of Parliament passed this year, every ship in Great Britain or his majesty's plantations in North America was compelled on first going to sea to be furnished with a complete suit of sails, made of sailcloth manufactured in Great Britain, under a penalty of fifty pounds. It was also enacted that every sail-maker in Britain or the plantations shall on every new sail affix in letters and words at length his name and place of abode, under a penalty of ten pounds.

By an order in council dated the 10th of February, 1747, established rank was first given to the officers in the Royal Navy, and a uniform clothing appointed to be worn by admirals, captains, lieutenants, and midshipmen. Hitherto they had dressed much as suited their fancy. The crew of a man-of-war must have looked more like a band of pirates than a well-ordered ship's company of the present day. Even in later days midshipmen sometimes appeared on the deck of a man-of-war in rather extraordinary costume, as the following account, taken from the journal of an old admiral, will show.

"As we midshipmen met on board the cutter which was to carry us to Plymouth, we were not, I will allow, altogether satisfied with our personal appearance, and still less so when we stepped on the quarter-deck of the seventy-four, commanded by one of the proudest and most punctilious men in the service, surrounded by a body of well-dressed, dashing-looking officers. Tom Peard first advanced as chief and oldest of our gang, with a bob-wig on his head, surmounted by a high hat bound by narrow gold lace, white lapels to his coat, a white waistcoat, and light blue inexpressibles with midshipman's buttons. By his side hung a large brass-mounted hanger, while his legs were encased in a huge pair of waterproof boots. I followed next, habited in a coat 'all sides radius,' as old Allen, my schoolmaster, would have said, the skirt actually sweeping the deck, and so wide that it would button down to the very bottom — my white cuffs reaching half-way up the arm to the elbow. My waistcoat, which was of the same snowy hue, reached to my knees, but was fortunately concealed from sight by the ample folds of my coat, as were also my small clothes. I had on white-thread stockings, high shoes and buckles, and a plain cocked hat, a prodigiously long silver-handled sword completing my costume. Dick Martingall's and Tom Painter's dresses were not much less out of order, giving them more the appearance of gentlemen of the highway than of naval officers of respectability. One had a large brass sword, once belonging to his great-grandfather, a trooper in the army of the Prince of Orange, the other a green-handled hanger, which had done service with Sir Cloudsley Shovel." The writer and his friends had to beat a precipitate retreat from the *Torbay*, as, with a stamp of his foot, their future captain ordered them to begone, and instantly get cut-down and reduced into ordinary proportions by the Plymouth tailors. This description refers to some thirty years later than the time we are speaking of. The tailor had taken his models, the writer observes, from the days of Benbow; or rather, perhaps, from the costumes of those groups who go about at Christmas time enacting plays in the halls of the gentry and nobility, and are called by the west-country folks "geese-dancers."

Vice-Admiral Anson, who had returned from his voyage to the Pacific, was now placed in command of a powerful fleet, and sent to cruise on the coast of France. He and Rear-Admiral Warren sailed from Plymouth on the 9th of April to intercept the French fleet, with which it fell in on the 3rd of May off Cape Finisterre, convoying a large number of merchantmen. Admiral Anson had made the signal to form line of battle, when Rear-Admiral Warren, suspecting the enemy to be merely manoeuvring to favour the escape of the convoy, bore down and communicated his opinion to the admiral, who thereon threw out a signal for a general chase. The *Centurion*, under a press of sail, was the first to come up with the rearmost French ship, which she attacked in so gallant a manner that two others dropped astern to her support. Three more English ships coming up, the action became general. The French, though much inferior in numbers, fought with great spirit till seven in the evening, when all their ships were taken, as well as nine sail of East India ships. The enemy lost 700 men, killed and wounded, and the British 250. Among the latter was Captain Grenville of the *Defiance*, to whom a monument was erected by his uncle, Lord Cobham, in his gardens at Stowe. Upwards of 300,000 pounds were found on board the ships of war, which were conveyed in twenty waggons by a military escort to London.

So pleased was the king with this action that, after complimenting Admiral Anson, he was created a peer of Great Britain, and Rear-Admiral Warren was honoured with the order of the Bath.

A sad accident occurred shortly afterwards in an action off the Azores, when the *Dartmouth*, Captain Hamilton, of 50 guns, while engaging for some hours the *Glorioso*, a Spanish ship of 74 guns and 750 men, caught fire and blew up, every soul with her brave commander perishing, except Lieutenant O'Bryan and eleven seamen, who were saved by the boats of a privateer in company. The *Dartmouth's* consort, the *Russell*, pursuing the Spaniard, captured her after a warm engagement.

As an encouragement and relief to disabled and wounded seamen in the merchant-service, an Act of Parliament was passed in this year authorising the masters of merchant-vessels to detain sixpence per month from the wages of seamen. It was extended also to the widows and children of such seamen as should be killed or drowned. A corporation was established for the management of this fund.

Admiral Hawke in command of another squadron, was equally successful, having captured in one action no less than six large French ships.

The war terminated at the peace of Aix-la-Chapelle in 1748. The total number of ships taken from the French and Spaniards amounted in all to 3434, while the entire loss of English merchant-vessels amounted to 3238.

In 1744 Admiral Sir John Balchen, whose flag was flying on board the *Victory*, was returning from Gibraltar, when, having reached the channel on the 3rd of October, the fleet was overtaken by a violent storm. The *Exeter*, one of the squadron, lost her main and mizen-mast, and it became necessary to throw twelve of her guns overboard to prevent her from sinking, while other ships suffered much. On the 4th the *Victory* separated from the fleet, and was never more heard of. She had on board nearly a thousand men, besides fifty volunteers, sons of the first nobility and gentry in the kingdom. It is supposed that she struck upon a ridge of rocks off the Caskets, as from the testimony of the men who attended the light, and the inhabitants of the island of Alderney, minute-guns were heard on the nights of the 4th and 5th, but the weather was too tempestuous to allow boats to go out to her assistance. The king settled a pension of 500 pounds per annum on Sir John Balchen's widow.

As an example of the danger those on board fire-ships ran, a fearful accident which happened to one of them must be mentioned. While the fleet of Admiral Matthews was engaged with the Spaniards in the Mediterranean, he ordered the *Anne* galley fire-ship, commanded by Captain Mackay, to go down and burn the *Real*. In obedience to his orders, that brave officer approached the Spanish admiral. Notwithstanding the heavy fire opened on his vessel, he ordered all his people off the deck, and boldly steered the fire-ship, with a match in his hand. As he approached, he found that the enemy's shot had such an effect that his ship was fast sinking; at the same time, observing a large Spanish launch rowing towards him, he opened fire on her with his guns, when, on a sudden, the fire-ship appeared in a blaze, and almost immediately blew up, but at a distance too great either to grapple or damage the *Real*. The gallant commander, with his lieutenant, gunner, mate, and two quartermasters, perished.

The Admiralty at this time appear to have considered that the best way of inducing naval officers to perform their duty was to shoot or otherwise severely punish them if they did not. On the 22nd of April, 1745, the *Anglesea*, of 40 guns and 250 men, commanded by Captain Jacob Elton, fell in with a French privateer of 50 guns and 500 men. After a severe action, in which the commander and his first lieutenant were killed, the ship being much disabled, and above sixty of her crew killed or wounded, Mr Barker Phillips, her second lieutenant, who succeeded to the command, surrendered her to the enemy. On his return to England, he was tried by a court-martial, and sentenced to be shot, which sentence was carried into execution on board the *Princess Royal* at Spithead.

The war again broke out in 1755, when information being received that the French were preparing a fleet of men-of-war to sail from different ports, the ministry immediately equipped a squadron, the command of which was given to Admiral Boscawen, who was ordered to proceed to North America. The first ships taken during the war were by the *Dunkirk*, Captain Howe, who after an engagement of five hours captured the *Alcide* and *Lys*, part of the squadron of M. de la Motte.

A fleet of ten ships, under the command of Admiral Byng, was sent out to the Mediterranean. With his squadron but imperfectly manned, he sailed from Spithead on the 7th of April. When off Minorca, then held by the English, and besieged by the Spaniards, a French fleet appeared in sight. The next day, the weather being hazy, the French fleet was not seen till noon, when Admiral Byng threw out an order to Rear-Admiral West to engage them, but he being at a distance did not understand these orders. He, however, with his whole division bearing away seven points, came up with the enemy, and attacked them with such impetuosity that several of their ships were soon obliged to quit the line. Byng's division not advancing, Admiral West was prevented from pursuing his advantage for fear of being separated from the rest of the fleet, which, from unskilful manoeuvring, gave the enemy time to escape. On his arrival at Gibraltar the unfortunate Admiral Byng found that commissioners had arrived to arrest him and Admiral West, who were accordingly sent prisoners to England. Sir Edward Hawke, who had brought out reinforcements, immediately sailed up the Mediterranean, but on arriving off Minorca, to his mortification, saw the French flag flying from the Castle of San Felipe. The French fleet took shelter in Toulon, while Sir Edward Hawke had the command of the Mediterranean. The fall of Minorca caused the greatest dissatisfaction in England, and though undoubtedly the ministry were to blame for not having sent more troops to Minorca, and given Byng a larger fleet, he committed an error in not taking greater pains to engage the French fleet. A court-martial pronounced him guilty of a breach of the twelfth article of war, and condemned him to death. He was accordingly, on the 14th of March, shot on board the *Monarch*, in Portsmouth harbour — a sacrifice to popular clamour. The court which condemned him, however, declared that his misconduct did not proceed from want of courage or disaffection, and added to their report of their proceedings a petition to the Lords of the Admiralty requesting their lordships most earnestly to recommend him to his majesty's clemency. The Government, however, having resolved on his death, allowed the law to take its course. The president of the court-martial was Vice-Admiral Thomas Smith, generally known in the service by the name of Tom of Ten Thousand. When he was lieutenant on board the *Gosport* in Plymouth Sound, and her captain on shore, Mr Smith directed a shot to be fired at a French frigate which, on passing, had neglected to pay the usual compliment to the flag. The Frenchman considering this as an insult offered to his flag, lodged a complaint against Mr Smith, who was tried by a court-martial and dismissed the service. His spirited conduct was, however, so much approved of by the nation, that he was promoted at once to the rank of post-captain.

In 1749 an Act of Parliament was passed authorising the Admiralty to grant commissions to flag-officers or any other officer commanding his majesty's fleet or squadron of ships of war, to call and assemble courts-martial in foreign parts.

The sudden possession of wealth by the capture of prizes had undoubtedly a deteriorating effect on the minds of many officers of the navy. We may understand the disappointment which was felt by those serving under Admiral Knowles, who was cruising off the Havannah to intercept the expected Plate fleet, when a Spanish advice-boat brought into the squadron informed the admiral that the preliminary articles for a general peace were signed. The unpleasant news caused a general dejection throughout the whole squadron. Dissensions among the officers had for some time before prevailed, and these at length terminated in various courts-martial. It was probably this lust of wealth which induced the officers of the *Chesterfield*, of 40 guns, commanded by Captain O'Brien Dudley, when off Cape Coast Castle, to mutiny. Samuel Couchman, the first lieutenant, John Morgan, the lieutenant of marines, Thomas Knight, the carpenter, were the ringleaders. They managed to seize the ship and carry her to sea while the captain and some others were on shore. By the spirited conduct of Mr Gastrien, the boatswain, and Messrs Gillan and Fraser, she was retaken from the mutineers thirty hours afterwards, and ultimately brought safe to Portsmouth, where the mutineers being tried, two of the principal officers were shot on board their ship. The four others and one seaman were hanged.

The animosity which had existed among the captains of the West India squadron was carried to serious lengths, and resulted in several duels, one of which was fought between Captains Clarke and Innes, in Hyde Park, when the latter was killed. Captain Clarke was tried, and received sentence of death, but his majesty granted him a free pardon. Another duel was fought between Admiral Knowles and Captain Holmes. After they had discharged two or three shots at each other, the seconds interfered, and they were reconciled. The king being informed that four more challenges had been sent to the admiral, ordered three of the officers to be taken into custody, which put an end to all further dissensions.

In 1753 an Act was passed to render more effectual the Act of the 12th of Queen Anne, for providing a public reward for such person or persons as should discover the longitude at sea.

In 1756 the Marine Society was instituted, owing to the patriotic zeal of the merchants of London, who entered into a liberal subscription to clothe and educate orphans or deserted and friendless boys to serve in the Royal Navy. It has proved of great advantage to the navy. In June, 1772, it was incorporated, and is governed by a president and six vice-presidents.

Among the most desperate engagements fought at this period the exploit of the *Terrible* privateer, commanded by Captain Death, deserves to be recorded. She carried 26 guns and 200 men. When on a cruise, she fell in with the *Grand Alexander*, from Saint Domingo, of 22 guns and 100 men, when, after an action of two hours, she captured her. Both vessels were considerably damaged; the *Terrible* had a lieutenant and sixteen men killed. While conducting her prize to England, and ill-prepared for a second engagement, she fell in with the *Vengeance* privateer, belonging to Saint Malo, of 36 guns and 360 men. The enemy having retaken the prize, manned her, and together bore down on the *Terrible*. Captain Death defended his ship with the greatest bravery against so unequal a force, but at length, he and half his crew being killed and most of the survivors badly wounded, the masts being shot away, she was compelled to strike. The enemy's ship was also a complete wreck; her first and second captains were killed, with two-thirds of her crew. The merchants of London, as a testimony of their high sense of the gallant behaviour of Captain Death and his brave crew, opened a subscription at Lloyd's coffee-house for the benefit of his widow; for the widows of the brave fellows who lost their lives with him, and for that part of the crew who survived the engagement.

Captain Fortunatus Wright, who had before been so successful in the Mediterranean, was now in command of the *Saint George* privateer cruising in the same sea. He had first a desperate battle with a French privateer twice his size, which he beat off, and then proceeded to Leghorn, where he was thrown into prison by the Austrian government. Admiral Hawke, on hearing of it, sent two ships to demand his immediate release. This request was complied with. Shortly afterwards the *Saint George* was overtaken by a furious storm, in which she foundered, her brave commander and crew perishing.

At this time, while Lord Clive was, by a series of victories, laying the foundation of the British Empire in the east, Admiral Watson commanded in the Indian seas. To assist the army the squadron entered the Hooghly, when a body of seamen was landed to attack the fort of Boujee. By a singular event it was carried without bloodshed. A seaman by the name of Strachan, belonging to the *Kent*, having drunk too much grog, strayed under the walls of the fort in the dead of night, and observing a breach, entered at it, giving loud huzzas. This alarmed some more of his comrades, who had also strayed the same way. They instantly mounted the breach, and drove the Indian garrison from the works. By this time the whole camp and squadron were alarmed, and the troops, flying to the fort, entered and gained possession of it without the loss of a man. After everything was quiet, Admiral Watson sent for Strachan to admonish him for his temerity, and addressing him, observed, "Strachan, what is this you have been doing?" The untutored hero, after having made his bow, scratching his head with one hand and twirling his hat with the other, replied, "Why, to be sure, sir, it was I who took the fort, but I hope there was no harm in it." The admiral then pointed out to him the dreadful consequences that might have resulted from so rash an act, and insinuated as he left the cabin that he should be punished. Strachan, highly disappointed at this rebuke from the admiral when he thought himself entitled to applause, muttered as he was leaving the cabin, "If I'm flogged for this here action, I'll never take another fort as long as I live."

A gallant action fought in the West Indies, in the year 1757, is worthy of note. Admiral Cotes, commander-in-chief on the station, despatched Captain Arthur Forrest, of the 60-gun ship *Augusta*, with the *Edinburgh*, Captain Langdon, of 60 guns, and the *Dreadnought*, Captain Maurice Suckling, of 60 guns, to cruise off Cape François, where the French were assembling a fleet of merchant-vessels for Europe. The French squadron consisted of two seventy-fours, one sixty-four, one fifty, one forty-four, and two of thirty-two guns. On the 21st of October, early in the morning, the *Dreadnought* made the signal for the enemy. On this, Captain Forrest summoned his captains, and on their arrival on the *Augusta's* quarter-deck, he observed, "Well, gentlemen, you see they are come out to engage us." On this, Captain Suckling replied, "I think it would be a pity to disappoint them." Captain Langdon being of the same opinion, the signal was thrown out to make all sail to close the enemy. So admirably were the three ships manoeuvred, and so well were their guns fought, that one of the enemy's ships was dismasted and the whole fleet much disabled, with the loss of nearly 600 men killed and wounded, when they made sail to leeward. The British ships were so much cut up in their sails and rigging that it was impossible to follow. The *Dreadnought* had lost 9 killed, 20 dangerously and 10 slightly wounded, while every yard and mast was greatly injured. Shortly afterwards, Captain Forrest captured a French convoy consisting of 9 ships, carrying 112 guns and 415 men.

Among the many dashing officers of those days was Captain Gilchrist. When in command of the *Southampton*, of 32 guns and 220 men, he was on his way from Portsmouth to Plymouth, with money to pay the dockyard artificers. Being attacked at eleven at night, off Saint Alban's Head, by five French privateers, two of them of equal force, he compelled them, after an action of two hours, to sheer off; his vessel being a perfect wreck, with several shot between wind and water, and ten men killed, and fourteen mortally wounded. The following September, when looking into Brest, a French ship came out, for which he waited. He reserved his fire till he got within twenty yards of her, when a most furious engagement began; the ships falling on board of each other. The enemy made an attempt to board the *Southampton*, but being vigorously repulsed, in a quarter of an hour after struck, and proved to be the *Emeraude*, a French frigate of 28 guns and 245 men, 60 of whom were either killed or wounded. The action was fought at such close quarters that the men used their handspikes, and two of the officers were killed by a discharge from Captain Gilchrist's own blunderbuss. The *Southampton* had her second lieutenant and 19 men killed, and every officer except the captain, and 28 wounded. While conducting her prize into port, the *Southampton* captured an 18-gun privateer belonging to Dunkirk.

Among the worst ships in the service at that time were the two-deck 40 and 50 gun ships, for when any heavy sea was running, they were unable to open their lower-deck ports, and were thus of even less force than vessels carrying only 20 guns. Numerous instances of this occurred, and among others the *Antelope*, of 50 guns, Captain Thomas Saumarez, fell in with a French privateer of 22 guns. The *Antelope* being unable at the time to open her lower-deck ports in consequence of the heavy sea, it took her two hours to capture the privateer, which even then would probably have got off, had not her mizen-mast been shot away.

An action, celebrated in naval song, was that between the *Monmouth*, of 64 guns, commanded by Captain Gardiner, and the *Foudroyant*, of 84 guns. Captain Gardiner had been flag-captain to Admiral Byng in the action off Minorca, in which the *Foudroyant* bore the French admiral's flag, and he had declared that if he should ever fall in with the *Foudroyant* he would attack her at all hazards, though he should perish in the encounter. In company with the *Monmouth* were the *Swiftsure*, 74, and the *Hampton Court*, 64; but the *Monmouth* soon ran her consorts out of sight, and at 8 p.m., getting up with the chase, commenced the action. Among the first wounded was the captain, but it being in the arm, he refused to go below. He soon knocked away some of the *Foudroyant's* spars, and then carried his ship close under her starboard-quarter, where for four hours the *Monmouth* maintained the unequal contest. At 9 p.m. the gallant Gardiner was mortally wounded in the forehead by a musket-ball, when Lieutenant Robert Carket took command. Shortly afterwards the *Monmouth's* mizzen-mast was shot away, on which the French crew cheered; but the *Foudroyant's* mizen-mast sharing the same fate, the British seamen returned the compliment, and in a little time down came the French ship's main-mast. Still, she continued working her guns till some time after the arrival of the *Swiftsure*, when she surrendered. Her captain presented his sword to Lieutenant Carket, thus acknowledging that he was captured by the *Monmouth*. To understand the disparity between the two ships, their comparative broadside weight of metal should be known. That of the *Monmouth* was 540 pounds, that of the *Foudroyant* was 1136 pounds. The *Foudroyant*, which was taken into the service, was looked upon for many years as the finest ship in the British Navy. She exceeded by twelve feet in length the *Chester* British first-rate, and measured 1977 tons. All her guns abaft the main-mast were of brass. Lieutenant Carket was deservedly promoted to command her.

We must pass over one of the most memorable events of this reign, the capture of Quebec by General Wolfe, in which Captain Cook, then a master in the navy, first exhibited his talents and courage, and briefly describe an important naval action, that of Sir Edward Hawke in Quiberon Bay. The admiral sailed from Spithead early in June, 1759, with a powerful fleet to cruise off Brest and in soundings. Hence he despatched three small squadrons to scour the enemy's coast. In November a heavy gale compelled Sir Edward Hawke to take shelter in Torbay. During his absence M. de Conflans got safe into Brest with his squadron from the West Indies. Believing that the coast was clear, he again put to sea on the 14th of November, and on the same day the British fleet sailed from Torbay. The next day Captain McCleverty, in the *Gibraltar*, joined Sir Edward, with the information that he had seen the French fleet about twenty-four leagues to the north-west of Belleisle, steering to the south-east. Sir Edward immediately shaped a course for Quiberon Bay. A strong wind forced the fleet to leeward; it shifted, however, on the 19th to the westward. The *Maidstone* and *Coventry* frigates were ordered to look out ahead. The French admiral seeing them, sent some of his ships in chase, but soon after perceiving the British fleet, he recalled them, and formed in order of battle. On the approach of the British ships he crowded sail and pushed in for the land, not more than four or five leagues distant, in the hopes of entangling them among the rocks and shoals. In this he was disappointed, as the van ships of the English fleet were close up to his rear at half-past two o'clock, and in a few minutes the engagement became general. The *Formidable*, carrying the flag of the French rear-admiral, was closely engaged by the *Resolution*, and having to sustain the fire of every ship that passed, was obliged to strike, he and 200 of his men being killed. Lord Howe, in the *Magnanime* attacked the *Thésée*, but the *Montague* running foul of the former so much disabled her, that she fell astern. Captain Keppel, in the *Torbay*, then attacked the *Thésée*, when a sudden squall coming on, the lower-deck ports of the latter ship not being closed, she filled and instantly sank. The *Superbe* shared a similar fate alongside of the *Royal George*. Lord Howe having got clear, bore down and attacked the *Hero* so furiously that he soon compelled her to strike. During the night, which proved very boisterous, she drove on shore and was lost. The enemy then endeavoured to make their escape; some succeeded, but several got ashore, as did the *Essex* and *Resolution*, but their crews were saved. The French admiral's ship, the *Soleil Royal*, had in the dark anchored in the midst of the British fleet, on discovering which he cut his cable, when he drove ashore. On the weather moderating the boats of the squadron were sent in to destroy the French ships. The *Soleil Royal* was set on fire by her own crew, and the *Hero* by the British boats. *La Juste*, of 70 guns, was also wrecked, but seven of the French ships, by throwing overboard their guns and stores, escaped into the river Yillaine.

The remnant of this fleet, under M. de Thurot, a celebrated privateer commander, escaped out of Dunkirk for the purpose of making a descent on the northern coast of England or Ireland. After taking shelter during the winter on the coast of Norway, he appeared with three frigates before the town of Carrickfergus, which he attacked and laid under contribution. Having supplied his ships with such necessaries as they were in need of, he re-embarked his men and took his departure. At that time Captain John Elliot, who was lying at Kinsale in the *Aeolus*, with the *Pallas* and *Brilliant* under his command, on hearing that M. de Thurot was on the coast, put to sea, and fortunately came up with him off the Isle of Man. A close action was maintained for an hour and a-half, when the gallant Thurot and a large number of his men being killed, the three frigates struck their colours. His own ship, the *Maréchal Belleisle*, was so shattered that it was with difficulty she could be kept afloat. *La Blonde* and *Terpsichore* were added to the British Navy.

The French at this time built a number of vessels on a new construction, to which they gave the name of prames. They were about a hundred feet long, quite flat-bottomed, and capable of carrying four or five hundred men. They were to be employed in transporting troops over for the invasion of England. Admiral Rodney fell in with and destroyed a number of them off Havre-de-Grâce.

During this year the French took 330 ships from the English, whereas the English took only 110 from the French. In reality, however, the gain was on the side of Great Britain, the French ships captured being chiefly large privateers and rich armed merchantmen, while those England lost were mostly coasters and colliers. The trade of France, also, was almost annihilated, and she in consequence employed the greater part of her seamen in small privateers, which swarmed in the channel, the vessels they captured being of like value.

George the Second had the satisfaction of seeing the arms of England everywhere prospering, when on the 27th of October, 1760, he breathed his last, in the thirty-third year of his reign and the seventy-seventh of his age.

Gallant as were the officers and brave as were the men of the navy, they were generally rough in their manners, and ignorant of all matters not connected with their profession. So they continued for many years, till the naval college was established, and schoolmasters were placed on board ships to afford the midshipmen instruction. It could scarcely have been otherwise, considering the early age at which young gentlemen were sent to sea, when they had had barely time to learn more than reading, writing, and arithmetic, while comparatively few had afterwards time or opportunity to improve themselves. Practices were allowed on board ship which would not have been tolerated in Elizabeth's days.

Chapter Fourteen.

George the Third — from A.D. 1760 to A.D. 1782.

On George the Third coming to the throne in 1760 he found the nation still at war with France.

Among the gallant men actively employed at this time, whose names were long as household words both in the navy and on shore, were Lord Anson, Sir Edward Hawke, Admiral Rodney, Captain Alexander Hood, Commodore Keppell, Captain Faulkner, Captain the Honourable Keith Stuart, Captain Richard Howe, afterwards Earl Howe, Captains Shuldham, Sir Hugh Palliser, the Honourable John Byron, Peter Parker, and Samuel Barrington.

The fleets of England were at this time distributed much, as at the present time, under flag-officers. The Nore, the Channel Fleet, the Mediterranean, Lisbon, North America, Newfoundland, the West Indies, the Leeward Islands, Jamaica, the East Indies, and occasionally on the coast of Africa.

We have numerous proofs that British seamen gained their victories as much by their proficiency in gunnery and their activity as by their strength and courage. Of this there are numberless instances, among others the following. In 1761, on the evening of the 13th of August, the *Bellona*, of 74 guns, and a crew of 550 men, Captain Robert Faulkner, and the *Brilliant*, a 36-gun frigate, Captain James Logie, on their passage from Lisbon to England, being off Vigo, came in sight of three large ships. The strangers were the French 74-gun ship *Courageux*, of 700 men, and the 36-gun frigates *Hermione* and *Malicieuse*. In consequence of seeing the British ships through the magnifying medium of a hazy atmosphere, they concluded that they were both line of battle ships, and dreading the issue of an engagement, took to flight. Captain Faulkner on this, suspecting them to be enemies, immediately made sail in chase, and kept them in sight all night. At daylight the next morning he and his consort were about five miles from the two ships, when the largest, throwing out a signal, took in her studding-sail, wore round, and stood for the *Bellona*. The two frigates at the same time closed, and at six brought the *Brilliant* to action. Captain Logie determined to find so much for them to do that the *Bellona* should have the *Courageux* to herself. So vigorously did he work his guns that the frigates received such injury in their sails and rigging as to be compelled to sheer off to repair damages. As the water was smooth and a light wind only blowing, the contest become one of simple gunnery. At half-past six the *Bellona* was closely engaged with the French 74. In nine minutes both their mizen-masts fell overboard, while the *Bellona's* braces, shrouds, and rigging were much cut up. Captain Faulkner, fearing that the enemy would seize the opportunity to sheer off, gave orders for immediately boarding, but the *Courageux*, falling athwart the bow of his ship, rendered this impracticable. The *Bellona* might now have been seriously raked fore and aft, but Captain Faulkner immediately set all his studding-sails to wear the ship round, when the crew flew to their guns on the side now opposed to the enemy, from which they fired away with so much rapidity for twenty minutes as almost to knock the *Courageux* to pieces, while the two frigates were unable, in consequence of the gallant way in which they were kept at bay by Captain Logie, to render her any assistance. Unable to withstand this unremitting fire, the *Courageux* hauled down her colours, her crew crying for quarter. The two frigates on this bore away and got off. Considerable as was the damage done to the *Bellona* in her rigging, she had suffered very little in the hull, and had lost only 6 killed and 25 wounded; while the *Courageux* had her foremast and bowsprit alone standing, her decks torn up in several places, and large breaches made in her sides; 220 of her men being killed, and half that number wounded, among whom was her captain, Dugué L'Ambert. The *Brilliant* lost her master and 5 men killed and 16 wounded. The *Courageux* had on board 8500 pounds in specie. She was carried by her captor into Lisbon to be refitted, and was added to the British Navy under the same name. Proverbially thoughtless as are British seamen, they have ever shown themselves equally kind and generous to those in distress. On this occasion the French crew being found destitute of means for their support when at Lisbon, a subscription was raised on board the *Bellona* and *Brilliant*, as well as among the merchants on shore, to enable them to return to France.

Still further improvements being made in Mr Harrison's timekeeper for finding the longitude at sea, the *Deptford*, of 50 guns, was sent out with the inventor on board. She made the island of Maderia at the exact time which he pointed out, and from thence proceeded to Jamaica, making that island with equal accuracy. On his return he found that the instrument had lost only 1 minute, 54 and a half seconds.

This year also the experiment for coppering ships' bottoms as a preservation against worms was introduced into the Royal Navy, and tried on the *Alarm* frigate, of 32 guns.

Another act of humanity deserves to be recorded. In November, 1762, Captain Clarke, commanding the *Sheerness*, of 24 guns, being closely pursued by five French ships of war, took refuge in the neutral bay of Villa Franca. One of the enemy's ships, *La Minerva*, continued the pursuit, and by way of bravado running in between the *Sheerness* and the land, attempted to anchor. In doing this she was driven on the rocks, and the sea running high was soon dashed to pieces. On this, although the other four ships were approaching, Captain Clarke, with much humanity, sent in his boats, and saved the greater part of her crew, twenty-five only perishing, although the whole would otherwise have been lost. Struck by this generous act, the French commodore went on board the *Sheerness* to thank Captain Clarke for the relief he had offered his distressed countrymen.

To the credit of the Spaniards, it must be told how they on another occasion exhibited much good-feeling. Two ships, the *Lord Clive* and *Ambuscade*, had been sent out to attack the Spanish settlements on the River Plate in South America. During the action the first blew up; her commander, and the whole crew, excepting seventy-eight, perishing. They, escaping the flames, swam to the shore, when instead of being looked upon as enemies who came to plunder the settlement, the Spaniards treated them with the greatest tenderness, and furnished them with clothes and every necessary refreshment.

On the 6th of June, 1762, Lord Anson died, and was succeeded as First Lord of the Admiralty by the Earl of Halifax.

The king's ships were especially fortunate in their captures this year. In the Mediterranean a rich Spanish ship from Barcelona, with 100,000 dollars on board, was taken; and the *Active* frigate, Captain Sawyer, and the *Favourite* sloop of war, Captain Pownall, while on a cruise off Cadiz, captured the *Hermione*, a large Spanish register ship from Lima. She was the richest prize made during the war, the net proceeds of her cargo amounting to 519,705 pounds, 10 shillings. The admiral received 64,000 pounds; the captain of the *Active*, 65,000 pounds; three commissioned officers of that ship, 13,800 pounds each; eight warrant officers, 4000 pounds each; twenty petty officers, 1800 pounds each; and each seaman and marine, 485 pounds. The officers and crew of the *Favourite* received in the same proportion. On arriving at Portsmouth the treasure was sent up to London in twenty waggons, decorated with the British colours flying over those of Spain, and escorted by a party of seamen. At Hyde Park corner they were joined by a troop of light horse, and proceeded through the city, amidst the acclamations of the people, to the Tower.

The Seven Years' War with France and Spain was now brought to a conclusion, and peace was signed at Fontainebleau on the 3rd of November. England was now possessed of the most powerful fleet in the world, while her resources were comparatively undiminished. By means chiefly of her navy, she had gained the whole of the provinces of Canada, the islands of Saint John and Cape Breton, the navigation of the river Mississippi, and that part of Louisiana which lies on the east of that river, the town of New Orleans excepted, permission to cut logwood and to build houses in the Bay of Honduras, and the province of Florida — though she had to restore the Havannah and its dependencies to Spain, as well as Martinico, Guadaloupe, Marie Galante, and Saint Lucia to France — while she was to retain the Grenadas and Grenadines, with the neutral islands of Dominica, Saint Vincent, and Tobago. In Europe she regained the island of Minorca and gave up that of Belleisle. In Africa she retained Senegal and restored Gorée. In Asia all her conquests made from France were restored, with the restriction that France was not to erect fortifications in the province of Bengal, and the fortifications of Dunkirk were to be demolished.

Popular as had been the war, Parliament had only voted 70,000 men for the navy, though in order that each ship should have had her full complement, fully 85,000 men would have been required. Many ships, indeed, went to sea imperfectly manned; the proper number of the crews being often made up of men sent from the jails, and landsmen carried off by the press-gangs. The ships themselves were also of a very inferior character.

Up to this time all 80-gun ships were three-deckers, but after 1759 no more were built. The building also of 70 and 60 gun ships was discontinued about the same period. The finest ships were those taken from the French and added to the Royal Navy. The first English 80-gun ship on two decks was the *Caesar*, launched in 1793.

The Marine Society at the peace came to the resolution of receiving and making provision for all boys under sixteen years of age who had been, or might be, discharged from his majesty's service, by putting them out apprentices in the merchant-service. 295 boys made application for employment, and were provided for.

A body of sailors presented a petition to the king requesting to have the D's, placed against their names for deserter, taken off. His majesty granted the request to all who had again entered on board a king's ship.

It appears that the whole number of seamen and marines employed during the war amounted to 184,893. Of these, only 1512 had been killed in action or by accident, while 133,700 had either died by sickness or were missing — probably, had deserted. Thus, on the books of the Navy Office but 49,673 remained. Of these, all except 16,000 were paid off at the peace. To pay them, Parliament granted 832,000 pounds; to pay the officers, including those on half-pay, 398,000 pounds.

In 1764 Mr Harrison's chronometer was again tried on board the *Tartar* frigate, commanded by Captain John Lindsay, who reported most favourably on it.

This year the officers of his majesty's navy were directed to act as custom-house officers on the coast of America, as well as in the British Channel, but, from the complaints made, the Admiralty released them from a service which they considered as degrading to their situation.

On the 3rd of July his majesty's ship *Dolphin*, of 20 guns, commanded by the Honourable John Byron, and the *Tamer* sloop of war, 14 guns, Captain Mouat, sailed from Plymouth on a voyage of discovery. On her return in 1766 the *Dolphin* was again despatched, under the command of Captain Samuel Wallis, and the *Swallow* sloop of war, Captain Carteret, was ordered to accompany her till she should have got through the Straits of Magellan.

In 1768 a pump, invented by Mr Coles in 1764, was tried on board the *Seaford* frigate in Portsmouth harbour, and it was found that with four men it pumped out a ton of water in 43 and a half seconds; with two men, in 55 seconds; and when choked with shingle ballast, it was cleared in 4 minutes: while the old pump, with seven men, pumped out one ton of water in 76 seconds.

Early this year the Royal Society presented a memorial to his majesty, expressing a wish that proper vessels might be appointed to sail to the southward to observe the transit of Venus over the disc of the sun.

The Admiralty accordingly, for this service, purchased the *Endeavour* barque, and placed her under the command of Lieutenant James Cook. Mr Charles Green was appointed astronomer, and Mr Banks and Dr Solander embarked on board her.

In the month of June, 1769, a French frigate having anchored in the Downs without paying the usual compliment to the British flag, Captain John Hollwell, the senior officer there, in the *Apollo* frigate, sent on board to demand the customary salute. The French captain refused to comply, upon which Captain Hollwell ordered the *Hawke* sloop of war to fire two shots over her, when the Frenchman thought proper to salute.

In 1771 Admiral Sir Charles Knowles obtained his majesty's permission to enter into the service of the Empress of Russia as admiral of her fleet. Though high payments were promised him, it appears that he was very inadequately rewarded. On his return in 1774, he found some difficulty in being reinstated to his rank as admiral.

A machine, invented by Dr Lynn, for making salt water fresh, was tried on board the *Resolution* at Deptford with great success, in consequence of which the Admiralty directed all ships of war to be fitted with a still and the necessary apparatus.

In 1772 Captain James Cook, who had lately returned, undertook a second voyage of discovery in the Pacific, on board the *Resolution*, accompanied by Captain Furneaux in the *Adventure*.

We now come to the first outbreak of hostilities with the revolted provinces of North America. At Rhode Island, his majesty's schooner *Gaspee*, commanded by Lieutenant Duddingstone, was attacked in the night by 200 armed men in eight boats, who, notwithstanding the defence made by her commander, seized the vessel, when he and several of his people were wounded, and the rebels taking out the crew, set her on fire.

In 1773 Lord Howe presented a petition to the House of Commons in behalf of the captains in the navy, soliciting an increase of half-pay. It was carried by a great majority, and two shillings a-day were added to the half-pay. The pay of surgeons was also increased, as was that of masters.

It was now evident that the ministry expected to be plunged into war. On the 26th of April the guard-ships were ordered to take on board six months' provisions, to complete their complement of men, and to prepare for sea. All the ships of war reported fit for service were got ready to be commissioned, rendezvous were opened for the raising of seamen, and a proclamation issued by his majesty offering bounties of 3 pounds to every able seaman who should enter the navy, 2 pounds to an ordinary seaman, and 1 pound to a landsman. On the 22nd of June his majesty reviewed the fleet at Spithead, consisting of 20 sail of the line, 2 frigates, and a few sloops, when he was saluted by 232 guns. It was the first of many visits. He knighted several officers, others received promotion, and sums were distributed among the dockyard artisans, the crews of his yacht, the poor of Portsea and Gosport, and the prisoners confined for debt in Portsmouth jail.

Another voyage was undertaken to the North Pole in the hopes of discovering a passage to the East Indies. The *Racehorse* and *Carcass* bombs, commanded by the Honourable Captain Phipps — afterwards Lord Mulgrave — and Captain Lutwidge, were equipped for the enterprise, but, unable to penetrate the ice, returned in the same autumn. On board the *Racehorse* sailed, in the capacity of captain's coxswain, one who was ere long to make his name known to fame — Horatio Nelson.

His majesty's ship *Kent*, commanded by Captain Fielding, was nearly destroyed while saluting the admiral as she was sailing out of Plymouth Sound, the wadding from the guns having communicated with some powder in the ammunition-chest on the poop. It blew up all the after-part of the ship, when most of the men on the poop were blown overboard, 50 of whom being killed or dreadfully wounded.

On the 29th of June, 1775, the Hibernian Marine Society in Dublin was instituted for maintaining and educating the children of decayed, reduced, or deceased seamen, and apprenticing them to the sea-service.

The news arrived of a conflict between the revolted provinces and a detachment of the king's troops at Lexington, when the latter were compelled to retire with considerable loss into the town of Boston. This was followed by the attack on Bunker's Hill on the 17th of June, when the British also lost a number of officers and men, and the flame of war now began to blaze over the whole of the continent. The incidents, however, of the American war of independence cannot but be briefly touched on. A fleet under Lord Shuldham and Commodore Sir Peter Parker was sent to blockade the principal naval ports, and both parties fitted out small vessels on Lake Champlain to carry on the contest. The English squadron was under the command of Captain Pringle, who found the Americans drawn up in an advantageous position to defend the passage between the island of Valicour and the main. As the enemy was to windward, he was unable to work up his large vessels, so that his gunboats and a schooner were alone engaged. He, however, succeeded in sinking the largest American schooner and a smaller vessel. At night, he called off the vessels engaged, and anchored his fleet in line, to be ready for an attack the next morning. General Arnold, who commanded the American squadron, finding it inferior, availed himself of the darkness of the night, and withdrew towards Crown Point. Captain Pringle followed him on the 13th, when another action ensued, and continued for two hours, the Americans being dispersed, leaving the *Washington* galley, with General Waterburn on board, in the hands of the British; others were run on shore and burnt by their own crews, the remainder effecting their escape to Ticonderoga.

Letters of marque and reprisal were now granted by the Admiralty against the thirteen revolted provinces. On the 18th of March the French king issued an edict to seize all British ships in the ports of France, and on the 13th of April a squadron of French ships of war under the command of the Comte D'Estaing sailed for North America. It was not, however, till the 5th of June that an English fleet under Admiral Byron was sent out in quest of it. The English fleet was dispersed by a heavy gale, when Admiral Byron alone succeeded in reaching the American coast. He found the French squadron already at anchor in the neighbourhood of New York.

Admiral Keppel was now appointed to the command of the Channel Fleet, and soon afterwards the *Milford* captured the *Licorne*, a French frigate of 32 guns, which, with three others, had been found reconnoitring the fleet. The *Arethusa* and *Alert* cutters pursued the other French vessels, and at night came up with the *Belle Poule*, when the first action of this war ensued, celebrated in song. Captain Marshall informed her commander that his orders were to conduct him to the British admiral, with which the French captain peremptorily refused to comply. Captain Marshall then fired a shot over her, which was instantly returned by a broadside from the *Belle Poule*. A desperate engagement took place, and continued with great obstinacy for two hours, by which time they were close in with the French coast. The *Belle Poule* then stood in to a small bay, from whence a number of boats came out and towed her into a place of safety. The *Arethusa's* main-mast fell over the side, and she was otherwise so disabled that it was with the utmost difficulty she could clear the land. The next morning she was towed back to the fleet by the *Valiant* and *Monarch*.

"The Arethusa."

Come, all you jolly sailors bold,
Whose hearts are cast in honour's mould,
While English glory I unfold,
Huzza to the Arethusa!
She is a frigate, tight and brave,
As ever stemm'd the dashing wave;
Her men are staunch
To their favourite launch;
And when the foe shall meet our fire,
Sooner than strike we'll all expire
On board of the Arethusa.

'Twas with the spring fleet she went out
The English Channel to cruise about,
When four French sail in show so stout
Bore down on the Arethusa.
The famed Belle Poule straight ahead did lie;
The Arethusa seemed to fly —
Not a sheet, or a tack,
Or a brace, did she slack,
Tho' the Frenchmen laugh'd and thought it stuff;
But they knew not the handful of men, how tough
On board of the Arethusa.

On deck five hundred men did dance,
The stoutest they could find in France;
We with two hundred did advance
On board of the Arethusa.
Our captain hailed the Frenchmen, Ho!
The Frenchmen they cried out, Hallo!
"Bear down, d'ye see, To our admiral's lee."
"No, no," says the Frenchman, "that can't be;"
"Then I must lug you along with me,"
Says the saucy Arethusa.

The fight was off the Frenchmen's land,
We forced them back upon their strand,
For we fought till not a stick would stand
Of the gallant Arethusa.
And now we've driven the foe ashore,
Never to fight with Britons more.
Let each fill a glass
To his favourite lass;
A health to our captain and officers true,
And all that belong to the jovial crew
Of the gallant Arethusa.

On the 23rd of June Admiral Keppel's fleet came in sight of that of the French under the command of the Comte D'Orvilliers. After an engagement of some hours, the French fleet took to flight during the night, and escaped into Brest.

It is impossible to relate the numberless gallant actions which from this period took place for many years between the ships of Great Britain and her enemies.

In consequence of charges exhibited by Sir Hugh Palliser against Admiral Keppel for his conduct in the engagement just mentioned, a court-martial was held at the governor's house at Portsmouth to try him, when the following sentence was pronounced: — "That in their opinion the charge against Admiral Keppel is malicious and ill-founded, it having appeared that the said admiral, so far from having, by misconduct or neglect of duty on the days therein alluded to, lost an opportunity of rendering essential service to the State, and thereby tarnished the honour of the British Navy, behaved as became a judicious, brave, and experienced officer."

On the following day Admiral Keppel received the thanks of both Houses of Parliament.

Not long after this the "gallant *Arethusa*" was wrecked upon the rocks near Ushant, in pursuit of an enemy. The crew were saved, and treated by the French with great humanity.

On the 15th of June, 1779, his Royal Highness Prince William Henry embarked on board his majesty's ship *Prince George*, 90 guns, to serve as a midshipman in the navy. The next day a proclamation was issued to commence hostilities against Spain, in consequence of the hostile attitude that country had assumed. The first Spanish ship captured during the war was taken by the *Pearl*, of 32 guns, commanded by Captain George Montague, during a cruise off the Western Islands. After an action which lasted from half-past nine till half-past eleven, she struck, and proved to be the *Santa Armonica*, a Spanish frigate of 32 guns and 271 men, 38 of whom were killed and 45 wounded. The *Pearl* had 12 killed and 10 wounded.

Admiral Byron, though a gallant officer, appears always to have been unfortunate. In the last engagement which took place while he commanded the British fleet on the American station, Comte D'Estaing managed to pass him and escape after severely mauling his ships, when 103 men were killed and 346 wounded, though the French loss amounted to 1200 men killed and 1500 wounded.

At this time the want of active flag-officers was severely felt. Promotions were exceedingly slow, so that it was not until officers were nearly superannuated that they attained to that rank. The junior captain promoted in 1779 to the rank of rear-admiral was Sir John Lockhart Rose, who had been twenty-three years on the list of post-captains. Others had been a still longer time.

The French ships also had a great advantage in being coppered, besides which, though respectively carrying the same number of guns as the British, they were much larger vessels.

Among the actions fought at this time, one deserves especially to be noticed. It ended disastrously to the English flag; although nothing could exceed the gallantry displayed by British officers and seamen on the occasion. Captain Richard Pearson, commanding the 44-gun ship *Serapis*, in company of the armed 22-gun ship *Countess of Scarborough*, Captain Thomas Piercy, was escorting the Baltic Fleet, loaded with naval stores, which were at that time of especial consequence to supply the dockyards, left almost destitute of them. The *Serapis* was one of a remarkably bad class of ships, worse even than the two-decked 50-gun ships. She measured 886 tons, and her armament consisted of 20 long 18-pounders on the lower-deck, 22 long 12-pounders on the main-deck, and 2 long 6-pounders on the forecastle, making in all 44 guns. These guns she carried on two decks, but the lower-deck ports were so close to the water's edge that it was dangerous to open them in a seaway, besides which the space between decks was so low that it was with difficulty they could be worked, while the upper-deck had only a light breast-high bulwark. From the length of the lower-deck guns they could not be easily run in, while the 12-pounders on the main-deck were so old and their vents so large that much powder exploded through them.

The convoy had already made the coast of England, and was close in with Scarborough, when information was received from the shore that a flying squadron of the enemy's ships had been seen the day before standing to the southward. Upon receiving this intelligence, Captain Pearson made the signal for the convoy to bear down under his lee, but they still kept stretching out from the land, till the headmost vessel caught sight of the enemy, when they tacked and stood inshore, letting fly their topgallant sheets and firing guns. Captain Pearson on this made sail to windward to get between the enemy's ships and the convoy. At one o'clock the strangers were seen from the mast-head of the *Serapis*, and at four were discovered from the deck to be three large ships and a brig. His consort, *Countess of Scarborough*, being at this time close inshore, Captain Pearson ordered her by signal to join him. The approaching ships were three fitted out in France, but carrying the American flag, and commanded by Captain Paul Jones. The largest had formerly been an Indiaman, and her name had been changed to that of the *Bon Homme Richard*. She is supposed to have measured about 946 tons, and to have carried on her main-deck about 28 long 12-pounders, on the lower-deck, 6 or 8 18-pounders, and 2 long 6-pounders on the forecastle. The other ships were the American 36-gun frigate *Alliance*, the French 32-gun frigate *Pallas*, the *Vengeance*, a French 14-gun brig, and the French *Cerf* cutter. As yet, however, the strangers' colours were not visible.

At about 7:20 the two-decked ship, soon known to be the *Bon Homme Richard*, brought to on the larboard bow of the *Serapis*, within musket-shot, when Captain Pearson hailed her, and asked, "What ship's that?"

"The *Princess Royal*," was the answer. Captain Pearson then asked from whence they came, and on an evasive answer being returned, declared that he would fire if his question was not directly answered. The stranger then fired a gun, on which the *Serapis* gave her her broadsides. Several broadsides were now exchanged, when the American ship hove all aback, and dropped on the quarter of the *Serapis*, evidently with the intention of raking her. Filling again, she ran the *Serapis* aboard on the weather or larboard quarter, and an attempt was now made to board her, but was at once repulsed. Captain Pearson now backed his yards to enable him to get square with his antagonist, but gathering too much stern-way, the *Richard* was able to fill and stand across his bows. Her mizen-shrouds, however, catching the jib-boom of the *Serapis*, and the spar giving way, the ships dropped alongside each other head and stern. Both ships were kept in this position in consequence of the spare anchor of the *Serapis* having entered the gallery of the *Richard*, when a furious cannonade was carried on, the muzzles of the guns touching each other. While in this position, the *Alliance* frigate coming up, sailed round the combatants, pouring in a galling fire on the *Serapis*, to which no return could be made. There could have been little doubt that even thus Captain Pearson would have gained the victory, had not some hand grenades been thrown on his deck, which set the ship on fire several times, one of them igniting a cartridge of powder, the flames of which communicated from cartridge to cartridge all the way off, and blew up the whole of the people and several officers who were quartered abaft the main-mast. By this time all the men on the quarter and main-decks were killed or wounded. Notwithstanding this, so furious had been the fire of the *Serapis*, that at ten the enemy called for quarter; but on Captain Pearson hailing to inquire if they had struck, and no answer being given, he ordered the boarders away. As, however, they reached the deck of the enemy, they found a superior number of men concealed with pikes in their hands ready to receive them. On this the crew of the *Serapis* retreated to their own ship, and instantly returned to their guns; but at the same moment the frigate again poured another broadside into her with such effect that the main-mast fell, and Captain Pearson being unable to get a single gun to bear on his antagonist, was compelled to strike his colours. He and his first lieutenant were immediately escorted on board the *Bon Homme Richard*. He found her condition to be even worse than his own; her quarters and counter were entirely driven in; the whole of her lower-deck guns dismounted, and she was also on fire in two places, with six or seven feet of water in the hold.

In the meantime Captain Piercy had been closely engaged with the *Pallas* and *Vengeance*, but perceiving another frigate bearing down on him, he also was compelled to surrender. The next day the *Bon Homme Richard* sank, and Paul Jones and the French frigate carried their prizes into the Texel. The two English captains had done their duty, and saved their convoy, which all escaped. Of the numerous crew on board the *Richard* no less a number than 317 were killed or wounded, while the *Serapis* lost 49 killed and 68 wounded, many others suffering from burns — while, from the ill-treatment the prisoners received, many of the wounded died.

On the return of Captains Pearson and Piercy, the former was knighted and the latter promoted, and both received testimonials from the London Assurance Company, as an acknowledgment of their skill and bravery, which had preserved the valuable fleet from capture. Had ships of sufficient force been sent out to convoy the fleet, the enemy would, in all probability, have been captured.

A considerable change was now about to be introduced in the character of the guns used on board ships of war. On the banks of the River Carron in Scotland, the ironworks of the Carron Company for some time existed. In these works, in the year 1779, a piece of ordnance had been cast, the invention of John Robert Melville, shorter than a 4-pounder, and lighter than a 12-pounder. It carried a shot of 68 pounds, and from its destructive effects, when fired against a mass of timber, its inventor called it the "Smasher." From the works in which it was cast, it soon obtained the name of "carronade." Several smaller pieces were shortly afterwards cast, to carry shot of 24, 18, and 12 pounds. These guns were eagerly purchased by the owners of privateers fitted out to cruise against the Americans, and the Lords of the Admiralty approving of them, directed some 18 and 12-pounder carronades to be placed on board a few frigates and smaller vessels of the Royal Navy. It was some time, however, before naval officers approved of them; some complained that the carronade was too short to allow its fire to pass clear of the ship's side, and that its range was not of sufficient extent to be of use; that one pair of their quarter-deck carronades being in the way of the rigging, endangered the lanyards and shrouds. The Board of Ordnance also asserted that the old gun, from the comparative length of its range, was superior to the carronade, notwithstanding the greater weight of the shot it carried. Thus, curiously enough, although a considerable number of carronades were placed on board ships of war, they were not reckoned for some time as belonging to the armament of the ship, and officers persisted in speaking only of the long guns they carried, and ignoring the carronades, although, in reality, far more destructive in their effects. Especially did they object to exchange any of their long guns for carronades. On board the larger ships, as the quarter-decks carried already as many guns as there was room for ports on each side, no additional pieces could be admitted; but the forecastle in most ships allowed of the opening of a pair of extra ports, and by strengthening the poop, it was found that three pairs of ports could be placed there. A 50-gun ship had room for three pairs of ports on her poop, one pair on her quarter-deck, and a pair on her forecastle. By similar alterations, a 44-gun ship was made to carry ten carronades, while on board the sixth-rates and the quarter-deck ship-sloop class, by building up bulwarks or barricades, they could be made to carry eight carronades.

Notwithstanding the fewer number of men with which carronades were worked, and the powerful effect of their shot at close quarters, it was some time before all British men-of-war were entirely furnished with them. At length it was determined to arm with them the 44-gun ship *Rainbow*, commanded by Captain Henry Trollope, who, with Lord Keith, then Captain Keith Elphinstone, and Admiral Macbride, were among the first patrons of the new style of gun. About March, 1782, she was equipped with 48 carronades — namely, 20 68-pounders on her main-deck, 22 42-pounders on her upper deck, 4 32-pounders on her quarter-deck, and 2 32-pounders on her forecastle, her broadside weight of metal being thus 1238 pounds, whereas in her former armament of long guns, the broadside weight of metal was only 318 pounds. Thus armed, with the above-mentioned officers and crew, she sailed on a cruise in search of an enemy; for some months, however, she was unable to come within gunshot of a foe, and it was not till the 4th of September of that year, when, being off the Isle du Bas, she came in sight of a large French frigate, to which she at once gave chase. The enemy proved to be the *Hébé*, mounting 28 18-pounders, and 12 8-pounders, 40 guns in all, and measuring 1063 tons, with 363 men on board, commanded by the Chevalier de Vigney. At 7 a.m. the *Rainbow* commenced firing her bow-chasers, which were returned by the frigate, and, as it proved, several shot falling on board, the enemy discovered their size. The French captain concluding that if such large shot came from the forecastle of the enemy's ship, larger ones would follow from her lower batteries, after exchanging a single broadside with the *Rainbow,* for the honour of his flag, wisely surrendered. During this short action the *Hébé's* foremast had been disabled by one of the 68-pound shot, her wheel had been knocked away, and her second captain and four men killed. No one was hurt on board the *Rainbow*. The *Hébé*, a beautiful ship, was purchased into the British Navy, and long served as a model to English shipwrights. No reflection could be cast upon the courage of the French captain, for had he continued the action, his ship would in a few minutes probably have been sunk, the *Rainbow's* broadside weight of metal being nearly four times that of the *Hébé*, though the number of guns she carried was only four less than that of his antagonist. This action went far to establish the reputation of the carronades.

Towards the end of 1779 information was received that the French had agreed to assist Spain in an attempt to retake Gibraltar, in consequence of which Sir George Rodney, who was about to sail to the West Indies with 20 sail of the line convoying a large fleet of merchantmen, was directed to relieve Gibraltar before he proceeded westward. Another squadron under Rear-Admiral Digby was also sent out, which was to return to England. For several years since 1773 a Spanish army had been kept before Gibraltar, but General Elliot, who commanded the fortress, had completely baffled all its attempts. Rodney on his way out, when off Cape Saint Vincent, caught sight of a Spanish squadron convoying a fleet of merchant-vessels. The enemy on discovering him crowded all sail to escape, on which he made a signal for a general chase. The English ships gained rapidly on the enemy. At about five in the evening the *Bienfaisant*, Captain John Macbride, got up with the Spanish 70-gun ship the *San Domingo*, but scarcely had she opened her fire when the latter blew up, and every soul on board, with the exception of one man, perished. The poor fellow was picked up by the *Pegasus*, but was so much injured that he expired shortly afterwards. The action was continued during the whole night, and at 2 a.m. the following morning Admiral Rodney finding that the enemy's ships were too much disabled to enable them to escape, hove to. Besides the one which blew up, the *Phoenix* 80-gun ship and five 70-gun ships were taken. The weather being bad, it was not without great difficulty that the fleet, which had got into shoal water, could work off again. Two of the prizes, on board of which prize-crews had been put, but from which on account of the bad weather it had been impossible to remove the officers and men, were recaptured by the Spaniards and carried into Cadiz. The small-pox raging on board the *Bienfaisant*, Captain Macbride, who had taken possession of the *Phoenix*, actuated by principles of humanity worthy of being recorded, to avoid the risk of infection spreading among the prisoners, sent the following proposals to Don Juan de Langara, who accepted them with thanks: —

"Captain Macbride consents that neither officers nor men shall be removed from the *Phoenix*, Admiral Langara being responsible for their conduct; and in case we shall fall in with any Spanish or French ships of war, he will not suffer Lieutenant Thomas Lewis, the officer now in command of the *Phoenix*, to be interrupted in conducting and defending the ship to the last extremity. And if, meeting with superior force, the *Phoenix* should be retaken and the *Bienfaisant* fight her way clear, the admiral and his officers and men are to hold themselves prisoners of war to Captain Macbride, upon their parole of honour, (which he is confident with Spanish officers is ever sacred). Likewise, if the *Bienfaisant* should be taken and the *Phoenix* escape, the admiral and his officers will no longer be prisoners, but freed immediately. In short, they are to follow the fate of the *Bienfaisant*."

This remarkable agreement was executed with the strictest honour.

Soon afterwards Captain Macbride, after a smart action, captured the *Comte d'Arotis*, private ship of war, mounting 64 guns, and 644 men, commanded by the Chevalier de Clonard.

Admiral Rodney, who had been joined by Rear-Admiral Sir Hyde Parker at Saint Lucia, gaining intelligence of the French fleet, which consisted of 25 sail of the line and 8 frigates, sailed in search of them. On the 19th of April, having come in sight of the enemy on the previous evening, about noon he threw out a signal for every ship to bear down, steer for them, and engage at close quarters her opposite in the enemy's line. At 1 the action became general, and continued until 4:15 p.m., when the French took to flight, the crippled state of the British ships rendering pursuit impracticable. Every exertion having now been made to repair damages, on the 20th the *George* again caught sight of the French, and pursued them without effect for three successive days. The French ran under Guadaloupe, where they had taken shelter. On the 6th, hearing that they had left their anchorage and were approaching to windward of Martinique, Rodney put to sea, and continued turning to windward between it and Saint Lucia until the 10th, when the enemy's fleet was discovered about three leagues to windward. Still the French studiously avoided coming to a general action. Sir George on this, to deceive them, directed his fleet to make all possible sail on a wind. This manoeuvre led the enemy to think he was retiring, and emboldened him to approach much nearer than usual. Rodney allowed them to indulge in their mistake, until their own ship had approached abreast of his centre, when, by a fortunate shift of wind, being able to weather the enemy, he made the signal to Rear-Admiral Parker, who led the van, to tack and gain the wind of the enemy. The French fleet instantly wore and fled under a crowd of sail, but would have been compelled to fight, had not the wind on a sudden changed. The *Albion*, Captain Bowyer, late in the evening, reached the centre of the enemy's line, and commenced a heavy cannonade, supported by the *Conqueror* and the rest of the van; but as the enemy continued under a press of sail, the remainder of the fleet could not partake in the action. Still, Rodney perseveringly followed up the enemy, and on the 19th the wind again changing gave him hopes of being able to bring on a general action. Before, however, he could close it again shifted; but the French admiral finding that his rear could not escape, suddenly took the resolution of risking a general action. As soon is his van had weathered the British, he bore away along the line to windward, discharging his broadsides, but at such a distance as to do little execution. The Frenchmen, however, could not avoid being closely attacked by the ships of the van, led by Commodore Hotham. After this the enemy continued under a press of sail to the northward, and on the 21st were out of sight.

In these several actions the British loss amounted to 186 killed and 464 wounded, including 7 officers in the former and 14 in the latter list.

On the 10th and 11th of October a dreadful hurricane blew over the West Indian Islands, during which eight ships were lost, with the greater portion of their crews, and six were severely damaged. The French were also great sufferers.

A squadron, under Rear-Admiral Rowley, on the passage to England with a convoy, also suffered dreadfully. The admiral, with five of his ships, returned to Jamaica dismasted. The *Berwick*, also dismasted, with difficulty arrived in England. The *Stirling Castle* was totally lost on the Silver Keys, near Hispaniola, and only fifty of her crew saved; while the *Thunderer*, which had separated from the fleet, foundered, and every soul perished. Several other ships were driven on shore, and eight lost their masts.

Towards the end of 1780 war was declared against the Dutch, who, it was found, were making preparations to attack England. On the 5th of August, 1781, Rear-Admiral Sir Hyde Parker fell in with the Dutch fleet off the Dogger Bank, when an action ensued in which both fleets were dreadfully cut to pieces, the Dutch escaping into the Texel. One of their ships, of 68 guns, the *Hollandia*, went down in twenty-two fathom water. Her pendant the next morning was seen above the surface, when Captain Patten, of the *Belle Poule*, struck it, and brought it to Sir Hyde Parker. The English lost 104 men killed and 339 wounded, among whom were 30 officers.

Sir George Rodney at the same time attacked the Dutch island of Saint Eustatia, which, with those of Saint Martin and Saba, at once capitulated, a richly-laden fleet falling into the hands of the English, as well as a vast quantity of merchandise stored up.

One of the most important events of this period must now be described. The hopes of the Spaniards had been raised in consequence of their recapture of the island of Minorca; General Murray, in command of Fort Saint Philip — the greater portion of his troops having died or been struck down with scurvy — after a heroic defence, having been compelled to yield. The Spanish army, which had so long been besieging Gibraltar, was now increased to 40,000 men, including 12,000 French, and, in addition, there were 47 sail of the line, 40 gunboats with heavy cannon, 40 bomb-vessels, each armed with 12-inch mortars, 5 large bomb-ketches, and 300 large boats to be employed in landing the troops as soon as a breach should be made — besides which, there were 10 large floating batteries, the invention of the Chevalier D'Arzon, a French engineer of great repute, on such a principle that they would not, he believed, be sunk or set on fire by shot. It was said that no less than 1200 pieces of heavy ordnance had been accumulated before the place, with 83,000 barrels of gunpowder, and shot, shells, military stores, and provisions in the same proportion. The chief reliance of the besiegers was, however, placed on the floating batteries. They were built of extraordinary thickness, and so fortified that they were proof from all external, as well as internal, violence. To prevent their being set on fire, a strong case was formed of timber and cork, a long time soaked in water, and enclosing a large body of wet sand; the whole being of such thickness and density that no cannon-ball could penetrate within two feet of the inner partition.

For this purpose, ten large ships, from 600 to 1400 tons burden, had been cut-down, and 200,000 cubic feet of timber worked in their construction. To protect them from bombs, and the men at the batteries from grape, or descending shot, a hanging roof was contrived; which was worked up and down by springs. The roof was composed of a strong rope-work netting, laid over with a thick covering of wet hides, while its sloping position was calculated to prevent shells from lodging, and to throw them off into the sea before they could burst. To render the fire of these batteries the more rapid, a kind of match had been contrived, so to be placed that all the guns in the battery could go off at the same instant. To defend them from red-hot shot, with which the fortress was supplied, the newest part of the plan was that by which water could be carried in every direction to neutralise its effect. In imitation of the circulation of the blood, a variety of pipes and canals perforated all the solid workmanship in such a manner that a continued succession of water could be conveyed to every part of the structure, a number of pumps being adapted to afford an unlimited supply. It was thus believed that these terrible machines, capable of inflicting destruction, would themselves be invulnerable. The largest carried 21 guns, and their complement of men was 36 for each gun in use, exclusive of officers and mariners for working the ships.

General Elliot, undaunted by the preparations made by the enemy, determined to try what he and his brave garrison could do to counteract them. Accordingly, at seven o'clock in the morning of the 8th of September, he opened a tremendous fire on their works with red-hot shot, carcasses, and shells. At ten o'clock the Mahon battery, with the one adjoining it, were in flames. By five in the evening both were entirely consumed; a great part of the eastern parallel, and of the trenches and parapet for musketry, were likewise destroyed. A large battery near the bay was so much damaged by having repeatedly been set on fire, that the enemy were compelled to abandon it, while they lost an immense number of men in their endeavour to extinguish the flames. The next day the French and Spaniards opened a new battery of 64 heavy cannon, which, with the artillery from the lines and mortars, continued to play upon the garrison without intermission the whole day. At the same time, seven Spanish ships of the line and two French, with some frigates and small vessels, passing along the works discharged their broadsides, until they had passed Europa Point, and got into the Mediterranean.

In the meantime, the English squadron being too small to compete with them, the seamen had been landed, under the command of Captain Roger Curtis, and had been placed in the batteries at Europa Point. Hence they had attacked the Spanish line-of-battle ships, and compelled them to haul off.

About eight o'clock in the morning of the 13th of September, the battering ships lying at the head of the bay, under the command of Rear-Admiral Don Moreno, got under sail to attack the fort. At ten o'clock the admiral having taken up his station off the king's bastion, the other ships extended themselves at moderate distances from the old to the new mole, in a line parallel with the rock, at a distance of about one thousand yards, and immediately commenced a heavy cannonade, supported by the cannon and mortars on the enemy's lines. On seeing this the garrison opened a tremendous fire; the red-hot shot were thrown with such precision that about two o'clock in the afternoon, the smoke was seen to issue from the admiral and another ship, the men in vain endeavouring to extinguish the fire by pouring water into the holes. By one o'clock the two ships were in flames, and seven more took fire in succession. Signals of distress were now seen flying on board the Spanish ships, while the launches came up for the purpose of taking the men out of the burning ships, it being impossible to remove them. When he saw this, Captain Curtis advanced with his gunboats and drew them up so as to flank the enemy's battering ships, which were annoyed by an incessant, heavy, and well-directed fire from the garrison. The Spanish boats were so assailed by showers of shot and shell that they would not venture on a nearer approach, and were compelled to abandon their ships and friends to the flames. Several of the enemy's boats were sunk; the crew of one of these were all drowned, with the exception of an officer and twelve men, who floated on the wreck under the walls, and were rescued by the English.

The scene was full of horrors. Numbers of men were observed in the midst of the flames, imploring relief; others were seen floating on pieces of timber; while even those on board the ships not on fire expressed the deepest distress, and were equally urgent in asking for assistance. Captain Curtis and his gallant sailors, though exposed to the greatest possible danger, eagerly boarded the burning ships to rescue the now conquered enemy from destruction. While they were thus engaged, one of the largest of the Spanish ships blew up, spreading its wreck far around. By this accident, one English gunboat was sunk, and another much damaged. A piece of falling timber struck a hole through the bottom of Captain Curtis' barge, by which his coxswain was killed and two of his crew wounded; the rest were saved from perishing by the seamen stuffing their jackets into the hole, which kept the boat afloat until others came to their assistance. While the ships were burning, numbers of Spaniards were seen floating on pieces of timber, liable every moment to be washed off, or destroyed by the shot from the garrison. As soon, however, as it was discovered that the enemy were defeated, the firing from Gibraltar entirely ceased, and every possible effort was made to save the Spaniards from death. Nine of these formidable batteries were burnt by the red-hot shot, and the tenth was set on fire by her crew, as it was found impracticable to carry her off. Even had the battering ships not taken fire, the Spaniards would have had no chance of success, as the works of the fortress, notwithstanding the tremendous fire directed against them, were scarcely damaged. During the nine weeks the siege had been going on, only 65 of the garrison had been killed, and less than 400 wounded, while the seamen had only lost two or three men.

A heavy gale coming on, several of the French and Spanish ships suffered material damage, and the *Saint Michael*, a 72-gun ship, carrying 650 men, was driven close under the works, and struck after a few shot had been fired into her. She was got off by Captain Curtis a few days afterwards, with the loss only of her mizen-mast.

On the 11th of October Lord Howe appeared with a large fleet, which the enemy endeavoured to avoid. After seeing the troop-ships which he had convoyed into the harbour, he went in search of the enemy's fleet, which, after a short engagement, hauled their wind and stood off to the north-west.

In the bomb-proof vessels above described we recognise the idea of our present floating batteries; while the result of their attack on Gibraltar might have shown our naval commanders in the Crimean war the slight hope there was of any advantage being gained by their attack on the batteries of Sebastopol.

The great object of the French was to capture the island of Jamaica. For this purpose, the Comte de Grasse, who commanded their fleet in the West Indies, was using every exertion to equip his fleet and to form a junction with the Spaniards. Sir George Rodney, with Sir Samuel Hood and Admiral Drake and Commodore Affleck under him, were on the look-out to prevent them. At length, on the 8th of April, while the English fleet was at anchor at Saint Lucia, Captain Byron, in the *Andromache* frigate, communicated to the admiral by signal that the enemy's fleet, with a large convoy, were seen coming out of Fort Royal Bay, and standing to the north-west. Sir George instantly made the signal to weigh, and on the morning of the 9th the enemy were seen forming a line of battle to windward, and standing over towards Guadaloupe. For some time the British fleet was becalmed, but as the breeze reached the van division, commanded by Sir Samuel Hood, he stood on and closed with the enemy's centre. At nine o'clock the action commenced, and was maintained with determined bravery for upwards of an hour by this division, the *Barfleur* having generally three ships firing upon her at once. At length the leading ships of the centre got the breeze, and were enabled to come up to the assistance of the van. These were soon after followed by the *Formidable, Bake,* and *Namur.* The action raged it for some time, much gallantry being displayed by the captain of a French 74-gun ship, who, backing his main-topsail, steadily received and returned the fire of these three ships in succession. The Comte de Grasse, seeing the remainder of the British fleet coming up, withdrew out of fire, and by the 11th his fleet was nearly hull down. All hopes of being able to keep up with them appeared to be at an end, when two French ships, which had been much damaged, were perceived about noon to leeward of their fleet. Chase was instantly made by the English, when the Comte de Grasse bore down to their relief. Sir George Rodney on this recalled the ships in chase, and formed a close line of battle, carrying sail to windward all night. At dawn of the 12th, a French ship of the line, the *Zélé,* 74 guns, was seen much disabled, and towed by a frigate. The Comte de Grasse, on perceiving that she must be taken, bore up with his whole fleet for her protection. He could now no longer avoid an engagement. At half-past seven Rear-Admiral Drake's division, which led, commenced the action, which soon became general from van to rear. Captain Gardner, in the *Duke,* having unsuccessfully attempted to force the enemy's line, in consequence of the loss of his main-topmast, Sir George Rodney, in the *Formidable,* supported by the *Namur* and *Canada,* broke through their line, about three ships from the *Ville de Paris,* and was followed by the ships in his rear, when he wore and doubled upon the enemy. By this manoeuvre the French line was broken and thrown into the utmost confusion; their van bore away, and endeavoured to re-form to leeward, but this, hardly pressed as they were, they were unable to accomplish. Sir Samuel Hood's division, which had been becalmed the greater part of the forenoon, now coming up, completed the victory. Several of the French ships struck. Captain Cornwallis, to whom the *Hector* had yielded, left his prize, and made sail after the French admiral in the *Ville de Paris.* The well-directed fire of the *Canada* so much annoyed her, and some other ships approaching, made it impossible for her to escape; but the Comte de Grasse seemed determined to sink rather than yield to anything under a flag. At length Sir Samuel Hood came up in the *Barfleur,* and poured in a tremendous and destructive fire. The brave Frenchman maintained the action for a quarter-of-an-hour longer, when finding further resistance vain, and that he was deserted by his second, hauled down his flag. The enemy's fleet continued going off before the wind in small detached squadrons and single ships, pursued by the British. On this, Sir George made the signal to bring to, in order to collect his fleet and secure the prizes. Some of the ships, however, not observing the signal, did not return till the next day. Before the prisoners could be shifted from the *Caesar*, she caught fire and blew up, an English lieutenant and 50 men belonging to the *Centaur*, together with 400 Frenchmen, perishing.

The French are supposed to have lost 3000 men killed, and double that number wounded, for, besides the ships' crews, the fleet had on board 5500 troops. It was said that at the time the *Ville de Paris* struck there were but three men left alive and unhurt on the upper deck, and that the Comte de Grasse was one of the three.

A story is told of a female sailor who fought in the action. While the battle was raging, one of the crew of a gun being wounded and sent below, a woman took his place. After the action she was brought before the admiral, when it was discovered that she was the sailor's wife, and had been concealed on board. She declared that she thought it her duty to supply her husband's place, and fight the French. Rodney threatened her for a breach of the rules, but privately sent her a purse of ten guineas.

A few days afterwards the admiral detached Sir Samuel Hood in chase of the crippled French ships, when two more were captured in the same gallant way by Captain Goodall of the *Valiant*. A frigate of 32 guns and a sloop of 16 were also taken.

For this action Sir George Rodney was created a peer of Great Britain; Sir Samuel Hood a peer of Ireland; and Admiral Drake and Commodore Affleck were made baronets.

These actions must be taken merely as examples of what the navy was about at that time.

Towards the end of 1782, negotiations for a general peace were set on foot, and it was finally concluded early in the following year.

Chapter Fifteen.

George the Third — from War with Republican France, A.D. 1792, to end of A.D. 1802.

We will briefly run over a few events which occurred previous to the breaking out of the first revolutionary war.

On May the 29th, 1782, the *Royal George*, of 100 guns, being heeled over at Spithead to repair a pipe which led under water, the lower-deck guns having been run out, the water rushed with such rapidity in at the port-holes that she filled and sank — Rear-Admiral Kempenfeldt, with more than half his officers, and four hundred persons, perishing, many of them the wives and children of the seamen and marines on board.

We are apt to consider that the uniform of the navy differed greatly from the army; but in an order dated the 11th of January, 1783, admirals, vice-admirals, and rear-admirals were directed to wear coats very similar to those worn by generals, lieutenant-generals, and major-generals respectively, in the army, with the exception of the crown and anchor buttons.

In the month of June, 1785, his Royal Highness Prince William Henry, who had now served his time as a midshipman, passed his examination, and was appointed third lieutenant of the *Hébé* frigate, of 40 guns.

In 1785 a debate arose in the House of Commons on the propriety of repairing the old 64-gun ships, and also suffering ships of war to remain in ordinary with the copper on their bottoms. Captain Macbride thought that the 64-gun ships should be either broken up or sold, and recommended in future none less than seventy-fours to be built for the line of battle. He also pointed out the mischievous effects that might ensue in suffering ships to be laid up with their copper on, alleging that the copper would in time corrode the bolts; in consequence of which the ships' bottoms might drop out. He had examined a coppered ship under repair, and found the bolts corroded and eaten away. Ships had, however, before this time, been fastened with copper bolts, and probably those seen by Captain Macbride were either iron bolts cased only with copper or composition.

The supplies granted by Parliament for the sea-service for the year 1789 amounted to 2,328,570 pounds.

On the 24th of November, 1787, the *Bounty*, of 215 tons, commanded by Lieutenant William Bligh, sailed from Spithead, for the Pacific Ocean, to obtain a supply of the bread-fruit tree. On the 28th of April, 1789, some of his officers and crew mutinied, and took possession of the ship, casting the commander and those who remained firm to him adrift in an open boat. The hardihood and judgment he displayed in conducting his boat's crew across the Pacific to Batavia are well known.

Many useful contrivances have been invented by inferior officers of the navy. Among others, Mr Hill, the carpenter of the *Active*, invented a machine for drawing bolts out of ships' sides. He also invented a method for stopping shot-holes.

In 1791 some experiments were made on board a ship in Portsmouth Harbour, when he stopped a shot-hole on the outside of the ship, four feet under water, in the space of one minute, without the assistance of any person out of the vessel. He stopped in the same manner a space in the ship's side, four feet under water, of four feet by four inches, in two minutes and a-half. During the time of effectually curing both leaks, the ship made only ten inches water in the well.

He also invented a wheel to work the chain-pump, which was much safer and less liable to get out of order than that before in use.

The French Revolution broke out in 1792. On the 21st of the following January, the French beheaded their king, Louis the Sixteenth; in consequence of which the French ambassador at the court of London was ordered to quit England. A short time before this the new Republic had exhibited its hostile spirit against England, and on the 2nd of January a shot had been fired from one of the batteries near Brest on the British 16-gun brig-sloop *Childers*. Though a 48-pounder shot struck her, no one was hurt.

On the 1st of February the National Convention declared war against Great Britain and the United Netherlands.

England at this time possessed nominally 135 ships of war in commission, and 169 in ordinary or under repair; 21 building or ordering to be built, and 86 harbour-ships; making in all 411 ships of 402,555 tons. Of these there was one of 100 guns, 12-pounders, of 2091 tons, in commission; two of 100 guns, 18-pounders, under repair; and two of 100 guns, 12-pounders, under repair. Of second-rates there were four 98-gun ships in commission, and eleven under repair; of 90-gun ships there was one under repair. Of two-deckers third-rate there was one 80-gun ship in commission and one under repair. Of seventy-fours there were 19 in commission and 61 under repair. Of sixty-fours there were only two in commission and 30 under repair, making a total of 113 line-of-battle ships. There were 75 frigates either in commission or under repair; but 23 of these carried 28 guns only. Of the most useless class of ships in the service, the 24 and 20 gun post-ships, there were 12 in commission or under repair. Of 18-gun ship-sloops and gun brigs there were altogether 40. Besides these there were 25 bomb fire-ships and cutters, either in commission or under repair, making a total of 304 vessels, exclusive of those building; but of these probably some were unseaworthy, and of those building or ordered to be built, many were not in a state to be launched for two or more years. However, in consequence of the expected rupture between Spain and Russia, in the previous two or three years upwards of 60 line-of-battle ships were in a condition speedily to go to sea, while the dockyards were well-stocked with imperishable stores. Thus, in a few weeks, 200 cruisers were commissioned and fit for use.

At that time we had admirals 17, vice-admirals 19, rear-admirals 19, post-captains 446, commanders 136, lieutenants 1417, and masters 197. The number of seamen and marines, including officers of all ranks, voted by Parliament for the service of the current year, was 45,000.

Portugal and Naples, who joined England, had the first six ships of the line and four frigates, and the latter four 74-gun ships.

The Spanish navy amounted to 204 vessels, 76 of which were of the line, carrying from 112 to 60 guns.

The Dutch navy at this time, though amounting nominally to 119 vessels, from a 74-gun ship to the smallest armed cutter, was of little use to England, a large number of the ships lying rotting in the different harbours, and those able to put to sea being of comparatively small size, and carrying but light guns.

The navy of France amounted to 250 vessels, of which 82 were of the line, nearly three-fourths in a serviceable state; and immediately on the outbreak of war, 71 new ships were laid down, including 25 of the line, and orders given to cast 400 brass 36-pounder carronades, the first guns of the kind employed by the French. One of the former was to mount 130 guns, and several old small-class seventy-fours were cut-down and converted into the most formidable frigates that had hitherto been seen.

Such was the French navy, with which the fleet of England was about to contend, not only for the dominion of the seas, but to protect the hearths and homes of the people from foreign invasion. Such, from the aggressive character of the French people, was the danger, it was soon seen, most to be apprehended. Never had the royal dockyards been so busy. Squadrons had to be sent off to reinforce stations at a distance from home, and to protect our colonies. Some months, therefore, elapsed before a fleet could be got ready to cope with the enemy. As soon as the ships could be fitted out, they were placed under the command of Admiral Lord Howe, who, on the 24th of July, set sail from Spithead with 15 ships of the line and a few frigates and sloops. For some weeks he cruised about in search of the French fleet, being joined in the meantime by more ships, till he had upwards of 30 under his command. He, however, was compelled to return to Spithead without meeting them.

In the meantime Lord Hood had proceeded to the Mediterranean and taken possession of Toulon. Before, however, we describe the events which took place there, we will follow Lord Howe, who, on the following May, received information that a valuable French convoy was expected from the West Indies, and guessing that the enemy's fleet would sail out for their protection, put to sea in the hopes of intercepting them. His force now consisted of 26 sail of the line and 13 frigates and sloops. On the morning of the 28th, being about 140 leagues west of Ushant, the enemy were discovered at some distance to windward. On their perceiving the British fleet, they bore down in loose order, but soon after hauled again to the wind, and began to form in order of battle. Several of the British ships, at a considerable distance to windward of the fleet, approached the enemy's rear. Lord Howe then made the signal for a general chase, and to engage the enemy. Rear-Admiral Pasley, of the *Bellerophon*, towards the close of the day, got up with the rear-ship of the enemy's line, a three-decker, on which he commenced a firm and resolute attack, supported occasionally by the ships in his division. The *Bellerophon*, being soon disabled, fell to leeward. The *Audacious* came up just at that time, and continued to engage the same ship for two hours without intermission, when the enemy's mizen-mast fell overboard, her lower yards and main-topsail yards shot away, and otherwise much shattered. The *Audacious*, however, having her rigging and sails cut to pieces, and the ship being for some time unmanageable, was unable to follow the Frenchman, who put before the wind and escaped. The night being dark, Captain Parker lost sight of the fleet, and being in too disabled a state to rejoin, was compelled to bear away for the channel. The next day a partial engagement took place between the two hostile fleets, which resulted in the British obtaining the weather-gage.

On the morning of the 1st of June, both fleets being drawn up in order of battle, at half-past seven Lord Howe made the signal for both fleets to bear up, and for each ship to engage her opponent in the enemy's line. In a short time a tremendous cannonade commenced from van to rear, which raged with unceasing fury for about an hour. The enemy's line having been forced through in many places, they began to give way, and their admiral, vigorously attacked by the *Queen Charlotte*, bore up, and was followed by all those of his ships that were able to carry sail, leaving the rest, which were dismasted and crippled, at the mercy of their enemies. Upon the clearing up of the smoke, eight or ten French ships were seen, some totally dismasted and others with only one mast standing, endeavouring to make off under their spritsails. Seven of these were taken possession of; one, *Le Vengeur*, sank before the whole of her crew could be taken out, not more than 280 being saved. A distant and irregular firing was continued at intervals between the fugitive and British ships till about four in the afternoon, when the French admiral, having collected most of his remaining ships, steered off to the eastward. The *Queen Charlotte* had lost both her topmasts, the *Marlborough* and *Defence* were wholly dismasted, and many of the other ships materially damaged. Earl Howe, therefore, brought to, in order to secure the prizes and collect his ships before dark. The loss sustained by the British in this action amounted to 281 killed and 788 wounded. Among the first was Captain James Montague of the *Montague*, while three admirals and four captains were severely wounded. The killed on board the enemy's ships that were captured amounted to 690, and 580 wounded, exclusive of 320 lost in *Le Vengeur* when she sank, the greater number of whom were wounded.

So important was this action considered, that on the return of the fleet to Spithead, the king himself came down to Portsmouth and personally presented Lord Howe with a sword; while various honours were bestowed upon the principal officers engaged, gold medals being struck to commemorate the glorious victory of the 1st of June; a liberal subscription being opened likewise for the relief of the wounded officers, seamen, and marines, and also the widows and children of those who fell in the action.

This victory early in the war was of the greatest consequence, as it raised the spirits and confidence of the British, while it proportionably depressed the enemy, and proved the prelude of that succession of victories which at length crushed the power of France and secured the safety of England.

After the English had held Toulon for some time, in consequence of the large force of republicans collected round the city, it was found impossible to retain it. Several thousand French royalists having been embarked, it was resolved to destroy the arsenal and ships of war. This dangerous task was undertaken by Sir Sidney Smith, having under his command three English and three Spanish gunboats and a tender, with the *Vulcan* fire-ship. He proceeded into the harbour at dark; the fire-ship was first placed across the outer men-of-war in such a position that she was certain to do effectual execution. Scarcely had the signal been made for setting the trains on fire, than the flames rose in all directions; a magazine, filled with pitch, tar, tallow, oil, and hemp, was quickly in a blaze; while the guns of the fire-ship went off in the direction the enemy were approaching. The destruction would have been more complete had not the Spaniards set fire to two ships laden with powder, which they had been directed to sink; on board one of them, the *Isis* frigate, there were some thousand barrels. In a few moments the explosion took place; the air was filled with masses of burning timber, which fell in all directions, and two of the British boats were destroyed. The crew of one was taken up, but in the other, Lieutenant Young, with three men, perished, and many were badly wounded.

Notwithstanding this, Sir Sidney and his brave companions destroyed ten of the enemy's ships of the line in the arsenal, with the mast-house, the great storehouse and other buildings.

After this, Lord Hood proceeded to Hieres Bay, leaving a small squadron to cruise before Toulon. Unfortunately, the *Moselle*, Captain Bennet, on her return from Gibraltar, passed through them, and not knowing that the place was evacuated, entered the harbour and was captured.

Some time after this, Captain Samuel Hood, in the *Juno* frigate of 32 guns, who had been sent to Malta for supernumeraries for the fleet — having been detained by a succession of foul winds — also ignorant of what had occurred, at ten in the evening stood into the outer road; not perceiving the fleet at anchor there, and concluding that they had taken shelter within the new harbour from a strong easterly gale which had lately been blowing, steered for it. Having no pilot on board, two midshipmen were stationed at each cathead to look out. Soon after, several lights were seen, which were supposed to be those of the fleet. The *Juno* accordingly stood on under her topsails till she made out a brig which lay off Point Grandtour, when the captain, finding that he could not weather her, set more sail. The brig, as he approached, hailed; but no one understood what was said. Captain Hood, in reply, gave the name and nation of his ship, upon which the people on board the brig shouted "Viva!" and soon after some one cried out "Luff." The *Juno's* helm on this was put a-lee, but before the ship came head to wind, she took the ground. Directly afterwards, a boat was observed to pull from the brig towards the town, but even then her object was not suspected. Happily, while the *Juno's* people were still on the yards, a sudden flaw of wind taking the ship, drove her astern. To help her off, the driver and mizen-staysail were hoisted, and directly the ship lost her way, an anchor was let go, but she still touched the ground abaft. Accordingly, to get her off, the launch and cutter were ordered to carry out a kedge-anchor ahead. While the boats were still away, a boat from the shore came alongside, out of which several officers hurried on board. One of them informed Captain Hood that it was the commanding officer's orders that the ship should go into another branch of the harbour to perform ten days' quarantine. From some of the remarks now made, suspicions were aroused, and they were confirmed when, on a midshipman exclaiming, "Why, those are the national cockades," the captain, looking at the Frenchmen's hats, discovered by the light of the moon the tricolours of the republicans. The captain again asking where Lord Hood's squadron lay, one of the French officers replied, "Soyez tranquilles. Les Anglais sont des braves gens; nous les traiterons bien. L'Amiral Anglais est sorti il y a quelque temps."

"Be calm. The English are brave people; we will treat them well. The English admiral sailed some time ago."

It may easily be conceived what were Captain Hood's feelings on hearing this. The alarming intelligence ran through the ship; some of the officers hurried aft to inquire if it were true. Happily, at this moment a flaw of wind came down the harbour, when Mr Welby, the third lieutenant, said to Captain Hood, "I believe, sir, that we shall be able to fetch out if we can get under sail." Captain Hood at once determined to try what could be done, and with great presence of mind immediately ordered the crew to their respective stations, and directed that the Frenchmen should be taken below. They at first began to bluster, but the marines appearing with their half-pikes, soon forced them down below. Such was the alacrity of the officers and crew, that in less than three minutes every sail in the ship was set, and the yards braced for casting. The cable, being hove short, was cut, the head sails filled, and the ship glided forward down the harbour. At the same time, her own boats and that of the Frenchmen were cut adrift, that they might not impede her progress. A favourable flaw of wind now coming, she got good way. The instant the brig saw the *Juno* under sail, she and one of the forts began to fire on her, and presently all the other forts, as their guns could be brought to bear, opened fire. Still the frigate stood undauntedly on; as she approached Cape Serpet, it was feared that she would not be able to weather it without making a tack, but the wind shifting so as to admit her lying up two points, she scraped clear of the cape, under a heavy fire from the batteries. As soon as Captain Hood was able to keep the ship away, he opened a brisk fire on the enemy, which he kept up till half-past twelve, when, being out of shot, he ceased firing.

Notwithstanding the heavy cannonade the *Juno* had passed through, not a man on board her was hurt; and though two 36-pound shot had struck her, no material damage had been inflicted, nor had her rigging and sails suffered much injury. Two days afterwards the *Juno* joined Lord Hood's fleet in the Bay of Hieres. The coolness and presence of mind which have been so often exhibited by British naval officers was signally displayed on this occasion; and when we recollect that the *Juno* was actually within the enemy's port, full of armed vessels, with formidable batteries on either side of her, we must acknowledge that the feat she accomplished is unsurpassed in naval annals.

We must pass over the numerous gallant actions between small squadrons and single ships. Great difficulties were experienced at this time in manning the navy; even the press-gangs failed to obtain a sufficient number of men. An Act was passed, therefore, on the 15th of March, 1795, for raising 10,000 men in the several counties of England, and on the 16th of April another was passed for procuring a supply from the several ports of Great Britain; and the more effectually to enforce the Act, an embargo was laid on all British shipping until the quota of men was raised. To encourage men to come forward, enormous bounties were offered by many of the counties and sea-ports, sometimes exceeding 30 pounds for each able seaman. An Act was also passed to enable those who came forward voluntarily to allot part of their pay to the maintenance of their wives and families. Seamen also were allowed to forward letters home on the payment only of a penny; half-pay officers and widows of officers were enabled to obtain their pay or pensions free of charge.

Early in January of the next year Sir Sidney Smith, while in command of the *Diamond* frigate, performed one of those exploits which made his name notorious. While attached to the squadron of Sir John Borlase Warren, he stood close into Brest, where he ascertained that the French fleet were at sea. As he was standing off, a corvette which was coming out of the harbour hove to and made a signal, which not being answered by the *Diamond*, she hauled her wind and worked in. Soon after this Sir Sidney passed within hail of a line-of-battle ship at anchor. She appeared to have no upper-deck guns mounted, and to be very leaky. He asked her commander in French if she wanted any assistance; to which he answered, "No, that he had been dismasted in a heavy gale, and had parted with the French fleet three days ago." Some other conversation passed, after which, Sir Sidney crowded sail and stood out to sea. So completely had he disguised his ship, that the Frenchman had not the slightest suspicion of her being an English man-of-war.

The following year, however, being on a cruise off Havre-de-Grâce, he discovered a lugger in the outer road. Having taken her with the boats of his squadron, he attempted to tow her off, but the flood-tide setting strong in, he was compelled to anchor. In the night the cable either parted or was cut by one of the prisoners, when the lugger, driving a considerable way up the Seine, was attacked by several gunboats and other armed vessels; and Sir Sidney, after making a gallant resistance, was compelled to surrender. He was carried to Paris, and for long shut up in the Temple; but, with the aid of friends, he effected his escape from prison, and reaching Havre-de-Grâce, put off in an open boat, when he was picked up by the *Argo* frigate, and landed safe in Portsmouth on the 5th of March, 1798.

On the 1st of June, 1795, an alteration was made in the uniform of naval officers, which continued for many years afterwards. Those who can remember it can scarcely fail to consider it the most becoming worn at any time in the service. The rank of officers was now distinguished by epaulettes. An admiral wore two gold epaulettes, with three silver stars on each; a vice-admiral had two stars, and a rear-admiral one; a post-captain of above three years standing wore two gold epaulettes, under three years, one on the right shoulder, a master and commander, one on the left shoulder, captains wore blue lapels and cuffs, with lace as before, but on the undress coat neither lace nor embroidery.

On the 4th of June his majesty appointed seven superannuated or disabled lieutenants of the navy to be poor knights of Windsor. This institution was founded by Samuel Travers, who, in 1724, left a residuary estate in trust for building or buying a house for their reception near the castle of Windsor, bequeathing to each knight 60 pounds per annum, 26 pounds of which is to be applied only for keeping them a constant table. The first knight was William Hogarth, whose commission bore the date of 1757, so that he had been nearly forty years a lieutenant; while the next three had been thirty years lieutenants.

In the same year the masters in the navy received an increase of half-pay, and their position was otherwise improved.

Towards the end of the year an improved system of telegraph, the invention of Lord George Murray, was introduced on several heights leading from the coast to London.

Post-captains were appointed as governors to the royal hospitals of Haslar and Plymouth, and lieutenants to those of Deal and Great Yarmouth.

One of the most gallant actions of the war was fought at the commencement of this year in the West Indies. The *Blanche*, a 32-gun 12-pounder frigate, commanded by Captain Robert Faulkner, was cruising in the neighbourhood of Guadaloupe, when she chased a French armed schooner, under a fort within a bay in the island of Desiradé. The schooner brought up with springs to her cables; but, notwithstanding the fire of the fort and some troops on shore, Captain Faulkner cut the schooner out with his boats, and triumphantly carried her off. Manning his prize, he sent her away to an English port, and was next day joined by the *Quebec* frigate, which, however, parted company. On the 4th at daybreak Captain Faulkner discovered the French 32-gun frigate *Pique*, lying at anchor just outside the harbour of Pointe-a-Pètre in Guadaloupe. Finding the French frigate, however, did not appear inclined to come out from under the protection of the batteries, the *Blanche* made sail towards a schooner, which she captured and took in tow. She then stood over for Dominico with her prize. Late in the evening, however, the French frigate was seen about two leagues astern, upon which, Captain Faulkner, casting off the schooner, tacked and made sail to meet her. At a quarter-past twelve the *Blanche* tacked and came up with her. When within musket-shot the enemy wore; Captain Faulkner seeing his intention was to rake him, wore also, when the two frigates closely engaged broadside to broadside. A fierce action now ensued for an hour and a-half, when, as the *Blanche*, shooting ahead, was in the act of luffing up to rake the *Pique*, her main and mizen-masts fell over the side. Directly after this, the *Pique* running foul of the *Blanche* on her larboard quarter, the French made several attempts to board. They were, however, gallantly repulsed by the British crew, and the larboard quarter-deck guns and such of those on the main-deck as could be brought to bear, were fired into the *Pique's* starboard bow, she answering in return with musketry from her tops, as also from some of her quarter-deck guns, which had been run in amidships fore and aft. The bowsprit of the *Pique* passing over the starboard-quarter of the *Blanche*, Captain Faulkner, aided by his second lieutenant and two others of his crew, was in the act of lashing the *Pique's* bowsprit to her capstern, when he was shot by a musket-ball through the heart. Soon after this the lashings broke loose, when the *Pique*, as she was crossing the stern of the *Blanche*, which began to pay off for want of after-sail, again fell on board on the starboard-quarter, her hawser having just before been got on deck, the *Pique's* bowsprit was lashed to the stump of the *Blanche's* mainmast. The first lieutenant, Mr Frederick Watkins, now took command, and kept the *Blanche* before the wind, towing her opponent, while a hot fire was kept up by the British marines on the French seamen who attempted to cut away the second lashing. This was returned from the forecastle and tops of the *Pique*, as well as from the latter's quarter-deck guns pointed forward. The *Blanche* having no stern-ports on the main-deck could only return the fire by two quarter-deck 6-pounders. Lieutenant Watkins accordingly resolved to venture on the somewhat hazardous experiment of blowing away part of the stern to allow a couple of guns to be run out. The firemen were called with their buckets ready to extinguish the flames should they burst out, and two 12-

pounders being pointed astern in the cabin, soon made a clear breach, through which a tremendous fire was opened on the *Pique's* decks. The French frigate had already lost her fore and mizen-mast, and about three hours and a quarter after midnight, her main-mast fell over the side. Thus the *Blanche* continued towing along her antagonist, which, notwithstanding the raking fire to which she was exposed, held out two hours longer; when at length some of the French seamen who had climbed on to the bowsprit cried out that they had struck. Neither of the frigates being able to put a boat in the water, Mr David Milne, the second lieutenant, and ten men, endeavoured to gain the prize by means of a hawser still attached to her. Their weight, however, bringing it down, they were compelled to swim on board. When the *Blanche* commenced the action, she had but 198 men and boys on board; of these, besides her gallant commander, she lost a midshipman, 5 seamen, and I marine killed, and I midshipman, 4 petty officers, and 12 seamen, and 4 marines wounded. The *Pique* had 279 men on board, of whom she lost 76 officers and men killed and 110 wounded, her brave captain, who soon afterwards died from his hurts, being among the number. The *Blanche* measured 710 tons and the *Pique* 906, while the weight of her guns was slightly in excess of that of the victor. The *Pique* was added to the British Navy, and Lieutenants Watkins and Milne were deservedly promoted. About a quarter-of-an-hour after the action had ceased, just after daylight, a 64-gun ship, the *Veteran*, was seen approaching, and the French officers afterwards refused to sign the usual head-money certificate unless the

CAPTURE OF "PIQUE" BY "BLANCHE."—p. 274.

233

Veteran was named as one of their captors, though they afterwards withdrew their objections, which were absurd, considering that though she had seen the flashes of their guns, she had not caught sight of the combatants until the *Pique* was in possession of her captors.

The change which had some time before been proposed in the armament of British ships of war had now taken place, though at first, as has been the case with other improvements, carronades were objected to on various grounds, there were now few ships in the navy without them. A whole class of ships, carrying 44 guns, were armed on the main-deck with 32-pounder carronades, instead of the long 6-pounders which they would otherwise have carried. A considerable increase was also made in the size of ships. The largest launched at this date, the *Ville de Paris*, to carry 110 guns, was somewhat smaller, however, than the French 80-gun ships. Fourteen ships of the line had been commissioned, and ten had been purchased from the East India Company and armed with 54 guns, but, though well fitted for merchantmen, were unsuitable for men-of-war. With one of them, however, one of the most gallant actions on record was fought, about the middle of this year, 1796. The *Glatton*, one of the purchased Indiamen, of 1256 tons, commanded by Captain Henry Trollope, and fitted on the main-deck with 28 carronades, 68-pounders, the rest of her guns being 32-pounders, making altogether 54 guns; but, as the ports were too small to allow the larger guns to traverse properly, and she had no bow or stern chasers, they could only be pointed right abeam. Having been appointed to reinforce the North Sea Fleet, under Admiral Duncan, she proceeded from Sheerness to Yarmouth Roads, whence, on the 14th of July, she was directed to sail to join a squadron of two sail of the line and some frigates, under the command of Captain Savage, of the *Albion* 64, cruising off the Texel. At one in the afternoon of the 16th, being about four or five leagues from Helvaetsluis, Captain Trollope discovered a squadron of ships of war, consisting of six large frigates, a brig, and a cutter. One of these, as far as could be made out, mounted 50 guns, two 36, and the other three 28. He was soon convinced, from the way in which they manoeuvred, and from not answering the private signal, that they were enemies. Not intimidated, however, by their vast superiority, he at once cleared for action, and bore down resolutely to attack them. The strangers on this shortened sail, backing their mizen-topsails, in order to keep their stations. At 10 p.m. Captain Trollope having got alongside of the third ship in the enemy's line, hailed her, and finding that she was French, ordered her commander to strike his colours. Instead of doing so, he immediately fired a broadside, on which the *Glatton* poured into her antagonist, at a distance of thirty yards, such a shower of shot as perhaps no ship had ever before received. Her crew being insufficient to man her guns on both sides, the allotment to each gun was divided into gangs. One of these having loaded and run out the gun, left the most experienced hands to point and fire it, while they ran across and loaded and ran out the gun on the opposite side. The two headmost French ships then tacked, one placing herself alongside to windward, and the other on the *Glatton's* bow, while the other ships engaged her on her lee-quarter and stern. A fierce cannonade was kept up, the *Glatton* engaging on both sides so near, that her yard-arms were nearly touching those of the enemy; the shrieks and cries which arose from them showing the terrible effect of the *Glatton's* shot — though the French commodore, at all events, exhibited no want of courage in the way he fought his ship. Close to leeward was the Brill shoal, on which the van-ship of the French, now tacking, endeavoured to drive the *Glatton*. The French commodore, with whom Captain Trollope had at first engaged, was still on his lee bow, when the pilot exclaimed, that unless the *Glatton* tacked she would be on the Brill. "When the Frenchman strikes the ground, do you put the helm a-lee," was the answer. Directly afterwards the commodore tacked, when, while he was in stays, the *Glatton* poured in a heavy raking fire, and then endeavoured to come about, but so damaged was she in her sails and rigging, that it was not without difficulty she could do so. Notwithstanding that her topmasts and yards were wounded, her crew, when ordered to shorten sail, flew aloft with alacrity, executing their task, in spite of the shot flying round them from the nearest of the Frenchmen able to continue the action. During this interval the *Glatton's* fire had ceased, and one of the French ships stood towards her, in the hopes, probably, of making her their prize, but the British crew hurrying to their guns, soon undeceived them, and compelled their still remaining antagonists to follow their consorts. In attempting to wear after them, Captain Trollope found his masts, rigging, and sails so much injured that all his efforts were ineffectual, or his gallantry would probably have been rewarded by a complete victory. The remainder of the night was spent in strengthening masts and yards, and in bending fresh sails, and by seven o'clock the next morning the ship was in a fit state to renew the action. The enemy were at this time seen steering for Flushing; Captain Trollope continued to follow them till nine o'clock, when, as he had no hopes of being joined by any other ships, and the wind was blowing fresh on shore, he was compelled to haul off and steer for Yarmouth Roads, where he arrived on the 21st. It was afterwards discovered that the French ships had all, more or less, suffered, some of those that had taken the chief part in the action being tremendously knocked about, their decks being ripped up by the *Glatton's* shot; one of them, indeed, sank on reaching Flushing harbour. The largest, with which the *Glutton* was chiefly engaged, was supposed to be the *Brutus*, armed with 46 24-pounders on the main-deck, and several 36-pounders on the quarter-deck and forecastle, while she was fully 300 tons larger than the *Glatton*. Though Captain Trollope might have relied on the weight of metal his ship carried, yet his courage and decision in sailing into the midst of six powerfully-armed opponents is worthy of all admiration, and justly entitled him to the honour of knighthood, which was conferred on him soon afterwards by the king, while the merchants of London presented him with a handsome piece of plate, to show their appreciation of his courage.

In September of this year, the *Amphion* frigate, of 32 guns, commanded by Captain Pellew, lay refitting at Plymouth. Her captain and two other officers were in the cabin at dinner, when a rumbling noise was heard. The captain, followed by his lieutenant, rushed into the quarter-gallery — the instant afterwards the ship blew up; the greater number of persons on board, amounting to nearly 300, perished, they and forty others only escaping with their lives, many of them being severely injured. Great as was the explosion, it had but a trifling effect on the ships near her. Her masts (excepting the mizen-mast) were shivered to pieces and forced out of the ship; four of her main-deck guns were cast upon the deck of the hulk alongside which she lay; and several bodies, pieces of the wreck, etcetera, were thrown as high as her main-topgallant mast-head.

Another gallant action was fought on the 13th of October by the *Terpsichore* frigate, of 32 guns and 215 men, commanded by Captain Richard Bowen. The *Terpsichore* having left thirty men at the hospital, the greater number being still dangerously ill on board, was cruising off Carthagena, when at daylight Captain Bowen discovered a large frigate to windward, apparently in chase of him. Though so near an enemy's port, that even in the event of a victory he could scarcely hope to carry off his prize, trusting to his well-tried crew, he determined to meet the foe. At half-past nine the stranger came within hail, and hauled up on the *Terpsichore's* weather-beam. A fierce action now ensued, and continued on both sides for an hour and twenty minutes, when the enemy's fire began to slacken, and she attempted to make off; but the superior skill of Captain Bowen frustrated the attempt, and in less than twenty minutes compelled her to surrender. When taken possession of she proved to be the *Mahonesa,* a Spanish frigate of 36 guns, besides cohorns and snivels, manned with a crew of 275 men. She was completely disabled, her main-deck guns were rendered entirely useless, the booms having fallen down upon them, while her standing and running rigging was cut to pieces, she having also lost thirty men killed and as many more wounded. The *Terpsichore* had only the boatswain and three seamen wounded. Captain Bowen spoke of the gallant way in which the Spanish captain, Don Thomas Ayaldi, had fought his ship, having held out as long as he had the slightest prospect of victory. Notwithstanding her crippled condition, Captain Bowen succeeded in carrying his prize to Lisbon, but she was considered too much battered to be worth the cost of a thorough repair.

Soon afterwards, Captain Bowen captured a French 36-gun frigate, *La Vestale,* all her masts and her bowsprit being knocked away, and a large proportion of her crew killed and wounded. Being close to the shoals that lie between Cape Trafalgar and Cadiz, the prize, with the *Terpsichore's* master, one midshipman, and seven seamen, it having been impossible to remove the French crew, drifted towards the shore, where the master at length brought her up, and during the darkness the *Terpsichore* lost sight of her prize. While attempting to tow her off the next day, the towrope got foul of a rock and was cut. Soon after this the Frenchmen rose on the prize-crew and again anchored close inshore. The next morning, when Captain Bowen stood in to look for her, he had the mortification to see her standing in to Cadiz, some Spanish boats having come off and taken possession of her. *La Vestale* was, however, captured in the year 1799 by the gallant Captain Cunningham, of the *Clyde.*

Passing over many interesting events, we come to one which cannot be omitted in the history of the British Navy. English seamen had long undoubtedly been subjected to much ill-treatment. A large proportion of a ship's company consisted of pressed men, compelled to serve against their will. They were often harshly treated by their officers; they were badly fed, and but poorly paid, and often punished; while their necessaries were embezzled, and they were cheated in a variety of ways. Towards the end of February, 1797, while Lord Howe was on shore, several petitions were sent up from the seamen at Portsmouth, asking for an advance of wages. They were forwarded to Earl Spencer, First Lord of the Admiralty, but as they were looked upon as forgeries, no notice was taken of them. Lord Howe being unable from sickness to go afloat, Lord Bridport took command of the fleet, when the seamen, supposing their complaints to be disregarded, refused to put to sea. On the 17th of March, every man in the fleet having sworn to support the cause, the mutiny broke out. Ropes were reeved at the foreyard-arms of the *Queen Charlotte*, and the mutineers were about to hang the first lieutenant of the ship, when Lord Bridport saved him. They, however, turned all the officers out of the fleet who had behaved in any way to offend them. Two delegates were appointed from each ship to represent the whole fleet, and the admiral's cabin in the *Queen Charlotte* was fixed upon as the place for their deliberations. On the 21st Admirals Gardner, Colpoys, and Pole went on board the *Queen Charlotte* in order to confer with the delegates. These men assured the admirals that no arrangement would be considered as satisfactory till it should be sanctioned by the king and parliament, and guaranteed by a proclamation for a general pardon. So irritated did Admiral Gardner become on hearing this, that he seized one of the delegates and swore that he would have them all hanged with every fifth man throughout the fleet. This so exasperated the crew that it was with difficulty Admiral Gardner escaped with his life from the ship. The red or bloody flag was now seen flying from the *Royal George*, and that of Lord Bridport was struck. The mutineers also loaded all the guns, keeping a watch the same as at sea; every officer being detained on board his respective ship. In a few days, however, the seamen, hearing that their petitions were likely to be attended to, returned to their duty. Admiral Bridport rehoisted his flag on board the *Royal George*, and informed the seamen that he had brought with him the redress of their grievances and his majesty's pardon for the offenders. It was now hoped that all matters in dispute were settled; but the seamen, fancying that notwithstanding the admiral's assurances, they were to be neglected, again refused when ordered to weigh anchor. Admiral Golpoys, on this, ordered the marines to prevent the delegates from coming on board. The latter attempted to force their way, when the marines fired, and five seamen were killed and one of their officers wounded. On this the crew of the *London* turned the guns in the fore-part of the ship aft, and threatened to blow the officers, and all who stood by them, into the water. Seeing that resistance was hopeless, the officers surrendered, and the admiral and captain were confined in their cabins. Happily, on the 8th of May, a resolution of the House of Commons was passed, and the king's free pardon being communicated to the seamen, they became satisfied, the red flag was struck, the officers were reinstated in their commands, and the whole fleet put to sea the next day to look out for the enemy. Lord Bridport had been ordered to keep at sea as much as possible, and only to return when necessary to refit or revictual. This plan succeeded, and the seamen generally obeyed their officers and conducted themselves properly.

At Plymouth the ships' companies exhibited a mutinous disposition, but, after a time, they accepted the terms offered to the seamen at Portsmouth, and tranquillity was restored.

While these things were occurring at home, Sir John Jervis, with about 15 sail of the line, 4 frigates, 2 sloops of war, and a cutter, after putting into the Tagus, was cruising off Cape Saint Vincent. While there, a Spanish fleet of 25 sail of the line, 11 frigates, and a brig, came through the Straits of Gibraltar, bound for Cadiz. On the 14th of February, before dawn, a Portuguese frigate brought intelligence to the admiral that a Spanish fleet was about five leagues to windward. The English fleet was formed in two compact divisions; in one of them was the *Captain*, with the broad pendant of Horatio Nelson. It appeared that the Spaniards had at first supposed that the fleet in sight was part of a convoy. Some days before an American, which had passed through the British fleet before Admiral Sir Hyde Parker had joined with five ships of the line, while another, the *Culloden*, was absent in chase, had given the information that the English admiral had only nine sail of the line. The morning broke dark and hazy, and the Spaniards obtaining but a partial view of the British fleet, were fully confirmed in their mistake, and believed that they should surround the whole British squadron and carry them in triumph into Cadiz. Notwithstanding the more just estimate that Sir John Jervis had of his opponents, he lost no time in endeavouring to bring them to action. The main body of the Spanish fleet came down under all sail, with the wind on the starboard-quarter, while the ships to leeward, close-hauled on the same tack, were endeavouring to join them there. Admiral Jervis formed his line close-hauled on the starboard tack, steering straight for the opening between the two divisions of the Spanish fleet. The *Culloden*, the leading ship, commanded by Captain Troubridge, had the honour of commencing the battle about half-past eleven; the other British ships following, effectually cut off a part of the Spanish fleet from the main body, and compelled them to form on the larboard tack, with the intention of passing through or to leeward of the British line; but they were met with so warm a reception from the centre of the British that they were obliged to tack, and were unable again to get into action till towards the close of the day. Admiral Jervis now devoted all his attention to the main body of the enemy's fleet to windward, which was reduced at this time, by the separation of the ships to leeward, to eighteen sail of the line. A little after twelve o'clock the signal was made for the British fleet to tack in succession, and soon after the signal for again passing the enemy's line; while the Spanish admiral's design appeared to be to join the ships to leeward by wearing round to the rear of the British line. The intention of the enemy was, however, soon perceived by Commodore Nelson, who, being in the rear, had an opportunity of observing this manoeuvre. In order to frustrate the design, he had no sooner passed the Spanish rear than he wore and stood on the other tack towards the enemy. In executing this bold and decisive manoeuvre, the commodore found himself alongside of the Spanish admiral in the *Santissima Trinidad*, of 136 guns. Notwithstanding this immense disparity, Nelson was not the man to shrink from the contest, though the Spaniard was ably supported by her two seconds ahead and astern, each of which was a three-decker. While Nelson sustained this unequal conflict, Troubridge in the *Culloden*, and Captain Frederick in the *Blenheim*, were coming to his assistance. Sir John Jervis had ordered Captain Collingwood in the *Excellent* to bear up, while he passed to leeward of the rearmost ships of the enemy. As he did so, he gave the *San Ysidro* so effectual a broadside that she was compelled to submit. Captain Collingwood then passed on to the relief of Nelson, but before he arrived, the Spaniard's mizen-mast fell overboard and she got entangled with her second, the *San Nicolas*, a ship of guns. On this, Nelson determined to board the *San Nicolas*, and the *Captain* was so judiciously placed by Captain Miller, her commander, that he laid her aboard on the starboard-quarter of the Spanish 84, her spritsail-yard passing over the enemy's poop, and hooking in her mizen-shrouds. Nothing can surpass Nelson's own description of what now took place. Calling for the boarders, he ordered them on board: — "The soldiers of the 69th regiment, with an alacrity which will ever do them credit, and Lieutenant Pearson of the same regiment, were almost the foremost on this service. The first man who jumped into the enemy's mizen-chains was Captain Berry, late my first lieutenant (Captain Miller was in the very act of going also, but I directed him to remain). A soldier of the 69th regiment having broken the upper-quarter-gallery window, jumped in, followed by myself and others as fast as possible. I found the cabin doors fastened, and some Spanish officers fired their pistols at us through the windows; but having burst open the doors, the soldiers fired, and the Spanish brigadier (or commodore) fell as he was retreating to the quarter-deck. I found Captain Berry in possession of the poop, and the Spanish ensign hauling down. I passed with my people and Lieutenant Pearson along the larboard gangway to the forecastle, where I met several Spanish officers prisoners to my seamen, and they delivered me their swords. At this moment, a fire of pistols or muskets opening from the admiral's stern-gallery in the *San Josef*, I directed the soldiers to fire into her stern. Our seamen by this time were in full possession of every part of the ship. About seven of my men were killed, and some few wounded, and about twenty Spaniards. Having placed sentinels at the different ladders, and calling to Captain Miller, ordering him to send more men into the *San Nicolas*, I directed my brave fellows to board the first-rate, the *San Josef*, which was done in an instant, Captain Berry assisting me into the main-chains.

"At this moment a Spanish officer looked over the quarter-deck rail, and said they surrendered. From this most welcome intelligence, it was not long before I was on the quarter-deck, when the Spanish captain, with bended knee, presented me his sword, and told me the admiral was dying of his wounds below. I asked him on his honour if the ship had surrendered. He declared she had; on which I gave him my hand, and desired him to call his officers and ship's company and tell them of it, which he did; and on the quarter-deck of a Spanish first-rate, extravagant as the story may seem, did I receive the swords of vanquished Spaniards, which, as I received, I gave to William Fearney, one of my barge-men, who tucked them, with the greatest *sangfroid*, under his arm."

Immediately on Nelson's return on board the *Captain*, he made the signal for boats to assist in disengaging her from the prizes, and as she was rendered incapable of further service until refitted, he hoisted his pennant for the moment on board the *Minerve* frigate. In the meantime Admiral Jervis ordered the *Victory* to be placed on the lee-quarter of the rearmost ship of the enemy, the *Salvador del Mundo*, and threw in so effectual a broadside that the Spanish commander, seeing the *Barfleur* bear down to second the *Victory*, struck his flag. He was very nearly capturing the *Santissana Trinidad*, but the rest of the Spanish fleet, hitherto uninjured, coming down, he found it necessary to secure his prizes and bring to. All these ships did was to open an ineffectual fire, and then to sail away, leaving the British to carry off their prizes in triumph. The English ships lost in killed and wounded only 300 men, while on board the ships captured the Spanish killed and wounded amounted to 697. Just honours were showered on the victorious admirals and captains; Sir John Jervis was created a peer of Great Britain, under the titles of Baron Jervis of Meaford and Earl Saint Vincent; and among others, Commodore Nelson, who had just before been made a vice-admiral, received the insignia of the Bath.

It had been believed that the mutinous spirit of the seamen had been quelled by the concessions made to them, but such, it was soon found, was not the case. On the 20th of May most of the ships lying at the Nore, and nearly all of those belonging to the North Sea Fleet, hoisted the red flag. The mutineers at Sheerness, like those at Spithead, had chosen two delegates from every ship, and had appointed as a president over them a man of the name of Richard Parker; while on board each ship was a committee of twelve men, who decided on all the affairs relative to its internal management. They declared themselves dissatisfied with the terms accepted by the seamen of Portsmouth, and demanded a more just division of prize-money, more regular and frequent payment of wages, and also permission to go on shore when in port, with several other conditions. This statement they required Vice-Admiral Buckner, whose flag was flying on board the *Sandwich*, of 90 guns, to transmit without delay to the Admiralty, and they declared that only when its conditions were complied with would they return to their duty. So bold did they become that they went on shore without interruption, parading Sheerness with music and flags, inviting the crews of other ships to join them; while they had their headquarters in a public-house, above which a red flag was hoisted. To put a stop to this, some regiments were sent for, when they thought it prudent to keep to their ships. All communication with the shore being stopped, the mutineers supplied themselves with water and provisions from the merchant-vessels which they brought to, while they allowed none to proceed up to London, completely blockading the port. Throughout the whole of the mutiny the seamen behaved respectfully to their superior officers, while the strictest discipline was kept up on board all the ships. On the king's birthday the seamen even exhibited their loyalty by firing a grand salute from all the ships, which were decorated in the manner usual on festive occasions.

Conciliatory measures for inducing the seamen to return to their duty were tried in vain. The Government, however, would not yield to any of their demands, and the seamen on board most of the ships at length finding their cause hopeless, hauled down the red flag. Some had previously made their escape from their midst. Ultimately, the crew of the *Sandwich* carried their ship under the guns of Sheerness, when a guard of soldiers coming on board, Parker, their ringleader, was delivered up. He, with the chief culprits, was tried, convicted, and executed; others were flogged through the fleet, and many were imprisoned for certain periods, a general pardon being granted to the seamen who had been misled by them.

Wide as was the spread of the mutiny, whole ships' companies remained true to their colours. Among these crews who remained loyal, that of the *Saint Fiorenzo* deserves especially to be mentioned, and an account written by the late Admiral Mitford, who was then a midshipman on board her, cannot fail to prove interesting. "She was," says Admiral Mitford, "the favourite frigate of his majesty George the Third, who, from his courtesy and kind manner towards the ship's company, had endeared himself to them. This may in some degree account for the loyalty of the men, strengthened by their unbounded attachment to one of the most humane, brave, and zealous commanders that ever walked a deck — one to whom every man looked up as a father, the late Admiral Sir Harry Burrard Neale. A better lesson cannot be given to a young officer to show that by kindness and firmness that desirable object may be attained which was so eminently proved during one of the most eventful periods of this country. The *Saint Fiorenzo* was at Spithead when the first mutiny broke out, and the red flag was hoisted on board the *Queen Charlotte*. The day before that event the men came and informed Sir Harry of what was to take place, but that he might rely on their loyalty, and as far as was consistent with prudence, that they would obey every order from the officers, to which resolution they most scrupulously adhered. While such was the state of affairs, the *Saint Fiorenzo* having received orders to proceed to Sheerness for the purpose of fitting out to carry over the Princess Royal, then Duchess of Hesse-Homburg, to Cuxhaven, after her marriage, the mutineers allowed her to sail without attempting to stop her. Their demands having been acceded to by the Government, the men, just as we were sailing, returned to their duty. Notwithstanding the loyalty of our crew, two of the delegates, thoroughly trustworthy men, had been chosen, with Sir Harry's permission, who regularly brought him all the information they could obtain. On our arrival at Sheerness, we found the red flag still flying on board the

Sandwich guard-ship, and supposing that her crew had not been informed of what had taken place at Spithead, our delegates went on board to explain, and were surprised and disgusted to find that fresh demands had been made by the North Sea Fleet, and of so frivolous a nature, that from some remarks made by our men, perhaps not very courteous, their zeal in the cause was suspected, and consequently the mutineers were very jealous of our crew. On returning on board, our delegates immediately communicated with the *Clyde*, an old fellow-cruiser, commanded by Captain Cunningham, who also enjoying the confidence of his ship's company, an agreement took place between the respective captains and their crews, that should the disaffection of the mutineers continue, they would leave them and run under cover of the forts at Sheerness. I should say that I believe a very small proportion of the men were disaffected, and, as on most public outbreaks, the majority were dictated to by a few desperate and disappointed men. Parker had been shipmate with a considerable number of the *Saint Fiorenzo's* crew, and they had a great contempt for him. He had been acting-lieutenant in some ship with them, and was dismissed for drunkenness. If a little energy had been used on some of the opportunities that offered, the whole affair might have been quashed.

"Having got leave to go on shore from the delegates of our ship, I landed and passed through the dockyard, followed by the whole of the delegates of the fleet, Parker and Davis walking together in procession. When outside the gates, they saw the Lancashire fencibles coming to strengthen the garrison, to whom they offered every insult they could devise. On this the officer in command halted his men, and coming up to the admiral and commissioner, who were standing opposite the gates, asked, so I understood him, whether he might be permitted to surround the delegates, complaining of the insults offered to himself and his men. On this I involuntarily exclaimed, 'Now's the time;' when the admiral asked me what I meant, and how I dared to speak? I said, 'These are all the delegates,' pointing out to them Parker and Davis and others. The fellows overheard me, and I have no doubt I became a marked man. I may congratulate myself on the event which carried us away from the fleet, otherwise I might have suffered what others did, and been yard-armed, tarred, and feathered; but I feel justified in saying that, had my suggestion been acted upon, there would have been an end of the mutiny at the Nore. Returning on board I found that every arrangement had been made, and the *Clyde* being the inshore ship, was to move first, which she did, and ran under the batteries; when, either from incompetency or fear, our pilot refused to take charge of the ship, and the tide being on the turn to ebb, Sir Harry Neale thought it advisable to wait for a more favourable opportunity. In the meantime we were visited by the delegates of some of the leading ships, who abused our crew for permitting the *Clyde* to escape without our firing upon her. So incensed did the men become at this, that one of the quartermasters, John Ainslie, came aft, and asked the first lieutenant whether they might not throw the blackguards overboard, which, I doubt not, a nod of assent would have effected.

"The mutineers now gave orders to our crew to place the frigate between the *Inflexible* and *Director*, to send our gunpowder on board the *Sandwich*, Admiral Parker as he was called, and to unbend our sails, with which orders our people agreed to comply. Sir Harry was immediately acquainted with the circumstances, and he at once arranged that the ship, instead of doing so, should run into Sheerness. When all was prepared, with springs to our cables to cast inshore, and we were ready to cut, in heaving the spring broke, and we cast outward. Sir Harry, whose presence of mind never forsook him, on this directed the quartermaster to take the command and he would dictate to him. All was sheeted home in a moment, and we stood in between the two line-of-battle ships, which had their guns double-shotted, their crews being all ready with lanyards in hand to fire upon us. The ship by that time had got good way, when Sir Harry gave the order to let fly all the sheets, which took the mutineers by surprise, and supposing that the ship was coming to an anchor, they did not fire. Sir Harry then ordered the helm to be put hard a-port, which caused the ship to shoot ahead of the *Inflexible*. He now came on deck and took the command, crying out to the ship's company, 'Well done, my lads!' when a loud murmur of applause was heard fore and aft; but we had no time to cheer. 'Now, clear away the bulkheads, and mount the guns,' he cried. By this time the whole fleet of 82 sail had opened their fire upon us. The shot fell like hail, but, whether intentionally or not, few struck our hull. It was reported that the *Director* fired blank cartridges or she might have done us more injury; but I believe that her crew, struck with awe at the idea of firing on their countrymen, and also with admiration of their bravery, fired wide. In little more than two hours the bulkheads were cleared away from the cabin door to the break of the quarter-deck, the whole space having been fitted up with cabins for the suite of her royal highness, the guns on both sides being also down in the hold. The guns were mounted and we were ready for action. The men now came aft and begged that, should the mutineers come after them, they might go down with the ship rather than return to the fleet at the Nore. Our master, although a good pilot, did not feel himself justified in taking charge of the ship within the boundaries of a branch pilot. We were therefore on the look-out for a pilot-vessel, when a lugger was discovered on the lee bow, and we were on the point of bearing down on her, when we saw the North Sea Fleet coming with the red flag flying, having left their station in a state of mutiny, the admiral and all the officers being under arrest. A frigate bore down to us, when Sir Harry gave the speaking-trumpet to the quartermaster Stanley, and when she hailed as to what we were doing there, he replied that we were looking out to stop the ships with provisions for the fleet. She then proceeded, and joined the fleet again, and we made sail after the lugger. The necessary signals were made, but not being answered, we gave chase, and, after a run of four hours, captured the *Castor and Pollux*, a French vessel of 16 guns. We were proceeding to Portsmouth with our prize, when she, being to windward, spoke a brig, who informed us that the mutiny had again broken out at Spithead. Sir Harry on this thought it prudent to anchor under Dungeness until he could communicate with the Admiralty. During the night, as we lay there, a ship was seen bearing down towards us, which, however, answered the private signals; but that could not be depended upon, as it was probable that the mutineers would have possessed themselves of them. We accordingly beat to quarters. The men again repeated their request to sink rather than surrender to the mutineers. The stranger appeared high out of the water, and we could not be certain whether she might not be a line-of-battle ship. The wind being very light, she closed slowly. The suspense was awful. The springs were hove on to keep our broadside to bear. Sir Harry hailed, and her answer was, 'The *Hussar* frigate, Lord Garlies, from the West Indies.' Having come from a long voyage, her appearance was accounted for. Seeing the lights at all our port-holes, those on board the frigate could not understand the necessity of such extreme precautions, being, of course, ignorant of the mutiny. When her men wore acquainted with our situation, they were so struck with the bravery and determination of the *Saint Fiorenzo's* ship's company that they immediately said, should any ship be sent to bring us back, they would share our fate. None, however, came, and in a few days we heard that the mutiny was at an end, and we sailed, I think, for

Plymouth, and another ship was ordered to take over the Princess of Hesse-Homburg."

By the daring and determination of another captain, Sir Henry Trollope, he prevented his ship's company from joining the mutineers. He had been removed from the *Glutton* to the *Russell*, 74, one of the North Sea Fleet, which lay in Yarmouth Roads. On hearing that his crew were about to join the mutineers, he came to the resolution of compelling them, by a proceeding of the most desperate character, to obey his orders. Providing himself with provisions and water, a compass and a chart, and a brace of pistols, he secretly entered the powder-magazine. Besides the door at the entrance, there was a grate, through which he could look into the outer apartment. Seating himself with his pistols in his hand, he sent for the delegates, and ordered them at once to get the ship under way, to carry her out to sea. "You know me, my lads," he said, calmly; "we have been ordered to proceed to the Texel, and these orders must be obeyed. Sooner than have her name disgraced, I will blow her and all on board up into the air. Return on deck and attend to your duty."

CAPTAIN SIR HENRY TROLLOPE AND THE MUTINEERS.—p. 291.

The mutineers looked aghast, but they knew their captain, and of what he was capable, too well to disobey him. They could not have

247

molested him, even had they dared. The crew, obeying their officers, while the captain sat far below in the magazine, their guiding spirit, got the ship under way, and stood out to sea — the rest of the ships, either not aware of what she was about, or not venturing to interfere with her. In a short time she joined Admiral Duncan, who, with his flag flying on board the *Venerable*, was blockading the Texel. He had been left with only his own ship and the *Adamant*, keeping in check a Dutch fleet of 15 sail of the line, under Admiral de Winter. In order to prevent the Dutch from coming out, Admiral Duncan made use of a ruse, frequently repeating signals, as if communicating with the main body of his fleet in the offing. At length he was joined by other line-of-battle ships, but his fleet, severely battered by bad weather, and being short of provisions, had to put back into Yarmouth Roads, while Captain Trollope remained with a small squadron to watch the enemy. He continued there till the 9th of October, when information was brought that the Dutch fleet was at sea. He immediately sailed, and having looked into the Texel, on the 11th the *Russell* and other ships were seen with the signal flying at their mast-heads that the enemy was in sight to leeward. The Dutch fleet stood away, however, towards the coast of Suffolk, when, finding that the English admiral was within seven leagues of him, he sailed back towards Camperdown, followed by the English look-out frigates. De Winter now formed a close line of battle, and resolutely awaited Admiral Duncan. The British fleet on this bore down on the enemy, with the signal flying for close action. The *Monarch*, leading the larboard division of the British fleet, first cut the Dutch line, pouring in well-directed broadsides on the ships on either side of her. The action soon became general; one after the other the Dutch ships were compelled to strike. One of them, the *Hercules*, catching fire, the crew threw overboard their powder, and were therefore obliged to surrender their ship. The Dutch admiral's ship, the *Vryheid*, held out gallantly to the last, but was at length compelled to yield, when the rest of the ships which had not yet struck their colours, did their best to make off. By this time the English were in possession of two seventy-fours, five sixty-fours, two fifties, and two frigates. The escaping enemy could not be pursued, for the land was close aboard, and the fleet in nine fathoms water. All the victors could do, therefore, was to secure their prizes, and to endeavour to get clear of the shore before nightfall. The Dutchmen had fought gallantly, aiming at the hulls of the British ships, which were fearfully shattered, and in all of them numerous shots were found sticking; though the masts and rigging were but comparatively little injured. The English lost 228 killed and 812 wounded, including many officers, and the Dutch 540 killed and 620 wounded. Of the whole Dutch fleet seven only escaped, and five of these were afterwards captured. With regard to the number of their guns, the two fleets were almost equal — the English ships carrying altogether 1150 guns, and the Dutch 1034; besides which, the latter had some corvettes and brigs which took part in the action, and greatly annoyed their opponents, though their guns were not counted. The victory of Camperdown was gained by the very men who had taken part in the mutiny. On the news reaching England, all those still under sentence were pardoned.

During this year occurred the unfortunate attack on Santa Cruz, in the island of Teneriffe, when, in attempting to land on the mole, Nelson lost an arm, and the gallant Captain Bowen, with several lieutenants, was killed, many of the boats being sunk and their crews perishing.

In the year 1798 the French made three attempts to land armies in Ireland, but on each occasion their fleets were driven back, and many of their ships were captured. A previous attempt had been made in 1796, when they were scattered and discomfited by the weather. The second succeeded in landing a body of troops; the greater number were killed, and the survivors were made prisoners. In the third, the *Hoche*, under the command of Commodore Bompart, was captured, as were several frigates of his squadron; while the fourth, finding the warm reception the troops would meet with should they attempt to land, put back into port.

At this time there were no less than 30,000 French prisoners in England, and by an agreement with their own government, which was to support them, it was arranged they should reside at Portsmouth, Plymouth, Norman Cross, Liverpool, Edinburgh, Chatham, and Stapleton. Arrangements were made towards the end of the war for the exchange of prisoners, but it was found that there were only 2800 English in France. The French Directory now issued a decree declaring that all persons natives of, or originally belonging to, neutral countries, or countries in alliance with France, serving on board any English ship, should be tried as pirates. The English Government, in retaliation, threatened to treat all subjects of the French Republic in the same manner, should the savage order be carried out. This threat had the desired effect.

Bonaparte had been for some time planning a campaign in Egypt. Sailing with a large fleet from Toulon, he first captured Malta, and then proceeded to Alexandria, wonderfully escaping Earl Saint Vincent and Vice-Admiral Sir Horatio Nelson. Napoleon having landed, his fleet, under Admiral Brueys, brought up in Aboukir Bay. Here Nelson found the French on the 8th of August, drawn up at anchor in order of battle, and at 3 p.m. he threw out the signal to prepare for the fight, followed an hour afterwards with orders to anchor by the stern with springs to their cables. Another signal was shortly afterwards made to signify that the admiral meant to attack the enemy's van and centre. At 6 p.m. Nelson signalised to the fleet to fill and stand on, which they did in admirable order, the *Goliath* leading; when, soon afterwards hoisting their colours, with the Union Jack in several parts of the rigging, the British ships took up the stations allotted to them. At 6:20 p.m. the *Conquirant*, followed by the *Guerrier*, opened her fire upon the *Goliath* and *Zealous*, which was quickly answered by those ships; but the sun had already sunk into the ocean before any other British ship had fired a shot. Loud cheers now burst from every ship of the English fleet, when the men, flying to their guns, opened their broadsides with a spirit which soon knocked away the masts and spars of their opponents, and spread death and destruction on board their ships. The action had continued for two hours, several French ships having struck, when a fire was perceived on board the *Orient*, which in an hour afterwards blew up with a tremendous explosion, the burning wreck falling far and wide around, and setting fire to several ships, friends and foes, in the neighbourhood. So awful was the effect, that for ten minutes not a gun was fired on either side. Thus the battle raged all night long, till soon after dawn the French frigate *Artemise*, after striking her colours, also caught fire, and with a terrific explosion blew up.

In the morning the enemy's ships still in a condition to make sail got under way and endeavoured to escape. Of the thirteen French ships of the line, by this time, one had blown up, eight had surrendered, and two had escaped. Of the remaining two, one, the *Timoléon*, was on shore, with her colours flying; the other, the *Tonnant*, lay about two miles from her, a mere wreck, but also with her colours up. On the approach, however, of the *Theseus* and *Leander*, she hauled them down; while the crew of the *Timoléon* set her on fire, and she soon afterwards blew up. Thus, in the memorable "Battle of the Nile," the French lost eleven line-of-battle ships, besides frigates. In this action the British lost 218 killed and 678 wounded. Among the latter was Horatio Nelson, who was struck above his already darkened eye by a splinter; while all the ships were considerably cut up. On board the *Orient* fell the Commodore Casa Bianca, as well as his gallant young son, who had refused to quit his post; and the French commander-in-chief, Brueys, who, after receiving two severe wounds, was nearly cut in two by a shot. While still breathing, he desired not to be carried below, but to be left to die upon deck, exclaiming in a firm voice, "Un amiral Français doit mourir sur son banc de quart."

"A French admiral ought to die on his quarter-deck."

While the ship was in flames, the boats of the British ships put off to save the hapless crew, seventy of whom were thus rescued. The heroic conduct of the captain of the *Tonnant*, Du Petit Thonars, deserves to be recorded. He first lost both his arms, and then one of his legs; even then, still able to speak, he gave his dying commands to his crew not to surrender the ship. Of the English fleet, the *Culloden* unhappily got on shore while going into action, and only by great exertions did she get off, after the battle was over. That the French fought with the utmost gallantry is acknowledged by all, while we must rank the victory of the Nile among the most brilliant achievements of the British Navy.

After the battle every effort was made to repair the damages the ships had received, and to fit the prizes for the voyage to England. Nelson sent the prisoners taken on board them on shore in a cartel, on their parole not to serve again during the war; but Napoleon, with his usual disregard for treaties, formed them into a battalion, which he called the "nautic." Three of the prizes, being in too shattered a condition to be refitted, were burnt; another, the *Peuple-Souverain*, being considered unfit to proceed farther than Gibraltar, was there turned into a guard-ship. The five remaining vessels arrived safely at Plymouth; three of them being new and magnificent ships, the *Tonnant, Franklin*, and *Spartiate*, were added to the British Navy, the name of the former being changed to *Canopus*. Rewards were liberally bestowed upon the victors; Sir Horatio Nelson was created a peer of Great Britain by the title of Baron Nelson of the Nile and of Burnham Thorpe, while a pension was settled on him of 2000 pounds a-year by the English Parliament, and 1000 pounds a-year by the Irish; the East India Company presenting him with 10,000 pounds.

After the defeat of his fleet at Aboukir, Napoleon determined to invade Syria. His plans, however, were thwarted by Sir Sidney Smith, who having captured the fleet which was bringing the battering-cannon and ammunition from Damietta for the siege of Saint Jean d'Acre, made use of it to fortify that town, into which, with a small body of seamen and a few officers, he threw himself, and put it into a state of defence, while he organised the Turkish troops who formed its garrison. Napoleon, obtaining fresh guns, in a short time laid siege to Acre. Though he made several desperate attempts to storm it, they were on each occasion repulsed by the valour of the Turks, aided by the fire from the English and sultan's ships. During one of the many engagements the *Theseus* frigate caught fire, and the poop and after-part of the ship was almost blown to pieces, several of her officers and men being killed. The fire was put out by the courage of the surviving officers and crew.

Napoleon, enraged at his defeat, made every effort to destroy Sir Sidney Smith. Two attempts to assassinate him, however, happily failed. At length an Arab dervish appeared with a letter to the pacha, proposing a cessation of arms for the purpose of burying the dead bodies, which in vast numbers were piled up under the ramparts. While this proposal was under consideration, with unexampled treachery, Napoleon attempted to storm the town; but the garrison were on the alert, and the assailants were driven back with great slaughter. The Arab tribes having been induced to cut off the supply of provisions for the French army, on the 20th of May Napoleon raised the siege, and leaving his guns behind him, precipitately retreated towards Egypt. Such is a brief outline of one of the most daring exploits ever performed by a naval man.

Of a very different character, though one in which consummate bravery was displayed, was the cutting-out of the *Hermione* frigate. She had been in the year 1799 under the command of Captain Hugh Pigot, one of those tyrant commanders who are truly said to make their ships "hells afloat." While cruising off Porto Rico, as the crew were reefing top-sails, the captain shouted that he would flog the last man off the mizen-topsail yard. Two, in their attempt to spring over their comrades' backs, missing their hold, fell on the quarter-deck and were killed. The captain, it is said, on seeing it, merely observed, "Throw the lubbers overboard." The crew, who were probably a bad lot to begin with, for such a captain could not have obtained a good ship's company, from a long succession of tyrannical acts, had become infinitely worse. The next day they rose on their officers, murdered the greater number, including the captain, and carried the ship into La Guayra, a port of the Spanish Main. Hearing that the *Hermione*, which had been fitted out by the Spaniards and strongly armed, was lying in the harbour of Puerto Cabello, Captain Hamilton, commanding the *Surprise*, a 28-gun frigate, determined to cut her out. Coming off the port on the 21st of October, he discovered her moored head and stern between two strong batteries on either side of the harbour, with her sails bent and ready for sea. After waiting off the port till the 24th without mentioning his intentions, he addressed his crew, reminding them of many enterprises they had undertaken, and pointing out to them that unless they should at once attempt the capture of the frigate, some more fortunate vessel would carry off the prize. Three hearty cheers showed him that he might depend on his crew. "I shall lead you myself," he added. "Here are the orders for the six boats to be employed, with the names of the officers and men to be engaged on the service."

CUTTING OUT THE "HERMIONE."

Every arrangement had been judiciously made. The crew were to be dressed in blue; the password was Britannia, the answer Ireland. The boarders were to take the first spell at the oars; then, as they neared the *Hermione*, they were to be relieved by the regular crews. The expe-

253

dition was to proceed in two divisions, the one to board on the starboard, the other on the larboard bow, gangway, and quarter. Sharp axes were provided for those who were to cut the bower cable, while others were told off to cut the stern cable, and certain men were to go aloft to loose the sails. In the event of their reaching the ship undiscovered, the boarders only were to board, while the boats' crews were to take the ship in tow directly the cables were cut; but should they be discovered, the crews of each boat were to board and all aid in the enterprise. The rendezvous was to be on the *Hermione's* quarter-deck. At half-past seven the boats were hoisted out, the crews mustered, and away they pulled from the *Surprise*. As it happened, within a mile of the *Hermione* the expedition was discovered by two gunboats, and the alarm being given, firing commenced. Captain Hamilton on this pushed for the frigate, believing that all his boats would do the same, but some, misunderstanding his orders, engaged the gunboats. On approaching, lights were seen at every port, with the ship's company at quarters. Captain Hamilton pushed for the bows, and climbing up, his foot slipped and his pistol went off; but he soon succeeded in gaining a footing on the forecastle, and those who had been ordered to loose the sails immediately got the foresail ready for bending and hauling out to the yard-arms, thus forming a screen to themselves, for not a Spaniard was there to interfere with them. On looking down from the forecastle, they saw the crew of the *Hermione* at quarters on the main-deck, firing away into the darkness, utterly unconscious that the enemy were on board. Captain Hamilton, with the gunner and fourteen men, now made his way to the quarter-deck — part of them, however, under the gunner, being driven back by the Spaniards, who gained possession of the forecastle. Another party of English also neglecting to rendezvous on the quarter-deck, the captain was left for some minutes to defend himself against the attack of four Spaniards, one of whom stunned him, when he fell. Happily, some of his men came to the rescue, and a party of marines climbing over the larboard gangway, now gave a favourable turn to affairs. The rest of the boats coming up, the marines formed, fired a volley, and ran down with fixed bayonets on the main-deck. About sixty Spaniards retreated to the cabin, and surrendered. For some time, however, fighting continued on the main-deck and under the forecastle. The cables were cut, the sails were loosed, while the gunner and two men, though severely wounded, standing at the helm, the boats took the frigate in tow, and she stood out of Puerto Cabello. The batteries immediately opened, and a Portuguese reported that he heard the Spanish prisoners threatening to blow up the frigate. A few muskets fired down the hatchway restored order, and in less than an hour after Captain Hamilton was on board, all opposition had ceased, and the *Hermione* was his prize. By 2 p.m. the ship was out of gunshot of the batteries, the towing-boats were called alongside, and her crews came on board. In this wonderful enterprise the British had only 12 wounded, while the Spaniards, out of a crew of 365, lost 119 killed and 97 wounded, most of them dangerously. The cutting-out of the *Hermione* may well be considered one of the most desperate services ever performed, and no man was ever more deserving of the knighthood he received than Captain Hamilton, who had planned every detail, and personally led the bold attack. He himself was among the most severely wounded; besides a blow on his head, he received a sabre wound on the left thigh, another by a pike in his right thigh, and a contusion on the shin-bone by grape-shot; one of his fingers was badly cut, and he was also much bruised.

For some time previously to this, detectives, if they may be so-called, were stationed at each of the ports to discover the members of the crew who had been on board the *Hermione* at the time of the mutiny. No mercy was shown to those who had taken part in it. A large number were hung; it used to be said, indeed, that more suffered than actually then belonged to her, though they might have done so at some former period.

Sir Edward Hamilton long lived to enjoy his honours.

The days when fabulous amounts of prize-money were to be picked up had not yet passed by, although the rich Spanish galleons which went to sea in the times of Drake were seldom to be found. In October of this year, 1799, fortune smiled on the officers and ships' companies of two British frigates. The *Naiad*, of 38 guns, Captain Pierrepoint, while cruising in latitude 44 degrees 1 minute north, and longitude 12 degrees 35 minutes west, came in sight of two frigates, to which, notwithstanding the disparity of force, he gave chase. They proved to be the Spanish 34-gun frigates *Santa Brigida* and *Thetis*, from Vera Cruz, bound to Spain. He followed them all night, when, early in the morning of the 16th, another ship was seen in the south-west, which hoisting her number showed herself to be the 38-gun frigate *Ethalion*, Captain James Young; and soon afterwards two other 32-gun frigates, the *Alcmène*, Captain Digby, and the *Triton*, Captain J. Gore appeared. The Spaniards, hoping to escape, steered different courses, but each were pursued by two British frigates, which, before long coming up with them, compelled them to haul down their colours. Fortunately, a breeze coming off the land, the captors with their prizes were enabled to stand off the coast, just in time to save themselves from being attacked by four large ships, which came out of Vigo. While the English frigates were preparing to receive the enemy, the four ships put back into port. The prizes were found to have on board a cargo of specie, besides other merchandise, to an amount which gave each captain upwards of 40,000 pounds, each lieutenant 5000 pounds, each warrant officer upwards of 2000 pounds, each midshipman nearly 800 pounds, each seaman and marine 182 pounds. Even the seamen and marines might have been well contented with the gold pieces they had to chink in their pockets; though in too many instances they were probably all dissipated before they had been many days on shore. Yet complaints were general of the uneven way in which prize-money was distributed. It was a common saying among sailors, that when the pay-clerk went on board ships to pay prize-money, he clambered with his money-bags into the main-top and showered down the money at random; all which remained upon the splinter-netting (a coarse rope netting spread as a kind of awning) was for the men, and all that went through for the officers. The captain of a ship not under the admiral's flag received three-eighths of the net proceeds. In this instance the three-eighths were divided among the four captains who assisted in the capture of the two Spanish frigates. On the treasure being landed, it was escorted in sixty-three artillery waggons, by horse and foot soldiers, and armed seamen and marines, attended by bands of music, and a vast multitude, to the dungeons of the citadel of Plymouth, whence it was afterwards removed, much in the same style, and deposited in the Bank of England.

Still more fortunate, a few years later, was Lord Cochrane, when, in command of the *Pallas*, he captured three rich prizes in succession, of which the value could not have been far short of 300,000 pounds. As, however, he only took one fourth, his share amounted to about 75,000 pounds. As it was, however, he nearly lost not only a large portion of his booty, but his liberty, as, while returning home after he had taken the last prize, three of the enemy's line-of-battle ships were seen. The wind freshening to half a gale, the *Pallas* was standing on, carrying all the sail she could, when it was found that the enemy were gaining on her. In this desperate emergency Lord Cochrane ordered every stitch of sail to be suddenly taken in, and the three ships of the enemy, one being on the weather, another on the lee beam, and the third nearly on the weather quarter, unable to get their canvas off and haul to the wind, shot miles away to leeward. The *Pallas* on this wore round and made sail on the opposite tack. The enemy, however, were soon again in chase, but night coming on, a lantern in a cask was put overboard, and the *Pallas*, altering her course, got clear of her pursuers, and reached Plymouth in safety. As he sailed up the harbour Lord Cochrane had a gold candlestick, five feet in height, fixed to the mast-head, and, as may be supposed, he never after this had any difficulty in manning his ship, when gold candlesticks were to be picked up, in addition to "pewter" and "cobs," the nickname given by seamen to silver and dollars. They have always been found ready to volunteer on board dashing frigates sent to stations where such prizes were supposed to abound.

The last important action was that known as the Battle of the Baltic. Napoleon had induced the Northern powers of Denmark, Sweden, and Russia to form a league, denominated an armed neutrality, for the French being unable to keep the sea, he hoped under their flags to obtain provisions and ammunition for his armies. To counteract this formidable confederacy, the English sent a fleet of 18 sail of the line, with a few frigates, and a number of bomb-vessels and gunboats, in the first place to attack the Danish fleet, and then to take in hand the other two confederates. After many delays, and attempts to induce the Danes to come to terms, on the 2nd of April, 1801, a portion of the fleet, which had been intrusted by Sir Hyde Parker to Lord Nelson, appeared before Copenhagen, and commenced an attack on the floating batteries and forts prepared by the Danes for the defence of their city. There is not space to give the details of the battle. The Danes fought heroically, their floating batteries being remanned over and over again from the shore. After three hours' cannonading, from which both parties suffered severely, Sir Hyde Parker, understanding that two of the British line-of-battle ships were in distress, threw out a signal for discontinuing the action. On its being reported to Nelson, he shrugged his shoulders, repeating the words, "Leave off action? Now, damn me if I do. You know, Foley, I have only one eye — I have a right to be blind sometimes;" then putting the glass to his blind eye, in that mood of mind which sports with bitterness, he exclaimed, "I really do not see the signal — keep mine for closer battle flying! That's the way I answer such signals. Nail mine to the mast."

At 1:30 p.m. the Danish fire slackened, and at 2 p.m. ceased along nearly the whole of the line. Among the British officers who fell was the gallant Captain Riou, who was cut in two while carrying his frigate, the *Amazon*, into action. After the flags of all the chief batteries had been struck, some of the lighter vessels that had got adrift fired on the boats which approached to take possession of them. Nelson prepared a letter to send to the Crown Prince of Denmark, threatening to destroy the prizes unless this proceeding was put a stop to. He concluded his letter, "The brave Danes are the brothers and should never be the enemies of England." A wafer was then given him, but he ordered a candle to be brought from the cock-pit, and sealed the letter with wax, affixing a larger seal than is ordinarily used, remarking as he did so, "This is no time to appear hurried and informal."

The remainder of the batteries having at length ceased firing, a flag of truce arrived from the shore, when the action, which had continued for five hours, was brought to a close, the total loss of killed being 255, and of wounded 688. The Danish loss amounted to between 1600 and 1800. The result of the victory was the secession of Denmark from the league, and the Emperor of Russia dying soon afterwards, the armed neutrality was dissolved.

Napoleon now began to hope more ardently than ever that he should ere long land his victorious legions on British ground. To carry them over, he had collected a large flotilla, chiefly at Boulogne. By Lord Nelson's orders, a desperate attempt was made by the boats of the squadron to destroy them. Some were gun brigs of between 200 and 250 tons; others were flats, vessels capable of carrying a crew of 30 men and 150 soldiers, with either a mortar or a long 24-pounder, as well as swivels and small-arms. Though some few were captured, all attempts at their destruction failed. The British cruisers, however, kept too good a watch to allow them to put to sea.

Numerous cutting-out expeditions took place during the war, in which both officers and men displayed the greatest possible amount of courage and determination. One of the most daring and successful on record was the capture of the French 20-gun ship-corvette *Chevrette*, while lying under some batteries in Camaret Bay, by the boats of the *Doris*, *Beaulieu*, and *Uremic*, forming part of the Channel Fleet under Admiral Cornwallis, stationed off Brest Harbour. At the first attempt the boats were discovered, and the *Chevrette* ran a mile and a-half farther up the bay, and took on board a party of soldiers.

Notwithstanding this, the next night, the 21st, the boats of the three frigates, joined by the barge and pinnace of the *Robust*, 74, amounting in all to 15, and containing about 280 officers and men, under the command of Lieutenant Losack, the second in command being Lieutenant Keith Maxwell of the *Beaulieu*, left their ships at 9:30 p.m. As they were pulling into the bay, Lieutenant Losack, with six boats, went in chase of a boat supposed to be sent as a look-out from the *Chevrette*, and as he did not return, Lieutenant Maxwell proceeded on without him. About 1 a.m. the flotilla coming in sight of the *Chevrette*, she opened a heavy fire on them of grape and musketry, and at the same time they were assailed by a fire of musketry from the shore. Undaunted by this, the British boarded the ship, some on the starboard bow and quarter, and others on the larboard bow, bravely opposed by the Frenchmen, who were armed with muskets and pistols, sabres, tomahawks, and pikes. Some, indeed, attempted to enter the boats, but were driven back by the British, who, having lost their pistols and muskets, made their way cutlass in hand. Some who had been directed to loose the sails, fought their way on to the corvette's yards. Here they found the foot-ropes strapped up, but, notwithstanding every obstacle, the sails were let fall in less than three minutes after the boarders had gained the deck. The cable having, in the meantime, been cut outside, a light breeze blowing from the land, and the quartermaster of the *Beaulieu*, Henry Wallis, fighting his way to the helm, and though bleeding from his wounds, taking charge of the wheel, the ship drifted out of the bay. On seeing the canvas loose, some of the Frenchmen leaped overboard, and others sprang down the hatchways, thus allowing the British to gain possession of the quarter-deck and forecastle, now nearly covered with the bodies of the slain. For some time, however, the Frenchmen who had fled below kept up a sharp fire of musketry, but the English, firing down in return, compelled them to yield. On her way out the prize was exposed to a heavy fire of round and grape from the batteries, but, the wind increasing, she got out of grape-shot. Not till then did Lieutenant Losack and his companions get on board. Two officers were killed, one of whom was Lieutenant Sinclair of the marines, while defending Mr Crofton, a midshipman, who had been severely wounded while boarding. The other, Robert Warren, a midshipman. Another, Lieutenant Waller Burke, was mortally wounded. Altogether, 11 were killed and 57 wounded, and 1 marine drowned in the *Beaulieu's* barge, which was sunk by a shot from the corvette. The gallantry of the boatswain of the *Beaulieu*, Mr John Brown, was also conspicuous. After attempting to force his way in to the *Chevrette's* fore-quarter-gallery, he climbed up over the taffrail, when standing up for some time exposed to the enemy's fire, waving his cutlass, he shouted out, "Make a lane there;" then, gallantly dashing among the Frenchmen, he fought his way to the forecastle. Here he continued driving back the French, who attempted to regain the post, all the time carrying out the orders he received from the quarter-deck, while he assisted in casting the ship and making sail as coolly as if he had been carrying on duty under ordinary circumstances.

During the war, which ended at the peace of Amiens, on the 27th of March, 1802, England had captured 80 sail of the line, and numberless other ships, besides various islands in the West Indies and other parts of the world, from the French, Spaniards, and Dutch. Though most of the latter were given up, the navy of England had gained a renown which can never be obliterated.

Chapter Sixteen.

George the Third — from A.D. 1803 to end of war A.D. 1814.

The "piping times of peace" were not destined to last long. Napoleon, indeed, had never ceased making preparations for war from the time the treaty of Amiens was signed. On the 16th of May the British Government, discovering his aims, issued letters of marque and ordered general reprisals; and at the same time Holland, being in reality a province of France, all ships belonging to the Batavian Republic in English ports were detained. Admiral Cornwallis, in command of the Channel Fleet, of 10 sail of the line and frigates, which was lying in Cawsand Bay, had his flag flying on board the *Dreadnought*, 98. With these he proceeded the next day to cruise off Ushant, and watch the motions of the French ships in Brest Harbour; other small squadrons being sent, as soon as they were ready, off the other French ports, containing either ships of the line or gunboats, of which Napoleon was collecting vast numbers for the invasion of England. In a short time that war, which was to last ten years, commenced in earnest. The French gunboats were, however, kept pretty close prisoners by the English cruisers, and whenever any of them ventured out from under the protection of their batteries, they were attacked, captured, driven on shore, or compelled to seek shelter in the nearest port under their lee; while many of them were gallantly cut out and carried off in triumph, even when moored in positions where they could receive assistance from the forts on shore.

Out of the numberless gallant deeds performed by the crews of boats and small vessels engaged in this service, one must be instanced for its singularity, and the bravery displayed by the commanding officer and his followers. A hired cutter, the *Sheerness*, carrying 8 4-pounders and 30 men and boys, under the command of Lieutenant Henry Rowed, while watching Brest Harbour, observed two chasse-marées close inshore. Having sent a boat with seven men and the mate to cut off one of them, the commander proceeded in the cutter in chase of the other, which was about five miles off, under the protection of a battery. A calm coming on, he, with the boatswain, John Marks, and three other men, jumped into a small boat and pulled away for the chase. The latter, after some time, ran on shore under the battery, where thirty soldiers were observed drawn up on the beach. Notwithstanding the heavy fire they at once opened, Lieutenant Rowed dashed alongside. The Frenchmen having deserted their vessel, he began making efforts to get her off; in this, as the tide was rising, he at length succeeded, and going ahead in the boat, towed her away from the shore. He had pulled about a third of a mile, when suddenly a French boat, with an officer and nine men armed with muskets, were seen alongside, having pulled up in the wake of the vessel. Before the French could have time to attack them, John Marks sprang on board the chasse-marée, and seizing a boat-stretcher, stood prepared to prevent any of the enemy from getting up the side. The astonishment of the Frenchmen gave time to the lieutenant and his three men to climb on board and to prepare their firearms and cutlasses. The French, who attempted to get up the side, were driven back, when they sheered off, but discharged their muskets at the English as they pulled away, while the battery also opened fire. Wonderful as it may seem, though forty-nine musket-balls were found sticking in the prize, not a man was hurt; and both chasse-marées were carried off.

For some time the principal fighting was between the English cruisers in the channel and the invasion flotilla, as Napoleon's gunboats were called; and as their stings might annoy, though they could not inflict serious injury, attempts were made to destroy them by fire-vessels or catamarans — which was the name given to a species of nautical infernal machine — though without much success. The catamaran consisted of a coffer of about 21 feet long and 3 and a half broad, somewhat in shape like a log of mahogany, wedge-shaped at each end. It was covered with thick planking, and lined with lead, thoroughly caulked and tarred, while over all was a coat of canvas, payed over with hot pitch. To give an idea of its size, the vessel weighed about two tons. Inside was a piece of clock-work, the mainspring of which, on withdrawing a peg placed on the outside, would, after going six or ten minutes, draw the trigger of a lock, and explode the vessel. Every other part was filled with about 40 barrels of gunpowder and other inflammable matter. As much ballast was placed in it as would keep the upper surface of the deck even with the water's edge. It had no mast, and had to be towed towards the scene of its operations. The tow-rope was at one end, and to the other was fixed a rope with a grappling-iron at its extremity, kept afloat by pieces of cork. This grappling-iron, it was intended, should hook itself to the cable of the vessel it was to destroy, and thus swing the catamaran alongside. It was, indeed, on a larger scale, though with less destructive power, something like Harvey's torpedo of the present day.

Lord Keith, who was with a squadron off Boulogne, first made use of four of the machines, in the hopes of destroying some of a flotilla of 150 vessels moored in a double line outside the pier. Three exploded one after another, doing very little harm; but a heavily armed launch, which had chased one of the boats towing a catamaran, ran foul of it, when the launch and every one on board was blown into the air.

Numerous other engagements took place, and frequently the portions of the flotilla moving from the different ports towards Boulogne were severely handled by the British cruisers. Occasionally, small English vessels, venturing too close inshore for the purpose of attacking them, were captured by the French.

At length Napoleon managed to collect a vast number of prames and gun-vessels, with other craft, the whole flotilla amounting to 2293, of which the larger were armed. These were intended to carry 163,645 men, of whom 16,783 were sailors, besides 9059 horses. This flotilla was organised in six grand divisions. One, denominated the left wing, was stationed at Étaples, to convey the troops under Marshal Ney from the camp of Mottrieux. Two other divisions were in the port of Boulogne, to convey the troops from the two camps on either side of it, under Soult. A fourth was at the port of Vimereux to carry the corps of Marshal Lannes. The Gallo-Batavian flotilla, assembled off Ambleteuse, formed the fifth grand division, destined to transport the troops under Marshal Davoust; while the sixth, at Calais, was to carry the Italian infantry, and various divisions of mounted and dis-mounted dragoons.

On the 3rd of August, 1805, Napoleon came to Boulogne to inspect the flotilla, and so completely organised was it by this time, that although the extremities of the camps were more than two miles from the point of embarkation, an hour and a-half only was occupied in getting men and horses on board. All he wanted was the arrival of his fleet under Villeneuve, to protect his mighty flotilla during its passage across the channel, and then, as his generals at all events believed, the conquest of England was certain.

Meantime Nelson, who at the breaking out of the war had been ap-pointed to the command of the fleet in the Mediterranean, was watch-ing Villeneuve, resolved to prevent him from appearing on the spot where his fleet was so anxiously looked for by Napoleon. On the 18th of May, 1803, he had hoisted his flag on board his old ship, the *Victory*, and on the 20th had sailed from Spithead, first bound to Brest, and from thence to the Mediterranean. Here he remained for nearly two years, without once setting foot on shore, watching and waiting for the Toulon fleet, endeavouring to induce them to come out and give him battle. At length, on the 18th of January, 1805, the French fleet did come out, but a heavy gale blowing. Nelson was then at anchor off the coast of Sardinia. Supposing that they had gone to Egypt, he sailed in chase, but found that they had put back into Toulon. Hence again Villeneuve sailed, and escaping through the straits, was joined by the Spanish fleet at Cadiz, which had 4500 troops on board. The combined fleet of the enemy now numbered 20 sail of the line and 10 frigates, while Nelson had but 10 sail of the line and 3 frigates. With these, however, he chased Villeneuve to the West Indies, where, after threatening several of the islands, he fled back to Europe, with Nelson after him. When about twenty leagues west of Finisterre, on

NELSON LEAVING SOUTHSEA.

264

the 22nd of July, the French admiral was attacked by Sir Robert Calder, with 15 line-of-battle ships, but escaped into Cadiz, with the loss of two of the Spanish ships. Nelson, meantime, had sought the enemy on the north-west coast of Ireland, and then came back into the channel, where his ships reinforced the fleet under Admiral Cornwallis off Ushant, and he himself, worn out with fatigue and anxiety, went on shore for a short rest.

It was now that Napoleon urged Villeneuve to come into the channel, ending with the words, "England desires us, we are all ready, all is embarked, appear, and within four-and-twenty hours all is finished." No sooner did Nelson hear that the French and Spanish fleet had entered Cadiz than, again offering his services, he arrived at Portsmouth on the 14th of September, and the next morning, putting off in his barge to the *Victory*, he bade his last farewell to England. On the 29th of September, his birthday, he was off Cadiz, and joining Collingwood, took command of the British fleet, then amounting to 27 sail of the line. Villeneuve had been waiting till the Spaniards were ready, and till a favourable wind would allow him to sail. On the 9th of October Nelson sent Collingwood his plan of attack, his intention being to advance towards the enemy in two lines, led by eight of his fastest three-deckers, and thus to break through the enemy's line. Collingwood, having the command of one line, was to break through the enemy about the twelfth ship from the rear, Nelson intending to lead through the centre, while the advanced squadron was to cut off three or four ships ahead of the centre. He would make few signals: no captain could do wrong who placed his ship close alongside that of an enemy. Not till the 19th did the admiral learn that Villeneuve had put to sea, when he at once concluded that he intended to enter the Mediterranean. Two days afterwards, the ever-memorable 21st of October, 1805, at daylight, when the English fleet was about seven leagues from Cape Trafalgar, Nelson discovered the enemy six or seven miles to the eastward, which had so manoeuvred as to bring the shoals of Trafalgar and San Pedro under the lee of the British fleet, while they kept the port of Cadiz open for themselves.

Nelson now hoisted the signal to bear down on them in two lines. Nelson led one in the *Victory*, Collingwood the other in the *Royal Sovereign*. On going into action he asked Captain Blackwood, who had come on board to receive orders, what he should consider a victory. "The capture of 14 sail of the line," was the answer. "I shall not be satisfied with less than 20," said Nelson.

Shortly afterwards up went the signal, "England expects every man to do his duty."

"ENGLAND EXPECTS EVERY MAN TO DO HIS DUTY!"—TRAFALGAR.—p. 312.

Notwithstanding the attempts made to induce Lord Nelson to allow the *Teméraire* to lead his line into action, the *Victory* carrying all sail, kept her station. Ahead of her was Villeneuve's flag-ship, the *Bucentaur*, with the *Santissima Trinidad* as his second before her; while ahead of the *Royal Sovereign*, the leader of the lee column, was the *Santa Anna*, the flag-ship of the Spanish vice-admiral. The sea was smooth, the wind very light; the sun shone brightly on the fresh-painted sides of the long line of French and Spanish ships, when the *Fougueux*, astern of the *Santa Anna*, opened her fire on the *Royal Sovereign*, which, at about ten minutes past noon, delivered her larboard broadside, with guns double-shotted, at the *Santa Anna*, and with such precision as to disable 14 of her guns, and to kill or wound 400 of her crew; while with her starboard broadside she raked the *Fougueux*. Just then Collingwood exclaimed to his captain, "Rotherham, what would Nelson give to be here;" and at the same moment Nelson was observing, "See how that noble fellow Collingwood carries his ship into action."

The wind now falling to almost a calm, the *Victory* and the ships in her wake advanced so slowly that seven or eight of the rearmost ships of the French van having opened fire upon the *Victory* before she had fired a single gun, 50 of her men were killed or wounded, and her main-topmast with her studdensail-boom shot away, and every sail, especially on the foremast, had become like a sieve. At about four minutes after twelve she opened with both her broadsides. Captain Hardy now informed Nelson that it was impossible to break the enemy's line without running on board one of their ships. "Take your choice — go on board which you please," was the answer.

The *Victory*, as she approached the *Bucentaur*, fired a 68-pounder carronade containing a round-shot and a keg with 500 musket-balls, from the larboard side of her forecastle, right into the cabin-windows of that ship; and as she forged slowly ahead, the whole of her 50 broadside guns, all doubly and some trebly shotted, so as completely to rake her, killing or wounding as many men as the *Bucentaur* had lost, and dismounting 20 of her guns. Receiving the fire of an 80-gun ship, the *Neptune*, the *Victory's* helm being put hard a-port, she ran on board the *Redoutable*, into which she poured a heavy fire, while with her aftermost starboard guns she engaged the *Santissima Trinidad*. Besides the heavy fire of great guns and musketry she was enduring from other ships, she received the shot of the *Redoutable's* main-deck guns, and also constant discharges of musketry from the three tops of that ship. It was from the mizen-top of the *Redoutable*, at about 1:25 p.m., that, as Nelson and Captain Hardy were walking the deck together, the admiral was shot by a musket-ball, which entered his left shoulder, and descending lodged in his spine. Hardy, who had just turned, saw him in the act of falling, with his left hand just touching the deck. He was removed by the sergeant of marines and two seamen to the cock-pit.

In the meantime the action raged furiously. Soon after the first four ships of the lee division had cut through between the centre and rear of the enemy's line. The remainder, as they came up, forced their way into the dense mass and engaged such ships as they could best attack. The weather division was doing the same, rather ahead of the centre, and at about 1:30 p.m. the battle was at its height. At about 3 p.m. the firing began to slacken, and two hours afterwards had wholly ceased, by which time 9 French sail of the line, including one burnt, and 9 Spanish were captured. Nine French and 6 Spaniards escaped, of which 4 French ships made sail to the southward, and 11, 5 of which were French and 6 Spanish, reached Cadiz, most of them much knocked about; while all the frigates and smaller craft also escaped.

Within twenty minutes after the fatal shot had been fired from her, the *Redoutable* struck her colours, and about three hours after Nelson had received his wound, he breathed his last.

In the whole action the British lost 449 killed and 1241 wounded, while several of the ships lost two of their masts, and five were totally dismasted. Lord Nelson intended to anchor the fleet and prizes, but this Lord Collingwood did not think fit to do, and a gale coming on from the south-west, some of the prizes went down, others were driven ashore, one escaped into Cadiz, some were destroyed, and only four by the greatest exertions were saved. To the credit of the Spaniards it must be recorded that the English prize-crews which landed from the wrecks were treated with the greatest kindness.

Although there were few trophies, the result of the victory was completely to disconcert Napoleon's plans, and to prevent him from invading England. Four ships which escaped after the action were captured by Sir Richard Strachan on the 4th of November, and not while the war continued did the French and Spanish navies ever recover the tremendous blow they had received off Cape Trafalgar. Thus, of the once formidable French and Spanish fleet of 35 sail of the line, 2 were taken by Sir Robert Calder, 4 of those captured at Trafalgar were carried into Gibraltar, as were the 4 taken by Sir Richard Strachan, 15 were sunk or were burnt or wrecked; 3 only fit for sea escaped into Cadiz; while 7, so severely battered as to be mere wrecks, got into the same port, making up the whole number mentioned. In vain for some time did Napoleon attempt to send another fleet to sea. His ships were either blockaded by the British squadrons, or, when they did manage to escape, were attacked and beaten by our fleets. At the same time small squadrons or single cruisers running out of port committed much havoc on English commerce; not, however, with impunity. Numerous actions between light squadrons and single ships took place. The enemy, indeed, were never safe, even in port; and expeditions to cut out vessels in the harbours or under the protection of forts were much in vogue.

The navy of England was, at the commencement of 1806, larger than it had ever before been, consisting of 551 cruisers in commission, of which 104 were line-of-battle ships; in addition to which 26 were building or being built, and 10 in ordinary, a large proportion of the rest being frigates carrying from 56 to 28 guns.

A new method had been introduced to strengthen ships by diagonal braces or by doubling or sheathing them with plank, and sometimes when they were in bad condition both bracing and doubling them. By this means 22 sail of the line, several frigates, and other smaller vessels had been made fit for active service.

In this year, also, was launched the first British ship of war constructed of teak. Two first-rate ships also were ordered, the *Nelson* and the *Caledonia*, of a tonnage and force double that of many of the old ships of the line. To man this large fleet Parliament made a vote of 120,000 seamen and marines.

The four ships captured by Sir Richard Strachan were carried into Plymouth, and were added to the British Navy, the *Formidable* having the name of *Brave* given to her, the *Duguay-Trouin* that of the *Implacable*, while the *Scipion* and *Mont Blanc* were allowed to retain their former names. The *Implacable* and *Scipion* were, however, the only ships considered as fit for service.

Notwithstanding the heavy loss France had sustained, Bonaparte managed to send to sea a fleet of 11 sail of the line, and a number of frigates, in two squadrons. One of these sailed for the West Indies early in 1806, while the other steered for the Cape of Good Hope. Admiral Duckworth, who, with 7 sail of the line, had been blockading Cadiz, came up with the former of these squadrons, consisting of 5 ships, 2 frigates, and a corvette, and after a severe action took or destroyed the whole of the five line-of-battle ships.

Among the gallant actions performed at this time was one which shows that seamen fight as well on shore as afloat. The British 38-gun frigate *Loire*, Captain Maitland, cruising off the coast of Spain, having chased a privateer into the Bay of Camarinas, situated to the eastward of Cape Finisterre, sent in three of her boats, under the command of Lieutenant James Lucas Yeo, to bring her out. Instead of one, they found two privateers, moored under a battery of 10 guns. Both were captured, in spite of the fire of the battery; but in order to secure the larger of the two, Lieutenant Yeo was compelled to abandon the smallest vessel. To recompense himself for her loss, he captured three merchant-vessels laden with wine on his way out. From his prisoners Captain Maitland learned that a French privateer of 26 guns was fitting out at Muros, and being acquainted with the navigation of the bay, he resolved on her capture or destruction. Accordingly, on the 4th of June, he stood into the bay, with springs on his cables, ready to attack the fort, and towing his boats, with fifty officers and men under the command of Lieutenant Yeo. On passing close to the shore, the *Loire* was exposed to a fire from two long 18-pounders, which considerably annoyed her. On this Captain Maitland ordered Lieutenant Yeo to land and spike the guns. The gallant lieutenant departing on this service, the *Loire* stood on, when, as she opened the bay, she discovered at anchor within it a large corvette pierced for 26 guns, and a brig of 10 guns; but as the armament of both vessels was on shore, they were unable to offer any resistance. The *Loire*, however, was now exposed to a hot fire from a fort of 12 long 18-pounders, from which, as she was less than a quarter-of-a-mile off, nearly every shot struck her hull. Finding that by standing on he should be exposed to a still hotter fire, Captain Maitland ran as close in as he could venture, and anchoring the frigate with a spring on her cable, opened her broadside. So strong, however, was the fort, that the frigate's shot committed little or no damage, while numbers of her crew were falling, some severely wounded. Lieutenant Yeo had in the meantime landed, and storming the 2-gun battery, put its defenders to flight. Having spiked the guns, Lieutenant Yeo discovered the large fort close to the town of Muros, which was severely annoying the frigate. Without hesitation, he resolved to attack it, and his men were eager to follow him. The garrison were so occupied in firing at the frigate, that not only was the approach of the British unperceived, but the outer gate had actually been left open. On the seamen rushing forward, headed by Lieutenant Yeo, the sentinel who only just then perceived them, fired his musket and retreated, followed closely by the storming party, which on reaching the inner gate was met by the governor, and those he had time to rally round him, sword in hand. With a blow of his cutlass, which was broken in the effort, the lieutenant laid him dead at his feet. A desperate struggle ensued in the narrow passage between the officers of the garrison and the British seamen, who, bearing down all opposition, drove the enemy before them to the farther end of the fort, many of whom in their terror sprang through the embrasures down upon the rocks below, a height of twenty-five feet. The garrison of the fort consisted of upwards of 100 men, composed of the crew of the corvette, 22 Spanish soldiers, and several Spanish volunteers. Of these, the governor, the second captain of the corvette, and a Spanish gentleman, with nine other men, were killed, and thirty wounded, before the survivors, finding all opposition useless, laid down their arms; when the British colours, greatly to the satisfaction of the frigate's crew, were seen flying on the flagstaff. Directly the fort was in the possession of the British, the seamen and marines did their best to assist the wounded prisoners, and were amply repaid by the gratitude which the unfortunate men's friends expressed when they came to carry them into the town. The guns being spiked and thrown over the parapet, and part of the fort being blown up, the British embarked, carrying off 40 barrels of powder, 2 small brass cannon, and 50 stand of arms. The corvette and brig, as also the Spanish merchant-vessel, were taken possession of, when Captain Maitland sent a flag of truce to the town, promising that should the stores of the two privateers be delivered up, he would not injure the town; he also refrained from capturing a number of small merchant-vessels which lay in the bay, considering that it was cruel to deprive the poor owners of the means of obtaining a livelihood. His terms were gladly accepted, and the bishop and one of the principal inhabitants of Muros came off to express their gratitude for the kind way in which their victors had treated them, and offering such refreshment as the place could afford to the British captain and his officers. The corvette was named the *Confiance*, and on his return home Lieutenant Yeo was appointed to her. Shortly afterwards he was raised to post-rank, the *Confiance* being rated as a post-ship, with an armament of 22 carronades, 18-pounders, and a complement of 140 men and boys, in order that he might still remain her captain.

Among the most remarkable of the gallant actions of this period between single ships was that fought in August, 1805, between the British 18-pounder 36-gun frigate *Phoenix*, Captain Thomas Baker, and the French frigate *Didon*, of 40 guns, Captain Milius. The *Didon* measured 1091 tons, and had a crew of 330 men, the weight of her metal amounting to 563 pounds; while the *Phoenix* measured but 884 tons, her crew numbering only 245 men, and the weight of her metal was 444 pounds. The *Didon*, which had three days before sailed from Corunna with despatches for the Rochefort squadron, and after escaping an action from another English frigate, had been visited by the skipper of an American merchant-vessel, who informed Captain Milius that a ship whose topgallant-sails were just then rising out of the water to windward was an English 20-gun ship, on board of which he had been the previous evening, and from what he had heard he was sure that she would venture to engage the *Didon*. Captain Milius, though ordered to avoid an action, believing that victory was certain, backed his mizen-topsail and kept his main-topsail shivering to allow the British ship to come up with him. The stranger was the *Phoenix*, and which was not only a smaller frigate, but Captain Baker had disguised her to resemble at a distance a sloop of war. The mistake into which Captain Milius had been led by his treacherous visitor was therefore not discovered until the *Phoenix* was close to the *Didon*, which ship, hoisting her colours, fired a gun to windward, and at 8:45 a.m. opened her broadside. Captain Baker, in order to prevent the *Didon* from escaping, had resolved to engage to leeward, but, from the manoeuvres of the French ship, unable to do this, he stood down right at her to windward with all sail set. By this bold measure he succeeded in bringing his broadside to bear on the *Didon* at pistol-shot distance, when a hot fire of round-shot, grape and musketry was exchanged between the combatants. The *Phoenix* from the press of sails she carried, ranged ahead of the *Didon*, which lay almost stationary, and before she could haul up, was raked by the latter; but as the crew were ordered to lie down, they escaped without damage. By the rapidity with which the crew of the *Phoenix* repaired her damaged rigging, they avoided an attempt made by the *Didon* to rake her with her starboard broadside. In a short time the *Didon's* larboard bow ran against the starboard-quarter of the *Phoenix*, both ships lying nearly in a parallel direction, the former having only one gun which could be brought to bear on her antagonist. At that moment the Frenchmen in vast numbers attempted to board the *Phoenix*, but were vigorously repulsed; while the marines of both ships exchanged a warm and destructive fire. At this juncture a young midshipman, Edward Phillips, observed a man upon the *Didon's* bowsprit end taking deliberate aim at Captain Baker, close to whom he was standing. Being armed with a musket, he, thrusting the captain on one side, fired. At the same moment the Frenchmen fell into the water, while the bullet intended for the captain's head tore off alone the rim of his hat. Several men who were sick below, leaving their hammocks, employed themselves in bringing up powder, while the acting purser, Mr John Colman, who might with propriety have remained to assist the surgeons in the cock-pit, appeared on deck with a brace of pistols in his belt and a broadsword in his hand, encouraging the crew by every means in his power. Still, the great superiority of the French made it doubtful which ship would gain the victory; when Captain Baker by great exertions brought the aftermost main-deck gun to a port which he had cut by enlarging one of the stern windows. Several of his men were killed by the French marines while the operation was going forward, but at length he succeeded in running it through the port, and, at his first discharge, sweeping the *Didon* from her larboard bow to her starboard-quarter, laid low twenty-four of her crew. The British marines were, in the meantime, keeping up so spirited a fire on the forecastle of the *Didon* that they prevented the Frenchmen from discharging the carronade placed on it. This work continued for half-an-hour, when the *Didon* fore-reached on the *Phoenix*, which, as she did so, brought her second aftermost gun to bear on her, and at its first discharge cut away the gammoning of her bowsprit and did other damage. Though the guns of the *Phoenix* were lighter than those of the *Didon*, they were fired nearly half as quick again. The *Didon* had by this time, as she passed out of gunshot, lost her main-topmast, while her foremast was in a tottering condition, and her hull severely shattered. The rigging of the *Phoenix* had also been so much cut about that she was almost unmanageable. Both frigates, which had gone into action with nearly all their sails set, now exhibited a melancholy appearance, their canvas riddled or in tatters, and rope-ends drooping from their masts and yards. Their crews were now employed in repairing their damaged rigging, and so well trained and diligent was that of the *Phoenix* that in a short time they had knotted and spliced her rigging and rove fresh braces. While so employed, about noon, they were encouraged by seeing the *Didon's* foremast fall over the side. Soon afterwards a light air of wind springing up, the *Phoenix*, trimming her sails, stood down towards the *Didon*, and having got within gunshot, was about to open her fire, when the French frigate, being utterly helpless, hauled down her colours.

The *Phoenix* had lost her second lieutenant, 1 master's mate, and 10 seamen killed, and 3 officers, 13 seamen, and 12 marines wounded; while the *Didon* had had 27 officers and men killed, and 44 badly wounded out of her crew of 330 men, who were looked upon as one of the most efficient in the French navy, while Captain Milius, who was known for his gallantry and seamanship, had fought his frigate with the greatest bravery.

The crew of the *Phoenix* had still a difficult duty to perform. Their prisoners greatly outnumbered them, and not only had they to refit the two ships, but to keep a strict watch on their captives. The *Didon's* main-mast was so severely wounded that it had immediately to be cut away, when the *Phoenix*, taking her in tow, steered for a British port. On the evening of the 14th she fell in with the *Dragon*, 74, which ship accompanying her, the next day they came in sight of M. Villeneuve's fleet. On this the *Phoenix*, with her prize in tow, made sail to the southward, pursued by several French ships; but after a time they tacked and left her and her prize to proceed unmolested. Having passed Lisbon, she was steering for Gibraltar, when, during a thick fog, the ringing of bells and firing of guns were heard. Meeting with the *Euryalus* frigate, Captain Baker learned that the sounds proceeded from the Franco-Spanish fleet. He accordingly again altered his course to the westward. He had a still greater danger to contend with. The French pilot belonging to the *Phoenix* overheard some of the prisoners talking of a plan for getting possession of the *Phoenix*. The intended mutiny was speedily crushed. Shortly afterwards the pilot brought aft Captain Milius' late coxswain, accusing him of being the ringleader. The French captain was very indignant, and demanded of the man whether he had any complaint to offer. On his acknowledging that he had none, Captain Milius besought Captain Baker to put the fellow in irons, declaring him to be a disgrace to the name of Frenchman. After this the prisoners remained quiet, and the *Phoenix* with her prize, having the advantage of a good wind, at length safely reached Plymouth Sound on the 3rd of September. The *Didon*, which was a beautiful and fast-sailing frigate, was purchased for the navy, but, without ever having been sent to sea, was unaccountably broken up in 1811.

Humane and brave as British officers have almost always proved themselves, tyrannical captains, who in most instances have been also deficient in courage and seamanlike qualities, have occasionally been found in the service. Among men of this class the Honourable Captain Lake, commanding the sloop of war *Recruit*, must be ranked. While at Plymouth he had pressed a young seaman, Robert Jeffrey by name, belonging to Polperro in Cornwall, out of a privateer. Shortly afterwards the *Recruit* sailed for the West Indies. While in those seas, the ship having run short of water, Jeffrey was accused of stealing, on the 10th December, a bottle of rum, and some spruce beer out of a cask. He was accordingly put in the black-list. Two or three days afterwards the *Recruit* came in sight of the desert island of Sombrero, eighty miles to the south-west of Saint Christopher. Captain Lake on seeing it suddenly took it into his head to maroon Jeffrey on the island. Accordingly, that very evening, he was conveyed on shore in a boat, commanded by the second lieutenant, who had with him a midshipman and four seamen. Even the buccaneers, when they thus treated a culprit, had the humanity to leave him arms, and food, and clothing; but Captain Lake ordered the unfortunate youth to be left on this uninhabited spot with no other clothing than that he wore, without a particle of food. The lieutenant, observing that his bare feet were cut by the sharp stones, obtained a pair of shoes from one of the men, and gave him a knife and a couple of handkerchiefs, contributed by himself and the midshipman. The lieutenant advising him to keep a bright look-out for passing vessels, then, according to his orders, leaving the poor fellow, pulled back to his ship. Soon after the arrival of the *Recruit* at the Leeward Islands, Sir Alexander Cochrane, the commander-in-chief, hearing what had occurred, sent her back to bring off the man, in case he should have survived. The officers on landing searched the island over, but could discover no traces of the marooned seaman. Jeffrey, however, was not dead. For eight days he had subsisted on such limpets as he could find among the rocks, and the rain water which he discovered in their crevices. He was growing weaker and weaker, for though he had seen several vessels pass, he was unable from weakness to hail them; till, on the morning of the ninth day, an American schooner, the *Adams*, of Marblehead, Massachusetts, hove in sight, and his signal being seen, the master came on shore and saved him from the death which probably would have soon overtaken him. He was landed at Marblehead, where he remained till 1810, when the English Government hearing of the occurrence, sent for him, and gave him his discharge, taking the big R off his name thus enabling him to receive all arrears of pay. On the whole circumstance being inquired into, Captain Lake, who acknowledged that he had landed Jeffrey upon Sombrero under the belief that it was inhabited, was deservedly sentenced to be dismissed from the British Navy. In 1807, it having become known that Napoleon intended to take possession of the Danish fleet, to recompense himself for the loss of his own, a British fleet of 17 sail of the line and 21 frigates, and smaller vessels, was despatched to the Baltic, under the command of Admiral Gambier. An army of 20,000 men was also sent at the same time, commanded by Lord Cathcart, and they were directed to demand the surrender of the Danish fleet, the English Government undertaking merely to hold it as a deposit, to be restored at a general peace. The fleet reached its destination early in August. After various skirmishes with the Danish gunboats and batteries, it completely surrounded the island of Zealand, when the troops were landed, and the Danish general, Peiman, refusing the terms offered, on the 2nd of September the English fleet and batteries opened fire on Copenhagen, which was ultimately set on fire. The bombardment continued for three days, with a short interval, in the hopes that the Danes would yield; but it was not till a number of the garrison and inhabitants had been killed, and a large portion of the city burnt down, that General Peiman sent out a flag of truce. Lord Cathcart's reply was, that no capitulation could be listened to unless accompanied by the surrender of the Danish fleet. This was at length agreed to, and the British were put in possession of the citadel and the ships of war, with their stores. In six weeks the whole of the fleet fit for sea was carried off, the remaining few ships being destroyed; while a large amount of naval stores was embarked, as was the army, without a casualty. On going down the sound, the *Neptunus*, one of the prizes, an 80-gun ship, got on shore, and was destroyed, as were also most of the Danish gunboats, in consequence of bad weather coming on. The fleet, however, without further accident, at the close of October, arrived safely at Yarmouth and the Downs. Whatever opinion may be formed of the legality or expediency of the enterprise, no one can deny that it was carried out with ability and promptitude; and as the Danes would undoubtedly have assisted Napoleon in his designs against England, she was certainly justified in thus summarily preventing Denmark from injuring her.

It was at this time that the Danish island of Heligoland was captured by the *Majestic*, 74, and the *Quebec* frigate, but being of no possible use, was recently handed over to Germany.

The next expedition on a large scale in which a British fleet was engaged brought neither advantage to the country nor honour to its leaders. The Turks having been tampered with by the French, Sir John Duckworth, in command of a squadron, had been sent to Constantinople to take possession of or destroy the Turkish fleet should the sultan not give a sufficient guarantee of his friendly intentions. According to his instructions, Sir John proceeded with his squadron up the Dardanelles, his ships being exposed to the fire of the forts on either hand. Altogether, the loss of the squadron amounted to 6 killed and 51 wounded. The Turks, however, were not to escape without punishment. Not far from the Castle of Abydos lay the Turkish squadron, which had the audacity to fire on the British ships as they passed. While four of the latter came to an anchorage to prevent their escape, Sir Sidney Smith, with three frigates, ran in and anchored within musket-shot of them, when, opening his fire, he compelled one of the Turkish sixty-fours and two frigates, and other smaller vessels, to run on shore, the only ones which did not do so being captured, a fort under which they had sought protection being also destroyed. Unhappily, one of the British ships, the *Ajax*, commanded by Captain Blackwood, caught fire during the night, and so rapidly did the flames extend, that no efforts availed to put them out, and upwards of 250 souls, among whom were two merchants and two women passengers, perished. It was supposed that the fire was caused by the spontaneous combustion of some coals stowed in the after-cock-pit.

Sir John, on arriving before Constantinople, lost a considerable time in diplomatic negotiations, while the Turks were doing their utmost to fortify their city and the island of Prota, which commanded the anchorage. Instead of attacking the city, Sir John sailed again down the Dardanelles, receiving on his way a hot fire from the Castle of Abydos and other forts on either hand. The Turks fired granite shot, one of which, weighing 800 pounds and measuring 6 feet in circumference, passed through the side of the *Active*, two feet above the water, and lodged on the orlop-deck, close to the magazine-scuttle, without injuring a man. So large was the aperture made by it, that Captain Mowbray, her commander, saw two of his crew thrusting their heads out of it at the same moment. Another shot of the same weight struck the main-mast of the *Windsor Castle*, and cut it more than three-quarters through. Other ships were struck by shot of equal dimensions. Four men on board the *Standard* were killed by one of these shot, which, at the same time striking a salt or ammunition box on deck, caused an explosion by which a lieutenant, 3 petty officers, and 37 men and 6 marines were wounded, and 4 seamen in their alarm leapt overboard — the total loss by this single shot amounting to 8 killed and drowned, and 47 wounded. The story is told of a seaman who thrust his head out of one of the shot-holes, and pertinaciously kept it there. When asked why he did so, he replied that he considered it the safest place, as he was sure no other shot would come in at that hole.

By great exertions the French had in the year 1809 fitted out 9 line-of-battle ships, in addition to the squadrons already at sea, which, under the command of M. Allemand, had arrived in Basque Roads.

Here they were for some time blockaded by the British Channel Squadron under Lord Gambier, whose flag was flying on board the *Caledonia*, of 120 guns, Captain Sir H. Burrard Neale. Lord Gambier had himself suggested the possibility of destroying the French fleet by means of fire-ships, though he considered, as his letter expresses it, "a horrible mode of warfare, and the attempt very hazardous, if not desperate." The Admiralty had, however, anticipated him, and had already ordered the construction of several fire-ships, which, on the arrival from the Mediterranean of Lord Cochrane, commanding the 38-gun frigate *Impérieuse*, were placed under his command. On his reach-

277

ing the fleet he was coldly received by the other captains, who were jealous of the appointment of a junior officer to conduct so important a service. Lord Cochrane remarks that two only, Rear-Admiral Stafford and Sir Harry Neale, received him in a friendly manner. Lord Cochrane was not a man to be disconcerted by such conduct, and felt thoroughly convinced that the plan he proposed would succeed. The French, aware of the danger of their position, had done their utmost to fortify it. The defences on Ile d'Aix were strengthened, and works were commenced on the Boyart Shoal on the opposite side of the entrance to the roads, while a boom half-a-mile in length, composed of spars and cables, had been laid down and secured by heavy anchors. This boom, forming an obtuse angle, occupied a deep channel between Ile d'Aix and the Boyart Shoal, and it was supposed would prove effectual against the passage of fire-ships. The French fleet was drawn up in two lines inside the boom, with three frigates in line ahead of them. The ships thus placed, aided by the batteries on shore, would have been sufficient to sink the British fleet had it attempted to force a passage. Besides the fire-ships, Lord Cochrane had constructed two explosion vessels. The largest contained 1500 barrels of powder, formed into a solid mass by wedges and wet sand rammed hard between the casks. On the top of this mass of gunpowder were 400 live shells with short fusees, together with as many hundreds of hand grenades and rockets.

The night of the 11th of April was fixed on for the enterprise. The fire-ships were ready, but one mortar-vessel, the *Etna*, alone had arrived. The *Impérieuse*, from whence operations were to be directed, anchored close to the inner end of the Boyart Shoal. The *Aigle, Unicorn,* and *Pallas* frigates, brought up in a line to the northward of her, in order to receive the crews of the fire-ships and support the boats of the fleet, while the *Etna* anchored off the north-east point of Ile d'Aix, covered by the *Emerald* frigate and four gun brigs. Two others, with screened lights hoisted, were to act as pointers for the guidance of the fire-ships. They were to pass between the two light vessels, and then shape a course for the boom. A strong wind from the north-west enabled the fire-ships to run about two points free for the boom. At 8:30 p.m. Lord Cochrane, accompanied by Lieutenant Bissell, embarked on board the largest of the explosion vessels, on the perilous undertaking, the other fire-ships followed. He was accompanied by a boat's crew of four volunteers only, in addition to the lieutenant. Having nearly reached the boom, he ordered the lieutenant and his men to get into the boat while he ignited the port-fires. It was supposed that the fusees would burn fifteen minutes, by the end of which time the boat might be well out of the range of the grenades; but scarcely five minutes had elapsed ere a terrific explosion occurred, throwing up a huge wave which nearly swamped the boat, while grenades and rockets were darting round them on all sides, shells and missiles of every description rising in the air. The escape of Lord Cochrane and his companions was almost miraculous, for not one of them was hit. The fire-ship, too, had performed her destined work, if not as completely as had been desired, sufficiently so to enable the *Mediator* fire-ship, Commander Woolridge, to force her way. In his eagerness to direct her against the enemy, he remained till the explosion actually occurred, when he, with two lieutenants, a seaman, and the gunner, who was killed, were blown out of the ship. So well directed were the six other fire-ships that two fell on board the *Ocean*, of 120 guns, and the *Regulus*, a 74, the former being compelled to cut her cables, and she soon afterwards, narrowly escaping the Pallas Shoal, ran on shore, where she again had a narrow escape from another fire-ship. So panic-stricken were the French crews that every effort to escape was made. The scene was indeed truly terror-inspiring, the darkness rendering the effect of the burning ships, the flight of shells and rockets, and the flashes of the guns awful in the extreme.

The danger in which the French ships were placed will best be understood from an account written by one of the officers of the *Ocean*, the French admiral's flag-ship. After the *Ocean*, narrowly escaping being blown up, had grounded, a burning fire-ship grappled her athwart her stern. Every effort was made to prevent the fire from catching the ship; the engine playing, completely wetted the poop, while spars were used to heave off the fire-ship, and axes to cut the lashings of her grapnels fastened to the end of her yards; but the *chevaux-de-frise* on her sides held her firm. The flames from the fire-ship covering the whole of the poop, it seemed impossible that the *Ocean* could escape. At this juncture two other line-of-battle ships, the *Tonnerre* and *Patri-ote*, fell on board her. The first broke her own bowsprit and destroyed the *Ocean's* main-channels. As the fire-ship athwart the stern was now about to drive forward along the starboard side, the *Tonnerre* was got free. Unless this had happened the fire-ship would have fallen into the angle formed by the two ships, and would inevitably have burnt them. The fire-vessel having now drifted under the bowsprit of the *Ocean*, was there held for some time. In order to afford the *Tonnerre* and *Patriote* an opportunity to get out of her reach, an attempt had been made to drown the magazine, but the flow of water was too slow for the purpose. In the efforts to clear the fire-ships upwards of fifty men fell into the sea and were drowned, the boats saving others.

Shortly afterwards another fire-vessel approached on the starboard-quarter, but the *Ocean's* guns cut away her main-mast, and wearing, she passed close alongside. For the remainder of the night vessels were seen burning on all sides. Daylight revealed the French fleet in a deplorable condition; the *Ocean* on the mud at a distance of half-a-mile to the south-east of the anchorage in Aix Road; to the south-east of her, about fifteen hundred yards off, on a rocky bed, lay the *Varsovie* and *Aquilon*, and close to them on somewhat better ground the *Regulus* and *Jemappes*. The *Tonnerre*, already bilged, and her main-mast cut away, and most of her guns hove overboard, lay at the entrance of the Charente, and at some distance off the *Calcutta*, close to the wreck of the *Jean Bart*. The *Patriote* and *Tourville* also lay not far from the channel of the Charente. Four frigates were also on shore in the same direction. All the grounded ships were more or less on the heel — those on the Pallas Shoal in a very desperate condition. Thus, although the fire-vessels had not caused the immediate destruction of any of the French fleet, they had been the means of reducing nearly the whole of them to a comparatively defenceless state. Lord Cochrane, in the *Impérieuse*, being the nearest English ship, was the first to perceive their condition, and immediately telegraphed, "The fleet can destroy the enemy — seven on shore;" at 6:40, "Eleven on shore;" and at 9:30, "Enemy preparing to heave off." At first it was hoped that Lord Gambier would immediately stand in and complete the destruction of the helpless enemy; and there can be little doubt, had such men as Sir Sidney Smith or Lord Cochrane himself been in command, such would have been accomplished; but Lord Gambier, afraid of risking the loss of the whole fleet by venturing among the shoals, called his captains on board, held a council of war, and allowed the favourable time to pass by. The tide rising enabled several of the ships to get afloat, and run up the Charente out of the way of danger. The *Impérieuse*, without waiting for orders, after signalling for assistance, stood towards three of the French ships, the *Calcutta, Varsovie,* and *Aquilon*. After some time she was joined by some gun brigs and bomb-vessels, and later by the *Indefatigable*, and other frigates. She had, in the meantime, compelled the *Calcutta* to cease firing, and the French-men to abandon her. Lord Cochrane then sent a midshipman and boat's crew to take possession, when, without orders, the midshipman set her on fire, and in the evening she blew up with a tremendous explosion. The *Tonnerre* was also set on fire by her own officers and crew, and blew up. The fire from the English ships compelled the *Varsovie* and *Aquilon* to submit at 5:30 p.m. Five other French ships lying on shore at the mouth of the Charente might also have been destroyed had there been any reserve of fire-vessels, but these were wanting, and though efforts were made to prepare three more, by the time they were ready the wind had shifted and they could not be used. The French lost the *Varsovie*, of 84 guns, the *Aquilon* and *Tonnerre*, of 74 guns, and the *Calcutta*, of 50 guns. The *Impérieuse* during the action had three seamen killed, and Mr Gilbert, an assistant-surgeon, Mr Marsden, purser, seven seamen, and two marines wounded, while the *Revenge* had three men killed and Lieutenant Garland and fourteen men wounded, she also receiving considerable damage in her hull from the batteries on Ile d'Aix. The French loss was much more considerable; the *Varsovie* especially, having 100 killed and wounded, while the captain of the *Aquilon* was killed in a boat of the *Impérieuse*, when seated by the side of Lord Cochrane, by a shot from the burning *Tonnerre*. The burning *Varsovie* and *Aquilon*, being supposed by the French to be fire-ships, created a further panic among them. The captain and crew of the *Tourville*, believing that the fire-vessel was bearing down upon them, deserted their ship, and hastened in their boats on shore. A gallant French quartermaster, however, of the name of Bourgeois, managed to get on board again before the boat shoved off, resolved to stand by his ship to the last. To secure his safety should the fire-ships grapple the *Tourville*, he at once began constructing a raft. He had just completed it when an English boat approached, the crew of which were ignorant that the ship was abandoned. Bourgeois hailed her twice, but receiving no reply, fired a musket which he found at the gangway. This was returned, but the intrepid fellow, hastening to the captain's cabin, where he found twenty loaded muskets, discharged them in quick succession, when, greatly to his satisfaction, the boat pulled away. After he had been on board an hour, he discovered three of his shipmates insensible from drink on the lower-deck. A short time after this three of the *Tourville's* boats, with a young midshipman, who now took the command, returned on board the *Ocean*, and he and the brave quartermaster prepared to defend their ship to the last. Fortunately for them, the English, not aware of what had happened, did not attack her, or she would undoubtedly have been added to the list of the French ships destroyed on the occasion Lord Cochrane still remained with the gun brigs, and the *Pallas*, Captain Seymour, her commander, having gallantly decided on rendering him assistance. At 8 a.m. on the 13th of April he despatched the brigs and mortar-vessel to attack the ships still aground. The *Etna* unfortunately split her mortar, and the other vessels could do the enemy but little harm. A strong wind and tide prevented the *Impérieuse* and *Pallas* from taking a part in the attack. At noon five other small vessels were sent in by Lord Gambier, who wrote to Lord Cochrane giving him leave to attack the *Ocean*, but observing that there was little prospect of success, and desiring to see him as soon as possible. Lord Cochrane replied, "We can destroy the ships which are on shore, which I hope your lordship will approve of." The *Impérieuse*, therefore, remained until the next day, when Lord Gambier, finding that Lord Cochrane would not quit his post as long as he had a shadow of discretionary authority, superseded him in the command of the fire-ships by Captain Wolfe, observing, "I wish you to join me as soon as possible, that you may convey Sir Harry Neale to England, who will be charged with my despatches." The *Impérieuse*, therefore, proceeded to Basque Roads, where Lord Cochrane had a disagreeable interview with the admiral, who insinuated that he desired to take all the merit of the service to himself. On his arrival in England Lord Cochrane, who had now a seat in Parliament, gave notice that he should oppose the vote of thanks about to be proposed to Lord Gambier. On hearing this Lord Gambier, on his arrival, demanded a court-martial. The evidence of Captain Pulteney Malcolm was much in favour of Lord Cochrane, but the other witnesses supported Lord Gambier, and sentence was pronounced, honourably acquitting him of all blame. From that day Lord Cochrane's prospect of success in the navy was destroyed. Though attempts were made by Lord Mulgrave to bribe him over, he refused to abandon what he considered his duty to his constituents and the country. The vote of thanks to Lord Gambier was carried by a majority of 161 to 39.

The following year, when Crocker, secretary to the Admiralty, brought forward the navy estimates, Lord Cochrane moved an address for certain returns relating to pensions on the civil list, contrasting them with pensions to naval officers; remarking in the course of his speech, "An admiral, when superannuated, has 410 pounds a-year, a captain 210 pounds, while a clerk of the ticket-office retires on 700 pounds a-year. Four daughters of the gallant Captain Courtenay, who was killed in action with the enemy when commanding the *Boston*, have 12 pounds, 10 shillings each; the daughters of Admiral Sir A. Mitchel and Admiral Hepworth have each 25 pounds; Admiral Keppel's daughter, 24 pounds; the daughter of Captain Mann, who was killed in action, 25 pounds; and four children of Admiral Moriarty, 25 pounds each. Thus thirteen daughters of admirals and captains, several of whose fathers fell in the service of their country, receive from the gratitude of the nation a sum in the aggregate less than Dame Mary Sexton, the widow of a commissioner."

Remarking on the pension list, he observed, "Captain Johnstone receives 45 pounds 12 shillings for the loss of an arm; Lieutenants Harding and Lawson, 91 pounds, 5 shillings each for a similar loss; Lieutenant Campbell, 40 pounds for the loss of a leg; and Lieutenant Chambers, RM, 80 pounds for the loss of both legs — while Sir Andrew Hammond retires on a pension of 1500 pounds per annum."

Amongst the most renowned exploits of the navy is that of the capture of Curaçoa. It having been reported to Vice-Admiral Dacres, then commander-in-chief on the Jamaica station, that the inhabitants of the island of Curaçoa wished to ally themselves to Great Britain, he despatched the *Arethusa*, 38-gun frigate, commanded by Captain Charles Brisbane, accompanied by the *Latona*, also of 38 guns, Captain Wood, and the *Anson*, 44 guns, Captain Lydiard. These, when close to the island, were joined by the *Fisgard*, of 38 guns, Captain Bolton. Captain Brisbane, suspecting that the governor and the troops garrisoning the strong forts would not be willing to yield them up as the inhabitants might desire, without waiting to enter into diplomatic negotiations, determined at once to run into the harbour of Saint Anne, the capital of the island, and to invite the authorities to yield under the muzzles of his guns. A favourable wind, which sprang up on the last day of the year 1806, gave him hopes of being able to carry out his project. On New-Year's Eve it was known that every true Dutchman would indulge in extra potations, and that by getting in at daylight, before the garrison had regained their senses, there would be every probability of catching them unprepared. Excellent arrangements were made; each frigate had her allotted station, and the larger portion of her crew was divided into storming parties, under their respective officers. The master, with the remainder of the hands, being left in charge of the ship. Each was to wear a distinctive badge, so that they might know each other during the fighting. The difficulties to be encountered were of no light description. The harbour, only fifty fathoms wide, was defended by regular fortifications; one, Fort Amsterdam, on the right of the entrance, mounting sixty guns in two tiers. On the opposite side was a chain of forts, and at the farther end an almost impregnable fortress, called Fort République, enfilading it almost within grape-shot distance. Besides these defences, a 36-gun frigate, a 20-gun corvette, and two large armed schooners lay athwart the harbour, which nowhere exceeds a quarter-of-a-mile in width.

At daylight the *Arethusa* leading, with a flag of truce at the fore, followed by the other three frigates, entered the port, receiving as she did so a warm fire from the Dutch, who, however, only at that instant aroused out of their beds, took but bad aim. In a few minutes the wind beaded the frigates, but shifting again, they stood on, and took up their stations in favourable positions, with their broadsides bearing on the Dutch forts and ships. So close in were the frigates that the *Arethusa's* jib-boom was over the wall of the town. Captain Brisbane now sent a summons to the governor, to the effect that the British squadron had come to protect, not to conquer the inhabitants, but that if a shot was fired, he should immediately storm the batteries. He wisely gave the governor but five minutes to make up his mind. Receiving no answer, Captain Brisbane ordered the ships to open their broadside, when each having fired three, he and Captain Lydiard boarded and carried the frigate and corvette. This done, they proceeded to storm Fort Amsterdam, which, though strongly garrisoned, was carried in about ten minutes, one party breaking open the seagate with crowbars, while another escaladed the walls. The citadel of the town, and several other forts, were carried with equal celerity. A fire was next opened upon Fort République, and preparations were made to attack it in the rear with a body of 300 seamen and marines, but so completely confounded were the garrison by the suddenness of the assault that, though they might have effectually resisted, and possibly blown the British ships out of the water, they yielded without firing a shot, and a little after 10 a.m. the British flag was hoisted on their walls. Two hours later the island of Curaçoa capitulated, and was taken possession of by the victors.

During this brilliant morning's work the total loss of the English amounted to only 3 killed and 14 wounded, chiefly in the capture of the ships; and the Dutch lost 5 killed and 8 wounded, besides nearly 200 men killed and wounded on shore.

Many other gallant actions were fought between light squadrons and single ships, and numerous cutting-out expeditions in boats were successfully undertaken. During these years the British line-of-battle ships attained a size far greater than had existed at any preceding period. The *Caledonia*, though ordered as far back as the year 1794, did not begin building till January, 1805, and was launched on the 25th of June, 1808. Though originally intended to carry only 100 guns, she was altered to a 120-gun ship, her draught being prepared by Sir William Rule, one of the surveyors of the navy. Her length on the lower gun-deck from the rabbet of the stem to the rabbet of the stern-post was 205 feet; her extreme breadth 53 feet 8 inches; her depth of hold 23 feet 2 inches; and she was of 2615 tons burden. Her net complement, including marines and boys, was 891. She was, and continued to be, the finest three-decker in the service. She excelled in all essential qualities, rode easy at her anchors, carried her lee-ports well, rolled and pitched quite easy, steered, worked, and stayed remarkably well, was a weatherly ship, and lay to very close, close-hauled under whole or single reefed top-sails. She went nine knots, and under all large sail eleven knots.

She was followed by the *Nelson*, of the same size, the *Britannia*, built at Plymouth, and the *Prince Regent* at Chatham. Two others of a somewhat similar size were subsequently added, the *London*, built at Plymouth, and the *Princess Charlotte* at Portsmouth, in the year 1813.

The prizes captured during the year 1807 nearly doubled that of any other period. At the same time, the losses sustained by the navy were greater than had ever before occurred, amounting to no less than 38 ships. Of these, no fewer than 29 foundered at sea or were wrecked, a large proportion of their crews perishing with them. The navy of England had, however, greatly increased. At the commencement of 1815 she possessed 124 line-of-battle ships, averaging each 1830 tons; whereas at the end of the previous century, they averaged only 1645 tons. If we take a glance back to a still more distant period, we shall judge better of the enormous progress made during the last two centuries. In the year 1641 the navy of England consisted of 42 ships, the aggregate tonnage of which was 22,411 tons. At the period of which we are writing it amounted to 966,000 tons, and within fifty years of that period, Scott Russell launched in the Thames one vessel of 22,500 tons, being in excess by 89 tons of the whole British fleet at the time of Charles the First. At that period about 8000 men were considered sufficient to man the navy, while in 1814, 146,000 men were voted; the navy estimates amounted to 18,786,509 pounds, and the burden of 901 ships amounted to 966,000 tons.

England, taught by the loss of several frigates captured by American ships of the same class, though vastly superior in size, began to construct frigates to compete with her foes. Three small-class seventy-fours, the *Majestic, Goliath,* and *Saturn,* were cut-down so as to retain their main-deck batteries, on which they were armed with 28 long 32-pounders, while on their lower-decks they received an equal number of 42-pounder carronades, besides two long 12-pounders as chase-guns; making 58 guns on two flush-decks, with a net complement of 495 men and boys. They thus, though denominated frigates, possessed a slightly increased weight of metal in broadsides to that which they before carried. It was hoped that with the aid of black hammock-cloths thrown over the waist of the barricade, they would be so disguised as to tempt any large American frigates they might fall in with to come down and engage. Such ships would have been more than a match for the heaviest of the American 44-gun frigates. They were in reality two-decked ships, but, as it turned out, they had no opportunity of proving their powers with any of the vessels with which they were intended to cope.

Several other fine 50-gun frigates were built; the *Endymion, Glasgow,* and *Liverpool, Forth, Liffey,* and *Severn* the three latter of fir, and the two before-mentioned of pitch-pine; the chief complaint made of them being that their quarters were rather confined. They had a complement of 350 men and boys. Other smaller frigates were constructed for economy's sake of yellow pine, most of them carrying medium 24-pounders, with a complement of 330 men and boys. To the British Navy were also added two classes of sloops of war; the largest, of about 430 tons, mounted 18 32-pounder carronades on the main-deck, and 6, 12, or 18-pounder carronades on the quarter-deck and forecastle, with two long sixes, making a total of 26 guns, with 121 men and boys. The second-class was the 18-gun brig-sloop. Another class of ship-sloops or corvettes were fitted out for sea while Sir Joseph Yorke was First Lord of the Admiralty, having a flush-deck, and carrying 18 32-pounder carronades and two long nines. They were fitted with stern chase-ports, but from the narrowness of their sterns there was no room to work the tiller, while the guns were pointed from the ports. They were defective also in having their masts too slight, while they were in other respects heavily rigged. The worst vessels, however, constructed at a later period, were the 10-gun brigs of war, small, narrow craft, so low between decks that the unfortunate commander, if a tall man, had to stand up, with his head through the skylight, and his looking-glass on deck, to shave himself. For many years commanders were appointed to them with a crew of upwards of 100 men, two lieutenants, and other gun-room officers, as well as midshipmen, whose berth measured seven feet by five. Being excessively crank, the greater number foundered, and gained for the class the unenviable title of "sea-coffins." They and frigates carrying 28 guns, generally known in the service by the name of "jackass-frigates," were the worst class of vessels belonging of late years to the British Navy. They existed, however, till steam power and the screw propeller caused those that had escaped destruction to be broken up or sold out of the service. For some years previously, however, the 10-gun brigs were commanded by lieutenants, with, of course, reduced crews.

Chapter Seventeen.

War with United States of America to war in Syria — from A.D. 1811 to A.D. 1840.

Much indignation had long been felt by the people of the United States in consequence of Great Britain claiming the right of searching neutral vessels for deserters from our ships. There existed, also, among them another cause of annoyance. It was this, that while the rest of the world were at war, the Americans had enjoyed the advantage of being the carriers for other powers, and that Napoleon, in the hope of crippling England, had declared all neutral vessels that had touched at any of her home or colonial ports liable to confiscation, thus virtually putting a stop to the commerce of the United States. Instead of complaining of France, the Americans put the blame on England, and hoped by going to war with her to regain the carrying trade they had lost. England had, besides, given great provocation as far back as the year 1807, when a small squadron of British ships was stationed off the American coast. Several men having deserted from the different ships, some of them were received on board the United States frigate *Chesapeake*. Hearing of the occurrence, the admiral at Halifax despatched the 50-gun frigate *Leopard*, commanded by Captain Humphries, with orders to the captains of any of the ships should they fall in with the *Chesapeake* without the limits of the United States to insist on searching her for deserters. Having delivered her despatches, the *Leopard* was lying with the rest of the squadron, when the *Chesapeake*, which was at anchor in Hampton Roads, put to sea on her way to the Mediterranean. On this, the *Leopard* received orders from the British commodore, to make sail in chase of her. Captain Humphries, shortly afterwards, falling in with the *Chesapeake*, hailed to say that he had a message from the British commander-in-chief. To this the American commodore, Barron, replied, "Send it on board — I will heave to." On the arrival of the *Leopard's* lieutenant on board the *Chesapeake*, Commodore Barron declared that he had no such men on board as were described. On the lieutenant's return, Captain Humphries again hailed the *Chesapeake*, and receiving unsatisfactory answers, observing also indications of intended resistance on board the American frigate, he ordered a shot to be fired across her forefoot. At intervals of two minutes he fired others, but evasive answers only being returned, and it being evident that the object of Commodore

Barron was only to gain time, the *Leopard* opened her fire in earnest. After she had discharged three broadsides at the American frigate the latter hauled down her colours, having only returned a few guns. On this a lieutenant from the *Chesapeake* came on board the *Leopard* with a verbal message from Commodore Barron signifying that he considered his ship to be the *Leopard's* prize. Without undertaking to receive her as such, Captain Humphries sent two of his lieutenants, with several petty officers and men, on board the *Chesapeake* to search for the deserters, and the crew being mustered, one of them, who was dragged out of the coal-hole, Jenkin Ratford, was recognised as a deserter from the *Halifax*. Three others were found, who had deserted from the *Melampus*, and about twelve more from various British ships of war. The first four, however, alone were carried on board the *Leopard*, when Commodore Barron again offered to deliver up his frigate as a prize; to this Captain Humphries replied that, having fulfilled his instructions, he had nothing more to desire, but must proceed to his destination. He, however, expressed his regret at having been compelled to attack him, and offered all the assistance in his power. The *Chesapeake* had indeed suffered severely from the broadsides of the *Leopard*, twenty-two shot being lodged in her hull, while her masts and rigging were greatly damaged. She had lost three seamen killed, while the commodore, one midshipman, and sixteen seamen and marines were wounded. Though nearly a hundred tons larger than the *Leopard*, and carrying a greater weight of shot, while her crew numbered fifty men more, she was almost unprepared for battle, so that no imputation could be cast on Commodore Barron for not continuing the engagement.

On arriving at Halifax the unfortunate Jenkin Ratford was found guilty of mutiny and desertion, and was hanged at the foreyard-arm of the ship from which he had deserted. The other men, though found guilty of desertion, were pardoned.

This untoward event was the cause of protracted diplomatic negotiations. Every apology was offered to the United States; and England gave up all claim to the right of searching men-of-war of other nations for deserters. About three years afterwards the British frigate *Guerrier* impressed out of an American merchant-vessel a man named Deguyo, said to be a citizen of the United States, and shortly afterwards two other native Americans in the belief that they all three were English subjects. At this time the 44-gun frigate *President*, belonging to the United States, lay moored in the Chesapeake. On receiving directions from his government, Commodore Rogers, who took the command, put to sea in search of the *Guerrier* on the 12th of May, 1811. Soon after noon of the 16th, from the mast-head of the *President*, a ship was descried standing towards her under a press of sail, which Commodore Rogers at once concluded was the frigate *Guerrier*. The stranger was, however, the British ship-sloop *Little Belt*, mounting 18 32-pounder carronades, and 2 long nines, with a crew of 120 men and boys, commanded by Captain Bingham, who at the same time made out the *President*. Captain Bingham, finding her signals unanswered, felt assured that the stranger was an American frigate, and continued his course round Cape Hatteras. By the time the evening was closing in, the *President* was up to her Captain Bingham hailed, asking, "What ship is that?" Commodore Rogers merely repeated the question. At that instant a gun was fired from the *President*, as was afterwards alleged, by chance. On this the *Little Belt* fired, and a furious action commenced, which lasted upwards of half-an-hour, with a short intermission. The after-sail of the *Little Belt* being shot away, and her rigging much damaged, she fell off, so that, being unable to bring her guns to bear on her antagonist, she ceased firing. Commodore Rogers again hailed, when he received answer that the vessel he had attacked was a British ship of war, but, owing to the freshness of the breeze, he did not hear her name. During this short engagement her masts and yards were badly wounded, and her rigging cut to pieces, while her hull was severely injured. She had lost a midshipman and 10 men killed or mortally wounded, and 21 wounded; while the *President* had only one boy wounded, and her rigging and masts but slightly injured. The *President* now hove to to leeward during the night, while the *Little Belt* was employed in stopping her leaks and repairing damages. Next morning the first lieutenant of the *President* came on board, expressing Commodore Rogers' regret at the unfortunate affair, and stating that had he known the size of the British ship he would not have fired into her. Captain Bingham inquired why he had fired at all; on which the lieutenant replied that the *Little Belt* had fired first. Captain Bingham denied this, and the subject was long a matter of dispute — though there can be no doubt that one of the *President's* guns went off, possibly by chance, and that Captain Bingham lost no time in replying to it. That Captain Bingham's conduct was considered most gallant was proved by his being immediately promoted to post-rank.

The following year the United States unhappily declared war against Great Britain. The American government had previously laid an embargo upon all their national ships and vessels during a space of ninety days, so that when war broke out on the 18th of June a large number of fast-sailing-vessels of all sizes were ready to issue forth as privateers; while Commodore Rogers, in command of the squadron, consisting of the *President, United States,* and *Congress* frigates, and two brigs of war, sailed in hopes of capturing a fleet of above 100 homeward-bound Jamaica men, known to be off the coast, under the convoy of a single frigate and brig. Fortunately for the merchant-vessels, Commodore Rogers discovered the British frigate *Belvidera,* of 36 guns, 18-pounders, commanded by Captain Byron, standing towards him. Captain Byron, having ascertained the character of the American squadron, tacked and made sail, not so much to escape as to lead the enemy to a distance from their expected prey. By consummate seamanship and gallantry, he kept them employed, carrying on a spirited action with his two long 18-pounders run through his stern-ports, and the two 32-pounder carronades on his quarter-deck, greatly galling the *President,* and afterwards the *Congress,* when that frigate got near enough to open her fire. So successfully did he manoeuvre, that after leading his pursuers a long chase, he escaped from them and got into Halifax. The *Belvidera* lost altogether 3 killed and 22 wounded. The *President,* which was cut up in her rigging, lost 2 midshipmen and a marine killed, and 22 officers and men wounded; while the Jamaica convoy reached England in safety.

The war between England and her former dependencies had now commenced in earnest. Since their independence, the United States had taken pains to construct an efficient, though small navy. Aware that it would be useless to attempt building line-of-battle ships to compete with the fleets of Europe, they had turned their attention to the construction of frigates, to act as ocean cruisers, of a size and armament capable of contending successfully with any possessed by England, or indeed any other maritime power. The result proved the wisdom and forethought of their naval authorities. Their most famed frigates were the *Constitution,* the *United States,* and *President.* The other two were of the same size and force as the latter vessel. The *President* measured 1533 tons: her sides and bulwarks were thicker, and her spars and rigging stouter than those of a British 74-gun ship, while she sailed admirably. She was pierced for 56 guns, but only mounted 52, of which 32 were long 24-pounders, and 20 42-pounders, her complement being 480 men. The other two mounted 54 guns, and the *Constitution* carried 32 instead of 42-pounder carronades.

On the 18th the *Constitution*, Captain Hull, then cruising off the Gulf of Saint Lawrence, having heard from an American privateer that a British ship of war was at a short distance to the southward, immediately made sail in that direction. The ship of which Captain Hull had heard was the British frigate *Guerrier*, commanded by Captain Dacres, an officer of known talent and gallantry. She carried 48 guns, including 30 long 18-pounders on the main-deck, 16 carronades, 32-pounders, and 2 long nines on her quarter-deck and forecastle. She measured under 1100 tons, and though her regular complement was 300 men and boys, she was nearly 40 men short. Seeing the *Constitution* approaching, at 4:30 p.m. on the 19th the *Guerrier* laid her main-topsail to the mast, to enable her the more quickly to close. She then hoisted an English ensign at the peak, another at the mizzen-top-gallant mast-head, and the Union Jack at the fore, and at 4:50 opened her starboard broadside at the *Constitution*. The American frigate being admirably manoeuvred, her heavy shot in a short time began to tell with destructive effect on the English frigate. The *Guerrier's* mizzen-mast was soon carried away, as it fell, knocking a large hole in the counter, and by dragging in the water, brought the ship up in the wind — thus enabling the *Constitution* to place herself on the *Guerrier's* larboard bow, in which position she opened a destructive fire of great guns and small-arms on the British frigate, who could only return it with her bow-guns. The riflemen in the *Constitution's* tops continued firing all the time with unerring aim. Captain Dacres was severely wounded, as were several of his officers. At length the *Guerrier's* foremast and mizzen-mast were carried over the side, leaving a defenceless wreck, rolling her main-deck guns in the water. From the rotten state of her breachings, many of her guns broke loose, but still Captain Dacres, having cleared away the wreck of his masts, continued the action, till the *Constitution*, having rove new braces, took up a position within pistol-shot of the *Guerrier's* starboard-quarter. Finding his ship utterly unmanageable, to prevent further sacrifice of life, Captain Dacres at 6:45 hauled down the Union Jack from the stump of the mizzen-mast, the only stick he had standing. The *Guerrier* in this desperate action lost 15 men killed and 63 wounded, 6 of the latter mortally; while the *Constitution*, out of her 468 men and boys, lost 7 killed and about double that number more or less wounded. Though the Americans might well be gratified at the result of the action, the English had no cause to be ashamed at the loss of the *Guerrier* to a ship the weight of whose broadside was nearly one-half heavier than that of her own, especially when a considerable number of the *Constitution's* crew were English seamen, and all had been carefully trained.

On the 25th of October the *Macedonian*, a frigate of the same size as the *Guerrier*, was captured by the *United States*, a frigate in all respects similar to the *Constitution*. Commodore Decatur, commanding the *United States*, used every effort to induce the crew of the captured frigate to enter the American service, though, to the credit of British seamen, the band alone, who were foreigners, and three or four others, said to be Americans, yielded to his persuasions.

The third British frigate, also of the size and force of the two preceding ones, captured by the Americans was the *Java*, taken by the *Constitution*, on the 29th of September. The *Java* was originally the French frigate *Renommée*, and had been commissioned at Portsmouth by Captain Lambert to carry out Lieutenant-General John Hislop, the governor of Bombay. Her crew, hurriedly got together, were inefficient in the extreme. They consisted of 60 raw Irishmen, 50 mutinous fellows sent from on board the *Coquette*, a body of 50 marines, several of whom were recruits, while the prison-ships and press-gangs furnished a large portion of the remainder. Exclusive of the petty officers, the best of the crew consisted of eight seamen, who were allowed to volunteer from the *Rodney*, indeed, scarcely fifty of the whole ship's company had ever been in action, while the ship herself was hurriedly fitted out, lumbered up with stores, and scarcely in a condition to put to sea. Meeting with a succession of heavy gales, it was not till the 28th December that Captain Lambert had an opportunity of exercising his men at firing the guns, when the *Java* fired six broadsides with blank cartridges, the first the greater number of his crew had ever discharged. While steering for Saint Salvador to obtain water, early the following morning, the *Java* sighted the *Constitution*, and made sail in chase. Standing to the wind, which was very fresh, the *Java* rapidly gained on her, and at length the two ships being within half-a-mile of each other, the *Constitution* fired her larboard broadside, which the *Java* waited to return till she got considerably nearer, when she fired her broadside, every shot of which took effect. The untrained British crew lost soon after this an opportunity of raking their powerful antagonist. Most gallantly Captain Lambert fought his ship, and his rigging being cut to pieces and masts injured, with several officers and men killed and wounded, he determined to board his antagonist as affording the best chance of success. His bowsprit, however, catching the starboard mizzen-rigging of the *Constitution*, his ship was brought up to the wind, and he lost the opportunity both of raking her or boarding. While in this position, Captain Lambert fell mortally wounded, when the command devolved on Lieutenant Henry Chads. The *Constitution* getting clear, had now the *Java* at her mercy. Still, animated by their officers, her crew, bad as they were, worked energetically at their guns, and seeing the *Constitution* standing off to repair damages, cheered under the belief that she was taking to flight. After the action had lasted rather more than three hours, the *Constitution* placing herself so as to rake the dismasted *Java*, Lieutenant Chads ordered the colours to be lowered from the stump of the mizzen-mast, and the frigate was taken possession of by the victor. The whole of the *Java's* boats, and all except one of the *Constitution's*, were knocked to pieces. The operation of conveying the prisoners on board the American frigate occupied a considerable time. As soon as it was accomplished, the *Java*, being much shattered was set on fire. Though the Americans behaved civilly to the British officers, the crew complained bitterly of being handcuffed and otherwise severely treated. The *Java* had her captain, 3 masters' mates, 2 midshipmen, and I supernumerary clerk killed, and 17 seamen and marines, and 102 officers and men wounded, among whom was her gallant first lieutenant.

Several brig-sloops and other small craft were also captured during the war by the Americans, who had every reason to be proud of the gallantry displayed by their seamen. Success, however, did not always attend on the "star-spangled banner," and, as was natural, the captains of the British 38-gun frigates were eager to fall in with one of the famed American forty-fours. Among others, Captain Philip Vere Broke, commanding the *Shannon* frigate, resolved, if possible, to show what a well-disciplined crew could do. He had from the time he had been appointed to her, several years before, diligently exercised his crew in gunnery, so that those who knew him and his ship's company felt confident of his success. The following lines, written soon after the commencement of the war, prove this: —

> *"And as the war they did provoke,*
> *We'll pay them with our cannon;*
> *The first to do it will be Broke,*
> *In the gallant ship the Shannon."*

The following song well describes the far-famed action: —

The "Chesapeake" and the "Shannon."

At Boston one day, as the Chesapeake lay,
The captain, his crew thus began on:
See that ship out at sea, she our prize soon shall be;
'Tis the tight little frigate the Shannon.
Oh, 'twill be a good joke
To take Commodore Broke,
And add to our navy the Shannon.

Then he made a great bluster, calling all hands to muster,
And said, Now boys, stand firm to your cannon;
Let us get under weigh without further delay,
And capture the insolent Shannon.
Within two hours' space
We'll return to this place,
And bring into harbour the Shannon.

Now alongside they range, and broadsides they exchange,
But the Yankees soon flinch from their cannon;
When the captain and crew, without further ado,
Are attacked, sword in hand, from the Shannon.
The brave commodore of the Shannon
Fired a friendly salute
Just to end the dispute,
And the Chesapeake struck to the Shannon.

Let America know the respect she should show
To our national flag and our cannon;
And let her take heed that the Thames and the Tweed
Give us tars just as brave as the Shannon.
Here's to Commodore Broke of the Shannon;
May the olive of peace
Soon bid enmity cease
From the Chesapeake shore to the Shannon.

In March, 1813, Captain Broke sailed from Halifax in company with the *Tenedos*, Captain Hyde Parker. Captain Broke, finding that the *Constitution* and *Chesapeake* were in Boston Harbour, the former undergoing considerable repairs, sent Captain Parker away, in hopes that the latter would come out and fight him. The *Chesapeake* was at this time commanded by a gallant officer, Captain Lawrence. Although Captain Broke captured several prizes, rather than weaken his crew, he destroyed them all, while he remained off the port waiting for the expected encounter. At length, having waited till the 1st of June, Captain Broke addressed a letter of challenge to Captain Lawrence, which begins: "As the *Chesapeake* appears now ready for sea, I request you will do me the favour to meet the *Shannon* with her, ship to ship, to try the fortune of our respective flags;" and added, "You will feel it as a compliment if I say, that the result of our meeting may be the most grateful service I can render to my country; and I doubt not that you, equally confident of success, will feel convinced that it is only by repeated triumphs in 'even combats' that your little navy can now hope to console your country for the loss of that trade it can no longer protect."

The *Shannon*, having stood in close to Boston Lighthouse, with colours flying, lay to, when the *Chesapeake* was seen at anchor. She shortly afterwards, under all sail, stood out of the harbour, accompanied by numerous yachts and a schooner gunboat, with several American naval officers on board. At half-past five in the afternoon the *Chesapeake*, with a large flag flying, on which was inscribed the words, "Sailor's rights and free trade," approached the *Shannon*, and soon afterwards, luffing up within about fifty yards of her starboard-quarter, gave three cheers. At 5:50 p.m. the *Shannon's* aftermost main-deck gun was fired, and the two combatants exchanged broadsides. The *Chesapeake*, however, coming sharply up to the wind, in consequence of all the men at her helm being killed, was exposed to a shot from the *Shannon's* aftermost gun, which took a diagonal direction along her decks, beating in her stern-ports and sweeping the men from their quarters. The *Shannon's* foremost guns also did considerable damage. In a few minutes the *Chesapeake* fell on board the *Shannon*, when Captain Broke, ordering the two ships to be lashed together, called away the main-deck boarders, and, followed by about twenty men, sprang on to her quarter-deck, which had been completely deserted. The British were, however, encountered on the gangways by some twenty-five or thirty Americans, who made but slight resistance, and being driven towards the forecastle, endeavoured to escape down the fore-hatchway, while others plunged overboard. The remainder threw down their arms and submitted. During this time the boarders were exposed to a destructive fire from the main and mizzen-tops, which continued till the main-top was gallantly stormed by a midshipman, William Smith, and five topmen. Having made their way along the *Shannon's* foreyard on to that of the *Chesapeake's* main-yard, another midshipman, Mr Cosnahan, climbing up on the starboard main-yard, fired at the Americans in the mizzen-top, when he compelled them to yield. Captain Broke, at the moment of victory, was nearly killed, having been cut-down by one of three Americans, who, after they had yielded, seized some arms and attacked their victors. The Americans, also, who had fled to the hold, opened a fire of musketry, which killed a marine. A still more unfortunate accident occurred; the *Shannon's* first lieutenant, Mr Watt, after being severely wounded, was in the act of hoisting the English flag, when the halliards getting entangled, the American ensign went up first, and, observing this, the *Shannon's* people reopened their fire, and he and several of those around him were killed before the mistake was rectified. Captain Broke, who had been assisted to a carronade slide, directed Lieutenant Faulkner to summon the Americans in the hold to give in if they expected quarter. They shouted out, "We surrender," and all opposition ceased. From the moment the first gun was fired till Captain Broke led his boarders on the deck of the *Chesapeake*, only eleven minutes elapsed, and in four minutes more she was his. Including the first lieutenant, her purser, and captain's clerk, the *Shannon* lost 24 killed and 59 wounded, two of these, her boatswain and one midshipman mortally; while the *Chesapeake* lost 47 killed, among whom was her fourth lieutenant, her master, one lieutenant of marines, and 3 midshipmen, and 14 mortally wounded, including her brave commander, and his first lieutenant, and 99 wounded. Other accounts state that the killed and wounded amounted to nearly 170. Among the 325 prisoners taken on board the *Chesapeake*, above 32 were British seamen. Several of the *Shannon's* men recognised old shipmates among their foes, and one of the former, when boarding, was about to cut-down an enemy, when he was stopped by the cry, "What! you Bill!"

"What! Jack!"

"Ay, Bill, but it won't do — so here goes," and the poor fellow sprang overboard, and was drowned, rather than meet the fate which might have been his lot, as he had deserted from the *Shannon* a few months before.

The two frigates were pretty equally matched, there being a slight superiority only in favour of the *Chesapeake*, which was 31 tons larger, and had a crew of fully 70 more men. The gallant Captain Lawrence and his first lieutenant, Augustus Ludlow, died of their wounds, the former on the passage to Halifax, the latter on his arrival, and were buried there with all the honours their victors could bestow. Their remains were shortly afterwards removed in a cartel to the United States.

Passing over a number of actions between smaller vessels, in which sometimes the English and at others the Americans were the victors, a celebrated combat in the Pacific between two frigates, the American being the smallest, must be mentioned. In October, 1822, the United States 32-gun frigate *Essex*, commanded by Captain David Porter, sailed from Delaware Bay on a cruise in the Pacific. Having captured several whale-ships, he named one of them the *Essex Junior*, and having visited the Marquesas, where he exhibited his prowess against the natives, he reached Valparaiso about the 12th of January, 1814. The British 36-gun frigate *Phoebe*, Captain James Hillyar, with the 18-gun ship-sloop *Cherub*, Captain Tucker, which vessels had sailed in search of him, standing towards Valparaiso, on the 8th of February discovered the American cruisers, with several prizes at anchor in the harbour. For a couple of weeks or more Captain Hillyar did his best to draw the American ships out of the port. Captain Porter, however, had considered that his most prudent course was to attempt to escape, and he and his consort were on the point of doing so, a strong wind blowing out of the harbour, when the *Essex* was struck by a squall, which carried away her main-topmast. She accordingly bore up and anchored, while the *Essex Junior* ran back into the harbour. The *Phoebe* and *Cherub* made sail towards them. The former at length got near enough to open her fire. Captain Hillyar now ordered Captain Tucker to keep under way, while he himself stood in closer with the intention of anchoring close to the *Essex*. The latter ship now cut her cable, and endeavoured to run on shore, but the strong wind from the land blew her off towards the *Phoebe*, and she had again to let go an anchor. By this time most of her boats were destroyed. The three boats from the *Essex Junior* were alongside, carrying off the specie and other valuables in the ship. Those of her crew who were English taking the opportunity of escaping, a report was raised at this juncture that the ship was on fire, and a number of her men leaped overboard during the confusion. At about 6:30 p.m. the *Essex* hauled down her flags, and the boats of the *Phoebe*, pulling for her, saved the lives of 16 of her crew who were in the water, though too late to rescue 30 others who perished; while between 30 and 40 reached the shore. The *Phoebe* lost 5 killed and 10 wounded, and the Americans 24 killed, including one of the lieutenants, and 45 wounded. As soon as the *Essex* could be repaired, the command of her being given to Lieutenant Charles Pearson, she and the *Phoebe* sailed for England, and anchored safely in Plymouth Sound, although Captain Porter had stated that the damage she had received would prevent her making the voyage. Of the prizes she had taken, not one reached the States, all having been recaptured, with the exception of three, which were burnt by the Americans, and one, the *Seringapatam*, the American prize-crew of which mutinied and carried her to New South Wales, whence she was brought to England and delivered to her former owners; while the *Essex* herself was placed on the list of the British Navy. Those who have read the journals of Captain Porter's cruise in the Pacific will feel very little pity for him on account of its result.

This miserable war, proved, on the whole, disastrous to the Americans. The ships of the English squadron on their coasts were employed in sailing up their rivers, destroying their towns, as also in despatching numerous boat expeditions to cut out their merchantmen, and to attack the gunboats prepared for the defence of their harbours. At the same time, both parties fitted out flotillas on the great lakes, where a number of engagements, often with heavy losses on either side, occurred. The principal British officer employed in this service was Sir James Yeo, who was sent with a small body of seamen to man the ships on these fresh-water seas. Some of these vessels were of large size; one named the *Prince Regent* measured 1310 tons, and carried 58 guns, with a complement of 485 men and boys. Another, the *Princess Charlotte*, measured 815 tons, and carried 42 guns. The larger number of vessels, however, were of much smaller size. The Americans had also several powerful vessels, and before the close of the war they had actually begun to build one 74 and a frigate, to vie with a ship built by the English called the *Saint Lawrence*, of 2305 tons, and intended to mount 102 guns. None of these large craft, however, went out of harbour. The whole of the gear and stores for these vessels had been brought overland at a considerable expense, and it was said that the Admiralty sent out a supply of water-casks, forgetting that their ships were to navigate fresh-water seas. To make any of the actions which took place intelligible, far more space would be required than can be afforded. Happily, by the end of 1814, this unnatural and ill-advised war was brought to a conclusion; the Americans finding that although occasionally victorious, they were in the end greatly the losers. It left, however, an amount of ill-feeling between the two nations which the war of independence had failed to create, and which it took many years to eradicate — though, happily, at the present time the people of both countries are too right-minded and enlightened to wish to see a recurrence of a similar contest, both convinced that it is to their mutual interest to remain in amity, and to cultivate to the utmost that good understanding which has for long happily existed.

After the conclusion of the war, the Caribbean Sea was infested by a number of piratical vessels manned by blacks and desperate characters of all nations, which committed great havoc among the British merchantmen. Though several were from time to time captured, the pirates still continued their depredations. Bad as they were, some proved themselves not altogether destitute of humanity. On one occasion a small vessel, tender to his majesty's frigate *Tyne*, commanded by Lieutenant Hobson, with a crew of 20 men, was surprised and captured by a powerful piratical craft. The pirates were, according to their usual custom, about to hang their prisoners; but seized with compunction, or dreading the consequences of their intended crime, they spared their lives, and allowed them to return to their ship. As it happened, the very men who had acted so humane a part were shortly afterwards captured, and the circumstance not being taken into consideration in their favour, they were hanged at Jamaica. At this time, a desperate character, named Cayatano Aragonez, commanded a schooner called the *Zaragonaza*, of 120 tons, carrying a long swivel 18-pounder, 4 long 9-pounders, and 8 swivels, with a crew of between 70 and 80 men. Hearing of the way his friends had been treated, looking upon it as an ungenerous act, he vowed to take fearful revenge on all the English he could capture. Summoning his men, he bound them under an oath never to spare an Englishman's life, and in the event of being captured, to blow up themselves and their enemies. Some time before, they had taken a black man, a native of Jamaica, who had been compelled to act as their cook. In order thoroughly to commit his crew, Aragonez resolved on the sacrifice of the hapless negro. In vain he pleaded for mercy; he was hauled out to the end of the spritsail-yard, when the miscreants commenced firing at him from the deck, and thus tortured him for twenty minutes before death put an end to his sufferings. Sir Charles Rowley, commander-in-chief in the West

Indies, having determined to put a stop to the exploits of the pirates, despatched the *Tyne*, under the command of Captain Walcott, accompanied by the sloop of war *Thracian*, to look out for and destroy them. Their chief places of rendezvous were known to be among the numerous keys or sandy islets off the coast of Cuba. Captain Walcott, after for a long time vainly searching for the pirates, was informed by the master of an American pilot-boat that a schooner supposed to be the *Zaragonaza* had been seen cruising off Barracoa, at the east end of Cuba. Captain Walcott endeavoured to bribe the American pilot to remain with him. He, however, declined the risk, declaring it was impossible to capture the schooner with boats, and as she was a remarkably fast sailer, she was sure to escape; should the enterprise not succeed, he would become known as the informer, and be no longer able to act as pilot in the Bahama Channel. This was a disappointment to Captain Walcott, who knowing that two Spanish men-of-war schooners were cruising off the coast, and that there were numerous trading schooners of the same appearance, feared that the pirates would escape. However, on the 31st of March, the two British ships discovered the vessel of which they were in search off Barracoa. Captain Walcott had disguised both ships as merchant-vessels, and their sails being set in a slovenly manner, they stood in towards the schooner. For several hours it was evident that the pirate did not suspect what they were. Before, however, they got up with her, she, setting all sail, steered for the harbour of Mata. On this the frigate and sloop crowded every stitch of canvas they could carry in chase. The wind, however, failed them before they could get up to the schooner, which, running in to the harbour, at 1:30 p.m., was seen moored head and stern athwart it, with the Spanish colours flying aloft. The entrance of the harbour not being more than a cable's length in width, even the *Thracian* could not venture to approach close enough to attack the schooner. Captain Walcott, therefore, ordered out the boats, which carried altogether forty-seven men, and believing that a desperate resistance would be made, and that should the attack fail the pirates would slaughter all they might capture, he determined to lead the expedition himself. As he shoved off, he desired Commander Roberts of the *Thracian* to get as close as possible, so as to render all the assistance in his power. The sea was calm, the boats were in full view of the pirate. Shoving off from the ship's sides, they pulled gallantly towards her. At 3 p.m. they arrived within gunshot, when up went the black flag, thus giving undoubted evidence of the character of the craft, while the schooner opened her fire, at the same time bullets came flying round the boats from a number of the pirate crew who had been landed, and been stationed under shelter among the trees which grew close to the shore of the harbour. Still the British boats pulled steadily on in two divisions, Captain Walcott's intention being to board the pirate on both sides at once. Each of the pinnaces carried carronades, which were now rapidly fired, while the marines began to blaze away, thus partially, by the smoke which circled round them, concealing the boats and preventing the pirates from taking exact aim. As the boats approached, the deck of the pirate was seen crowded with men, and boarding nettings triced up. Three-quarters of an hour had the British seamen been exposed to her fire, as well as to that from the men on shore, when Captain Walcott issued the order to dash alongside. For a few moments the pirates ceased firing, being employed in loading all their guns in the hopes of sending their assailants with one broadside to the bottom. Three hearty cheers were given, and so rapidly did the boats approach that the shots flew over them, and before the schooner's guns could be reloaded, the boats were up to her, and the seamen began climbing on board — no easy matter, for the sides were unusually high, and had been greased all over so as to render it as difficult as possible. At that moment the pirate crew losing heart, began to leap overboard and swim towards the shore, in the hopes of preserving their lives. Many, however, were cut-down before they could make their escape, while others were captured in the water. Among them Aragonez himself was taken, with 27 besides, 10 were killed, and 15 wounded; while the English lost 1 man killed and 4 wounded in this most gallant affair. Captain Walcott then sent a requisition to the governor of Barracoa, which induced him to dispatch a party in search of those who had escaped into the woods, when sixteen more were captured and immediately put to death by the Spaniards. The *Tyne* then sailed with her prisoners for Jamaica, when two of them turning king's evidence, their chief and the remainder of the miscreant band were executed. The affair may well take rank with any of the most brilliant boat services on record, and Admiral Rowley expressed in a general order his sense of the admirable skill and courage with which the enterprise had been carried out. That most graphic of writers, Michael Scott, who spent many years in the West Indies, had evidently heard of it when he wrote "Tom Cringle's Log." The capture of Lieutenant Hobson by the pirates, and his subsequent release, afforded him the idea of the captive of his hero by the picaroon, while the destruction of Obed's schooner in a harbour off Cuba, with not a few additional touches, was also taken from the account of the capture of the *Zaragonaza*.

The piratical cruisers belonging to Algiers had long been the terror of the merchantmen of all nations. The Algerines not only plundered but massacred the crews of the vessels they captured, and it was supposed that many hundreds had fallen into their power. Their crowning act of atrocity was the murder of the crews of three hundred small vessels engaged in the coral fishery off Bona, near Algiers, who, being Christians, had landed to visit a church. At length the British Government determined to put a stop to their proceedings, and Lord Exmouth, who had just returned to England, after having compelled the Dey of Tunis to restore 1792 slaves to freedom, and to sign a treaty for the abolition of Christian slavery, was appointed to the command of a fleet which sailed from Plymouth on the 28th of July, 1816, with his flag flying on board the *Queen Charlotte*, of 100 guns, Captain James Brisbane. During the passage out, every ship in the fleet was exercised with the great guns, firing at a target hung from the end of the fore-topmast studdingsail-boom rigged out for the purpose, so that they became unusually expert. Lord Exmouth's fleet consisted of only five line-of-battle ships, with the 50-gun ship *Leander*, four frigates, and several sloops of war and bomb-vessels. Misled by the charts, which were altogether defective, Lord Nelson had required ten sail of the line, and the same number of bomb-vessels, when he proposed to attack Algiers, but the harbour and fortifications had lately been surveyed by Captain Warde, who had found the entrance of the harbour much narrower than had been supposed. The fortifications were, however, formidable in the extreme, the batteries defending the town bristling with several tiers of heavy guns, while powerful forts commanded the approaches. On the mole alone were upwards of 200 guns, and altogether 500 guns, few being smaller than 24-pounders, defended the piratic city. On reaching Gibraltar, Lord Exmouth found a Dutch squadron, Vice-Admiral Van de Cappellon, who entreated leave to co-operate with him, commanding it. After some delay owing to contrary winds, on the 14th of August the English and Dutch fleets, accompanied by several additional gunboats, sailed for Algiers. On their way they met the *Prometheus* sloop of war, Captain Dashwood, which had on board the wife, daughter, and infant child of the British consul, Mr McDonnell. The two ladies, disguised in midshipmen's uniforms, had with great difficulty escaped, but as they were passing through the gateway the infant, who had been concealed in a basket, uttering a cry, was detained and carried to the dey. It should be recorded as a solitary instance of his humanity that it was sent off the next morning to its mother by the dey. The surgeon of the *Prometheus* with three midshipmen and the crews of two boats, consisting in all of eighteen persons, had been detained.

The fleet being becalmed, Lord Exmouth sent a lieutenant in one of the *Queen Charlotte's* boats with a flag of truce to the dey, demanding the immediate liberation of the British consul and the people belonging to the *Prometheus*, the abolition of Christian slavery, the delivery of all Christian slaves in the Algerine state, and the repayment of the money exacted for the redemption of Neapolitan and Sardinian slaves, and peace with the King of the Netherlands. Before the answer had been received, a breeze sprung up, and the fleet standing in to the harbour, the ships took up their appointed positions before the city. The *Queen Charlotte* made herself fast to the main-mast of a brig on shore close to the mole. Near her lay the *Leander*, while the other ships arranged themselves to bring their guns to bear on different parts of the city, the lighter vessels bringing up abreast of any openings they could find in the line of battle. Scarcely had the *Queen Charlotte* brought up, when a shot was fired at her from the city, followed by two other guns, when Lord Exmouth seeing a large body of soldiers standing on the parapet of the mole, watching the ships, mercifully waved his hand to them to make their escape, and as they were leaping down, the *Queen Charlotte* opened her starboard broadside, the other ships following her example. So admirably were her guns served that her third broadside completely levelled the south end of the mole, when, changing her position, she attacked the batteries over the town-gate, and brought the guns on it tumbling over the battlements. Soon after this an Algerine frigate was boarded by the flagship's barge, under Lieutenant Richards, and her crew driven overboard. Till about ten at night the ships kept up a furious fire at the town and forts; and by this time all the Algerine ships and vessels within the harbour were burning, as were the arsenal and storehouses on the mole, while several parts of the city were in flames. A fire-ship, which had been prepared at Gibraltar, was now, under the conduct of Captain Herbert Powell, run on shore, close under the semicircular battery, to the northward of the lighthouse, and exploding, committed great damage to the enemy. At length, the fire from most of the forts being silenced, and the batteries on the mole being in a state of dilapidation, the ammunition of the attacking ships falling short, Lord Exmouth took advantage of a light air of wind off the land to cut his cables, and stand out of fire, ordering the other ships to follow his example. Severe as had been the punishment inflicted on the Algerines, the allied squadrons suffered considerably, the British having lost 128 killed and 690 wounded, and the Dutch 13 killed and 52 wounded; while many of the ships had had their masts injured, and the *Impregnable* and *Leander* had received numerous shot in their hulls – the first ship to the number of 233; an 18-pound shot had entered the bulwark, passed through the heart of the main-mast, and had gone out on the opposite side. The Algerines were said to have lost between 4000 and 7000 men. Next morning a boat was again sent on shore with a note to the dey, repeating the demands of the preceding morning. She was met by an Algerine officer, who declared that an answer, yielding to all demands, had been at once sent. Finally, the dey agreed to the terms, and upwards of 1200 Christian slaves were delivered up, besides the British consul and the people from the *Prometheus*, 30,000 dollars to the British consul for the destruction of his property, and an apology to him, the restoration of the 382,500 dollars for the slaves redeemed by Naples and Sicily, and peace with the King of the Netherlands.

Numerous promotions followed as rewards to the officers engaged in this most important expedition, the objects of which were so fully attained. As a proof of the disinterestedness of the British, it should be known that of all the slaves liberated few, if any, were English. The Dutch admiral and his officers behaved with the greatest gallantry, each ship taking up her position as close to the enemy's batteries as she could get. It was the first time that wooden ships were fairly matched against stone walls; the result proved that, provided the ships can get close enough, the advantage will be on their side, unless the stone batteries are of far greater thickness than any that had hitherto been erected.

Severe as had been the lesson received, scarcely eight years had passed by before the Algerines had again sent their cruisers to sea. In consequence of this, Sir Harry B. Neale, then the British admiral in the Mediterranean, received directions to inflict a fresh punishment on them. Before proceeding to extremities, however, he despatched the *Naiad*, Captain Spencer, to destroy a large 16-gun piratical brig, which had taken shelter under the fortress of Bona. The service was performed in the most gallant way by Lieutenant Quin, first lieutenant of the *Naiad*, with her boats, he having pulled in under a tremendous fire from the fortress, boarded and blown up the brig. Sir Harry then appeared off the place with his squadron, and the dey, without the slightest resistance, yielded to all his demands.

Six years after this the French, landing a powerful army, captured the fortress by attacking it in the rear, and took possession of the country.

First War with Burmah — 1826.

England had been at peace for nearly nine years, when the aggressions of the Burmese on the territories of the East India Company induced the Government to send an expedition into the Irrawaddy, a deep river which runs past Ava, the capital of the country, for several hundred miles into the sea, with many important places on its banks. British troops, under the command of Sir Archibald Campbell, and a small squadron, under the command of Commodore Grant in the *Liffey*, sailed for Rangoon. The other ships were the *Larne*, Commander Frederick Marryat, the *Slaney*, of 20 guns, and *Sophie*, an 18-gun brig, four of the Company's cruisers, and a number of small craft to serve as gunboats.

Rangoon having been bombarded by the squadron, the troops landed, and drove the enemy, after some severe fighting, from their stockades. The English flotilla was actively engaged in capturing cargo-boats, which, being cut-down, served well for landing the troops. Captain Marryat, the celebrated novelist, on all occasions especially distinguished himself, showing that he could fight as well as write. Sickness, however, attacked both the seamen and soldiers. In a short time 749 of the latter had died, and thousands were in the hospital; while Commodore Grant and a large number of the seamen had also succumbed to disease. Captain Marryat having been promoted into the *Tees*, happily for himself, left the expedition. Captain Chads now commanded the squadron, to which, at the recommendation of Captain Marryat, the *Diana* steam-vessel had been added. Though she was unarmed — for at that time no one thought that steamers could carry guns — she was of great service during the harassing warfare in towing vessels and boats. Still the fever increased to an alarming degree, though some of the invalids when removed to places near the sea, and to floating hospitals, which were established at the mouth of the Rangoon river, recovered.

Though generally successful, the troops were repulsed in an attack upon the pagoda of Keykloo, with a loss of 21 officers and men killed, and 74 wounded, while 28, who had been made prisoners, were found fastened to the trunks of trees on the roadside, mangled and mutilated in the most horrible manner. Sir Archibald Campbell having determined to attack Rangoon, a flotilla of gun-vessels and a mortar-boat were sent up under Lieutenant Keele, the command of the land force being confided to Lieutenant-Colonel Godwin. Lieutenant Keele and those under him behaved most gallantly, destroying thirty of the enemy's war-boats and opening a heavy fire on the stockades, while the troops stormed and carried the fortress. The Burmese were next driven from Kemerdine, a fortified village above Rangoon. Their war-boats gave considerable trouble, some of them being of large size and carrying a long 9-pounder apiece, with a crew of 76 oarsmen, besides warriors. A squadron of boats, however, captured a considerable number, sank others, and put the rest to flight. The steamer *Diana*, on board which several carronades had been placed, with a party of small-arm men, did good service under the command of Lieutenant Kellet. The enemy, not aware of the rapidity of her movements, were overtaken, and upwards of forty of their boats were captured.

Early in 1825 Captain Alexander, of the 28-gun frigate *Alligator*, arrived out and took command; but he was shortly superseded by Sir James Brisbane — he, however, having to leave the station on account of ill-health, Captain Chads again took the command of the flotilla. The army advanced, and the little squadron pushed up the river; Donabew and Proom were taken, on each occasion the squadron acting an important part. Meaday was next captured, and before the close of the year the force reached Melloone, which also quickly fell. Still pressing forward, the army and squadron arrived at Yandaboo, forty-five miles only from Ava — the Burmese, whenever they were met, being completely defeated. For nearly a year the naval officers and their men were away from their ships, rowing and tracking their boats by day against a rapid stream, and at night protected only by awnings, and often hard-pressed for provisions. For upwards of two months they were entirely destitute of fresh meat. Still, all behaved admirably. The defeat of his army, and the rapid approach of the British, at length induced the King of Ava to sue for peace; and Sir Archibald allowing him only ten hours to decide, he agreed to enter upon a commercial treaty upon the principles of reciprocal advantage, to send a minister to reside at Calcutta, to cede certain provinces conquered by the British, and to pay a million of money as an indemnity to the British, a large portion being immediately handed over. This was brought down the Irrawaddy, a distance of 600 miles, and conveyed to Calcutta by Captain Chads. The Companionship of the Bath was bestowed upon the leaders of the expedition, and all the lieutenants and passed midshipmen were promoted — an acknowledgment of the admirable way in which they had performed their duties during the long and arduous service in which they had been engaged.

The Second Burmese War — 1851-52.

After a time the Burmese forgot the lesson they had received, and having frequently violated the treaty of 1826, it became necessary to bring them to order. An army of about 6000 men, under General Godwin, who had taken a leading part in the previous operations, was sent out; while the commander-in-chief on the Indian station despatched a small squadron, under the command of Commodore Lambert, of the *Fox*, 40 guns, with the *Serpent, Rattler, Hermes,* and *Salamander,* to which the East India Company added 13 steamers. A naval brigade was formed, and served on shore, under Lieutenant D'Orville, first of the *Fox*. Most of the places which had before been taken had again to be attacked, and were captured much in the same way as before, though not without severe fighting. The squadron was further increased by the arrival of the *Winchester*, Captain Loch. Whereas before only one steamer belonged to the squadron, it now consisted of a number of well-armed steam-vessels, suited for the navigation of shallow waters. The boats belonging to the ships co-operated on all occasions, while the troops were carried to their destinations by the steamers.

A most important expedition was sent up the river Irrawaddy under the command of Captain Tarleton, on board the *Medusa*. He had with him three Company's steamers. They proceeded to Konnoughee, a short distance below Proom, where a strong force, which appeared on shore, was put to flight by the shells thrown from the vessels. Higher up they found a Burmese army of 10,000 men assembled to guard the passage to Proom and the capital. The river here divides into two channels, one of which the Burmese believed to be too shallow for the passage of the steamers. Captain Tarleton, however, having ascertained that there was water enough for his vessels, pushed through it during the night, leaving the Burmese general and his army in the rear, and by daylight came off Proom. As there were no troops to defend the place, he carried off a number of heavy guns from a battery at the south end of the town. The iron ones were sunk in deep water, and the brass taken on board, to the number of twenty-three. Captain Tarleton had been directed merely to explore the river, or within four days he might have appeared before Ava, and in all probability have captured the city. On his return he was attacked by a large flotilla of war-boats, forty or fifty of which he either captured or destroyed. In consequence of his report, a body of troops was sent up the river on board steamers to Proom, which was quickly captured. Several other expeditions were made up the river, most of them under the command of Captain Granville Loch. Unhappily, he led one on shore against a robber-chieftain, Mya-Toon, who with other chiefs of the same character, had been committing depredations in all directions. The party consisted of about 300 men of the 67th Bengal Native Infantry, 62 marines and 185 seamen, with 25 officers. Having landed at Donabew, they marched inland through a jungle till they reached the robber's fortress. Before it was an abattis of sharply-pointed bamboos, the road being so narrow that it was impossible to deploy the whole strength of the column. Concealed by their breast-works, the Burmese opened a murderous fire on the British force. In vain Captain Loch endeavoured to force his way across the nullah or trench. At length he fell mortally wounded, while several other officers and a considerable number of men were killed and wounded. At length Commander Lambert, on whom the command devolved, gave the order to his followers to retire. The two field-pieces they carried with them were spiked, and the carriages destroyed, and they commenced their march back to Donabew, carrying their wounded companions, but they were compelled to leave the dead on the field. They were bravely covered by the grenadier company of the 67th, who kept the enemy at a distance till, almost worn out, after twelve hours' march, they reached their boats. The gallant Captain Loch expired on board the *Phlegethon* about forty hours after he had received his wound.

This disaster had no effect on the war, and the Burmese monarch being defeated at all points, agreed to open the Irrawaddy to British trade, and, shorn of much of his power, he has since remained at peace with England.

Battle of Navarino — 1827.

Unhappy Greece had long groaned under the tyranny of the Turkish yoke, her efforts to throw it off having proved unavailing, and been crushed by the most barbarous cruelty; when at length, in 1827, England, France, and Russia combined to emancipate her, the latter influenced by other motives than those of humanity. Vice-Admiral Sir Edward Codrington was appointed to the command of the British squadron in the Mediterranean, and he was directed to mediate between the contending parties. As he was about to leave England, he received, as it was said, a hint from the Lord High Admiral how he was to conduct his negotiations, with the memorable words, "Go it, Ned!" The French and Russian squadrons, which afterwards joined him, were placed under his command. Sir Edward, on inquiring from Sir Stratford Canning how he was to act, received the following reply: "You are not to take part with either of the belligerents, but you are to interpose your forces between them, and to keep the peace with your speaking-trumpet if possible; but in case of necessity, with that which is used for the maintenance of a blockade against friends as well as foes — I mean force;" and he further added, "When all other means are exhausted, by cannon-shot."

The harbour of Navarino is in the form of a horse-shoe, about six miles in circumference, with an island stretching across it, the only passage into it being about six hundred yards wide. The Turco-Egyptian army was encamped on the mainland, close to the fortress of Navarino, while on the opposite side was a strong fort, mounting 125 guns. Within this bay the Turkish and Egyptian fleets, consisting of 3 ships of the line, 4 double frigates, and 13 frigates, and a large number of corvettes, brigs, and other small craft, besides a number of transports, were at anchor, drawn up in the form of a crescent. Sir Edward Codrington's flag was on board the *Asia*, of 80 guns. He had with him the *Genoa and Albion*, seventy-fours, the *Glasgow*, 50, the *Cambrian*, 48, the *Dartmouth*, 46, and the *Talbot*, 28 guns, besides a corvette, 4 brigs, and the *Hind* cutter, tender to the *Asia*. The French had 4 line-of-battle ships, a frigate, and 2 corvettes, and the Russians about the same number. The allied fleet was therefore superior to that of the Turks, except in point of numbers. The combined fleet being formed in two columns, the British and French in the weather or starboard line, and the Russians in the lee line, entered the harbour. The *Asia* led, followed by the *Genoa and Albion*, and anchored close alongside a ship of the line, bearing the flag of the Capitan Bey, another ship of the line, and a large double-banked frigate, each thus having their opponent in the front line of the Turkish fleet. The French squadron was directed to attack the Turks to leeward, and the Russian to fill up the interval, while the English brigs were to look after six fire-vessels at the entrance of the harbour. Positive orders were given that not a shot should be fired unless the Turks set the example. The first three English ships were permitted to pass the batteries, and to moor without any act of hostility taking place. A boat, however, was sent shortly afterwards from the *Dartmouth* to request the Turkish fire-vessels to move farther out of the way, when Lieutenant Fitzroy and several of her crew were shot at and killed. On this the *Dartmouth* and the French admiral's ship opened a fire of musketry on the Turkish vessel, when one of the Egyptian ships fired a cannon-shot, which was immediately answered by the *Dartmouth's* broadside. The ships opposed to the *Asia*, however, did not for some time fire, and Sir Edward sent a pilot on board the Egyptian admiral's ship to express his desire of avoiding bloodshed, when, as he was alongside, he was killed by some of the Egyptian crew, and soon afterwards his ship fired into the *Asia*. The action now became general. The Turks fought with the greatest bravery, but their ships, one after the other, were quickly destroyed, several blowing up. Two of the fire-ships were soon in flames, a third blew up, and a fourth was sunk by the *Philomel*. A gallant officer, Lieutenant Maine Lyons, a brother of Sir Edmund Lyons, afterwards Lord Lyons, belonging to the *Rose* corvette, was mortally wounded while endeavouring to tow a fire-ship in flames clear of the French *Armide*. Commodore Bathurst of the *Genoa* was also mortally wounded, after having previously been severely hurt by a splinter soon after the commencement of the action. One of the Turkish ships fell foul of the *Albion*, when the crew of the former attempted to board, but being repulsed, the Turk was boarded instead by Lieutenant John Drake, who compelled her crew to cry for quarter. Unhappily, before he could rescue some Greek prisoners in her hold, she burst into flames, when he was compelled to retire, and her cables being cut by one of the *Albion's* midshipmen, she drifted clear of that ship and soon afterwards blew up. Among the many acts of gallantry was one performed by Lieutenant Robb, in command of the *Hind* cutter. She had arrived after the commencement of the action, when entering the bay she took up a raking position at about the distance of forty yards across the stern of a large frigate, and opened a rapid fire.

After remaining here for three-quarters of an hour, and receiving the fire of various smaller vessels, her cable was cut by a shot, and she drifted between a large corvette and a brig, which she engaged till the brig blew up. Her last cable being cut, she drifted into the hottest part of the action, till her main-boom ran into one of the main-deck ports of a Turkish frigate, the crew of which made several attempts to board her, but were repulsed by Lieutenant Robb and his crew. The Turks after some time sent a large strongly-manned boat to attack the cutter. Just as the boat got alongside the *Hind* two carronades, charged with grape and canister, fired into her by the latter, knocked her to pieces. The cutter after this fortunately drifting clear of the frigate, escaped the destruction which might have been her fate. Besides receiving numerous round-shot in her hull, she lost a master's mate and 3 men killed, and a midshipman and 9 men wounded. Every ship in the squadron behaved well, and was ably supported by the Russians and French. A small number only of the Turco-Egyptian fleet escaped destruction, though it was larger than Sir Edward Codrington had at first supposed. The very doubtful advantage gained by the action was purchased at the heavy loss of 75 killed, including several valuable officers, and 195 wounded, while the French and Russians together lost still more. The usual rewards were bestowed on the victors; though a new ministry coming in, the action was spoken of in the royal speech as "that untoward event." However, its ultimate result undoubtedly was the liberation of Greece from the Turkish yoke. Another result was the suppression of the office of Lord High Admiral by the Duke of Wellington, who, on becoming Prime Minister, requested the Duke of Clarence to resign, finding that his royal highness, having a will of his own, was not sufficiently subservient to the government. To the credit of our sailor-king, he never exhibited the least ill-feeling in consequence towards the duke for this apparent slight.

Warfare in Syria with Mahomet Ali.

Mahomet Ali, who, from a common soldier, had raised himself to a high command in the Turkish army, having been sent to Egypt, had deposed the pacha of that province and slipped into his shoes. Nothing stopped him in his ambitious career. Finding the Mamelukes troublesome, he invited about 500, all he could collect, to a feast in the citadel of Cairo, where, with the exception of one chief, who leaped his horse over a high wall and escaped, he caused the whole band to be massacred. Consolidating his power, he made himself independent of the Ottoman Empire, and began to consider the possibility of mounting the throne of the caliphs. To effect this object he assembled a large army, which he sent under his adopted son, Ibrahim Pacha, into Syria. Ibrahim Pacha, on his successful march northward, was encouraged, it is supposed, by the French, when England, with Prussia, Austria, and Russia, thought it time to interfere. The Turks were almost helpless. A large army sent against Ibrahim Pacha had been defeated, and the Turkish fleet had joined that of the Egyptians. The four powers now sent an ultimatum to Mahomet Ali, offering him the hereditary sovereignty of Egypt, and the pachalia of Saint Jean d'Acre for life, provided he would withdraw his troops from Syria, notifying that if he refused he would be compelled to assent by force of arms. Mahomet replied that the territories he had won with the sword he would defend with the sword. An English fleet was accordingly sent out to the Mediterranean under the command of Admiral Sir Robert Stopford, who was joined by some Austrian and Turkish ships, and the ports of Syria and Egypt were blockaded. Captain Charles Napier was appointed to the *Powerful*, as commodore, with the *Ganges, Thunderer, Edinburgh, Castor,* and *Gorgon* under his command. On fitting out the *Powerful* at Portsmouth, he had the following characteristic announcement placarded on the walls: "Wanted active seamen for the *Powerful*, Captain Napier. The *Powerful* is a fine ship, and in the event of a war will not fail to take her own part." Captain Napier's character being well known, the *Powerful* soon obtained an efficient crew.

The attitude taken up by France was so doubtful that it was expected that at any moment war might break out, and the officers of the British squadron were cautioned to be on their guard against surprise. It was, indeed, the most exciting time since the last war. While Sir Robert Stopford was blockading Alexandria, Napier's squadron anchored off Beyrout on the 12th of August, 1840. At this time Suleiman Pacha, at the head of 15,000 Egyptian troops, occupied Beyrout. Ibrahim was at Balbec with 10,000 more; the garrison of Sidon consisted of 3000 men, that in Tripoli of 5000, while between 40,000 and 50,000 Egyptians were scattered through various parts of Syria. A small Turkish squadron had been fitted out and placed under the command of Captain Baldwin Walker, who was known as Walker Bey. After Napier had been employed some time in examining the coast, Admiral Stopford, who was commander-in-chief of the land as well as sea forces of the allies, in consequence of the illness of Lieutenant-Colonel Sir Charles Smith, appointed him to take the direction of the military force on shore. This was much to the taste of Napier, who was as fond of fighting on land as at sea. Heading the troops on a small pony, in his usual free and easy dress, he carried all before him, and the Egyptian troops being put to flight, the mountaineers crowded in numbers under the standard of the sultan. It was determined to bombard Beyrout; the bombardment of Algiers had shown what could be done against stone walls. A new power was now introduced into naval warfare — a considerable number of steam-ships being among the fleet. They were the *Gorgon, Cyclops, Vesuvius, Hydra, Phoenix,* and *Confiance.* At that time little confidence was placed in them as vessels of war, though it was acknowledged that they might prove useful in towing line-of-battle ships into action, or in acting as despatch-boats, or as transports for throwing troops on shore at any particular point.

On the refusal of Suleiman Pacha to yield up Beyrout, the bombardment commenced, and continued for several days. In the meantime the *Carysfort*, Captain Martin, with the *Dido*, followed by the *Cyclops* steamer, with a body of 220 marines and 150 mountaineers, was despatched to attack the strong castle of D'jebl, to the northward. The ships having bombarded the place for an hour, a body of seaman under Captain Austin, and some marines, under Captain Robinson, were landed, protected by the fire of the ships, and proceeded to the assault. They advanced with their usual gallantry, but when they had got within thirty yards of the strong and lofty towers, a destructive fire was opened on them from a crenelated outwork, with a deep ditch in front. In vain the commanding officers looked for some part of the castle which might prove practicable; the muzzles of the enemy's muskets were alone visible through the loop-holes. As the men were falling rapidly without a prospect of success, it became necessary to draw them off, it being evident that the place could not be taken until a breach had been made in the walls, though the immense solidity of the building prevented much hope of this being done. As the party were on the point of re-embarking, it was discovered that an English flag, which had been planted on a garden wall by the pilot of the *Cyclops* as a signal to the ships, had been left behind. On this Lieutenant Grenfell, and McDonald, a seaman of the *Cyclops*, undertook to bring it off, and set out on their hazardous expedition. They were seen from the decks of the ships, and their object being understood, were watched with intense anxiety. Pushing on amid the bullets levelled at them, they reached the garden wall, seized the flagstaff, and escaping the bullets, hastened to the shore. Loud cheers greeted them as they returned on board uninjured with their prize. The next morning it was found that the garrison had evacuated the castle. Five marines were killed in the attack, and eighteen men wounded, including Lieutenant Gifford, R.N., and Lieutenant Adair, of the marines.

Beyrout still held out in spite of the battering it was receiving. Suleiman Pacha proved that he was as courteous as he was brave, for the Indian mail arriving by way of Bagdad, he ordered a flag of truce to be hoisted, and on a boat being sent on shore, delivered the mail, with a polite message, assuring the British that all letters to and from India should be carefully forwarded. Admiral Stopford immediately sent in a letter of thanks to the pacha, and accompanied it with some cases of wine which had been seized in an Egyptian vessel directed to Suleiman, rightly conjecturing that it would not prove an unwelcome present.

Firing was then resumed. Information having been brought by an Egyptian gunner, a deserter, that a train had been laid along the bridge to the eastern castle, where a large quantity of powder was concealed, he undertook to guide a party to cut the train and seize the powder. Commander Worth, who immediately offered to perform this dangerous service, was joined by numerous volunteers. The party embarked in one of the boats of the *Hastings*, and, protected by the *Edinburgh's* launch and pinnace, as well as by the fire from the ships, dashed on in face of a heavy fire of musketry, and landed on the bridge. Having succeeded in cutting off the train, they forced their way into the castle, over the walls of which they threw some sixty or seventy casks of powder, and succeeded in bringing off upwards of thirty more. In this exploit, unfortunately, a midshipman of the *Hastings*, Mr Luscombe, was killed, and the Egyptian guide, with three seamen, were wounded.

Commodore Napier, at the head of his marines and Turks, had a gallant skirmish on the Kelbson, or Dog River, when he dispersed the Egyptian forces, and took between 400 and 500 prisoners. Next day he returned on board his ship.

While talking with Sir Robert Stopford on the 25th of September, he remarked that Sidon was not yet in our possession, and, according to an article in the *Malta Times*, said to the admiral, "If you like, I will go down and take it, and be back in eight and forty hours." He started with the *Thunderer, Cyclops, Gorgon*, and *Hydra*, with 500 marines and 800 Turks. On his way he fell in with the *Stromboli*, from England, with a detachment of 200 marines. These he took with him, and after firing shot and shell at the town for a couple of hours, he made a breach and landed at the head of his men. The struggle was a sharp one, but after a great number of the enemy, who would neither give nor receive quarter, had been killed, as well as the Egyptian commander, who, although the bayonets of two marines were at his breast, resisted, the Egyptian troops, to the number of 500, threw down their arms. Fifteen thousand were afterwards taken. The commodore put himself at the head of the British marines, and breaking into the barracks, as soon as Captain Henderson and another party had lodged themselves in a house above the building, he marched his battalion along the wall from the upper gate, waving his hat at the point of his sword, and cheering on his men, and seized the castle. Among other acts of gallantry must be mentioned a race which took place from the spot where they landed, between Mr James Hunt, a midshipman of the *Stromboli*, and Senhor Dominica Chinca, a midshipman of the Austrian frigate *Guerriera*, each striving who should first plant his colours on the walls of the town. It was won by the English reefer. Without in any way detracting from Mr Hunt's gallantry, it is right to state that Lieutenant Anderson, of the marines, had already planted a Union Jack nearly on the same spot, but which he had afterwards carried to a higher part of the town. The Turkish troops were gallantly led by their colonel, accompanied by Walker Bey and Captain Austin, under a heavy fire, as were the English marines under Captain Whylock and Lieutenants Anderson and Hockins, the latter, who had just landed from England, being unfortunately killed. The Egyptians held out till their leader was killed, when nearly 2000 laid down their arms. The remainder retired through the streets, pursued by the attacking parties, and at length took refuge in a vaulted barrack, where upwards of a thousand men were found lying down ready for a sortie. They at once yielded, and thus in five hours from the commencement of the bombardment, Sidon was captured. The total loss to the allies and Austrians was 4 killed and 21 wounded, while only 12 Turks were wounded.

At what is called the Battle of Boharsof, Commodore Napier, with his gallant aides-de-camp, Lieutenants Bradley and Duncan, and Mr Pearn, master of the *Powerful*, at the head of his Turks and marines, attacked Ibrahim Pacha, posted in the neighbourhood of Mount Lebanon, among rugged and almost inaccessible rocks. The Egyptians' position was stormed, and Ibrahim's army took to flight, he, with a few men, escaping, and leaving 600 or 700 prisoners in the hands of the victors. Beyrout, in consequence of this victory, was abandoned, and taken possession of by the Turks. Thus the gallant old commodore, in about a month, freed nearly the whole of the Lebanon, took 500 prisoners, and gained over an equal number of deserters.

On the 17th of September Caiffa was bombarded and captured by the *Castor* and *Pique*, and a Turkish frigate, under Captain Collier. By the same ships, in a similar manner, Tyre was taken on the 24th, without the loss of a man. On the 25th of September Tortosa was attacked by Captain Houston Stuart, commanding the *Benbow*, in company with the *Carysfort* and *Zebra*, he having been informed that a large quantity of provisions was stored in the place, and should they be destroyed the troops in the neighbourhood must evacuate the country, and leave open the communication with the mountains, whose inhabitants were anxious to join the Turks. Unfortunately, when the boats were sent on shore to storm the place, it was found that a reef of rocks, or a sunken mole, would allow only the smaller ones to reach the beach. A gallant party, under Lieutenants Charlwood and Maitland, with scarcely thirty men, were able to get on shore, and both they and the larger boats were exposed to a heavy fire of musketry from numerous loopholes and crevices from the fortress. Lieutenant Charlwood having broken open several stores, which he in vain attempted to set on fire, the ammunition of the marines, who had followed Lieutenant Maitland, being wet, they were ordered by Captain Stuart to retire. In this disastrous affair 5 were killed and 17 wounded.

The celebrated fortress of Saint Jean d'Acre, which, when held by Sir Sidney Smith, had resisted the arms of Napoleon, had been captured by Ibrahim Pacha in 1837, and still held out. Sir Robert Stopford having received orders to attack it, the ships of the allied fleet proceeded thither, and arrived off it on the 2nd of November. They consisted of the *Princess Charlotte*, of 104 guns, the *Powerful* and *Thunderer*, 84, *Bellerophon*, 80, *Revenge*, 76, *Benbow* and *Edinburgh*, 72, *Castor*, frigate, 36, and the *Carysfort*, 26, the *Gorgon*, *Phoenix*, *Stromboli*, and *Vesuvius*, steam-frigates, and the Austrian flag-ship, an Austrian frigate and corvette, and the Turkish flag-ship, an 84. Rear-Admiral Walker — the *Pique* and *Talbot* frigates, the *Hasard*, 18-gun sloop, and the *Wasp*, 16-gun brig — had been there for some days. The fortress of Acre stands on a point of land, thus presenting two sides to the sea, one facing the east, and the other the south-east. In consequence of this, it was necessary that the squadron should attack in two divisions. Sir Robert Stopford went on board the *Phoenix* to superintend the attack. Napier led the way in the *Powerful* to the northward, closely followed by the *Princess Charlotte, Thunderer, Bellerophon,* and *Pique,* while Captain Collier, of the *Castor,* commanded on the south. The *Powerful,* followed by the other ships, having got round a shoal which lies off the city, bore up and ran along shore towards the north angle, anchoring about 700 yards distant from the sea wall, considerably inside the buoys which had been laid down to assist the ships in taking up their stations. As the ships successively brought up, they opened a tremendous fire on the batteries and sea wall, where the shot was so well directed that it would have been almost impossible for any human beings to have stood their ground. The Egyptians, supposing that the ships would anchor close to the buoys, had pointed their guns too high; consequently most of their shot flew over the decks of the ships, wounding chiefly the rigging and spars, while the clouds of smoke which immediately enveloped the fleet prevented them from remedying their mistake. The *Revenge* had been ordered to keep under way as a reserve, but Napier signalled to her to take up a position ahead of him, to attack a heavy battery of five guns. This Captain Waldegrave did in gallant style.

In the meantime Captain Collier's squadron were engaging the batteries on the south, well supported by the Austrians, and Admiral Walker, who, running inside all the squadron, took up a warm berth abreast of a new and strong work. The steamers were not idle, as they kept up a hot fire of shot and shell, doing much execution. While the fleet were thus engaged, an incessant roar showing the rapidity of the firing, and clouds of smoke filling the air, a thundering sound was heard — for an instant the whole fortress was illumined with an intense blaze of light, which was as suddenly succeeded by a dense cloud of smoke, dust, bursting shells, and large fragments of stone hurled upwards and in every direction. The principal magazine, containing many thousand barrels of gunpowder, had exploded, in consequence, as was supposed, of a shell having been thrown into it by one of the steam-ships. A large number of the garrison were blown up by the explosion, and many more probably were buried amid the ruins. Notwithstanding this catastrophe, the five guns opposed to the *Revenge* continued their fire, and kept it up to the last. About sunset the signal was made to discontinue the engagement, but Napier fired away for some time after dusk, lest the enemy should be tempted to re-man their guns. At length the admiral's flag-lieutenant brought an order for the ships to withdraw. The *Revenge*, slipping her anchor, made sail without difficulty. The *Princess Charlotte* picked up both hers and made sail, but, casting the wrong way, nearly got on shore. She was, however, conducted in a most seamanlike manner, not a word being heard on board her. The *Powerful* was towed out by the *Gorgon*. The *Thunderer* and *Bellerophon*, as also the southern squadron, remained at anchor.

During the night a boat brought off information that the Egyptian troops were leaving the town, and, in consequence, at daylight, 300 Turks and a party of Austrian marines landed and took unopposed possession of it. The casualties of the allies amounted to only 14 English and 14 Turks killed, and 42 wounded. Notwithstanding the long continued fire to which the ships had been exposed, they escaped with slight damage. The havoc caused by the bombardment on the walls and houses was very great, while it was calculated that the explosion had destroyed between one and two thousand persons, two entire regiments being annihilated, with a number of animals. On the 4th another explosion took place, by which a marine was killed, and Captain Collier had his leg fractured.

This was the first occasion on which the advantages of steam had been fully proved in battle, by the rapidity with which the steamers took up their positions, and the assistance they rendered to the other ships, as also by the destruction the shells thrown from them produced. The survivors of the garrison, amounting to 3000, were taken prisoners, while nearly 200 guns and mortars and field-pieces were captured. Ibrahim's army, which in September had amounted to 75,000 men, had now dwindled to 20,000, who, hard-pressed, were making their way back to Egypt. On the fall of Acre, Napier proceeded to Alexandria, where he entered into a convention with Mahomet Ali, who agreed to evacuate Syria and to restore the Turkish fleet as soon as he had received final notification that the sultan would grant him the hereditary government of Egypt, which, the Turkish fleet being given up, the sultan soon afterwards did. On the return of the *Powerful* to the fleet, before proceeding to Malta, the ships manned the rigging and cheered, the bands playing "Charlie is my darling."

This terminated the duties of the fleet on the coast of Syria.

Chapter Eighteen.

First War with China, and efforts to suppress the Slave-Trade — A.D. 1840.

The Chinese had long designated the English, as well as all other Europeans, the "outer barbarians," and treated them in the most insulting manner. At length the Chinese government, finding that silver alone was given in exchange for opium, was afraid that the country would be drained of that precious metal, and resolved to put a stop to the importation of the drug. Commissioner Lin was sent to Canton for that purpose, and, to prove that he was in earnest, he ordered the first Chinese opium smuggler he could catch to be strangled, shut up the British merchants in their factories, and then demanded the delivery of all the opium ships in the river. At the same time the British flag was fired on, British ships were detained, and a Chinaman having been accidentally killed by a British seaman, the life of a British subject was demanded in return. Captain Elliott, R.N., acting at that time as chief superintendent of trade, immediately sent home an account of the state of affairs, summing up altogether a long list of complaints against the Chinese. On receipt of the news a squadron was sent out of 3 seventy-fours, 2 forty-fours, 3 38-gun frigates, and several sloops of war and brigs, which, on their arrival, were joined by 4 of the East India Company's armed steamers, and to meet them on their arrival about 4000 troops were despatched from India. Before this the *Volage* and *Hyacinth*, while lying in Canton River, had a sharp engagement with a fleet of war-junks, under the Chinese Admiral Kwang. Gallantly as Kwang behaved, in a short time one of his junks blew up, three sank, several were shattered and deserted by their crews, and the remainder fled in the greatest confusion, Kwang's junk being in a sinking condition. Captain Smith, not wishing to cause any unnecessary bloodshed, retired with his ships to Macao, where he embarked a number of British residents. Kwang, in consequence, boasted that he had gained a great victory, and was covered with honours, his countrymen being encouraged to persevere in the contest. The Chinese also issued a proclamation offering 20,000 Spanish dollars to any one who would capture an English 80-gun ship, and 5000 dollars to the man who took alive a foreign mandarin or captain, and so on in proportion to the rank of the captives; while a third of the sum was to be paid for killing them. The Chinese, determined to resist, prepared fire-ships, exercised their troops, and got up sham fights, dressing some of their men in red clothes, who were always soundly beaten, to teach the Celestials to conquer the barbarian English. They had likewise purchased the *Cambridge,* an old East Indiaman, of 900 tons, and armed her with thirty-four guns, and had built some curious craft with paddle-wheels, in imitation of English steamers. It was said even that they had funnels, with fires below them to create a smoke, in order to deceive the barbarians. They also threw up forts along the banks of their rivers, sometimes facing them with thin boards or canvas, painted to look like stone, in order to frighten their invaders.

A CHINESE JUNK.

A considerable squadron, under the command of Rear-Admiral Elliott, in the *Melville*, 74, now arrived. When at Singapore, Captain Maitland had drilled 350 of her seamen to act as light-infantry troops, and had brought them into an admirable state of efficiency. While one part of the fleet blockaded the mouth of the Canton River, the remainder proceeded to the northward to look into different harbours. On her way the *Blonde* came off Amoa, near which she observed batteries thrown up, and in a short time a number of large armed junks came down as if to attack her. On a boat being sent on shore with a flag of truce, she was fired on by the Chinese. On this the *Blonde* opened her broadsides, soon knocked the forts to pieces, and compelled the war-junks to run up the harbour.

The *Wellesley*, with a part of the squadron, then appeared off Chusan. Commodore Bremer was in hopes that his overwhelming force would induce the Chinese to yield, but their fleet was commanded by a tough old admiral, who, ignorant of the power of the English, had no intention of doing so without a fight. During the night the Chinese were seen by the light of thousands of painted lanterns throwing up embankments, and placing fresh guns in position, while numberless merchant-junks, loaded with goods, women, and children, were observed making their way down the river to escape. After giving the Chinese several opportunities of negotiating for peace, the *Wellesley* opened her fire. It was answered by the whole of the Chinese line of defence. The rest of the fleet than began bombarding the place, and in seven or eight minutes it was reduced to ruins. On the smoke clearing away, the principal battery was seen to be knocked to pieces, as were four war-junks, a few wounded men only being visible, among whom was the brave old admiral, who had lost his leg from a round-shot. On the troops being landed, possession was taken of the abandoned fortifications, and the British flag floated on the first military position in the Chinese Empire captured by her majesty's forces. An inner fortress was, however, discovered, from which the Chinese soldiers which crowded it, opened their fire, beating their tom-toms and gongs, waving banners, and beckoning the English to attack. A few shells having been thrown into it, the Chinese evacuated the place during the night, and with many of the inhabitants fled into the country. Several persons were found to have been killed, and the governor of the town drowned himself in despair. Chusan was held for some months, at the cost of the lives of many of the soldiers, who suffered from the poisonous exhalations from the paddy-fields, having nothing to do to employ their minds; while the seamen of the *Melville*, which had been hove down for repairs, kept their health during the six weeks they were employed on her. The squadron got as far north as the great wall of China. On the passage the *Pylades* corvette, Captain Anson, fell in with three junks. As his boats ranged up alongside of them, upwards of 100 men, who had been concealed, started up and commenced firing and hurling spears and stink-pots on the crews. On this the British shoved off to a short distance, and pouring in some well-directed volleys, killed half the pirates, the remainder jumping overboard and making for the shore — though many were drowned. The other two junks escaped.

One of the favourite exploits of the Chinese was to kidnap the English. A Madras officer of artillery, Captain Anstruther, had been carried off while taking a survey near Chusan. The crew of a merchant-vessel, the *Kite*, wrecked on the coast, and Mrs Noble, the captain's wife, were also captured. Near Macao a Mr Staunton had been been carried away, on which Captain Smith, then the senior officer on the station, sent to demand his release. It being refused, and the Chinese being observed strengthening the barrier which runs across the isthmus, joining Macao to the mainland, he considered it probable that the enemy would attack the city. Taking, therefore, the *Larne* and *Hyacinth*, with the *Enterprise* steamer and *Louisa* cutter, he ran up close to the barrier and opened so warm a cannonade on the Chinese works and barracks, that the enemy's fire was silenced in about an hour. Some blue-jacket small-arm men and soldiers being then disembarked, they drove the Chinese from every one of their positions, spiked the guns, and burnt the barracks and other buildings. This was the last hostile proceeding of the British in the year 1840. The Chinese, wishing to gain time, induced Admiral Elliott to agree to a truce, shortly after which he resigned command from ill-health, and returned to England, leaving Sir Gordon Bremer as commander-in-chief. At the commencement of 1841 the squadron was further increased by the arrival of the *Nemesis* steamer, commanded by Mr W.H. Hall, then a master in the navy, and the *Sulphur*, Commander Belcher. The *Nemesis*, though not commissioned under the articles of war, most of her officers were in the Royal Navy; but she belonged to the East India Company. She was built by Mr Laird at Birkenhead, and although of about 630 tons burden, with engines of 120 horse-power, with all her armament complete, she drew only 6 feet of water. Her extreme length was 184 feet, her breadth 29 feet, and her depth 11 feet. She had no fixed keel, and was almost perfectly flat-bottomed. She had, however, two sliding or movable keels, made of wood, each about 7 feet in length, one being placed before and the other abaft the engine-room, and, being enclosed in narrow cases reaching to the deck, they could be raised or lowered at will by means of a winch. With the exception of the great paddle-beams across the ship, the planks of the deck, and the cabin fittings, with a few other portions, she was built entirely of iron. As, from her form, she could not have been steered by an ordinary rudder, a movable rudder was attached to the lower part of the true or fixed rudder, descending to the same depth as the two false keels, and, like them, could be raised or lowered at pleasure. Another striking peculiarity of her construction was that she was divided into seven water-tight compartments by means of iron bulkheads, so that, in fact, she resembled a number of iron tanks cased over, a contrivance which saved her from the almost certain destruction which would otherwise have been her lot. By some cleverly-contrived leeboards her leeway, under sail, was reduced fully one-half. It was found, however, that the want of a fixed keel was a great detriment to her seaworthy qualities.

After a voyage, during which she encountered many dangers, she arrived safely in China, the first iron steamer which had ever performed so long a voyage. From her shallow draft of water she was enabled to play a conspicuous part in most of the operations in the Chinese seas.

Finding that the Chinese, though carrying on negotiations, were making strenuous preparations for war, Sir Gordon Bremer resolved to attack Canton. The entrance of the Canton River is called the Boca Tigris, on either side of which were lines of defences known as the Bogue Forts, supposed to be of great strength. These it was necessary to silence. The marines and other troops were sent on shore to assault the fort of Chuenpee, on the land side, while the ships battered it from the sea. The fort having been attacked by the troops, many of the Chinese were shot, and a large number, not aware that quarter would be granted, threw themselves from the battlements. Fort Tykocktow, on the opposite side of the river, was at the same time attacked by the *Samarang*, with three other vessels, and a breach being effected, the boats of the squadron, with a body of seamen, were sent on shore, who soon mastered the place. On the Chuenpee side was Anson's Bay, at the entrance of a small river, here protected by an island at its mouth. A Chinese fleet of about 15 war-junks lay moored in shoal water, under the command of Admiral Kwang. The *Nemesis*, with the boats of several other ships, was joined by Captain Belcher, of the *Sulphur*, with two of his ship's boats, and by Lieutenant Kellett, of the *Starling*, while the *Nemesis* soon got close enough to bring her 32-pounder pivot-guns to bear; and at the same time one of the *Larne's* boats, under Lieutenant Harrison, made her way outside the island to cut off the junks in the rear. The first Congreve rocket fired from the *Nemesis* having entered a large junk near that of the admiral, she almost immediately blew up, pouring forth a blaze like the rush of fire from a volcano, and destroying all on board. This so terrified the Chinese that, after a few discharges of round-shot had been fired into other junks, the crews of many jumped overboard, while others cut their cables in the hopes of escaping on shore. Some were immediately captured, others escaped up the river, pursued by the *Nemesis*, which succeeded in bringing one down and burning another which had grounded.

The next day Admiral Kwang sent off a boat with a flag of truce, in which were an old man and woman, bearing proposals for the cessation of hostilities. They came to request Captain Elliott to meet Commissioner Keshen, who finally agreed that the island of Hong-Kong should be ceded to the British, on condition that the Bogue Forts should be given up, and that, on the English captives being set at liberty, Chusan should be evacuated. To these terms Captain Elliott, the superintendent of trade, agreed, and Hong-Kong was taken possession of on the 26th of January. These terms having been rejected by the emperor, the fleet proceeded, on the 26th of February, to the attack of the remainder of the Bogue Forts. Their defenders were either put to flight or yielded themselves prisoners, and in a short time the British colours were flying on the whole chain of those celebrated works. The next day, the 27th, the light squadron, consisting of the *Calliope* and *Herald*, and the *Alligator, Sulphur, Modeste, Madagascar*, and *Nemesis* steamers, under Captain Herbert, were sent up to destroy any fortifications they might meet with. On reaching Whampoa Roads, a large armed fort, mounting 47 guns, was seen on the left bank, and extending across the river was a line of rafts secured to sunken junks, on the other side of which were forty large junks and the *Cambridge*, carrying the admiral's flag. The steamer pushing on, opened a heavy fire on the Chinese fleet, as well as on the batteries. For about an hour the Chinese held out, and when their fire was nearly silenced, the marines and small-arm men being landed, stormed the works, driving before them upwards of 2000 Chinese troops, and killing nearly 300. The *Cambridge* and some of the junks still held out, when Lieutenant Watson, first of the *Calliope*, having gallantly succeeded in dragging one of the boats across the raft, launched her on the other side. As soon as she was in the water, Mr Brown, master of the *Calliope*, Mr Hall and Mr Galbraith, of the *Nemesis*, and Mr Saint Leger, got into her with nine or ten men, and pulled away for the *Cambridge*. So confused were the Chinese that, as the boarding party climbed up on the port side, they jumped overboard on the other, and many were drowned in attempting to swim on shore. A number of dead and wounded were found on her decks. As she was an old ship, she was doomed to destruction, and the wounded being removed, she was set on fire, and soon afterwards blew up with a terrific explosion, the sound of which must have reached Canton. Numerous other forts were destroyed in succession, as were also a considerable number of junks. The steamers had many difficulties to encounter, as thick stockades had been placed across the channel, through which they had to force their way. At length the squadron came to an anchor off Whampoa, when the *Nemesis* was despatched with a letter to the Chinese authorities. Captain Bethune having undertaken to deliver it, pushed off in a boat with a white flag, when a shower of grape and shot was discharged on her from a fort. In consequence of this the ships pushed on to Canton, and opened a hot fire on the batteries which protect the city. After the bombardment had continued about an hour, the marines were landed, immediately stormed, and completed the capture of the enemy's works, notwithstanding a determined resistance on the part of the Tartars. Captain Bourchier, in command of the blue-jackets on shore, prevented any outbreak of the population, and he observing a number of burning junks drifting down on the suburbs, to which they would inevitably have set fire, by the most energetic exertions of his officers and men towed them away from the spot. The *Herald* getting up later in the day, by her imposing appearance contributed to bring the Chinese to reason, and in a short time the British colours were hoisted on the flagstaff of the factory by Commander Belcher. Thus one of the most important cities of China fell into the hands of the British, with a loss of only seven men wounded.

A truce was now agreed to, and trade was again opened, but the Chinese very soon began to rebuild their fortifications, and to fit out junks and fire-rafts. The main body of the fleet having retired, a small squadron remained in the neighbourhood of Canton. The night of the

21st of May was unusually dark; a sharp look-out was therefore kept, the officers lying down in their cloaks on the decks of the ships, ready for service. The *Modeste* being a little in advance, one of her sentries observed several dark-looking masses dropping down with the stream. On his hailing, they were immediately set on fire by the Chinese, and the flames bursting forth, pointed out the danger to the other vessels. In nine minutes the *Nemesis* had her steam up, and was running towards the fire-rafts to assist the boats in towing them away. These rafts were formed of boats chained together, so that, drifting down with the stream, they might hang across the bows of the ships, from which they would with much difficulty have been cleared. The Chinese batteries at the same time opened on the squadron, which of course fired in return, while the small-arm men picked off the people on the fire-rafts. In the morning the Shameen battery was taken, and 43 war-junks and 32 fire-rafts were destroyed. During these operations a Congreve rocket, which had been placed in a tube and ignited, hung within it instead of flying out. In another moment it would have burst, scattering destruction around, when Mr Hall thrust his arm into the tube and forced it out from behind. The rush of fire, however, severely burnt his hand, and caused him much suffering. Several other attempts to destroy the squadron by fire-ships were defeated by the vigilance of the officers and crews. On one occasion, the *Wellesley*, anchored at the Bogue, was attacked by 20 fire-vessels, filled with gunpowder and a variety of combustibles, and chained in twos and threes. Captain Maitland was absent with most of her boats and a large number of her crew and officers, and it was not without great exertion that Commander Fletcher, who had only three boats left on board, was able to tow them clear of the ship.

As it was evident that the Chinese still intended to hold out, the fleet proceeded to attack Canton. The troops and the blue-jackets, who had been landed quickly, stormed the outer defences, while the smaller vessels of the squadron bombarded the batteries on the river-front of the city. The Chinese again made use of fire-vessels, but as they drove down rapidly towards the fleet, the boats pushing off, towed them clear and carried them on shore, when they set fire to the suburbs. Several naval officers lost their lives, and others were wounded. Lieutenant Fox and Mr Kendall, mate, both of the *Nimrod*, each lost a leg; and Mr Fitzgeorge, mate of the *Modeste*, was killed. Lieutenant Fox died the same evening.

In the course of three days the whole of the fortifications of Canton were in the power of the British, and though the city contained an immense army, flags of truce were waved from the walls, and the Tartar generals came alongside humbly suing for peace, and offering six millions of dollars for the ransom of the city. This sum was accepted, and sent on board the ships of war, when 18,000 Tartars marched out of Canton. Many officers and men suffered from the fatigues they underwent, and Sir Humphrey Le Fleming Senhouse died in consequence of the exertions to which he had been exposed.

The fleet now proceeding northward, on the 26th of August captured Amoy, a place of considerable importance, about 300 miles north of Hong-Kong. The Chinese fought with more courage and stubbornness than usual, but were driven out of their fortifications by the ships, when the troops, the blue-jackets as usual playing their part, stormed and carried the place. Chusan, which had been given up to the Chinese, was next recaptured, after which Chinghai, a strong place situated at the mouth of the Takia River, was attacked. It was surrounded by a wall 2 miles in circumference, 37 feet thick, and 22 feet high, mounted by 69 heavy guns and numberless jingalls. A lofty and precipitous hill, with a citadel on the summit, commanded the town; stockades had been driven into the water in front of all the batteries and landing-places, and an army of 10,000 men lay encamped, with numerous guns, a short distance from the bank of the river. The ships approached till they touched the ground, when they opened their fire, and a breach was soon effected in the citadel. On this it was stormed by the blue-jackets and marines, when the garrison effected their escape into the city, the walls of which were then scaled in two places, and Chinghai was captured. Ningpo, higher up the river, was taken with even less difficulty. A desperate attempt was afterwards made to recapture the latter place, but the Chinese were repulsed with dreadful slaughter; while another attempt to burn the ships of war by fire-vessels was also defeated. Not less than 50 or 60 fire-rafts were seen coming down together, burning furiously, but the boats of the ships were ready, and grappling them bravely, towed them clear of the fleet.

Still, as the Chinese showed no readiness to come to terms, another town, which lies on the opposite side of the bay in which Chinghai is situated, called Chapoo, was attacked. Sir William Parker landed with a battalion of seamen and marines under Captain Bourchier, while the troops, headed by Sir Hugh Gough, drove the enemy before them. A large body of Tartars had thrown themselves into a building of considerable strength, and in attempting to enter it, Colonel Tomlinson, of the 18th, and a number of his men were killed. Mr Hall, Lieutenant Fitzjames, and other naval officers made several gallant attempts to force their way in. At length the gate was blown open by a powderbag; many of the defenders were destroyed, and fifty captured. The loss of the British was considerable. The Chinese wounded received great attention from the British medical officers; a conduct appreciated by the governor of Chapoo, who thanked the admiral and general, and when some English fell into the hands of the Chinese, they in return were treated with every kindness.

Before the expedition left Chapoo, all the Chinese prisoners were set at liberty, each man receiving three dollars; when the Chinese, not to be out-done in liberality, restored all the persons they had kidnapped, giving thirty dollars to each white man and fifteen to each native of India.

As the numerous places which had hitherto been taken were at a distance from the capital, the emperor still hoped that he might set the British at defiance. It was determined, therefore, to attack Nankin itself, the second city in the empire, situated about 200 miles up the great river Yang'tse Kiang, or Yellow River. The difficulties of the navigation had hitherto been considered an insuperable obstacle; although the river is of great size, the current runs with prodigious force, and there are numerous shoals and rocks in its course. The river, however, was surveyed by Commanders Kellett and Collinson, and as they reported that water for the largest ships was found right up to Nankin, the admiral undertook to carry the whole of the fleet up to the walls of that city. Woosung and Shanghai, situated on the banks of a river which falls into the sea at the entrance of the Yang'tse Kiang, were first captured, and on the 6th of July, 1842, a fleet of nearly 80 sail, including among them the *Cornwallis*, of 72 guns, Sir William Parker's flag-ship, in five divisions, sailed up the mighty stream on their voyage of 200 miles into the very heart of China. Before reaching Nankin they came off the large city of Chin Keang Foo, near which passes the great canal of China. It was captured on the 20th by the troops, aided by a body of seamen and marines under Captain Peter Richards, who scaled the walls on one side while the soldiers got over on another. The Tartars fought with the most determined bravery, holding every house and street, resolved to sell their lives dearly. Frequently, on being defeated, they put an end to themselves, and often destroyed their wives and children. Lieutenant Fitzjames distinguished himself in the attack, having brought up some rockets which, fired among the enemy, threw them into confusion. The gate of the city was just then blown open by powder-bags, when Sir Hugh Gough, who was with the third brigade, accompanied by Sir William Parker, dashed over the ruins. They were met, after fighting their way for some distance, by a sudden fire from a body of Tartars, when Lieutenant Fitzjames and several men were wounded. The British, however, uttering a loud cheer, attacked the Tartars with such fury that they were soon put to flight, when numbers fell by their own hands. The British were speedily in entire possession of the city. Every means was taken to spare life, to prevent plunder, and to restore order. During these operations several vessels of the fleet were employed in blockading the mouths of the great canal, in capturing all the trading junks which came in sight, and in preventing provisions being carried to the city. Still, it was necessary in order to bring the emperor to reason, for the fleet to appear before the walls of Nankin. Having been detained by contrary winds, it was not till the 4th of August that the ships could get up, carrying 4500 troops, besides marines and bluejackets. The *Cornwallis* and *Blonde* then took up their positions within one thousand paces of the Ifung Gate of Nankin, and every arrangement was made for the troops to attack the city. Before the British proceeded to extremities, the emperor having been informed the true state of affairs, authorised his commissioner to treat for peace, and on the 29th of August the treaty for which the British had been so long contending was signed on board the *Cornwallis*. Among other clauses, China agreed to pay twenty-one millions of dollars; Canton, Amoy, Foo-Chow, Ningpo, and Shanghai, were thrown open to British commerce, Hong-Kong was ceded in perpetuity to Her Britannic Majesty; all British subjects imprisoned in China were to be released, and correspondence was in future to be conducted on terms of perfect equality between the officers of both governments. Thus the war in which the navy of England had played so conspicuous a part was terminated. Its greatest achievement, however, was the passage of the fleet 200 miles up the river, and its return without the loss of a single vessel. This, however, could not have been effected without steamers, which, besides towing the sailing ships, performed important parts in all the operations of the war. Among those who especially distinguished themselves by their activity were Commander Belcher, afterwards Sir Edward Belcher, Mr Hall, of the *Nemesis*, who was deservedly made a lieutenant and commander, and is now Admiral Sir W.H.

Hall, Commanders Kellett, Collinson, and Fitzjames, well known as Arctic explorers, Lieutenant Mccleverty, and the bravest among the brave, Captain Loch, who fell in Burmah.

Destruction of Pirates in the Indian and China Seas.

For many years the pirates of the Eastern Archipelago and China seas had committed depredations on the commerce of the more peaceably-disposed people of that part of the world, and had frequently attacked merchant-vessels belonging to the English, as well as those of other nations, generally treating the prisoners they captured with the greatest barbarity. So audacious had they become that in 1836 the Governor-General of India determined to put an end to their proceedings, and Captain Chads, of the *Andromache* frigate, was sent into those seas to destroy as many piratical fleets and strongholds as he could fall in with. The pirate proas are vessels of considerable size, upwards of 60 feet in length and 12 in beam; though, as they draw scarcely four feet of water, they can run up into shallow rivers and escape. Each proa carried about 80 men, with a 12-pounder in the bows, 3 or 4 smaller pivot-guns, besides jingalls, stink-pots, spears, and the murderous kris which each man wore at his side. The crew in action were protected by a bulwark four or five feet high, thick enough to withstand musket-balls and grape-shot. They sailed in fleets of twenty or thirty vessels together, and were thus more than a match for any British merchantman, even though well-armed, they were likely to fall in with. The boats of the frigate, however, pursued them into their strongholds, and piracy in the neighbourhood of the Malay peninsula was for a time put a stop to. It existed, however, to a far greater degree in other parts of the Eastern seas, and it was not till 1843, that Rajah Brooke had established himself at Sarawak, on the western side of Borneo, that far more strenuous efforts than heretofore were employed against those pests of commerce. Several of the ships of war which had been engaged in the operations against China, on the conclusion of peace, were despatched to the assistance of Rajah Brooke in his noble and philanthropic object. Among the officers employed in the service were the Honourable Captain Keppel, of the *Dido* frigate, Sir Edward Belcher, of the *Samarang*, Captain Nicholas Vansittart, of the *Magician*, Captain Edward Vansittart, of the *Bittern*, Commander Fellowes, of the *Rattler*, Captain Mundy, of the *Iris*, besides many others. The *Nemesis* and *Phlegethon*, which had been so actively engaged in China, were sent with other steamers belonging to the East India Company. Sir Thomas Cochrane, commander-in-chief on the Indian station, also visited Borneo in his flag-ship the *Agincourt*, to superintend the operations which were now energetically pursued for the destruction of the pirates. There is no space to give more than an example of the sort of service in which the smaller vessels and the boats of the squadron were chiefly engaged against the common enemy.

The chief of a piratical band, Sherif Osman, had entrenched himself in a strong position on the banks of the River Songibusar, which falls into the bay of Malludu, near Labuan, in Borneo; and as it was of the greatest importance to destroy him, an expedition, under the command of Captain Talbot, was sent up the river for that purpose. It consisted of the *Vixen, Nemesis*, and *Pluto* steamers, and the boats of the *Agincourt, Daedalus, Vestal, Cruiser*, and *Wolverine*, several of them carrying guns in their bows, and another furnished with rockets. Altogether, the force consisted of 350 blue-jackets and above 200 marines. After working his way up the river, Captain Talbot came in sight of the enemy posted in two forts, mounting about twelve guns, and protected by a strong and well-contrived boom. Before the fight commenced, Sherif Osman sent a flag of truce begging to confer with Rajah Brooke, and hearing that he was not present, he invited Captain Talbot to meet him, offering to admit two gigs to be hauled over the boom. This being declined, the enemy opened their fire. Before the boats could advance, it was necessary to cut away the boom. While thus employed, axe in hand, a gallant young officer, Gibbard, of the *Wolverine*, fell mortally wounded. All the time the boats were under a heavy fire, to which they replied with their guns. The boom was fastened to the chain-cable of a vessel of three or four hundred tons. It was at length cut through, when the marines and small-arm men landing, carried the place after a desperate resistance, with a loss of 6 killed, 2 mortally wounded, and 15 severely wounded. The loss of the enemy was proportionably great. Sherif Osman was wounded dangerously, and though he managed to get off, it was supposed that he soon afterwards died in the jungle. In the forts were discovered numerous evidences of the piratical character of the defenders; several chain-cables, two ships' bells, a ship's long-boat, and ships' furniture of various descriptions. Some piratical Illanun and Balagnini boats were burnt, and twenty-four brass guns and several iron ones captured. Thus this piratical nest was completely destroyed.

In the year 1846, several chiefs friendly to the English and opposed to piracy having been cruelly murdered by the Sultan of Brunei Sir Thomas Cochrane determined to destroy his city. There being sufficient water over the bar of the river, the *Agincourt*, towed by the *Spiteful* steamer, entered it and anchored within Moarra Island. The smaller vessels being lightened, proceeded up the river, carrying a force of 200 marines and 600 blue-jackets armed as light-infantry, accompanied by the boats of the squadron towed by the steamers. On turning an angle of the river four batteries were seen, two of which were directly ahead, while the stream was staked across. As the squadron was making its way through the piles, the enemy's fire opened at a distance of 1000 yards. The round and grape passed between the masts of the *Phlegethon* and beyond the *Spiteful*, without striking. The guns having been pointed at the stakes, the *Phlegethon* immediately returned the compliment with rockets and her pivot-guns. After an hour's cannonade, Captain Mundy shoved off in the gunboats, Lieutenant Patey being ordered to pull for the shore and to storm the batteries which were erected on a precipice nearly a hundred feet in height from the bank of the river. So heavy, however, had been the fire from the steamer and gunboats that the resolution of the enemy failed them, and the gallant crews forced their way through the embrasures. In capturing the enemy's flag a skirmish took place between their rear-guard and the leading party of the British, while the former were endeavouring to escape into the jungle. Three handsome brass guns were carried off, the iron guns were spiked, and the magazines destroyed. The steamer then taking the *Royalist* and gunboats in tow, passed two other batteries and anchored half-a-mile below the city, when all hands went to dinner. At half-past one the expedition was again in motion, working up against an ebb tide of three knots. As the *Phlegethon* opened round the point, the city battery and hill forts mounting 18 guns, commenced firing, and two men were killed and several wounded on board the *Phlegethon*. She, however, opened a hot fire, and Captain Mundy shoving off in the gunboats, attacked the batteries at close quarters; but before he could reach them, the enemy fled. Nine shot had entered the *Phlegethon's* side below the water-line; and had she not been divided into compartments, she would inevitably have sunk. The marines were now landed and occupied the heights above the sultan's palace, the batteries on which had been silenced by the rocket and field-piece party under Lieutenant Paynter. The pirates had in the meantime manned the batteries already passed, on which Captain Mundy was sent down with the gunboats to destroy them. This he partially did in five hours, but so great was their strength that it would have taken days to do so effectually. Thirty-nine guns, mostly of large calibre, nineteen of them being of brass, fell into the hands of the British. The sultan and his boasted army had taken to flight. He was accordingly pursued by a party under Captain Mundy, to whom Lieutenant Vansittart acted as aide-de-camp. Having gone as far as they could in the boats, they landed, and in their progress destroyed several newly — erected forts. The natives now observing that no injury was done to private prop- erty, joined them and offered their services as guides. On their way they fell in with two houses belonging to the sultan, containing shields, arms, and magazines of powder. They were accordingly set on fire and destroyed, but the sultan himself escaped for the time, though his power was completely broken.

The towns of Pandassan and Tampassuck, notorious haunts of Illaun pirates, were destroyed by Captains McQuhae and Mundy, and nu- merous piratical proas captured, sunk, or burnt. The fierce and des- perate character of the pirates was shown on all occasions. The *Ring- dove*, Commander Sir William Hoste, having taken a proa, she was brought under the counter of the brig. From the way in which the crew behaved, it was doubted whether she was really a pirate, but as a protection a guard of three marines and several seamen was placed over them. Suddenly, during the night, they rose without the slightest warning and flew simultaneously with their krises upon the seamen and marines, and before the latter could defend themselves, one ma- rine was killed and the remainder of the guard severely wounded. As the unfortunate marine fell into the hold of the proa, the pirate chief seized his musket and fired it at the officer standing at the gangway. Another desperado, lunging his spear through the after-port of the brig, mortally wounded the master. The pirates then cut the hawser, and seizing their paddles, made off for the shore. The boats were im- mediately manned and sent in chase, when in ten minutes the proa was boarded, upon which the pirates retreated below, and with their long spears through the bamboo-deck made a desperate defence, but finally, refusing quarter, were slain to a man, and the proa was sunk by the guns of the pinnace.

The piratical fleets cruising off the coast of China committed even greater depredations on commerce, as well as on the population of the sea-board, than even those in the Indian seas. Captain Edward Vansit- tart, in command of the *Bittern*, was sent against them with two steamers fitted out by the Chinese merchants. The latter were manned chiefly from an American frigate, the *Macedonian*, then cruising off the coast. After a search of some days he discovered a flotilla of nearly forty junks, which bore down on him with tom-toms beating, evidently intending to fight. In order to draw them off the shore, he stood away, but as they would not follow the *Bittern* out of shoal water, she again steered towards them, yawing to bring her guns to bear, while they kept up a steady fire on her. She, however, sank or disabled eight of them, but the rest for a time escaped. Commander Vansittart was, however, able to set free a number of merchant-vessels up different rivers in the neighbourhood, which had been afraid to put to sea on account of the pirates, who had demanded 1200 dollars for the ransom of each vessel. The following day he captured twelve more, each carrying 10 guns with a crew of 50 men. Proceeding northwards, he reached the mouth of the Yang'tse Kiang, where he heard that a strong squadron of pirates had been blockading the island of Potoo, in which place a party of English ladies had taken refuge. On pursuing them, towed by the *Poushan* to Sheepoo, he discovered twenty-two junks lashed head and stern together across the entrance to the harbour. As the *Bittern* approached, the pirates commenced a vigorous cannonade, to which she, however, returned so hot a fire that in little more than an hour she had knocked the greater number to pieces, one junk alone being in a condition to carry off. No prisoners were made, but the pirates as they escaped to the shore were put to death by the inhabitants. Commander Creswell, in the *Surprise*, and Captain N. Vansittart, in the *Magician*, were equally successful in other directions. The latter had under his command the *Inflexible*, Commander Brooker, with the *Plover* and *Algerine* gunboats. As he proceeded, reports reached him of the atrocities committed by the pirates, and the natives were everywhere ready to give him accurate intelligence of their hiding-places. As they saw the British squadron, they took refuge when they could on uninhabited islands; when they escaped to the mainland the people of the country put them to death without mercy. As he was engaged in burning some captured junks, a sound of firing from the shore reached him. Immediately landing with a party of his men, he pushed in the direction from which the firing proceeded. He did not allow a gun to be discharged till he was within pistol-shot, so that the enemy were not aware of his approach. The whole of his party then opened their fire, and the pirates taken by surprise, scampered off without an attempt at resistance. The British having clambered over a formidable stockade, found themselves in a battery of 14 heavy guns, which must have contained a garrison strong enough to offer a successful resistance had the pirates fought with any courage.

Six large junks were soon afterwards met with, the whole of which were captured, and the crews of every one killed or made prisoners, besides which upwards of twenty prisoners taken by the pirates were released. Soon afterwards, while pursuing a pirate up a creek, his own light gig being far ahead of the heavier boats, he came up with the chase, which with his small party he gallantly boarded, several of her crew being killed, among which was Chappoo, a pirate chief long the terror of those seas. Altogether, in a week's cruise he had destroyed a 14-gun battery and 100 piratical craft, and had taken upwards of 200 guns and 36 pirates, besides having killed nearly 400 more. He had, in addition, retaken six vessels and liberated sixty prisoners captured by the pirates.

One more example alone can be given of the expeditions against the pirates of those seas. On the 30th of January, 1849, news was brought to Sir James Brooke that a large fleet of pirates had attacked the neighbouring village of Palo, and had threatened with destruction the inhabitants of the Sarabas River. A force, consisting of H.M. brigs *Albatross* and *Royalist*, with the *Nemesis* and *Renée*, under the orders of Commander Farquhar, immediately got under way, accompanied by a native flotilla, under Rajah Brooke, and proceeded to meet them. The *Nemesis* steamed out to sea to prevent their escape in that direction, and as soon as she was descried by the pirates they made at once for the Kaluka River, where they were intercepted by the native boats and those commanded by Lieutenants Welmshurst and Everest. The pirates then made a dash to reach their river, when they came in contact with the men-of-war's boats. It being now dark, there was considerable danger that the latter would fire into each other, or into the craft of their native allies. The password was "Rajah," and the Malays screamed this out at the top of their voices when they thought any of the Europeans were near them. Commander Farquhar seeing two large proas escaping seaward, ordered the steam-tender to chase. The nearest one, having barely escaped one of her 6-pounder rockets, made for the river, but in her course was encountered by the *Nemesis*, which dealing death and destruction to all around her, ran her down, and a fearful scene took place as her crew, above sixty in number, came in contact with the paddle-wheels. A large Congreve rocket from the smaller steamer entered a proa which had stood out to sea, and completely destroyed her. The battle continued till past midnight, when Commander Farquhar, taking the boats in tow, commenced the ascent of the Sarabas, to prevent the escape of the pirates by the Rembas branch. At daylight the whole bay presented one mass of wreck, shields, spears and portions of destroyed proas, extending as far as the eye could reach, as well as on the sandy spit which extends a considerable distance seawards. On the left bank of the Sarabas were upwards of seventy proas, which the natives were busy clearing of all valuables and destroying. Of 120 proas which are said to have started on a piratical expedition, more than 80 were destroyed, with 1200 men. No more convincing proof of the inhuman disposition of the pirates need be cited than the fact that the bodies of women, supposed to have been captives taken by the pirates, were found on the beach decapitated and gashed from the shoulder to the feet. On sailing up the river the force destroyed a piratical town, some villages and warproas, and then passing the Rejang River, chastised another tribe of pirates. Some prisoners were secured, among whom was a child, apparently of European origin. In other districts hostages were taken for the future peaceable demeanour of the inhabitants. By this severe example it was hoped that the piratical habits of the people would be effectually checked, and an opportunity given to the nascent civilisation of those regions to develop itself.

African Coast Blockade.

The horrible traffic in slaves has been carried on from the west coast of Africa to the American continent since Sir John Hawkins shipped his first cargo of blacks for the Spanish settlements, to supply the loss of the mild and yielding natives of the New World destroyed by the avarice and cruelty of their task-masters. The vessels which trafficked in slaves ran down the coast, touching at all the principal native settlements, and purchased such slaves as were offered for sale until their cargoes were completed. Sometimes a well-armed slaver carried off by force the negroes on board another slaver ready to sail, and unable to defend herself. After a time, regular slave-dealers established themselves on the coast, and induced the natives to make war on each other, in order that those captured might be brought to them for sale. There were at convenient points along the coast forts and stations established by the British and other European Governments for the very purpose of facilitating the slave-trade. At length, by the indefatigable efforts of Wilberforce and other philanthropic men, the

British public were taught to look on the slave-trade in all its dark and revolting colours. The British slave-trade was abolished on the 1st of January, 1808. At first only a fine was inflicted on those convicted of slave-dealing, but in 1824 the offence was declared to be piracy, and punishable by death. In 1837 the punishment inflicted on British subjects for trading in slaves was changed to transportation for life. On the trade being declared illegal, it was abandoned at all European settlements, with the exception of those belonging to the Spaniards and Portuguese, who, determining to persist in it, had adopted a new mode of operations. They had erected barracoons on those parts of the coast where slaves could be collected with the greatest ease. At stated periods vessels visited them, and took away the slaves without being detained on the coast more than twenty-four hours, and often a less time. They had from forty to fifty points where barracoons were placed, and many thousands of slaves every year were exported from them. A slave factory consists of several large dwelling-houses for the managers and clerks, and of huge stores for the reception of goods, sometimes to the amount of 100,000 pounds. To these are attached barracoons or sheds made of heavy piles driven deep into the earth, lashed together with bamboos, and thatched with palm-leaves. In these barracoons the slaves, when purchased, are imprisoned, till shipped on board a slave-vessel. If the barracoon be a large one, there is a centre row of piles, and along each line of piles is a chain, and at intervals of about two feet is a large neck-link, in one of which each slave is padlocked. Should this method be insufficient, two, and sometimes when the slaves appear unusually strong, three are shackled together — the strong man being placed between two others and heavily ironed; and often beaten half to death beforehand to ensure his being quiet. The floor is planked, not from any regard to the comfort of the slave, but because a small insect being in the soil might deteriorate the merchandise by causing a cutaneous disease. Night and day these barracoons are guarded by armed men, and the slightest insubordination immediately punished.

In building a slaver, the Spaniards and Portuguese spare no expense in order to make her light and buoyant. Her timbers and beams are small, and screwed together. When chased, the screws are loosened, to give the vessel play. Within her hold are erected huge water-casks called leaguers, on these are stowed the provisions, wood, etcetera; above this is the slave-deck. Thirty-six inches may be considered a medium height, but they sometimes measure 4 feet 6 inches, though occasionally only 14 or 18 inches, intended for the stowage of children. The upper-deck is generally clear, except of the sweeps or oars for calms, there is a covered sleeping-place, about 6 feet long by 3 feet wide, on each side, for the captain and pilot. Some used to carry guns, but of late years few do so. They mostly have but one small boat. The sails, on account of the frequency and force of the tornados, are very low and bent broad. Thus, the foreyard of a brig of about 140 tons, taken by H.M. ship *Dolphin*, was 76 feet long, and her ropes so beautifully racked aloft that after a cannonade of sixty shot, in which upwards of fifty had taken effect, not one sail was lowered. The following are the articles by which a slaver can be condemned if found on board: — A slave-deck, or planks ready for a deck; slave irons and slave coppers, which are a large cooking apparatus for the slaves and crew, standing generally amidships on the upper-deck; an extra quantity of farina, rice, water, or other provisions, which cannot be accounted for. The horrors of a full slaver almost defy description. Arrived on the coast and the port reached, if no man-of-war be on the coast, two hours suffice to place 400 human beings on board. On the slaves being received, the largest men are picked out as head-men, and these dividing the slaves into gangs, according to the size of the vessel, of from ten to twenty, keep them in order. A slave-deck is divided into two unequal parts, the larger for the men, the other for women and children. The stowage is managed entirely by the head-men, who take care that the strongest slaves should be farthest from the ship's side, or from any position in which their strength might avail them to secure a larger space than their neighbours. The form of stowage is that the poor wretch shall be seated on the beams, and the head thrust between the knees, so close that when one moves the mass must move also. The slaves feed twice a-day, and in order to give room, one-half are allowed at a time on deck at the hour of the meal. They are arranged into messes, and when all is ready, at a signal from the head-men, they commence. The food consists of either rice, carabansas, a kind of bean, or farina, the flour of the cassava boiled. After each meal they are made to sing to digest their food, and then the water is served out, the fullest nominal allowance of which is one quart to each daily, though seldom more than a pint. Irons are seldom used on board, only in case of a mutiny, or if closely chased by a man-of-war, in which case the condition of the slaves becomes truly dreadful; they are all barred below for fear of their rising, are seldom watered till the chase be over, that may last two or three days, while everything that can be thought of to make the vessel sail is done, whatever misery it may cost the cargo. Often some of the unfortunate wretches are thrown overboard in empty casks or lashed to floats, in the hope that the cruiser will stop to pick them up, and thus delay the chase. In many instances, when slaves have been captured, twenty or thirty, or even more, have been found dead on board, while the rest have been in a most horribly suffering condition. Indeed, the operation of taking off the hatches of a captured slaver, from the effluvium which arises, is sufficient to try the strongest stomachs, while the hearts of the captors cannot fail to be touched by the dreadful sufferings of their fellow-creatures which they are doomed to witness. Of late years the slave-trade from the West Coast has been carried on chiefly by fast steamers, but as the men-of-war engaged in the blockade are also steamers, the slave-dealers have found the trade a losing one, so that on the whole of the West Coast there are very few points from which slaves are shipped. From the early part of the century, British men-of-war have been employed on the African coast blockade, but for a long time, as only a few 10-gun brigs, and they inefficient vessels, were sent out, and as there were scarcely ever more than six cruisers at a time on the coast, during twenty years, from 1819 to 1839, only 333 slave-vessels were captured; whereas after that period a superior class of 16 and 18-gun brigs and sloops of war, and latterly fast screw-steamers, fitted for sailing as well as for steaming, were employed; and during the next eleven years 744 slave-vessels were captured. As up to probably two-thirds of those engaged in the trade escaped, we may have some idea of the vast number of blacks carried into captivity to America and the West Indies.

As for many years to blockade a coast-line of 3000 miles and upwards, only a few 10-gun brigs were employed, they being generally slow craft and very crank, in the open sea the fast-sailing slavers managed easily to escape from them. Captures, therefore, were mostly effected by their boats, which were sent up the rivers to lie in wait for the slavers, or to attack them when they were known to be at anchor. This species of service caused a great mortality among their crews, as a night spent in the pestiferous miasma of an African river was sufficient to produce fever among all those exposed to it, while the hot sun of the day was almost equally trying to English constitutions. Thus for many years the mortality among the blockading squadron was very great, and vessels have been known to return home with scarcely men sufficient to work them, and under charge of a master's assistant, or on one occasion the purser's clerk, all the superior officers having died or been invalided. Sometimes the boats were sent away for days, and even weeks together, to watch for slavers, and were thus often successful in capturing them when their ships had failed to do so. In this way a mate of the *Hyacinth*, Mr Tottenham, who was a remarkably good shot, in a four-oared gig chased a slave-brig, armed with a long gun and a number of muskets. Having succeeded with his rifle in picking off four of the slaver's crew, he compelled her to run on shore to avoid being boarded; the survivors of the crew, eighteen in number, then abandoning her, she was hove off by the *Hyacinth*, and proved to be of 200 tons, fitted for carrying a thousand slaves, and armed with two guns, and a number of muskets, swords, and bayonets.

Prizes were carried to Sierra Leone for adjudication, often with several hundred negroes on board. To preserve the rescued blacks in health was an onerous care to the captors; and instances have occurred where the greater number of the prize-crew have died from fever. Such was the case with the *Doris*, a small schooner captured by the *Dolphin*; her gunner, who was put in charge, with nearly all his men having died, so that she was found boxing about some twenty miles below Acra, without any one to navigate her. Lieutenant Augustus Murray, with a crew of two men and two boys, and a black who had survived the fever, was then put on board on August the 12th. Sickness attacked the lieutenant and his small crew, heavy gales came on, the schooner became so leaky that it was with difficulty she was kept afloat, she narrowly escaped capture by a slaver, the canvas was blown away, and finally calms came, succeeded by terrific storms, so that almost five months elapsed before the sorely-battered craft and her almost starved crew reached Sierra Leone.

Experience at length taught the officers of the squadron the means of combating the deadly effects of the climate, and preserving the health of their crews. The men were not allowed to leave the ship early in the morning without taking hot cocoa and an ample supply of nourishing food. They were clothed in thick flannel suits, were not allowed to remain up the rivers at night, and the use of quinine was introduced. By these means the crews were preserved in health, and only during very sickly seasons was there any great mortality among them; indeed, of late years, vessels have returned from the coast without the loss of a man.

GALLANT CONDUCT OF THE "BLACK JOKE."—p. 404

Most of the slavers were unarmed, and those carrying guns rarely attempted to defend themselves when overtaken, although they might have fired to knock away the spars of their pursuers. Occasionally, when attacked by a vessel inferior to themselves, or by one or two boats, a slaver's crew fought desperately. One of the most gallant actions was fought by the *Black Joke*, a schooner, commanded by Lieutenant Ramsey. She carried but one long heavy pivot-gun and a carronade, and had, all told, a crew only of 44 officers and men. Lieutenant Ramsey got intelligence that a brigantine, the *Marinereto*, of large size and great speed, and armed with five Impounder guns, and a crew of nearly 80 men, was lying in the Old Calabar River with a cargo of slaves destined for Cuba. She was commanded by a determined fellow, who had vowed he would never be captured, it was said, and was especially anxious to meet the *Black Joke* to punish her on account of the slavers she had already taken. Lieutenant Ramsey at once stood down for the Calabar River. As she could not enter it, he kept close off it by night, and stood away from the land during the day, that the slaver, not knowing of his presence, might venture to put to sea. After waiting for some days, the slaver was seen under all sail coming down the river. The *Black Joke* at once lowered her canvas, that she might remain concealed from the slaver's view as long as possible. On again hoisting it, the *Marinereto*, notwithstanding her commander's boastings, made all sail to avoid her, while Lieutenant Ramsey, setting all the canvas he could carry, stood after her in chase. Still, as the *Marinereto* was by far the faster vessel of the two, there was every chance of her escaping; when, fortunately, a calm came on, and both vessels got out their sweeps. The *Black Joke* had now an advantage, as, from her small size, her crew were able to row her rapidly through the water. Keeping the chase in sight all night, by the next morning Lieutenant Ramsey got her within range. Knowing, however, that she had a closely-packed cargo of slaves on board, he refrained from firing for fear of injuring them, although the brigantine was cutting his rigging to pieces with her shot. At length he got sufficiently close to aim only at the slaver's decks, and having loaded his guns with grape, and ordered two men to be ready to lash the vessels together directly they touched, he directed the rest of the crew to lie down to avoid the enemy's shot. He now ran the chase on board, discharging into her both his guns, and, under cover of the smoke, gallantly sprang on her deck, followed by a portion of his crew. The greater number, however, were prevented from boarding, as no sooner did the *Black Joke* strike the slaver than the force of the collision drove her off, and the gallant lieutenant, with only ten of his people, found himself opposed to the eighty miscreants who formed the slaver's crew, several of whom were either Englishmen or Americans, who, consequently, fought with the greatest desperation. In spite of the gallantry of the British, they ran a great risk of being overpowered, but, happily, a midshipman, Mr Hinds, then scarcely fifteen years old, had the presence of mind to order the crew to get out their sweeps, and, succeeding in again getting alongside the slaver, she was securely lashed to the *Black Joke*. Young Hinds then calling on his companions to follow, dashed on board the slaver, and, after a desperate hand-to-hand conflict, during which one of the British crew was killed and seven wounded, they cut-down and killed fifteen Spaniards, and wounded a good many more, the survivors, who still greatly outnumbered the victors, leaping below and crying out for quarter. Nearly 500 blacks were found on board, but as the hatches had been fastened down directly the *Black Joke* had been seen, and the chase had lasted upwards of twenty-four hours, above twenty of the blacks had died, and sixty were dying, from want of air. The prize was carried to Fernando Po, where the survivors were liberated. Lieutenant Ramsey was immediately promoted to the rank of commander. The officers and crews engaged in the service had to go through no common dangers. A Brazilian schooner, the *Felicidade*, had been captured by the *Wasp*, when, with the exception of the captain of the prize and another man, the crew were transferred to her, and Lieutenant Stupart, with Mr Palmer, midshipman, and a crew of fifteen seamen, remained in charge of the slaver. On her way to Sierra Leone the *Felicidade* chased and captured the *Echo*, with a crew of 28 men and 430 slaves. Lieutenant Stupart taking charge of the more valuable prize, left Mr Palmer in command of the *Felicidade*, with 7 Englishmen and 2 Kroomen. Unfortunately the captain and several of the *Echo's* crew were sent on board her as prisoners. Some days afterwards the *Felicidade* was seen by H.M. ship *Star*, Commander Dunlop, and on being chased made every effort to escape. When boarded the crew fled below; many of them were wounded, while there were evident traces that a severe struggle had taken place, and articles belonging to English seamen being found, there could be no doubt that the prize-crew had risen on Mr Palmer and his men, and murdered the whole of them. Captain Dunlop taking out the prisoners, left Lieutenant Wilson and nine men in charge of the *Felicidade*, with directions to proceed to Sierra Leone. She never reached her destination, having shortly afterwards been capsized, when she sank, a portion of her bow-rail alone remaining above water. To this Lieutenant Wilson and his people clung, and contrived to form a raft, on which two Kroomen and three of the seamen perished, but Lieutenant Wilson, with four survivors, after remaining twenty days on their raft, being supported chiefly by the flesh of a shark caught with a bowling-knot, were picked up after undergoing fearful hardships, and ultimately recovered their health.

Not only were the squadron engaged in capturing slavers at sea, but whenever it could be legally done, the boats were sent on shore to destroy the slave barracoons, and to set the occupants at liberty. This was often dangerous work, for whenever the slave-dealers thought they could do so with success, they did not scruple with their armed men to fire on their assailants. One of the most important services, however, rendered by the squadron was the capture of Lagos, in the Bight of Benin, under Commodore Bruce, in 1851. It had hitherto been one of the chief slave-marts, and its rulers had encouraged the tribes in the interior to make war on each other, for the sake of the captives they might bring to them. Two brothers, the younger of whom, Akitoye, had succeeded by his father's will as king, the elder, Kosako, having for misbehaviour been banished, it gave an opening for the interference of the English. Akitoye having recalled Kosako, the latter rebelled and usurped the government, compelling Akitoye to take refuge at Badagry. On this Kosako was preparing to attack Badagry, and would certainly have invaded Abbeokuta, the centre of Christianity and civilisation in that part of Africa, when Mr Beecroft, the British agent on the coast, applied to Commodore Bruce for a force to destroy Lagos. The *Bloodhound*, steamer, with a small squadron of boats, was accordingly sent up, but was fired on by Kosako's people. In consequence, the town was attacked and entered, with the loss of two British officers and several men wounded. As their force was inadequate to hold the place, the English were compelled to retire. As soon as a sufficient number of vessels could be collected, another expedition was sent against Lagos, which arrived before it on the 26th of December, 1851. As neither the *Penelope* nor the flag-ship of Commodore Bruce, nor any of the larger vessels, could cross the bar, the *Bloodhound* and *Teaser* only, with the boats of the squadron strongly armed, were sent in, under the command of Captain Lewis Jones, of the *Sampson*, with Commander Henry Lister, of the *Penelope*, as his second. The expedition was joined by the ex-king Akitoye, and upwards of 600 men, who were landed in some canoes captured by Lieutenant Saumarez. Lagos was strongly fortified; the people also had long been trained to arms, and possessed at least 5000 muskets and 60 pieces of cannon, so that the work undertaken was of no contemptible character. As the *Bloodhound* and *Teaser* with the boats approached the stockades, they were received with a hot fire from the guns, jingalls, and muskets of the negroes, which was returned with round-shot and rockets from the steamers and boats. An attempt at landing was made by a party under Lieutenant Saumarez with the boats of the *Sampson*, but so hot was the fire through which they had to pass, that before they got on shore, Mr Richards, a gallant young midshipman, was killed, and 10 men severely wounded. An attempt was then made to force their way through the stockades, but, after some men had been hit, Lieutenant Saumarez among them, he was compelled to retire. The *Teaser* having unfortunately got on shore, was exposed to the fire of the enemy; as the only way of saving her, a party was sent under Captain Lister to capture the guns directly pointing at her. After some severe fighting, and the loss of several men, they forced their way into the stockade and drove out the enemy, when all the guns were spiked. During this operation one of the life-boats was captured by the blacks, and in an attempt to retake her with several other boats, another midshipman, Mr Fletcher, was killed. Commander Hillyar and several other officers and men were severely wounded, as was Lieutenant Corbet, in endeavouring to cut the chain-cable of the *Victoria*, Mr Beecroft's boat, under a hot fire from the blacks. The life-boat was after all left on shore, when some forty blacks getting into her to carry her off, Mr Balfour threw a rocket from the first cutter, which, entering her magazine, blew it up. In the evening the *Teaser*, after great exertions, was got off. The next morning the attack was renewed, when at length the rockets from the squadron, admirably thrown, set the town on fire, and, the conflagration extending, the magazine was blown up, the whole place being shortly in a general blaze. A welcome reinforcement of the boats of the *Volcano* and *Water-witch*, under Commanders Coote and Gardner, arriving, after an interval of Sunday, preparations were made for another still more formidable attack on the place, when it was found that Kosako had abandoned it, and Akitoye, who with his people had absconded when affairs appeared unfavourable to his cause, was brought back and installed as king. Since then Lagos has become a possession of the British Empire.

A small squadron is still kept on the west coast, and but a very limited number of slaves are shipped from any part of it.

British ships have also been employed in the West Indies and along the eastern coast of South America in capturing slavers carrying blacks either to Cuba or to the Brazils. The Cuban slavers, large well-armed vessels, manned by ruffians of all nations, were frequently guilty of acts of piracy, and often fought desperately before they yielded. As the Brazilian laws now prohibit the importation of slaves, the steam-cruisers on the station have completely put a stop to the traffic.

Dhow chasing on the East Coast of Africa.

The slave-trade is, however, still carried on to a lamentable extent on the east coast of Africa, to supply the Arabian and Persian markets, and has been the chief cause of all the depopulating wars which have taken place on that side of Africa, reducing whole districts inhabited by an industrious people into howling deserts. A squadron, consisting entirely of steamers, has now for some years been stationed on that coast for its suppression.

Though not sanctioned by the Portuguese government, their officials in their possessions at the mouth of the Zambesi and other places along the coast have taken an active part in the trade, as have also the French, who, though they do not call their captives slaves, equally encourage the slave-dealers and internal warfare, by purchasing the blacks taken in battle and carrying them off under the name of ap-prentices to their possessions in the Southern ocean. The service on this coast, though less unhealthy, provided the crews do not sleep on shore, is often severe in the extreme, the boats being sent away for considerable periods to watch for slaving-dhows as they sail along the coast. These dhows are large, swift-sailing craft, commanded and manned by Arabs, savage fellows, who frequently fight desperately when attacked by the boats. With a strong breeze they often manage to elude even steamers. When hard-pressed, with a full cargo of slaves on board, they will run their vessels through the surf on shore in the hopes of carrying off some of their unfortunate captives who may escape from the wreck, being very indifferent about those who may be drowned. The Arabs themselves generally manage to get on shore, though sometimes the whole of their black cargo is sacrificed.

From the following account by an eye-witness some of the lesser hor-rors of the slave-trade on the east coast may be conceived. It exhibits, also, the spirit in which our gallant officers and seamen carry on the duty imposed on them.

Her Majesty's steamer *Vulture*, Commander Cay, was, in 1874, cruis-ing off Madagascar, when, it being almost calm, a dhow was seen standing for the port of Majunga. Although she had every appearance of an honest trader, a boat was sent to board her, carrying one of the officers and an interpreter, with directions to hail the *Vulture* should any slaves be found. All was suspense till the cry came from the dhow of "She's a slaver, sir!" Three hearty cheers were given by the *Vulture's* crew. "How many has she on board?" asked the captain. "Two hundred, sir," was the answer. A hawser was soon passed on board the slaver, and she was hauled alongside. Then began the sickening task of transferring the poor captives from the dhow to the ship. The British seamen behaved nobly; even the regular grumblers forgot their complaints and came forward to assist in transporting the weak and helpless creatures from their prison. So cramped and emaciated were they that many had to be carried in the arms of the men. Tenderly and carefully did these strong, rough fellows bear their helpless burdens, notwithstanding the filth which had accumulated on them during their long imprisonment in the pestilential hold. Now and then a baby appeared, and was eagerly lifted on board by the men. There were seven, and as the little ones were borne along they opened their eyes with wonderment. One baby had been born on board the dhow, and another had lost its mother during the fatal voyage. Those who had suffered most were children whose ages ranged from three to seven years. They had been evidently unable to hold their own against the stronger ones in the scramble for food which had taken place at feeding time; the stronger thrived, while the weaker starved. Of the hapless cargo thirty were at death's door, and thirty others little more than skeletons. Many of the unhappy beings had scarcely tasted food during their imprisonment in the dhow. In they poured, a living stream, until the ship's decks were covered with a black mass of human beings of all ages, including women so old that it was difficult to understand what object those dealers in human flesh could have had in shipping such worthless articles for the slave-market. At last the stream stopped. "They're all out of the dhow, sir," exclaimed the seamen who remained on board the vessel. "Have another look and make quite sure," answered the commander. Well it was that they did so, for in a dark corner of the hold, buried all but the head in the sand which the dhow carried for ballast, lay a poor old woman. She was dug out and borne on board.

DHOW CHASED BY MAN-OF-WAR.

In the meantime the Arabs came on board the *Vulture*, but these, having suffered no privations, were able to walk, and as they came over the side the ship's corporal and corporal of marines stripped them to search for arms or money. Nothing being found, they had their clothes returned, and were marched on to the poop and placed under a sentry's charge to wait till they could be turned over to the tender mercies of the Sultan of Zanzibar — a fate they dread very much. There were two women on board who seemed past hope of recovery; the one who was dug out of the sand, and another with an infant at her back, in which way these people carry their children. The greater portion were suffering dreadfully. Forty-one men, 59 women, and 137 children were taken out of the dhow from between her decks, where they had been packed, unable to move during the whole voyage. The young and good-looking women, who were the most profitable portion of the cargo, appeared to have been well fed, while the men and boys had been starved. The first care was to remove the filth with which they were covered. Those able to bear it were passed under the steam hose, the few rags they had on being taken away as they entered the stream, and as they passed out dry coverings were wrapped round them, contributed by the officers and seamen, such as shirts, towels, sheets, flannels, etcetera. The weaker ones were washed in warm water with soap. Nothing could exceed the gentleness with which the hardy tars handled these poor creatures. By the time they had all been washed the food was ready, and they were made to sit down in circles of from twelve to twenty. Large bowls of boiled rice and beans were placed in the centre of each group; this was the signal for the most dreadful din; each fearing his or her neighbour would get a larger share, crammed the food into their mouths, fighting, squalling, crying, and shouting being carried on all the time until the dishes were empty. It showed what must have been the state of things in the dhow, where there was no room to portion them off, neither would the lazy Arab disturb himself to see justice done to each. The sick were cared for by the doctor and his attentive sick-bay man, assisted by all the officers. Preserved milk, port wine, brandy and water, and preserved fowl were pressed upon these suffering ones, who were almost too far gone to care for anything, except to be allowed to die in peace. The difficulty was to berth them; it was impossible to let them go below, their filthy habits making it necessary that they should remain on the upper-deck, where plenty of water could be used for washing down. They were accordingly made to lie close to each other, when sails were covered over them and screens were hung round, while the awning was stretched over the top of all. Sleep was out of the question, even for the weary seamen; the groans and cries were most heartrending. The doctor and his assistant were up all night attending to the poor captives. At Majunga calico was purchased to clothe them. In the morning they went through the same cleansing process as the night before, when the warm sun, and decks washed down, made things look more cheerful. The dhow having been burnt, the *Vulture* stood away for the Seychelles. Cold nights told upon the exhausted frames of the poor captives, fifteen of whom passed away in spite of every care before the ship had completed half her voyage to the Seychelles. Happily the weather remained remarkably fine. Altogether seventeen deaths occurred among the slaves during the twelve days they were on board before the ship reached her destination. Six of these were children. The two women most despaired of were landed in a much improved state.

Frequently the slaving-dhows captured are in a far more horrible state than in the instance above given. The Arabs have been known to murder and throw into the sea every slave on board, in the hopes of preserving their vessel when they have seen no chance of escape. Very often half the slaves die on the voyage between the coast of Africa and the Persian Gulf. Probably, for every slave captured ten human lives have been lost, either in the attack on their native villages or on the journey to the coast, or by the attempts made to land them through the surf when chased by men-of-war, or by starvation and sickness on board. Still, as long as the Arabs have any hopes of making the voyage profitable, they will pursue the traffic, and the only way to put a stop to the horrible system is by making the chances of capture so great that they will be compelled to abandon it in despair. This can most effectually be done by keeping a large squadron of fast steamers, well supplied with boats, under zealous and active officers, with orders to board and thoroughly examine every dhow they can fall in with, and not to allow one to pass which has the slightest indication of being destined for the slave-trade.

British ships of war, mostly steamers, now traverse the whole of the Pacific, one of the chief services in which they are engaged being the prevention of the kidnapping system which has been carried on to a great extent to supply the Fiji Islands and Queensland with labourers. Nothing could be more abominable than the system which has been pursued. Small-armed vessels have been fitted out, and have, by fraud or violence, got the natives of different islands to come on board, when, shutting them down under hatches, they have carried them off and disposed of them, though nominally as free labourers, yet in reality as slaves. By the efforts of the naval officers engaged in the service, the practice has nearly, if not entirely, been suppressed.

These satisfactory results have not been produced without the sacrifice of the lives of many gallant officers and seamen, the destruction of the health of many more, and by a large expenditure of money. The question to be asked is, "Will England be content, when contemplating all that she has done, that slavery and the accursed slave-trade shall exist in any part of the world where she by means of her navy has the power to put it down?" We are confident that from every part of the British dominions the answer will be, "No! at every cost we will continue the noble work we have commenced, and not rest while a single nation dares to assert her right to enslave our fellow-men."

We hold it as one of the most glorious privileges which England possesses that a slave once setting foot on British soil or reaching the deck of a British man-of-war is a slave no longer, and must not be delivered up to the man who calls himself his owner while an English soldier or sailor remains alive to defend him, or a plank of the ship in which he has sought refuge still floats above the surface. More, we would say that should the fugitive slave place his hand on the gunwale of the smallest boat above which the flag of England flies, protection should be afforded him, even though his pursuers were at his heels. Let other nations know that England denies that one man can justly enslave his fellow — acknowledges not the right of ownership in slaves, but is resolved to strike off the fetters from the captive wherever he can be reached, whether on shore or afloat. But her task is only yet partly accomplished — she has still a great and glorious work before her, and to enable the officers of our ships to perform their duty as they would wish to do it, they must be hampered by no vexatious restrictions, or be allowed to feel that they are liable to heavy fines or censure should they overstep the strict line of their orders. Let them rather be assured that the nation fully understands the difficulties with which they have to contend, and will afford them support should they err in exhibiting their zeal in the repression of the evil traffic. The west coast still requires watching; each harbour on the east coast from which slaves are shipped must be blockaded, till every Arab dhow manned by a slave-trading crew is captured and destroyed. Our fleet of gunboats could not be more usefully employed than in such an undertaking, and in a few years, or months even, under active officers, they would render slave-trading too precarious a pursuit to be followed.

Expedition up the Niger.

To assist in the suppression of the slave-trade on the west coast of Africa, an expedition was organised in 1841, and placed under Captain Henry D. Trotter, commanding H.M. steam-vessel *Albert*, Lieutenants Fishbourne and Stenhouse. She was accompanied by H.H. steam-vessel *Wilberforce*, Commander William Allen, with Lieutenants James Strange and H. Harston, and H.M. steam-vessel *Soudan*, Commander Bird Allen. These vessels were built for the purpose by Mr Laird, of Liverpool. The two first were 139 feet 4 inches in length on deck, 27 feet breadth of beam, 11 feet depth of hold, 6 feet draft of water, and 457 tons measurement, and each was armed with one long brass 12-pounder, two brass 12-pounder howitzers, and 4 brass 1-pounder swivels, besides small arms. They had lofty masts, and were square-rigged forward and schooner aft; but though excellent sea-boats when hauled on a wind, from being flat-bottomed, they made much leeway. The *Soudan* was smaller, and drew only 4 feet 6 six inches. They were fitted with ventilating machines, and every means that science could devise was employed for the preservation of the health of the crews. On reaching the mouth of the Niger, a party of Kroomen were taken on board. After proceeding some way up the Niger against a strong current, they reached a spot fixed on for estab-lishing a model farm, when the stores for the purpose were landed. Unhappily, the paddle-box boat of the *Wilberforce* got adrift and sank in the centre of the river, whence she could not be recovered. Soon afterwards sickness attacked the crews of all the ships, and so rapid was the progress of the fever that the little *Soudan* had only six per-sons able to move about. All more or less suffered; nothing but mut-tering, delirium, or suppressed groans were heard on board the ves-sels. Nearly every person, even those unattacked, complained of the enervating effects of the climate. On the 18th of September the num-ber of the sick had increased to sixty, and many had died. Captain Trotter now decided to send back the *Soudan* to the sea with the sick on board, under the command of Lieutenant Fishbourne. The medical officer being of opinion, however, that by ascending higher up the river a more healthy climate would be reached, resolved to proceed in that direction in the *Albert*, while the *Wilberforce* also returned to the coast. There appeared every prospect of the expedition proving a bles-sing to the long-benighted inhabitants on either bank of the mighty stream — but Providence ordered it otherwise. In spite of the heroic courage displayed by all the naval officers employed, Captain Trotter was at last compelled to order the ship's head to be put down the stream, and on his arrival at the coast, as the only chance of saving his fife, the medical officers ordered his return to England.

Notwithstanding the fearful loss of life which had already been in-curred, Commander William Allen, now senior officer of the expedi-tion, hearing that Mr Carr, the superintendent of the model farm, had been murdered, and that the people were in danger of an attack from the surrounding natives, resolved at once again to ascend the river. He was on the point of starting, when H.M. steamer *Kite* arrived with despatches stopping all further explorations. He was, however, directed to send one of the steamers with a black crew, and only the number of white people and officers necessary to navigate her, to bring away the people from the model farm. Lieutenant Webb at once volunteered, and succeeded in carrying out his instructions, with the loss, unhappily, of Mr Webb, clerk in charge, and Mr Waddmgton, boatswain, a fine specimen of the British seaman, all the rest of the whites suffering also from fever. Such was the unhappy termination of an expedition undertaken with the most noble and philanthropic objects in view, and which, had it not been for the deadly climate, must, from the determination and zeal of all those engaged, have been fully successful.

Chapter Nineteen.

Warfare in the Nineteenth Century —
from A.D. 1845 to A.D. 1900.

Rarely has England been called on to interfere in any of the quarrels which have been so frequent among the states of South America. However, in 1842, General Oribe, president of the Banda Oriental, having been expelled from Monte Video, induced General Rosas, dictator of Buenos Ayres, to support his cause. Monte Video was therefore besieged both by sea and land by the Buenos Ayrean squadron and army; but the siege was raised chiefly by the efforts of the foreigners residing in the country, among whom was Garabaldi, who then first made himself known, at the head of a regiment of 500 Italians, whom he had raised from among the crews of the coasting vessels in the river. He and his followers appeared in the red shirts which have since become so famous. The English and French ministers residing in the Banda Oriental having vainly endeavoured to induce Rosas to keep the peace, their respective governments sent out a squadron under the commands of Admirals Inglefield and Laine. The fleet of Buenos Ayres was captured, and the invaders were driven out of Colonia, a town of which they had taken possession. Though thus defeated, Rosas still held out on the banks of the Parana, and had strongly fortified a place called Obligado, rather more than a hundred miles from its mouth, having erected batteries of great strength, and thrown a barrier consisting of a number of empty vessels secured together by iron cables across the whole width of the stream, guarded by an armed schooner and some gunboats. The admirals accordingly sent a detachment of their squadrons to attack the fortress, and then to proceed up the Parana to release a large fleet of merchant-vessels which had been detained some hundred miles from its mouth. The British squadron consisted of the steam-frigate *Gorgon*, Captain Charles Hotham, who had under him the *Firebrand* steam-frigate, Captain J. Hope, the *Philomel* surveying brig, Commander B.J. Sulivan, and the *Comus, Dolphin*, and *Fanny*, the latter commanded by Lieutenant A.C. Key. The French force was under Captain Terehouart, commanding the *Saint Martin*, of 10 guns, who had with him the *Fulton* steamer and three other vessels. After having been detained for some time by bad weather, the squadron arrived opposite the fortress, on which the vessels gallantly opened their fire. It was returned by a tremendous shower of shot, shell, grape, and rockets, by which a number of the English and French were killed. The Spaniards, letting loose their fire-vessels, endeavoured to destroy the ships, but they were towed clear by the boats, while Captain Hope, with a party of men trained for the purpose, under a tremendous fire from the shore, cut through the chains, and opened a way for the passage of the vessels up the stream. The marines and blue-jackets were then landed, when they attacking the batteries, the enemy took to flight, pursued by Lieutenant Key, at the head of a light company of seamen, who carried a wood into which they had thrown themselves. In a few minutes the remainder of the dictator's vessels were pursued up the streams in which they had sought refuge, and were destroyed. Commander Sulivan, of the *Philomel*, who had carefully surveyed the river, now undertook to pilot the squadron up to Santa Fé, the appointed rendezvous of the merchantmen. On their passage most of the vessels were attacked by batteries thrown up on the bank, and, unhappily, several officers and men were killed. While the squadron and their convoy were remaining at Santa Fé, Rosas had thrown up a line of heavy batteries on the summit of some high cliffs, at a place called San Lorenzo. It was clear that the fleet would be exposed to considerable danger while passing these batteries. Lieutenant Mackinnon, of the *Alecto*, having observed that opposite the batteries was a narrow island covered with reeds, grass, and small trees, though otherwise completely commanded by the batteries, proposed landing during the night preceding the day the squadron was to descend, with a number of Congreve rockets, which he suggested should be fired into the fort so as to distract the defenders, while the ships of war and merchant-vessels passed under it. His proposal was adopted. Fortunately, a bank was found parallel with the stream, which was of sufficient height to conceal the rocket party. Having made their way across the island to it during the hours of darkness, the rocket-stands were planted, and all was ready for the passage of the fleet. As Lieutenant Mackinnon was watching the battery from his place of concealment, he observed a sentry suddenly stop, one of the men having incautiously exposed himself, and eye the spot narrowly. "Hold fast," he whispered to the man; "don't move, as you value your life." The man obeyed, and the sentry moved on. At length, the wind being fair, the signal that the fleet were approaching was heard, the *Gorgon, Fulton,* and *Alecto* leading. As they approached, Lieutenant Mackinnon, jumping on the embankment and waving his cap, while the British flag was hoisted under the very nose of the enemy, sang out, "Pepper, lads! pepper, lads! pepper, pepper, pepper!" and pepper away the men did with a vengeance. In one minute forty rockets, admirably directed, were poured into the opposite battery, compelling the dismayed enemy to desert their guns. Terrific must have been the slaughter among them. The steamers meantime taking up their position under the batteries, the fleet of merchantmen passed quickly down under the showers of rockets which were fired without cessation. The sternmost ships of the squadron being out of range, the rocket party prepared to retreat, while the enemy, misled by the flagstaff, which was erected at some distance from their place of concealment, fired away at that. A better-conducted or more successful exploit was never performed. The rocket party got back to their boat without the loss of a single man, and, pulling rapidly down the stream, rejoined their ship. The British and French squadron, on their return to Monte Video, defeated an attack made on the city by some of the allies of Rosas, a party of marines and seamen being landed to assist in placing it in a better position for defence.

FORCING THE BATTERIES OF SAN LORENZO.—p. 420.

Captain Loch's expedition up the Saint Juan De Nicaragua.

In 1848 Captain Granville G. Loch led a boat expedition up the Saint Juan de Nicaragua, which was as spiritedly carried out as any in the times of the previous war. It consisted of the boats of his own ship the *Alarm* and the *Vixen*, Commander Rider; and its object was to punish a certain Colonel Sales of the Nicaraguan army, who, after carrying off two British subjects and committing various outrages, had fortified himself in the town of Serapaqui, situated about thirty miles up the river. The current runs at the rate of five knots an hour, and the fort was situated at the head of a long reach, its defences consisting of six angular stockaded entrenchments eight feet in height, of considerable thickness, one side of each looking down the reach and the other across the river, completely commanding the only landing-place. Notwithstanding the strength of the current, Captain Loch commenced the ascent with twelve boats, carrying 260 officers and men, accompanied by the consul in his own boat. Passing over numerous downfalls and rapids, by immense exertions the party, at the end of seventy-two hours, got almost in sight of the fort. Unhappily, the consul and a friend accompanying him fell overboard during the night, and both were drowned. The next morning on approaching the fort the boats were received by a tremendous fire from it and from both banks of the river, which riddled them with shot, broke nearly half the oars, killed two men, and severely wounded Mr Turner, a midshipman, and several others. Notwithstanding this, pulling on against the strong current for an hour and forty minutes, they got past the batteries, and then, dropping down to the landing-place, sprang on shore, and the crews, uttering a loud cheer, stormed the stockades. The Nicaraguans withstood them for some time, but at length giving way fled into the forest, leaving twenty dead behind them, while twice that number were wounded, and two officers and seven men captured. The boats returned down the river, and arrived safely on board the ships.

Attacks on Pirates.

It is impossible to mention one-tenth part of the services performed by our men-of-war in all parts of the world of late years in capturing slavers, destroying pirates, and punishing outrages committed on British subjects. In 1848 an English merchant-vessel, the *Three Sisters*, was taken possession of by the notorious Riff pirates, and towed close in to the shore on the coast of the Mediterranean, after her master and the crew had fortunately escaped. Commander McCleverty, of the *Polyphemus*, was at once despatched to retake the brig. On approaching the shore he found a force of 500 men drawn up to defend their prize. The pirates on this daringly opened a hot fire of musketry upon the steamer, which she returned with doses of grape and canister, and quickly dispersed them. The boats, under the command of Lieutenant Allen Gardner, were then sent to bring off the brig, but as they got up to her a gun opened fire on them, and the pirates returning commenced blazing away from behind the rocks at them and the ship, by which Lieutenant Wasey and seven men were wounded. Lieutenant Gardner, notwithstanding, got hold of the brig, and towed her to the *Polyphemus*, which steamed off with her to sea.

The punishment inflicted on the Riff pirates was soon forgotten, and they continued their depredations on British commerce. In 1851 they captured the brigantine *Violet* and the schooner *Amelia*, killing the masters and several men among their crews, while the survivors were carried into slavery. On information of the outrage being received at Gibraltar the *Janus*, Captain Powell, started immediately to punish the pirates. Both vessels were found total wrecks on shore. The *Janus* could therefore only retaliate by firing on the piratical boats, which she did, totally destroying the whole of those seen. She afterwards came in sight of another large pirate fleet. The boats were sent on shore to destroy them, but the Riff people collecting in overwhelming numbers, attacked them so furiously that they were compelled to return to the ship, Captain Powell himself and seven men being wounded. The *Violet's* crew were, however, liberated.

War with China — 1856.

The seizure of the *Arrow*, sailing under British colours, by the Chinese, and their haughty refusal to make any reparation, compelled the British minister at Canton to apply to Sir Michael Seymour, commander-in-chief on the China station, to try the efficacy of his guns in inducing the commissioner, Yeh, to yield to his demands. The admiral's flag was flying on board the *Calcutta*, 84; he had under him the *Winchester*, of 50 guns, the *Sybil* and *Pique*, of 40, and the *Hornet* and *Encounter*, screw-steamers, the first of 17 and the other of 15 guns, and three paddle-wheel steamers and three sloops of war. He was in a short time reinforced by the *Sanspareil*, of 70 guns, the *Nankin*, of 50, the *Amethyst*, of 26, several screw-steamers, and a considerable number of gunboats, well suited for navigating the Chinese rivers. The English admiral first sailed up to Canton, and took possession of all its outer defences, one of which, the Macao fort, situated in the middle of the river, he garrisoned with a force of marines. The Barrier Forts, armed with 150 guns, were stormed and captured, the guns spiked, and the buildings destroyed. These proceedings, however, had no effect on Yeh, and he still held out. Accordingly, bringing up other vessels, the admiral ordered an attack on Canton itself. The ships soon made a breach in the walls, when a body of seamen and marines under Captains Elliott and Stuart and Commanders Holland and Bate stormed the place, and in a short time the gallant Bate having scaled the walls at the head of one detachment, waved the British ensign on the top of the breach; the gate of the city was blown open, and in less than an hour Canton was in possession of the British. The blue-jackets and marines abstained from all acts of plunder, and treated the inhabitants so well that they came fearlessly alongside the vessels, bringing fresh provisions of all kinds. The admiral, not considering it advisable to retain the city, withdrew his men, leaving only a force sufficient for the protection of the factory. This place the Chinese attempted to burn, and made every effort to destroy the fleet with fire-rafts and enormous explosive machines, some of which, it is said, contained 3000 pounds of gunpowder. They were invariably, however, towed clear of the ships. Yeh then one night sent a fleet of 23 war-junks in the hopes of surprising the fleet. Getting news of the intended attack, the admiral despatched the *Barracouta* with a fleet of boats under Captain Wilson of the *Winchester*, the admiral himself afterwards joining, and in half-an-hour the whole of the fleet was destroyed, with the exception of the admiral's vessel, carrying 60 guns, which was brought off.

Still Yeh refused to yield, and Sir Michael therefore attacked the Bogue Forts, which now mounted upwards of 200 guns, and the whole were captured with trifling loss the mandarins having run away and deserted their men, who began in their terror to throw themselves into the sea, till they were persuaded by Captain Hall that they would not be injured.

Meantime, the Chinese were beginning to repair the Barrier Forts, which, as they commanded the river, the admiral resolved to destroy. Two of them, the French Folly and Dutch Folly, were successively attacked. Captains Wilson and Cochrane landing at the head of 850 seamen and marines, stormed the latter, and blew up it and the 30 guns with which it was armed. The Dutch Folly was garrisoned by 140 seamen, under the command of Commodore Elliott, while, to protect the squadron, two strong booms were thrown across the river, one above and the other below it. This terminated the year 1856.

Early in the following year the Chinese having collected a fleet of 90 large junks and 30 row-boats, advanced from three different quarters, hoping to overwhelm the British squadron; but the ships, opening their fire, soon put them to flight, when they were followed by the boats and several more destroyed. For several months no active operations took place. Unhappily, the Honourable Captain Keppel's ship, the *Raleigh*, on her way to Hong-Kong, struck on a rock and was totally wrecked. Sir Michael, however, gave him command of the *Alligator*, and placed under him the *Bittern* sloop and the hired steamers, *Hong-Kong* and *Sir Charles Forbes*, attached to the *Raleigh* as tenders. As soon as active operations were commenced, a squadron of gunboats towing about 20 ship's boats, most of them armed with a heavy gun, was despatched up the Escape Creek in search of a large fleet of Chinese war-junks. As soon as the Chinese saw them, they took to flight up a shallow creek, where the gunboats pursuing them, grounded; but the officers jumping into the boats, continued the pursuit, when Commander Forsyth captured ten, and Mr Brown, mate of the *Hornet*, with a single boat's crew, attacked and carried three large ones in succession. Altogether, ten were taken and seventeen destroyed.

Several smaller expeditions were made with the like success. Still, the main fleet of the Chinese remaining in safety in Fatshan, the admiral resolved to lead against it an expedition he had organised of 11 gunboats and between 50 and 60 boats of the fleet, carrying 2000 men. Each division of boats was commanded by the captains of the ships to which they belonged. The fleet they were to attack consisted of 80 of the largest junks, manned by 6000 of the best Chinese sailors and warriors. It was drawn up under heavy batteries on either bank; across the stream 50 junks were found moored side by side, the large guns in their bows pointed down it. The admiral waited till dead low water, the most favourable time for making his attack, and he hoped that the junks would be unable to move till he got up to them, while should any of his own gunboats take the ground, they would soon again be afloat with the rising tide. The Chinese had further strengthened their position by sinking junks laden with stone, against one of which the *Coromandel*, carrying the admiral's flag, grounded. He, on this, landing with a party of blue-jackets and marines, stormed one of the batteries, the garrison of which soon took to flight. Meantime, the

Haughty, the leading gunboat, attacked the largest of the junks; her crew jumping overboard, the example was followed by those of the rest of the fleet, when the whole squadron was immediately set on fire. Commodore Keppel attacked and carried a second battery, and then sent his division of boats against another squadron of junks. These having been destroyed, he pushed on three miles till he saw before him the main body of the largest junks moored compactly across the stream with their heavy bow-guns pointing at him. These opened so tremendous a fire that in a few moments every boat was hit. The commodore's coxswain was killed, and scarcely a man in the boat escaped. While Lieutenant Prince Victor of Hohenlohe was engaged in attending to a wounded man, a shot whizzed between him and the commodore, and had he not been bending down, he would have been killed. So full of water was the boat that Keppel had to jump on the after-thwart to keep his legs out of it, when another round-shot passed through both sides of the boat scarcely an inch below him. At length, as the boat was on the point of sinking, he and his companions, taking the wounded men, got into one of the *Calcutta's* boats. The rest of the flotilla had suffered in the same way, and numerous officers and men had been killed or wounded. The commodore, seeing that there was little hope of success at that moment, ordered the boats to retire, and the deck of the *Hong-Kong* was soon covered with the wounded men brought on board. The fire of the Chinese still reaching her, several more men were killed on board. The admiral, however, hearing the firing, had sent up reinforcements, and Commodore Keppel, calling to the rest of the boats to follow, again dashed forward in the *Raleigh's* cutter, in a style which so daunted the Chinese that, cutting their cables, they pulled away up the stream. The British seamen cheered and, opening fire from their big guns, were soon up to the sternmost junks. These were quickly captured, their crews in many instances leaping overboard. The rest were pursued for seven miles, till the British boats found themselves almost in the middle of the large city of Fatshan. Here the commodore landing put a considerable body of troops to flight, and would have captured and held the town had not the admiral considered the enterprise useless. He contented himself, therefore, with towing away five large junks, the only portion of the Chinese fleet which had escaped destruction. This success was purchased at the cost of 84 men killed and wounded. Chuenpee, further down the river, was next captured without difficulty, for though considerably strengthened, so disheartened were the Chinese that they did not attempt to defend it.

Considerable reinforcements were now sent out from England, including the *Shannon*, Captain W. Peel, the *Pearl, Sanspareil*, and numerous gunboats; but news of the Sepoy mutiny having reached the admiral, he immediately despatched them to Calcutta with a force of Royal Artillery and other troops. During the eventful struggle which ensued, the crews of the *Shannon* and *Pearl*, formed into naval brigades, did good service. In November, 1857, the Indian mutiny being nearly quelled, operations in China were recommenced. Yeh proved as obstinate as ever, and to bring him to reason Canton was again attacked. Besides 800 regular troops, the British force consisted of the marines and 1550 blue-jackets, well trained to act on shore. They were formed into three divisions under Captains Stuart, Key, and McClure, the command of the whole being confided to Commodore Elliott. The French, who had now joined the English, had also a naval brigade of less size. The smaller vessels and gunboats having arrived before Canton, began and kept up a ceaseless fire on the walls as well as on the heights both inside and outside the city, replied to by the cannon, jingalls, and rockets of the Chinese. On the morning of the 29th the naval brigade stormed and captured a large temple close to the walls, and at daylight the artillery, which had been landed, opened fire and soon effected a breach. The signal was now given for the scaling parties to advance, and rushing forward with ladders in hand they were quickly up to the walls. The French had the honour of getting over first, not having waited for the signal. The British seamen in different directions were not long after them, Commander Fellowes, of the *Cruiser*, being the first to mount. The Chinese fought bravely, and many of the British seamen fell. Among them was Captain Bate, of the *Actaeon*, who was killed while about to mount a scaling ladder. Captain Key with his brigade seizing a battery turned its guns upon the foe; and division after division having got over, swept the Chinese before them, till by nine o'clock the city was won. So large was the city that it took some days before it could be thoroughly occupied. Among those captured were Yeh himself and several other mandarins of rank. As a punishment for his conduct he was sent as a prisoner to Calcutta. The whole loss of the allies was under 130 men killed and wounded, the larger portion belonging to the naval brigade. After this the fleet proceeded to the Peiho, at the mouth of which stands the town of Taku, to which the emperor had despatched a new commissioner named Tau, to negotiate with Lord Elgin. As, however, Tau behaved exactly as Yeh had done, the English and French admirals sent a squadron to capture the forts which guard the entrance to the river.

They had been of late greatly strengthened, and from the ditches and wide extent of mud spread before them, were truly formidable. The force consisted of the *Cormorant*, Commander Saumarez, the *Nimrod*, *Slaney*, several French vessels, and a number of the smaller British gunboats, *Opossum, Bustard, Staunch*. The two admirals going up on board the *Slaney*. The *Cormorant* leading, broke through a boom of great strength, passed across the river, and various vessels quickly taking up their position, opened their fire on the forts, which, though defended for some time, at length yielded, their garrisons taking to flight. A squadron of gunboats, with the English and French admirals on board, then made their way up to Tientsin, a large city midway between Pekin and the sea. The emperor, now fearing that his capital itself would be attacked, came to terms. The fleet, however, remained ready to compel him to keep to them, should he attempt to evade fulfilling his engagements. In the meantime a small squadron, consisting of the *Retribution*, Captain Barker, the *Furious*, Captain S. Osborn, the *Cruiser*, Commander Bythesea, the gunboat *Lee*, Lieutenant Jones, and surveying-vessel *Dove*, Commander Ward, made a voyage up the Yang'tse Kiang, 600 miles above Nankin, to a city of importance called Hang-keo. From the shallowness of the water the larger vessels frequently grounded, and on passing Nankin, then in possession of a formidable army of rebels, which attacked them, they had to fight their onward way. At length the *Retribution* could proceed no farther, but Osborn leading the rest reached Hang-keo in safety. On their way back the larger vessels again grounded, but being released by a flood, the whole succeeded in returning to Shanghai.

Sir Michael Seymour returning home, was succeeded by Admiral J. Hope, with his flag on board the *Chesapeake*. Besides six larger vessels, he had under his command a squadron of nine gunboats. Each boat was armed with two long guns and two howitzers, and before they went into action the admiral sent on board each from the *Chesapeake* an additional 32-pounder and an organised crew to work it. Those who knew the Chinese best were very sure, as the result proved, that the emperor did not intend to keep the terms of the treaty. Admiral Hope arrived off the Peiho on the 8th of June, and as soon as he attempted to ascend it for the purpose of proceeding to Pekin to announce the arrival of the British ambassador, he discovered that the forts had been greatly strengthened, and that obstructions of all sorts had been placed across the river. Strong booms had been carried from side to side, and iron stakes driven into the bottom at intervals, reaching within two feet of high-water mark. The Chinese having neglected to remove the obstructions, after the admirals had waited several days, Mr Bruce and the French ambassador having arrived, the admiral sent in to say that unless his demands were immediately complied with he should force his way. A force of blue-jackets and marines 700 strong were told off to storm the forts, and the admiral, shifting his flag to the *Plover*, led his squadron of gunboats, accompanied by those of the French, towards the forts. During the night Captain Wills with three boats had broken the first boom with barrels of gunpowder, and pushing on, was examining the inner one, when the moon rising revealed his position to the Chinese, who opened so warm a fire on him that he was compelled to retire. The plan proposed was to attack the works on the river side with the gunboats, and the batteries being silenced, to storm with the landing-party. The gunboats, as far as they were able, took up the position allotted to them, but from the shallowness of the water, the *Starling* and *Banterer* got aground. No sooner did they open fire than the Chinese began blazing away from a line of heavy guns, which, in a short time, played havoc among them. The *Plover* was almost knocked to pieces, and her commander killed, 30 of her crew being killed or wounded, and the admiral himself severely hurt. He, however, shifted his flag on board the *Opossum*, whose commander was shortly afterwards wounded, and her screw becoming fouled, she drifted down the stream. On this Admiral Hope went on board the *Cormorant*, and on her deck, lying in his cot, issued his directions till overcome by loss of blood. Captain Shadwell then took the command. The engagement continued with great fury on both sides, but the *Lee* and *Haughty* were both nearly destroyed. The tide having sunk several feet, the English guns produced less effect on the fort than at first. At the end of four hours, however, nearly all the Chinese guns on the left bank were silenced, though those on the right still continued their fire. It was determined, therefore, to storm the forts on that side, and late in the evening the force destined for that purpose was landed, led by Captains Shadwell and Vansittart and Colonel Lemon, of the marines, and supported by Commanders Commerell and Heath. The gallant Captain Tricault led a body of French, and the boats of an American man-of-war assisted in landing the men. Scarcely, however, had they jumped on shore, unable to obtain the slightest shelter, than the Chinese opened a tremendous fire on them with jingalls, rifles, and muskets, and every gun that could be brought to bear. In a few minutes numbers were hit, Captain Vansittart was mortally wounded, Captain Shadwell's foot was smashed, and Colonel Lemon fell, severely hurt. The command now devolved on Commerell, who gallantly led forward his men; but two ditches and a wide extent of mud intervened between them and the fort, and so thickly did the shot rain down on them that, before they got twenty yards, 300 were killed or wounded, and they were compelled to retreat — many unfortunate fellows being suffocated in the mud. Of the numerous vessels which had run on shore, all were got off with the exception of the *Cormorant, Plover,* and *Lee,* which were knocked to pieces to prevent them falling into the hands of the Chinese. In this disastrous affair above 80 men had been killed and 350 wounded, many of whom died from their hurts.

The Chinese were not allowed, however, for any length of time to boast of their victory. The Peiho was again entered, the town of Pehtang was occupied and the Taku Forts again attacked from the sea and land. Though the army lost a good many men in the operations, not one on board the gunboats was killed. The booms across the river were broken through, the iron stakes drawn, and Admiral Hope pushing on in the *Coromandel* with a squadron of gunboats, arrived before Tientsin, which yielded to the first summons.

After this the duties of the steamers consisted chiefly in conveying the heavy siege trains of baggage and provisions for the supply of the army in the neighbourhood of Pekin, when after his army had been thoroughly defeated, and at the moment that his city was about to be stormed, the emperor yielded to all the demands of the allies. The emperor had acted with great treachery in the negotiations for peace, imprisoning and torturing the English envoys and escort, so as a lesson to him and his people, his celebrated Summer Palace was burnt to the ground, thus showing them that had they thought fit Pekin itself might have been treated in the same manner.

Russian War — 1854-55.

Russia had shown her evident intention of laying violent hands on Turkey, by destroying with a treachery unworthy a civilised nation a Turkish squadron at Sinope, and England and France being bound by treaty to protect the Ottoman Empire, without delay each despatched a fleet into the Black Sea. That of England was under the command of Admiral Dundas, who had his flag on board the *Britannia*, of 120 guns, his second in command being Rear-Admiral Sir Edmund Lyons, whose flag flew on board the *Agamemnon*, of 91 guns, a name known to fame. The other ships were the *Trafalgar*, of 120 guns, the *Queen*, of 116, the *Albion*, 91, *Rodney* and *London*, 90, *Vengeance*, 84, *Bellerophon*, 80, *Sanspareil*, 70, *Arethusa* and *Leander*, 50, *Tribune* and *Curacoa*, 31, *Retribution*, steam-frigate, 28, *Diamond*, 26, *Terrible* and *Sidon*, steam-frigates, 22, *Highflyer*, steam-sloop, 21, *Furious* and *Tiger*, 16, the former a steam-frigate, the *Niger*, 13, and nine steam-sloops. The French fleet consisted of 15 sail of the line, and 21 frigates and smaller vessels.

From the first Admiral Lyons contemplated an attack on Sebastopol, and in order to ascertain the strength of its fortifications, Captain Drummond, of the *Retribution*, before war was actually declared, was sent there with a despatch for the Russian governor. He ran in during a fog, and had brought up before even his presence was discovered. Having sent his despatch on shore, he waited for an answer, making good use of his time, and when it arrived, having exchanged salutes with the governor, he stood out again with the valuable information he had obtained. Peace not having been actually broken, the *Furious*, Captain Loring, was sent to Odessa to bring off the British consul, or any British subjects who might wish to leave it. As the frigate was receiving them on board, the garrison, notwithstanding the flag of truce she carried, fired on her. This treacherous conduct deserved a prompt punishment. A fleet accordingly on the 17th of April sailed for that port, off which they anchored on the 20th. The line-of-battle ships could not get close enough to the walls, and a squadron of English and French steam-frigates under Captain Jones, of the *Sampson*, stood in and delivered their broadsides. Having done so, one after another in succession steamed rapidly round out of gunshot, to return again and fire as before. The Russian guns returned the compliment with red-hot shot, which set the *Vauban* on fire. Captain Mends, of the "gallant *Arethusa*," remembering the fame of her name, though he had only his sails to depend on, ran in as close as the depth of water would allow, and opened a heavy fire from his 9-inch shell guns, and repeated his manoeuvres till recalled by a signal from the flag-ship. Ultimately some gunboats with rockets were directed to try their powers; at last flames burst forth from several parts of the works, and at one o'clock the magazine in the principal fort exploding cast destruction around. The batteries having been now silenced, the squadron stood closer in and destroyed moat of the vessels which had taken shelter behind the mole. Soon after the fleet retired from before Odessa, the *Tiger*, which had been stationed off the coast, ran on shore.

While attempts were being made to get her off the Russians brought down a field battery, from which they opened so brisk a fire that Captain Gifford, being mortally wounded, and several of his men hit, he was compelled, in order to save their lives, to haul down his flag.

Another visit to ascertain the strength of Sebastopol was paid by Captain Tatham, of the *Fury*. Disguising her like an Austrian packet, which he knew was expected in the harbour, he boldly stood in on the 10th of May, running past two brigs of war, and having sufficiently looked about him steamed as calmly out again, hoisting the British colours as soon as he had got out of shot. While still in sight of the batteries he captured a Russian schooner, and was carrying her off, when some frigates getting under way, chased him and compelled him to abandon his prize. The fleets now proceeded off Sebastopol, sending away some of their ships in order to induce the Russians to come out and fight them. All their efforts proved vain, and Sir Edmund Lyons scoured the Black Sea till not a Russian vessel of any size remained on its bosom.

Some months thus passed, when the army having been collected at Varna, Sir Edmund Lyons, to whom the task was intrusted by the commander-in-chief, embarked them on board the transports destined for their reception. Admirably were the arrangements made, both for their embarkation and landing on the shores of the Crimea. Indeed, difficult as were both operations, they were carried out without the loss of a man, and with that only of one or two horses drowned. While the army marched towards the Alma, the fleet proceeded along the shore. Some of the steamers standing in, put to flight the few Russian troops their guns could reach. For some time it was hoped that the Russian ships would come out of Sebastopol and give battle to the allied fleets; but all hopes of their doing so were lost when the Russians, having arranged some of their finest line-of-battle ships across the harbour, scuttled them, and their masts were seen slowly descending beneath the surface. No hopes remaining of a naval engagement, each ship supplied a contingent of men, who were formed into a naval brigade, under Captain Stephen Lushington, a body of the French seamen being employed in the same manner. None of the brave fellows employed in the siege performed a greater variety of duties, or behaved with more gallantry, than did the British blue-jackets on shore. They fought in the batteries, armed with some of their own heavy ship's guns dragged up by themselves from the shore, carried the scaling-ladders in many an assault, assisted to land the stores, and were for some time the principal labourers in forming a road between Balaclava and Sebastopol. Led by the gallant Captain Peel, they took an active part in the assault on the Redan, on which occasion they lost 14 killed and 47 wounded. They were ever-active in succouring those who had been left on the field of battle, whether blue-jackets or red-coats, and many who might have perished owed their lives to their courage and activity. During the engagement known as the Little Inkerman, on the 26th of October Mr Hewett, mate of the *Beagle*, while in command of a Lancaster gun, was greatly instrumental in the de-feat of the Russians. Having received a message by a sergeant from an officer, who thought the battery would be taken in reverse, to spike his gun and retreat, he replying that he only received orders from his own captain, got his gun round to bear on the Russians, and blowing away the parapet, poured his fire down on them in a way which com-pelled them to abandon their object.

As soon as the troops on shore were ready to open with their batter-ies, the combined fleets prepared to perform their parts in attacking the sea faces of Sebastopol. By this time Admiral Dundas had given up the command of the fleet to Sir Edmund Lyons, who, as before, directed all the operations. The *Agamemnon* and *Sanspareil* were the only line-of-battle ships fitted with screws, but there were steamers sufficient to tow all into action, or to assist them out again if neces-sary. The final arrangements were made on the 16th between the Eng-lish and French admirals, when it was settled that the French and Turks should attack the forts on the south side of the harbour, and the English those on the north. Early on the morning of the 17th the order to weigh was given — the fleets having been collected in Kazatch Bay, some distance to the north of the city. The French and Turks, who formed one line, naturally led; the *Britannia* followed, close to the *Charlemagne*, the rearmost of the French line. An inshore squadron had been formed, consisting of the *Agamemnon, Sanspareil*, and *London*, which was afterwards joined by the *Albion* and other ships. The *Bri-tannia*, the most southern of the British ships, took up her position opposite Fort Constantine; next to her in succession were the *Trafalgar, Vengeance, Rodney*, and *Queen*. The *Agamemnon*, piloted by Mr Ball in the little steam-tender *Circassia*, glided on till she was about 750 yards from Fort Constantine, close to a shoal, which prevented her nearer approach. The *London, Sanspareil*, and *Albion* followed her, but were unable to get quite as near the fort as she was. The admiral had warned Mr Ball that his little vessel would probably be sunk, and promised to keep a boat ready to save him and his crew should she go down; but undaunted by the danger, he stood on amid a perfect shower of shot and shell, sounding as he went, till the line was cut from the leadsman's hand by a shot from the batteries; but another leadsman immediately took his place, and the *Circassia*, without a man killed, though frequently hulled, steamed out of harm's way. Immediately the *Agamemnon's* anchor was dropped, she opened her fire, as did the other ships in succession. Fortunately, from being so close in, the Russian shot mostly passed over her, as the guns had been trained for a longer range; but the ships to the north of her suffered considerably. Happily, one of the first shells she fired reached the powder-magazine in the fort, which, blowing up with a tremendous explosion, drove the Russians from their guns, and though they again returned, it was to find that a large number of them had been dismounted, while the upper part of their works were crumbling to pieces from the effects of the fire from the British ships. From their lower batteries, however, and from various forts on the heights, so hot was the Russian fire, that the *Albion* and *London*, terribly shattered, were compelled to haul off. The *Sanspareil* also brought up so close to the *Agamemnon* as to be unable to use her foremost guns, and had to get under way to take up a better berth, and for a time the *Agamemnon* stood the brunt of the battle in her part of the line. The *Sanspareil*, however, again quickly came to her support, and the *Albion*, having repaired some of her damages, returned; but as the *London* was unable to do so, the admiral signalled to the *Rodney*, the *Queen, Bellerophon*, and *Arethusa*, to come to his assistance. A short time afterwards the *Queen*, set on fire by a shell, was compelled to retreat, and the *Rodney* got on shore at the end of the bank; but a large portion of her crew having joined the naval brigade, she had but few men on board, and therefore fought only her main-deck guns, and though in so exposed a position, escaped with comparatively little loss. For five hours the whole fleet kept up perhaps the most tremendous cannonade that has ever been fired from British or any other ships, when night coming on, the *Agamemnon* made the signal for the fleet to retire, she herself being the last to leave her station. Though during that time the upper portions of some of the Russian batteries had been knocked away, and a large number of people killed and wounded in them, the furious cannonade which had been so long kept up produced no result to compensate the British for a loss sustained of 44 killed and 266 wounded, besides the damages received by many of the ships, two of which, the *Albion* and *Arethusa*, had to go to Malta to be repaired. Though the French ships suffered more than ours, they lost under 200 men killed and wounded. The steamers had gallantly performed their part in towing the ships in and out of action, notwithstanding the showers of shot and shell directed at them. Altogether, the admirals came to the conclusion that it was useless attempting to batter down the stone walls of the fortifications, or to again expose their ships to such a fire as they had that day endured.

A portion of the allied fleets still remained before Sebastopol, and harassed the garrison by sending into the harbour two fast, strongly-armed steamers night after night, which, always keeping in motion, fired their shot into the city, and rapidly steamed out again before the enemy could get their guns to bear on them. On one of these occasions the admiral's son, while directing the course of his vessel, was so severely wounded that he died shortly afterwards.

During the winter months of 1855 no operations were undertaken by the fleet, but as soon as the finer weather allowed the ships to navigate the Black Sea, an expedition sailed for Kertch, a town of importance at the extreme eastern point of the Crimea, containing immense magazines of corn, with which from thence the beleaguered garrison was supplied. Just as the expedition was sailing, however, Canrobert, who had supreme authority over the French naval forces, forbade Admiral Brueys from proceeding, and Sir Edmund magnanimously gave up the enterprise for a time at the earnest request of his colleague. A fortnight afterwards, however, General Pelissier succeeding Canrobert, authorised the French admiral to proceed in support of the English. An overpowering fleet accordingly sailed towards the entrance of the Sea of Azov. As soon as the ships appeared off Kertch, the Russians blew up their fortifications without firing a shot, and evacuated the place. The only officer who had an opportunity of distinguishing himself was Lieutenant McKillop, commanding the *Snake*, of 4 guns. Perceiving a Russian steamer in the offing, he obtained leave to chase her, which he did till she got under the forts of Yeni-kale, when both fort and steamer opened their guns on him. Undaunted, he returned the salute, throwing his shells upon both his opponents, and in three-quarters of an hour set the steamer on fire. He was still blazing away at the fort, when three other steamers were seen approaching, and they also, as he refused to run, began to attack him, the guns of each one of them being of heavier calibre than his. He continued engaging them till assistance sent by the admiral arrived, when the whole of the Russian vessels were captured.

While the larger ships proceeded in various directions along the coast, a squadron consisting of the smaller vessels and gunboats were sent into the Sea of Azov, under Captain Lyons, of the *Miranda*, to attack the numerous stores of corn and other provisions accumulated at different spots along the shores. On the return of the *Miranda* to Sebastopol, Captain Lyons was succeeded by Commander Sherard Osborn in the *Vesuvius*. Although the duties imposed on the squadron were not apparently of a very heroic character, they were attended with a considerable amount of risk, and were carried out in a most spirited and gallant manner. In several places the magazines and stores were protected by large bodies of the enemy, who fought courageously in their defence, but were invariably defeated by the determination and activity of the British seamen. Taganrog and other places were protected by heavy batteries, which, however, did not prevent the little squadron from attacking them and coming off victorious. For many months the steam-vessels were thus employed moving about from one place to another. Wherever they were least expected, the officers landed with parties of men, and did not hesitate to proceed either up the rivers or some way inland wherever they gained intelligence that storehouses existed, and in no instance failed to set them on fire. Many hazardous and gallant acts were performed. In this way the squadron were of the most essential service to the allies, and by almost depriving the garrison of Sebastopol of their means of support, were mainly instrumental in the reduction of the great fortress. In a short time scarcely a Russian trading-vessel on those waters had escaped destruction or capture. The vessels of the squadron were everywhere, and often, when espied by troops of Cossack cavalry from the shore, there would be a race between them and the vessels who should first arrive at the store-houses, which the latter had destined to destruction, while the steamers' long guns played on the Cossacks, and generally sent them galloping away inland out of range of fire, so that when they reached the store-houses they found them burnt to the ground. One of the last places attacked was Gheisk, in the neighbourhood of which, extending for fully four miles along the shore, were collected in huge stacks quantities of corn and hay; while close to the town, under the protection of its batteries, were large piles of timber, cured fish, numerous boats, and naval stores of all descriptions. The place was protected by a strong force of infantry and cavalry. Notwithstanding, Captain Osborn proceeded to attack it with the gunboats *Grinder, Boxer, Cracker,* and *Clinker;* but the shallowness of the water would allow them to get only just within range of the batteries.

The squadron was, however, supplied with a number of large boats which could carry heavy guns, and these he brought close in to the shore in order to cover the landing-parties, distributing them in four divisions, under Commander Kennedy and Lieutenants Ross, Day, and Strode, with directions to land at intervals of a mile from each other, and then driving the Russians before them to set fire to the stores. To protect the stores, the Russians had thrown up light breast-works along the whole of their front, but they were not such as to arrest British blue-jackets for a moment. Fortunately, the wind blew directly on shore, and thus as soon as the boats opened fire the smoke was driven in the faces of the enemy. The seamen quickly landing, notwithstanding the warm fire with which they were received, drove the Russians before them, and the stacks being at once ignited, the dense volumes of smoke which arose from them completely concealed the movements of the British, whose only object being to destroy the corn and hay, did not follow the enemy. Success attended every one of the operations; in a little more than six hours every stack was blaz-ing, as were the piles of timber, the boats, naval stores, and dried fish, under the protection of the batteries at Gheisk — the whole work be-ing accomplished with the loss only of five men wounded.

To prevent the escape of any of the Russian ships on the fall of Sebas-topol, the allied squadron brought up across the harbour, when the enemy having already sunk the remainder of their line-of-battle ships, set fire to all their steamers, thus with their own hands destroying the whole of their fleet. The English and French fleet then sailed for Kin-burn, standing on the shore of a shallow bay full of shoals. On their way they appeared off Odessa, in order to mislead the Russians, and then proceeded direct for their destination. The troops, consisting of 5000 British, and a large number of French, were landed on the 15th, and some of the gunboats stood in, and began firing to distract the garrison. The roughness of the sea, however, prevented the ships from commencing the grand attack till the 17th. The smaller steamers and gunboats then advanced, circling round and delivering their fire in rapid succession, silencing the Russian guns, killing the men, and forcing them to take refuge under ground. About noon the line-of-battle ships, English and French, entered into action in magnificent order close to the batteries, while a squadron of steamers, led by Sir Houston Stuart and the French rear-admiral, approached the forts on the northern side, and began pouring in their broadsides. Not for a moment was there a cessation of the thundering roar of the guns, while the whole fleet and doomed fortress became shrouded in dense wreaths of smoke, the gunboats on the other side keeping up their fire with fearful effect. The fire from the French floating batteries, which had lately been sent out at the suggestion of Napoleon, was most effective, while their power of resistance was fully as great as had been expected, the heavy shot by which they were frequently struck falling harmless from their iron sides, while the shells shivered against them like glass. The bombardment from the larger ships had continued scarcely a quarter-of-an-hour when a white flag was seen flying from the ramparts as a token of submission, and as if by magic the firing ceased. In a short time afterwards the old Russian general appeared to deliver up his sword, and he and a large staff of officers, who were permitted to retain their swords, became prisoners.

The Russians themselves blew up Oczakov, which was to have been attacked, while Sir Houston Stuart led a squadron up the Boug, and destroyed a battery on its shore. Had not the Russians soon afterwards come to terms, not a place of importance on their southern coasts would have been left in their possession.

Operations in the Baltic.

While one British fleet was attacking the Russians on the southern shores of their empire, another of still greater power was sent up the Baltic to prove to them that no part of their coasts was safe. Great results were naturally expected from it, and, indeed, England had never before sent so really powerful a fleet to sea — not on account of the number of the ships, but from their means of inflicting injury, most of them possessing steam power, while their guns were more effective than any which had before been used. The fleet consisted of the *Duke of Wellington*, of 131 guns, *Neptune, Saint George*, and *Royal George*, 120, *Saint Jean d'Arc*, 101, *Princess Royal, James Watt, Nile*, and *Majestic*, of 91, *Caesar* and *Prince Regent*, of 90, *Monarch*, 84, *Cressy*, 80, *Boscawen* and *Cumberland*, 70, *Edinburgh, Hogue, Blenheim*, and *Ajax*, of 60, *Impérieuse* and *Euryalus*, of 51, and *Arrogant*, of 46, besides frigates, sloops, and numerous paddle-steamers, the whole under the command of Admiral Sir Charles Napier. Gallant and energetic as he had always proved himself, he was now sixty-eight years of age, and those who knew him best feared too truly that his energies had begun to fail him, and that he would have acted more wisely by remaining on shore. The French also sent a considerable fleet to take part in the operations. The first portion of the fleet entered the Great Belt on the 25th of March, and proceeding to the Gulf of Finland, established a rigorous blockade. Napier then, moving towards Helsingfors, prevented a junction of the two portions of the Russian fleet, while in the meantime Admiral Plumridge, scouring the Gulf of Bothnia, captured a large number of merchantmen.

One of the first exploits in the Baltic was performed by Captain Yelverton, of the *Arrogant*, and Captain W.H. Hall, of the *Hecla*, who, running up a narrow creek, made their way to the town of Ekness, eight miles from the sea, where, after a sharp engagement with some batteries, they carried off a large merchant-vessel under the noses of the enemy. The fleets then appeared off Cronstadt, the approaches to which had been carefully surveyed by the indefatigable Captain Sulivan, of the *Lightning*, but the strength of the fortifications induced the admirals to believe that it would be useless to attack it, and they in vain endeavoured to tempt the Russian fleet to come out and give them battle. Bomarsund was the first place of importance assailed. It was attacked on the land side by the English artillery and French troops, as well as by the English and French marines, with a brigade of seamen who were landed after a fort which was in their way had been blown to pieces, while thirteen ships of the allied fleet assailed it from the sea. The ships directed their fire against a large circular fort mounting nearly 100 guns, with a garrison of 2000 men, when the shot soon shattered the huge masses of stone, which literally crumbled away before them, and in a short time the garrison, seeing that resistance was useless, yielded, and Bomarsund was taken possession of. It was, however, said that the works, though apparently strong, had been constructed by contract, and were therefore less able to withstand the shot hurled against them than the other fortresses which Russia possessed on her sea-board. Still, if such was the case, it does not detract from the praise due to those who had made the attack. The whole fortress was forthwith blown up, with the exception of one portion, which was allowed to stand for a few days to enable the *Edinburgh* to try some of her heavy guns against it, and it was finally levelled with the rest of the works.

The winter season coming on, compelled the fleet to return to England. Whatever may be said of the gallant old admiral's conduct during the war, it was acknowledged that the crews of his ships, though inexperienced when they set sail, returned in a high state of efficiency.

While these proceedings were taking place in the Baltic, in order as much as possible to annoy the Russians in all portions of their vast territory, a small British squadron, consisting of the *Eurydice*, Captain Ommaney, the *Miranda*, Captain Lyons, and the *Brisk*, Commander Seymour, were sent into the White Sea, where, though they found it impossible to attack Archangel, they destroyed several government establishments. The *Miranda* also, steaming up the river Kola for thirty miles, attacked the capital of Russian Lapland, of the same name, and, with her yardarms almost over the walls, set the city on fire and destroyed most of the public buildings and magazines. In spite of the hot fire with which his ship was assailed from the batteries, Captain Lyons returned from his gallant enterprise without losing a man, and, after capturing a fleet of merchant-vessels, rejoined Captain Ommaney.

The most unfortunate event of the whole war occurred on the Pacific coast, when a small English and French squadron, in attempting to take a number of Russian vessels anchored off Petro Pauloffsky, they were driven off, while by bad management the whole of the Russian vessels escaped.

The following year Admiral Dundas, being appointed to the command in the Baltic, sailed in the *Duke of Wellington*, of 130 guns, with Rear-Admiral Sir Michael Seymour as his second in command in the *Exmouth*, of 90 guns, and numerous other line-of-battle ships, block-ships, and smaller vessels, nearly all fitted with the screw, and upwards of twenty gunboats. At the end of May the fleet arrived off Cronstadt, when the two admirals, going on board the *Merlin*, which, under the command of Captain Sulivan, had been actively surveying that and other places in the Baltic, stood in to examine the works and the Russian fleet protected by them. They were not long in coming to the conclusion that the place, if not impregnable, would be most difficult to assail, while it was ascertained that a vast number of torpedoes had been placed in all directions in the shallow waters over which the ships must pass. Many had been put down in the preceding year, but, though looked for, none had been discovered; this year, however, several were fished up, and one was brought on board the *Exmouth*, when, while Admiral Seymour and his officers were examining it, it exploded in their midst. Though the admiral was wounded, as were several other officers and men, not one was killed. The *Merlin*, also, while passing over a shallow, exploded two, one of which drove in her side, breaking or disabling everything in that portion of the ship, though, happily, without committing any further damage. The greater number discovered had not been properly set, and thus had become injured from various causes. The boats, by carefully creeping wherever they were likely to be placed, ultimately discovered nearly the whole which it was supposed had been laid down. Very different would have been the result had they been constructed as torpedoes are at the present day, when in all probability many of our ships would have been destroyed.

The Russian fleet kept securely within their fortifications while the English and French remained off Cronstadt. All intention of attacking it being abandoned, the allies proceeded in different directions. The smaller vessels cruised off the coast, destroying all the government magazines and stores they could reach, and capturing innumerable merchant-vessels; while the admirals were preparing for an attack on the fortress of Sveaborg, which had been considerably strengthened since the preceding year. It stands on three islands, round the whole circumference of which the works form an almost unbroken line, and within them are vast arsenals full of all descriptions of warlike stores; while in front of the fortress lies a cluster of rocky islets. The passages between these islets had been carefully surveyed by Captain Sulivan, and on each of those nearest the fortress, mortar batteries were now placed, while the mortar-boats formed in a line outside them. The gunboats and mortar-vessels in different divisions were directed to stand in among the islets, where there was sufficient room for their movements, while the whole were covered by the frigates, which took up their stations outside. Some of the principal buildings in the fortress had been selected as targets, and so well had Captain Sulivan placed the mortar-vessels, that the shells thrown from them fell exactly on the spots at which they were aimed, as was ascertained by the cloud of smoke which rose from each. Hitherto it had been considered necessary not to fire more than seven shots in an hour from a mortar, but Captain Wemyss, who had charge of the mortar-vessels, considering that should such a plan be adopted, the enemy would have time to extinguish the flames they produced, determined to allow a much less interval to elapse, and sent no less than thirty shells an hour from each mortar. The gunboats were in the meantime performing their part, moving rapidly in circles, each boat firing as she brought her guns to bear on the fortifications. Besides their ordinary armament, each vessel had received on board from the line-of-battle ships a 10-inch gun, and two of them, the *Snapper* and *Stork*, had been armed with long

377

Lancaster guns. These were detached to attack a large three-decker at anchor between the islets, and so furious a fire did they open that flames several times burst out from her, while in a short time nearly seventy of her crew had been killed. The Russians, with their numerous guns, fired away rapidly in return. Though the gunboats were within range, their small size and quick movements made them difficult marks to hit, and only one or two were struck. The batteries thrown up on the small islets were throwing shells at the same time, while the *Arrogant, Cornwallis, Hastings,* and *Amphion* attacked the Drumsio and Sandham batteries, and kept them amply employed. About noon, some shells fell into several powder-magazines, which blew up with successive explosions, casting huge fragments of masonry and numberless shells into the air, proving the destruction which had been produced. The bombardment continued during the whole day, and not till sunset did Admiral Dundas withdraw the gunboats, or till some time afterwards the mortar-vessels, when the boats of the fleet, armed with rockets, were sent off to attack Vargon and the other principal islands, under Captain Caldwell, of the *Duke of Wellington*. Thus fearfully the unhappy garrison were annoyed during the whole night, and at daybreak the gunboats and mortar-vessels again began to play on the batteries. The mortars, however, were so considerably worn by the firing of the previous day, that one or two burst, and none were so effective as before. East Svarto, which had before escaped, was now attacked by a division of English and French mortar-boats, placed by Captain Sulivan considerably nearer the fortifications than they had hitherto ventured. Their fire was replied to by some heavy guns, which the enemy had brought up, but no damage was received from them. In a short time, dense columns of smoke and forked flames ascending in all directions showed that the buildings, magazines, and arsenal were being destroyed, and when night came on, one unbroken sheet of flame ascended from the fortress. To prevent the enemy from attempting to extinguish it, the rocket-boats were again sent in, and effectually performed their object. The conflagration continued, raging all night, and on the morning of the 11th there was no sign of its abatement. The admiral was therefore satisfied that the work he had undertaken was accomplished, and as the Russians had ceased to fire, he discontinued the action. The whole of the operation had been accomplished without the loss of a single man killed, and scarcely 16 in the British fleet wounded; but the slaughter among the unfortunate Russians was prodigious. Of one whole regiment but few had survived, and at Vargon and Svarto a large number of the garrison had been killed. Had shells not been used, and an attempt simply been made to destroy the fortress with the ships' heavy guns, the allies would probably have been driven away with severe loss, without making any impression on its massive walls. It was the first time in the history of war that shells had been thrown from a distance at which the besiegers could not be reached by the enemy's shot, or that shot had been discharged from vessels moving at so rapid a rate as to render it scarcely possible for the besiegers to strike them. These circumstances, with the use of torpedoes, showed that a new era in marine warfare had commenced, and that from henceforth the style of fighting which had existed down to the period of Algiers and Navarino was about entirely to be changed.

No other operation of importance was undertaken, and the winter approaching, the admiral sent home the sailing-vessels and gunboats, though he did not finally quit Kiel till the first week in December, when soon afterwards the whole fleet arrived safely in England. Happily, the various reverses he had experienced induced the Emperor of Russia to see the hopelessness of continuing the war, and to sue for peace.

From the time of the Crimean war and onwards, the British Navy has happily never had occasion to engage in warfare with the ships of any of the other great Powers. Individual ships and "naval contingents," however, have taken part in operations of more or less importance, and the first action in which a British vessel was opposed to an iron-clad, took place in 1877, when the cruiser *Shah* engaged for some hours the Peruvian turret-ship *Huascar*.

In the course of one of the numerous revolutions that so often convulse the South American Republics, the latter vessel had become little better than a pirate, by levying contributions on various seaport towns, but having been venturesome enough to deal with British vessels in the same way, the *Shah* and the *Amethyst* were sent to demand satisfaction. The *Huascar*, however, paid no attention, and at last the British ships opened fire on her.

The *Shah* was a fast cruiser armed with heavy guns, but was wholly unarmoured, while the *Amethyst* was only a small sloop, also unarmoured. The *Huascar* was a small, low, turret-ship of the *Devastation* type, with only one ten-inch gun mounted in her turret, but she was thickly armoured, and obtained a great advantage by taking up such a position that the *Shah* had frequently to cease fire for fear of sending her shot into the adjacent town of Ylo.

The combat continued for three hours without result, as the *Shah* had to keep at long-range; her shot repeatedly struck her opponent, but without result, owing to her armour. One shell however pierced the armour, and bursting inside, killed one man and wounded several more. None of the *Huascar's* shot struck the *Shah* although they fell close on every side. Night put an end to the combat, and enabled the *Huascar* to escape. In the course of the action the *Shah* fired the first Whitehead torpedo ever used in actual warfare; the distance however, was too great and it failed to reach the mark. Next day the *Huascar* surrendered to her own government.

The next occasion on which British warships were engaged was at Alexandria in July 1882. There had been trouble in Egypt for some time, and a month previously many Europeans had perished at the hands of the Alexandrian mob. A "National" party, headed by Arabi Pasha, was preparing revolt, and it was found that the fortifications of Alexandria were being strengthened, which would give serious trouble if marines had to be landed again to give protection to the Europeans. As the French declined to co-operate in any way, the British Government were left to deal with the matter alone, and, as the Egyptians declined to surrender the forts, pending the restoration of order, notice was given that the forts would be bombarded unless the demands were complied with. No answer being forthcoming, seven of the most powerful ironclads proceeded to bombard the forts, and after firing the whole day, drove the Egyptians from their guns and silenced the forts, blowing up a couple of magazines, and dismounting many of the guns. A large number of the Egyptians were killed, while on our side, only six men were slain, the armour giving efficient protection. The armour of the flag-ship however, was once perforated by a 10-inch shell, which dropped smoking on the deck, but a brave gunner, named Israel Harding, rushed upstairs, flung water on it to extinguish the fuse, and then dropped it into a bucket of water. For this brave deed, he was awarded the Victoria Cross.

Later on, our sailors gave great assistance during the expedition sent to relieve General Gordon in Khartoum, manning the gunboats which advanced up the Nile to that city, only to find that he had been murdered whenever it became known that they were at hand.

Chapter Twenty.

The Evolution of the Modern Warship.

We may now pass on from the history of the doings of the British Navy to the history of the ships themselves, and the appliances with which our sailors fought. We have seen that in the time of King Alfred, when the Navy, properly so-called, came into existence, ships had but one deck, or were nearly altogether open, and had but one or two masts with large square sails, being propelled in calms and contrary winds by long oars. For purposes of offence they were fitted with beaks or rams to pierce the sides of the enemy, and were provided with catapults or other engines for hurling missiles, and with tubes for projecting Greek fire to create smoke and set their opponent on fire. The main tactics of the time, however, consisted in grappling with the enemy and transforming the combat into a hand-to-hand mêlée.

When cannon were first mounted on board ship, about the year 1335, they were fired over the bulwarks, and the gunners were thus fully exposed to the enemy's fire. About the year 1500, however, the Dutch introduced the modern practice of pointing the guns through ports in the ship's side, so that the gunners would be sheltered from all shot that could not pierce the sides. This improvement was soon universally adopted, and by the beginning of the sixteenth century, ships resembling on the whole the sailing ship of modern times had been evolved, having one or two tiers of guns. But as the fight was still at comparatively close quarters — owing to the guns being small, and of no great range, — warships were fitted with cumbrous "forecastles" and "aftercastles" (see illustration on page 69), and with heavy tops on the masts, to contain musketeers, in order to command the enemy's deck. These features greatly detracted from their seaworthiness, and made them unwieldy, cumbrous craft.

As the centuries went on, experience gradually remedied the mistakes of the earlier builders. Artillery also was improved, and tactics no longer depended to the same extent on boarding and hand-to-hand fighting. High "forecastles" and "aftercastles," and heavy tops, thus became of little use and were discarded, as were also the oars used on smaller craft, as the art of sailing became better understood and vessels more seaworthy. For similar reasons the navigating and fighting sections of the crew, hitherto distinct, were merged into one, only a small number of "marines," as they are now called, being retained to perform military duties for which fully trained seamen were not required.

English naval architects seem to have had little inventive genius till a late period. The early ships were all imitations from the Genoese or other maritime people of the Mediterranean, while latterly the best vessels were either taken from the French or else copied from them. For instance the model for all the 80-gun ships built at the beginning of the nineteenth century was the *Canopus*, which was taken from the French, under the name of *Franklin*, at the Battle of the Nile in 1798. The *Belleisle*, a "74," captured in 1795, bore a conspicuous part in the battle of Trafalgar. Many frigates also, whose names are known to fame, were acquired in the same way and performed useful service against their former possessors.

In the early part of the eighteenth century British men-of-war were of insufficient size for the guns they were made to carry, with the result they worked and sailed heavily, while in heavy weather their lower batteries could seldom be used. The smaller the vessel the thinner is her planking, and the more liable are her crew and structure to suffer from the shot of the enemy. Other nations realised this long before we did, especially the Americans, who built forty-four gun frigates almost as large as our "seventy-fours," while their planking was even thicker. This, of course, told heavily against us in the war with the United States, but we were taught a lesson which perhaps helped us later on. In truth Britain's battles were won not because her ships were superior in size or armament to those of other nations but on account of the pluck, courage, determination, and good seamanship of British officers and crews, and because the latter had been well trained to use their guns.

At last British naval architects woke up from their long lethargy and began to think for themselves. Till the end of the eighteenth century the ships were flat-sterned with heavy "quarter-galleries" projecting from the side at the stern, while their bows below water were bluff with long projecting beak-heads which, to avoid weight, were but flimsy structures, affording no protection whatever to the crew. In 1805 Sir Robert Seppings remedied this defect by constructing a solid circular bow right up to the main-deck, thus protecting the crew from raking shot. A dozen years later the same designer abolished the quarter-galleries, and introduced the neater and stronger circular stern. From this time forward, improvements were considerable and rapid until about 1860, when the ironclad settled the fate of the "wooden walls" that had protected England for well-nigh a thousand years.

But, while the sailing ship was being brought to its highest perfection, it was on the eve of being supplanted altogether. In 1769, Watt took out his first patent for the steam engine, and in October 1788 Mr Miller, of Dalswinton in Scotland, first applied the new motive power to propel a vessel. An engine was placed on a frame, fixed between two pleasure boats, and made to turn two paddle-wheels, one in front of the other — the invention of William Symington — which drove the improvised steamer across Dalswinton Loch, at the rate of five miles an hour. The first practical steamer, however, was not built till 1801, when Lord Dundas, taking advantage of Mr Miller's labours, after spending 7000 pounds on experiments in two years, built the *Charlotte Dundas*. It was intended to work her on the Forth and Clyde Canal, but the proprietors having objected that she would damage the banks, she was laid up, as was a second boat.

In 1804, John Stephens of Hoboken, near New York, built a small vessel 22 feet in length, which ran at the rate of seven or eight miles an hour, and Fulton soon afterwards introduced steamers on the Hudson. In the year 1812 the *Comet* was launched by Henry Bell, a ship carpenter of Helensburgh, and began to ply on the Clyde, being the first British steamer that ran regularly with passengers. The *Comet* was of 40 feet keel, 25 tons burthen, and 3 horse-power. The second steamer launched on the Clyde was the *Elizabeth*, in 1813, and the year following, Mr Fife of Fairlie launched the *Industry*, which was in use for upwards of fifty years. After this, steam navigation rapidly increased, steamers being introduced on the Thames in 1815.

The first war steamer ever built, was constructed by Fulton during the war between the United States and Great Britain in 1814, It was a large vessel after the plan of the first experimental steamer, two vessels with the paddles between them, evidently to protect them from the enemy's shot. This vessel was intended to carry 30 guns, and was fitted with machinery to discharge hot water through the port-holes, by which the ammunition of the enemy would be rendered useless, and her crew scalded to death, if they attempted to come to close quarters. She was also said to be armed with numerous cutlasses and pikes moved to and fro by machinery, so that the boarding would be impossible, while it was supposed that her paddles would enable her to keep ahead or astern of her enemy, so that the broadside guns could not be trained on her. It is doubtful, however, if this marvellous production was ever actually completed, and as her machinery could only have been imperfectly protected, she might have been disabled and left at her enemy's mercy.

Some years later the Americans had the honour of performing the first Atlantic voyage under steam, with the *Savannah*, which arrived at Liverpool on July 15th 1819, after a voyage of 26 days from New York. Six years later the *Enterprise*, an English vessel, made the longer voyage to India.

Some years passed before it occurred to the Admiralty that steamers could be of any use to the Navy, and it was not till 1823 that they purchased the *Monkey* tug, which, not withstanding its undignified name and humble employment, had the honour of being the first steam-vessel belonging to the Royal Navy. She was a vessel of about 212 tons, and 80 horse-power, and did good service in her day. Both Admiralty and naval officers held steamers, − "smoke-jacks," or "tea-kettles," they were generally called − in great contempt, supposing that their only possible use would be as despatch-boats, or as tugs. It was reasoned that paddles would be so readily disabled in action, that it would be useless to fit them to fighting ships. However, after a year or so, several steam-sloops and frigates were built which took some part in the Syrian and Chinese wars, as also in operations in the Parana. In none of these wars, however, were they subjected to any severe test of their liability to damage under fire.

All possible difficulties on this latter score, were solved in 1834, when Mr Francis Pettit Smith invented the screw propeller, which works wholly under water. He succeeded in propelling a small model by this means on his father's horsepond at Hendon, in Middlesex, and in 1836 he took out a patent for his invention. The idea was old; in 1775, Bushnell, an American, had utilised it to propel a submarine boat, but up till then, practical difficulties in working had not been solved.

Smith was neither a naval man nor an engineer, and for some time, neither Admiralty, engineers, nor naval men believed that the invention would work with sufficient power to drive a ship against the wind. Fortunately others thought differently, and in 1836, a vessel of 10 tons, with an engine of 6 horse-power, was built and successfully tried, first on the Paddington Canal, and then on the Thames. Finally, it put out to sea, and demonstrated by its behaviour in severe weather, that the screw was equally successful in rough water.

This turned the scales in favour of the screw. A larger boat was built, which showed her powers to the Lords of the Admiralty, by towing their barge to Blackwall and back, at the average rate of 10 miles an hour. Still they were not convinced, and it was not for a couple of years or so that they took the matter up, after a successful voyage made by the *Archimedes*, the first sea-going screw steamer. They then built a small craft called the *Bee*, fitted with both paddles and screw, to try which was the better means of propulsion. The screw had the best of it, and after the further experiment of building two vessels of the same size and power, the one with paddles the other with a screw, and finding the screw still superior, it was finally adopted as an auxiliary to the sails. Little thought the naval experts of that period, that another fifty years or so would see both sails and wooden ships quite obsolete — as far as the Navy was concerned at any rate.

These experiments showed clearly that the screw was absolutely essential to every warship, as in a calm, the finest sailing ship would be at the mercy of any small steamer, armed with long-range guns. Thus while new vessels were laid down specially designed to carry screws, wherever it was found possible to do so, all the efficient battleships and frigates were fitted with auxiliary engines. Of course these converted sailing ships, not having been designed for the purpose, could only carry engines of small power, still, it was a case of half a loaf being better than no bread, and was the best that could be done under the circumstances.

The first propellers were in the form of an ordinary screw thread, but it was soon found that separate fans were equally satisfactory, and more convenient to make. Much discomfort was caused by the excessive vibration caused by the early screws, but various improvements in their design reduced this. The fans of the screws are now attached by means of; bolts to a hollow sphere on the end of the shaft, and should a fan be damaged, it can be readily replaced. At first all screws were so constructed, that they could be lifted up through a well when sails alone were being used, so that it would not impede the ship. The funnels, too, being made to shut up like a telescope, a steamer could thus be easily turned into a sailing ship.

At the very time that the screw propeller was initiating a revolution in the method of steam propulsion, another revolution was taking place in shipbuilding material. Iron barges had been used as far back as 1787, and an iron steamer had been built at Tipton about the year 1821, but for another twenty years iron ships were not viewed with favour, and only began to force their way to the front about the beginning of the reign of Queen Victoria. Even then they were deemed utterly unsuitable for war vessels, as being very difficult to repair and keep afloat when perforated by the enemy's shot, as they must inevitably be in action. But in the course of time, the iron vessel naturally raised the possibility of protecting warships by armour, and the matter, was forced to the front when gunmakers followed the lead of the shipbuilders and engineers, and set themselves to see what could be done in the way of improving ordnance, that had remained practically unchanged for hundreds of years, saving for more accurate workmanship.

Up till this time, only solid round-shot had been used on shipboard. An attempt had been made to get Napoleon the First to sanction the use of shells for naval use; fortunately, for some reason or other, he declined to do so, and thus our great struggle for naval supremacy was carried on with the solid round-shot that had been in vogue from the earliest introduction of cannon. The smooth-bore cannon from which they were fired, could not be relied on to project them with accuracy to distances greater than about 1500 yards; beyond this range, their flight became so erratic, that it was simply a waste of ammunition to fire them. Whitworth and Armstrong set themselves to solve the problem of how to make cannon shoot better.

The experiments of Whitworth and Armstrong resulted in the production of rifled guns, based on a principle that had already been tried with success in small-arms. The rifling enabled long conical shot to be fired with far greater accuracy than the old round-shot, and as these conical shot were two or three times as heavy as the round-shot that could be fired from a gun of the same bore, the guns of a given bore had only to be rifled to be suddenly raised to a much heavier grade, supposing them to be strong enough to stand the heavier charge of powder required. Not only that, but their range would be much greater, and their shot would pass through both sides of the stoutest ship in existence. For, when fired at wooden targets identical in material and thickness with the side of a ship, the projectiles went through them as if they had been paper, or, if shells were used, tore them to pieces. Even strong iron plates failed to withstand their impact. The thinner plates they tore open; as the thickness was increased, they first buried their heads in the metal, but stuck fast; then indented it only; and finally glanced off, but not until the plate had been made 4 or 5 inches thick.

Further progress was also made by the invention of breech loaders, which gave an increased rate of fire to these already formidable weapons, and to make matters still worse, much larger guns than had ever been made before could now be constructed without difficulty, and naval men justly began to feel uncomfortable about the safety of our "wooden walls."

In 1859, the French led the way by constructing the *Gloire*, which was covered with thick iron plates, and our Admiralty had to face the task of constructing ironclad ships, and of armouring existing ships, pending the construction of others. One thing was very plain; the existing high-sided ships could not carry the weight of even the thinnest armour that would be of any service.

In 1861, the *Warrior* was produced in answer to the French *Gloire*. She was a frigate-built vessel doing 14 knots, and carried thirty-two heavy guns, 200 feet only of her length of 310 feet were armoured with iron plates 4 and a half inches thick — which was proof against any guns then existing — as it was thought that her seaworthiness would be impaired if the great weight of the armour were extended to the two ends. But to protect the vessel from raking shot — that is, shots fired

THE "WARRIOR," THE FIRST BRITISH IRONCLAD; BATTLESHIP OF 1861.
Length, 310 feet; Displacement, 9210 tons; Speed, 14 knots;
Armament, 32 guns of 9 and 6½ tons.

at her when bow on, or stern on, to the enemy — armoured partitions, or "bulkheads", as they are called, were provided.

In 1861, ships of the type of the *Minotaur* were built, armoured from stem to stern. These were considered monster ships at the time, as they had a displacement of, 10,627 tons and were 400 feet in length. Their speed was 14 or 15 knots, attained by engines of 6,700 horse-power. The bow was constructed on the ram principle, projecting some distance under the water, and her sides were covered with iron plates 5 inches thick, tapering off in thickness, however, as they approached the bow. Further, she was divided into many compartments below water, with watertight doors, so that if pierced, either in action or by grounding, she might still be kept afloat. She was fitted with five masts, made partly of iron, while her armament consisted of thirty-four 12-ton and 18-ton guns. Her cost was, 478,000 pounds but she and her sister ships the *Agincourt* and *Northumberland* did not come up to their expectations, being found unwieldy on account of their great length, while in a few years it was found that their armour was not thick enough to withstand the more powerful guns that were being manufactured.

THE "SULTAN," BATTLESHIP OF 1871.
Length, 325 feet ; Displacement, 9,290 tons ; Speed, 14 knots ;
Armament, 12 guns of 12½ and 18 tons.

THE "MINOTAUR;" BATTLESHIP OF 1863,
Length, 400 feet; Displacement, 10,627 tons; Speed, 15 knots;
Armament, 34 guns of 18 and 12 tons.

The next type of design was that of the *Hercules*, the prototype of the "citadel" design. This ship was protected from end to end by much thicker armour than had hitherto been used, but instead of carrying the armour right up to the upper deck, to save weight it was in the form of a narrow belt protecting a few feet above and below the water line only, except amidships, where it was carried up to the upper deck, forming a "citadel," inside which her ten 18-ton and 12-ton guns were well protected. In this way her guns, waterline, and engines — or "vitals," as these are known for short — were fully protected at the expense of less vital parts of the ship. Though smaller and less expensive than the *Minotaur* she was a far more efficient ship. Her broadside was 1818 pounds. The *Sultan*, another ship of much the same type, had a broadside of 1964 pounds. During the early sixties another type of vessel came to the front. Captain Coles had invented the "turret," which consisted of a turn-table or revolving platform, round which was a shield of thick armour, turning with it: the top was also closed in. In the shield was a very small port for the gun — which was aimed by revolving the turret till it pointed at the required object. The crew was thus completely protected from the enemy's fire.

In the American Civil War the Federals or Northerners, had provided two of their wooden frigates with these turrets and sent them to attack the *Merrimac*, a cut-down wooden frigate which had been armoured and provided with a ram. The *Merrimac* steamed up to the *Congress*, delivering her fire with awful effect, and then proceeding towards the *Cumberland*, ran into her near the bow, ripping an enormous rent in her side, and hung on by her own sharp prow while she fired into the fractured chasm. She then backed out and repeated her tremendous onslaught, suffering little from the fire of her enemy, till the latter went down. She next attacked the *Congress* with shells, which killed the greater number of the Federal crew, and in half-an-hour the few survivors hauled down their colours.

Later on the *Merrimac* was attacked by the armoured *Monitor*. The two ships hammered away at one another for many hours without result; only five men were killed after a five hours action, for the armour beat the gun.

The result of these actions made it clear that turret-ships to be of any use must be armoured, and as a first experiment it was decided to cut-down the *Royal Sovereign*, a ship of the size of the *Duke of Wellington*. Her masts and her three upper decks were taken off, her lower-deck alone remaining, so that she was cut-down almost to the water's edge. Massive plates of iron were fastened to her sides and deck, thus converting her into an ironclad, while four turrets were sunk into the deck in a line fore and aft, three of them containing one huge gun each, firing 300-pound shot, while the fourth and foremost turret contained two guns. The muzzles of the guns were only a little way above the deck, and the bulwarks were hinged so that when the guns were to be fired they could be dropped over the side so as not to be in the way.

THE TURRET-SHIP "DEVASTATION," BATTLESHIP OF 1872.
Length, 285 feet; Displacement, 9330 tons; Speed, 14 knots;
Armament, 4 guns of 35 tons.

Amidships was a circular armoured box, rather higher than the turrets, called the "conning-tower." Here the captain took his stand in time of action, communicating with the engines, turrets, and other parts of the ship, by speaking tubes. In more recent ships the vessel is also steered from the conning-tower in time of action. Such was our first converted ironclad turret-ship. She was, however, found to be of little value, drawing too much water to serve for harbour defence, and not being handy enough at sea in manoeuvring.

Turret-ships, as first constructed, were very heavily, armoured, and in consequence rather unseaworthy. Being intended for coast defence only, they always had a harbour available in bad weather, and sails were not required as they were never far from a coal supply.

In 1869, however, Sir Edward Reed designed the first sea-going turret-ships, properly so-called, taking the bold step, as it seemed then, of providing no sails. These were the *Devastation* and *Thunderer*, which, despite many faults, proved to be serviceable ships for over thirty years. These were ships of, 9,330 tons, and 14 knots speed, and the annexed picture gives their general appearance. Their hulls were protected by 12-inch armour, and the turrets by 14-inch armour, while an important improvement was introduced by providing what is called a "protective deck," that is, a horizontal deck, of armour several inches thick, which prevents shot from penetrating to the engines, etcetera, below. Their armament consisted of four 35-ton guns firing 600-pound shot, and as all these guns could fire on either side, their broadside was, 2,400 pounds. Their crews were composed of only 300 men, and though they cost about 150,000 pounds less than the *Minotaur* they were far more efficient and powerful warships. They lay very low in the water, their bows rising only 9 feet above it, while the stern was even lower, being only 4 and a half feet above the waterline. Amidships, however, the deck was raised some 6 or 8 feet higher.

THE TURRET-SHIP "MONARCH," BATTLESHIP OF 1869.
Length, 330 feet ; Displacement, 8330 tons ; Speed, 15 knots ;
Armament, 7 guns of 25 and 12 tons.

DIAGRAMS

SHOWING THE CHANGES IN THE METHOD OF PLACING THE ARMOUR ON

BATTLESHIPS.

(The side armour is shown by shading and by thick lines.)

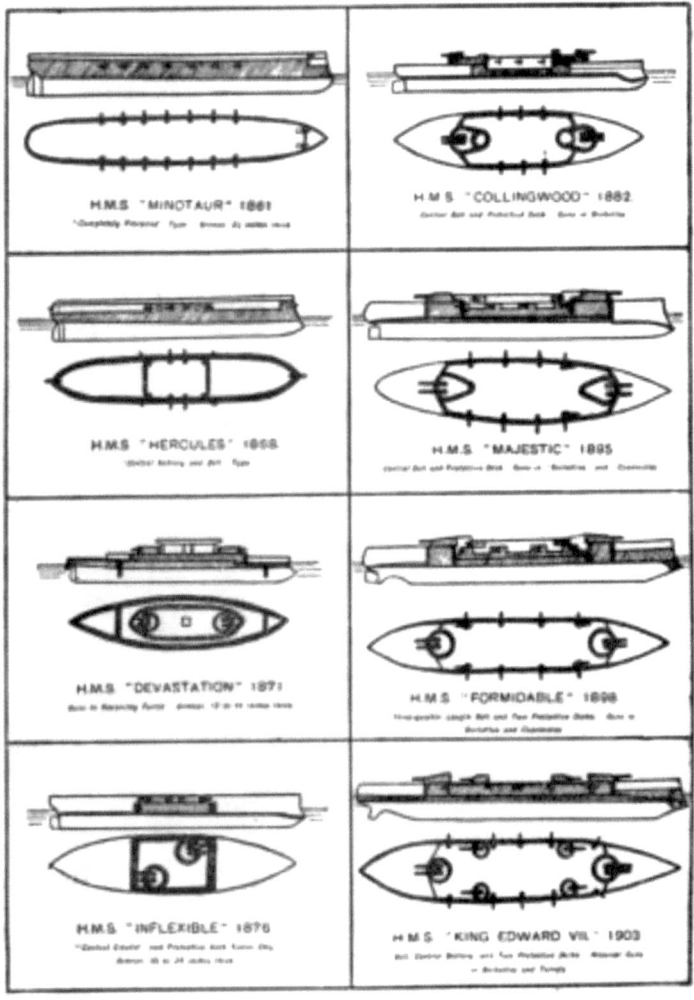

H.M.S. "MINOTAUR" 1861

H.M.S. "COLLINGWOOD" 1882

H.M.S. "HERCULES" 1868

H.M.S. "MAJESTIC" 1895

H.M.S. "DEVASTATION" 1871

H.M.S. "FORMIDABLE" 1898

H.M.S. "INFLEXIBLE" 1876

H.M.S. "KING EDWARD VII." 1903

Between the two turrets was a large superstructure, the walls of which curved outwards all over the top. A passage passed through it from side to side, in which were the doors leading to the hatchways and to the hurricane deck above, on which were the conning tower, wheels, etcetera. The boats were also carried on this deck, high above the water, so that there was no obstruction to the firing of the guns in the turrets below.

It might have been supposed, that a ship so low in the water could not venture out to sea in rough weather, but, though her forecastle was frequently completely submerged in a heavy sea, she has behaved very well.

Other turret ships, however, had been built a year or two earlier with masts and sails, and bows of ordinary height. At first these ships were over-masted and canvassed, but after one of them, the *Captain*, capsized during a gale in the Bay of Biscay, this defect was remedied. This class was represented by the *Monarch*, completed in 1869, a vessel of 8930 tons, and 15 knots speed. She carried seven guns, those in the turrets weighing 25 tons.

The turret-ship reached its highest development in the year 1876, when the *Inflexible* was designed. By this time, guns had so greatly increased in power, that the thickness of armour required to withstand their shot was very great, and, as this involved an enormous addition to the dead weight that had to be carried, some means had to be devised whereby an efficient protection could be carried. The "central citadel" form of design was that finally adopted, in which the armour was concentrated on a citadel in the centre of the vessel, amply protecting the engines, turrets, and other "vitals" of the ship, the rest of the hull being left wholly unprotected, save for a "protective deck," about the level of the waterline. This deck being horizontal, would always be struck by shot at a very oblique angle, hence its thickness afforded a much greater amount of protection — about double — than if placed vertically on the sides.

THE TURRET-SHIP "INFLEXIBLE;" BATTLESHIP OF 1881.
Length, 320 feet; Displacement, 11,880 tons; Speed, 12½ knots;
Armament, 4 guns of 80 tons.

The *Inflexible* was a ship of 11,800 tons, and was driven at a speed of nearly 13 knots, by engines of 6,500 horse-power. The turrets were arranged one on each side of the ship, and thus enabled to fire both ahead and astern or on the broadside. These turrets were protected by armour 18 inches thick, and each carried two 80-ton guns, firing a 1700-pound shot to a distance of eight miles. These monster muzzle-loading guns were loaded from outside the turret, by means of hydraulic machinery. The armour on the sides was 2 feet thick, and the vessel was divided into 135 compartments, so that she would not be readily sunk. The *Inflexible* was the last of the turret-ships properly so-called. She was not the success that had been hoped; her engine power, which gave only 12 and a half knots, had been sacrificed to obtain heavier armament and protection, and as she was slower than much older ships, she was laid aside before vessels launched earlier than she was. About this time, the combination of several important factors worked a revolution in warship design. The Russo-Turkish war of 1878-79, taught that a torpedo was a more important element in naval warfare than had been imagined. Launches going at the rate of 18 or 20 miles an hour, covered a mile in about three minutes, and if they attacked at night, were so small, quick-moving, and indistinguishable, that they could attack the most powerful battleship with little risk of being hit by the snap shots of the few slow-firing heavy guns, with which modern ships were armed.

THE "MERSEY;" STEAM CRUISER OF 1862.
Armament, 20 guns.

The machine gun was first introduced to meet this danger; it could send a continuous shower of rifle bullets at the approaching boat, and riddle and sink her before she got near enough to do mischief; but when torpedo boats began to be armoured with iron plates, proof not only against rifle bullets, but even against the heavier Hotchkiss and Nordenfeldt half-pounder guns, except at very close ranges, it was seen that an armament of small guns was desirable to repel torpedo boats, or to be used against unarmoured cruisers, whose superior speed would soon take them out of danger from the slow-firing heavy guns. Another factor was the introduction of longer guns, and what are termed "slow burning" powders. These last do not explode with such sudden violence as the ordinary powder, so that there is less sudden strain on the gun, while a steadier pressure on the shot is kept up. The long gun enables the pressure of the gases formed by the burning powder to act longer on the shot, with the result that a higher velocity is given to it, not only increasing its range, but also its penetrative power.

The result of these improvements was to some extent a repetition of what had taken place when rifled guns were first introduced. Guns could be made lighter, and yet be much more powerful than the old patterns of the same bore, and it was seen that a ship could with advantage be provided with a "secondary" armament, as it is called of these smaller yet powerful guns. Armour, too, was being improved, so that it could be made thinner and yet equally effective; higher speeds were also called for, and it was evident that warships must be designed on different lines to meet or take advantage of the new conditions.

The first ship designed on the new lines was the *Collingwood*, a vessel of 9,500 tons, 16 and a half knots speed, and 7,000 horse-power. She was the first ship of what was called the "Admiral class," — several sister ships named after famous admirals. The four heavy guns of the *Devastation* type of turret-ship were retained, mounted fore and aft, but instead of placing them in turrets, the turret armour was fixed to the deck, forming what is known as a "barbette," or breastwork, over the upper edge of which the gun fired. Inside the barbette the gun revolved on its turn-table; its breech, together with the gunners, was protected by a hood of armour which revolved with the gun. This arrangement is probably less liable to be knocked out of action by the enemy's shot than the turret.

Amidships was the "secondary" armament of six 6-inch breech-loading guns. All the guns were mounted well above the water, enabling them to be used even in a heavy sea, which could not be done in the case of ships lying low in the water like the *Devastation*.

A further impetus was given to the development of the secondary armament by the introduction of "smokeless" powder — which, however, gives a *very* slight smoke, — and the "quick-firing gun." By simplifying the breech mechanism, using metal cartridge cases for the ammunition instead of silk bags — which necessitated the sponging out of the piece after each shot to remove the smouldering fragments — arranging the "sights" of the gun so that it could be aimed while loading was going on, and other ingenious arrangements, it was found that 6-inch 100-pounder guns could be fired many times per minute without any mechanical appliances. About the same time also, means were found of firing with safety what are called "high explosives," that is, explosives of far greater destructive power than the same weight of gunpowder. Similar improvements were naturally extended to the larger guns, and thus there has been a reversion to the type of ships mounting a fair number of guns, the lighter ones, firing shells of 100 pounds, being intended to wreck the unarmoured portions of the enemy, and demoralise his crew; the heavier ones, 200-pounders, 380-pounders, and 850-pounders, being adapted to pierce the armour and destroy the guns or the machinery. Some idea of the terrible power of modern quick-fire guns may be obtained when it is mentioned that a modern ship, armed with *one* 6-inch 100-pounder gun could fire — and hit every time too, at three-quarters-of-a-mile range — a greater weight of metal per minute than could be kept up by the 52 guns on the broadside of Nelson's *Victory*, or even by the broadside of the more modern *Britannia*.

Such are the types of the principal battleships constructed up to nearly the end of the nineteenth century, and we may now glance at the cruisers.

The frigate of the olden days, used for scouting and cruising, was the favourite ship in the great wars, as they bore off the greatest proportion of prize-money, and afforded their commanders greater opportunities of gaining promotion and distinction. As already mentioned, the French built faster and finer craft of this description than we did, and Nelson was always complaining that we had not a sufficient number of swift frigates to keep down whose of the enemy.

The frigates had from 28 to 50 guns, and did not vary much in general design, although the Americans taught us to build them of larger size and of thicker planking. When steam was introduced, engines were fitted to these cruisers, and they were given a few knots superior speed to the line-of-battle-ships. To enable them to keep the sea for long periods without their bottoms becoming fouled by marine growths — which decrease the speed — their iron hulls were sheathed wood, which in its turn was covered by copper. Ships of this type were not armoured. The *Shah*, which fought the *Huascar* in 1877, was a ship of this description; she carried 26 heavy guns, and had a speed of 16 knots.

Other vessels were specially designed as rams. The sinking of the powerful battleships *Vanguard*, in the Irish sea, and *Victoria*, in the Mediterranean, after accidental collision with the ram of another ship in the squadron, shows the terrible effect of this weapon when it can strike home. But torpedoes render it highly improbable that the opportunity of using it will ever arise. Modern naval battles will probably be fought and decided, at the *minimum* range of 2 miles, or thereby.

Chapter Twenty One.

Modern Engines of War.

For many centuries after the invention of gunpowder, little change took place in the weapons used in naval warfare, the chief developments being in the way of better workmanship and material, and the production of guns of larger size.

About the end of the eighteenth century, however, the period from which so many of our modern improvements begin to date, inventors began to plan new and improved methods of disposing of the enemy. About the year 1770, the American Bushnell conceived the idea of what his fellow-countryman Fulton afterwards called the "torpedo." This weapon consisted of a case of powder which was to be attached to the bottom of the enemy's ship by the aid of a submarine boat, leaving it to explode later on by means of a clock inside.

The submarine boat was actually made in 1775; it was egg-shaped in form, and held one man. It was propelled through the water by means of a screw propeller, worked by manual power; a similar screw, arranged vertically, enabled the boat to rise or sink at will. With this boat, during the War of Independence, he, or some other operator, succeeded in getting under a British man-of-war lying at anchor near New York. Without her crew having the slightest suspicion of his presence, he attempted to screw his torpedo to her bottom, but his auger encountered what appeared to be a bar of iron. When shifting to another position he lost the ship altogether, and being unable to find her again was forced to cast off the torpedo and make away, as the clock-work inside had been arranged to explode soon afterwards. And about an hour later the crew of the warship were first roused to their danger by the explosion of the torpedo at no great distance from them, and they were the more alarmed as they were wholly unable to account for it.

In the beginning of the nineteenth century another American, named Fulton, having borrowed Bushnell's ideas, came over to Europe and endeavoured to get the French government to take up his plans for submarine warfare. After long delay he was at length given the sum of 10,000 francs, with which he successfully constructed a submarine boat. In this boat he remained under water for more than four hours, and having been required to blow up a small vessel had no difficulty in getting under her and in blowing her to pieces with his torpedo. The torpedo in a highly developed form is now one of the most important weapons in naval tactics.

In spite of the success of Fulton's experiments, his plans were not adopted, either by Napoleon or by the British Admiralty, to whom Fulton afterwards offered them. The great European wars having been brought to an end by the downfall of Napoleon, the torpedo for a while sunk into oblivion, although during the Crimean war the Russians used submarine mines to protect their harbours. But during the American Civil War the torpedo was again brought to the front, and the Southerners, or "Confederates," used vast numbers of them, to the great damage of the Northerners, or "Federals."

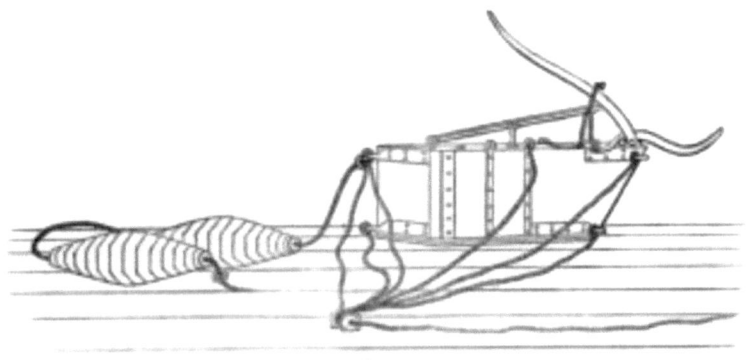

HARVEY'S TORPEDO.

At first these torpedoes proved so harmless — so few exploding out of the hundreds laid — that the Federal officers paid little attention to them. But as the war went on, better methods of exploding them were devised, and vessel after vessel was sunk in a few minutes, often with great loss of life. Some of these were sunk by submarine mines fired by electricity, others by floating torpedoes drifted down by the current or tide; others again by torpedoes at the end of a long spar carried in a small launch. In one instance, a submarine boat was employed, propelled by a screw worked by eight men. Instead of running just beneath the surface, however, her crew insisted on keeping the hatchway just above water, and open, with the result that the wave caused by the explosion of her torpedo rushed in and swamped her, so that she went to the bottom with all on board.

Another night a large frigate was blockading Charleston harbour when a *David* — as these torpedo boats were then called — was seen approaching. The frigate, which carried a crew of 700 men, slipped her cable and made off at full speed, although she was only being attacked by a small launch, manned by four men, armed with a few pounds of powder extended on a spar in front of her! In spite of a fierce fusillade aimed at her, not a shot struck the *David*, which returned in safety to Charleston.

The Russo-Turkish War afforded several additional examples of the same kind, which, as already mentioned, had not a little to do with the alteration in naval design and tactics that took place during the last two decades of the nineteenth century.

Torpedoes were of three kinds: the first were really submarine mines, and were placed in a river channel, being fired by electricity when the vessel came over them. The second kind was the floating or Harvey's torpedo, consisting of a long narrow, but deep wooden case from 44 to 60 inches in length, which contained 30 to 80 pounds of gunpowder, inside a copper lining. It had two levers projecting on the outside, which, on striking an object, set off the explosive inside. This torpedo was used in two ways: the first by setting it adrift on a river, or where there was a well-marked current setting towards the enemy's ships, when the current carried it to its destination; the other way was by towing it at night, by means of a long line, across the bows of an enemy's ship; it exploded whenever it came in contact with the ship.

The third kind of torpedo was practically a Harvey's torpedo attached to a long boom, or pole, about 28 feet long. This was carried at the gunwale of a fast steam launch at night; on nearing the enemy's ship this boom was pushed forward so as to bring the torpedo ten feet below the surface and well in advance of the boat. The torpedo exploded when it struck the ship, and to prevent the torpedo-boat from being sunk by the huge wave raised by the explosion, it had to be covered in front by a shield.

The experiences of the two wars already mentioned showed the difficulty of dealing with torpedo boats at night, and "search lights" are now installed on all modern warships. These consist of an electric arc lamp of 25,000 candle-power, combined with a reflector, which concentrates the light so that it brilliantly lights up objects at a great distance. Torpedo boats can be readily discovered when a mile or more

distant and, at the same distance from the light, the rays are so powerful that a newspaper can be read with the greatest ease.

Torpedo attack, however, has been revolutionised by the invention of
"Whitehead's torpedo," which can be used from a distance. In shape it
is exactly like a huge cigar, 12 to 18 inches in diameter, and 6 to 10 feet
long. At the head is the explosive; behind this is a reservoir containing
air compressed to an enormous pressure, which drives engines contained in a third compartment, and which in their turn work a screw
propeller at the back of the torpedo. There is also mechanism which
automatically adjusts the depth at which the torpedo travels below
the water, and other mechanism which ensures that it will keep going
in the direction in which it was fired. Such a torpedo is now effective
up to two miles, and it will traverse this distance in about six minutes.

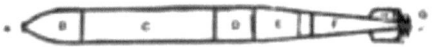

A. Trigger; B. Explosive; C. Compressed air chamber; D. Balance chamber for regulating depth; E. Engine chamber; F. Buoyancy chamber; G. Propellers; H. Rudders.

WHITEHEAD'S TORPEDO.

Torpedoes are discharged from what are called "torpedo tubes" by
means of compressed air. These tubes are to all intents and purposes,
guns made of thin steel, the torpedo being put in at the breech. Those
used on board torpedo boats or similar light fast craft are mounted on
a swivel on the deck; in larger vessels they are usually placed below
the waterline so as to be free from the serious consequences that
would ensue if the tube were struck by the enemy's shot, while a torpedo was in it. Torpedoes have also been invented which are steered
by electricity.

The problem of protecting ships against torpedoes is a difficult one,
and no satisfactory solution has yet been arrived at. All large warships, however, are provided with "torpedo nets" of thick iron wire,
which are hung round her at the end of long poles, which, when not
in use, are tied up alongside. But mechanism has been invented by
which the torpedo will cut through the netting, if it encounters it, so
that at present the torpedo is master of the situation, within its range.
In fairly shallow water a torpedo will throw a column of water nearly
200 feet into the air, by the impulse of the gases generated by the ex-

plosion, and no ship yet built would be able to withstand its enormous shock.

Reference has already been made to the huge guns of the *Inflexible*, and to the improvements in both powder and guns made later on. The modern gun is what is called a "wire gun," from its method of construction. Round a central tube of steel, several layers of immensely strong steel wire is tightly wound; a second steel tube is then slipped on above the wire, and as this tube is hot when first put on, when it cools it contracts and binds the layers of wire tightly together, forming a gun of very great strength — as, indeed, it would need to be, seeing that it has to withstand a pressure of over 16 tons to the square inch.

The projectiles fired from naval guns are of three kinds, solid shot for piercing the thickest armour, — as on the conning-tower, or barbettes; "armour piercing shell," with very thick walls and small bursting charge, which can only penetrate armour, two-thirds of that piercible by solid shot; lastly, "common shell," in which the shell walls are much thinner, and can thus only be used with effect against the lighter structures of the enemy. By placing a small "cap" of iron on the points of ordinary shot, "capped shot" are produced; and thus provided, they will pierce a much greater thickness of hard-faced armour than the ordinary ones. Against soft armour, however, they are not so efficient.

The armour of modern ships has also been greatly improved in resisting power. The *Inflexible* of 1881 was protected by wrought-iron plates 24 inches thick, which weighed 2,400 tons, or a fifth of her total weight, yet only a third of her length was protected. Soon after her completion, "compound" armour plates, — with a hard steel face on a backing of wrought-iron — were introduced, which enabled a third of the weight of the armour to be saved, yet leaving the amount of penetrability unchanged. Later on, "Harvey" armour, made of steel alloyed with nickel, still further reduced the weight, and recent improvements now make the best armour equal in resisting power to three times its thickness of wrought-iron. It may be mentioned also that the coal bunkers are now arranged so as to further protect the engines, being reckoned equivalent to about three inches of wrought-iron.

THE "MARLBOROUGH;" STEAM BATTLESHIP OF 1855.
Armament, 121 Guns.

Facing page 464 are two "sections" of warships, which will, no doubt, interest the reader. The first is of an old steam battleship, such as the *Marlborough*, the other, that of a modern second-class cruiser, like the *Minerva*, which could blow the *Marlborough* to pieces before the latter could get her within the range of her guns. Notice the enormous difference in the space devoted to the engines and boilers. The modern vessel gives a general idea of the arrangement in all classes of modern warships. The conning-tower will be seen below the bridge, in front of the foremast. The magazines are at the bottom, right below the forward and aft guns, which in this type of vessel, are protected by a shield only, with armoured ammunition hoists going down from it; the barbettes of the more powerful vessels would simply be iron breast-works, extending all round these guns. The curved protective deck is also seen, about the waterline, and the projecting ram, while at the stern is the curiously shaped rudder, made in this form, because it takes less power to work, than that of the ordinary type.

Chapter Twenty Two.

The British Navy of to-day.

In giving a brief outline of the general features of the battleships and cruisers composing the present British navy, it must be remembered that the navy is made up of ships built during a period of fifteen or twenty years; the newest being a great advance upon the older ones, yet differing but little from those launched a few years before.

The indications at present are for fast ships of very large size, the battleships — intended to act in squadrons — possessing the maximum of offensive and defensive power; the cruisers — intended for scouting and similar purposes — possessing a high rate of speed, heavy armament, and a certain amount of protection; and, as the travelling speed of a fleet is limited to that of the slowest vessel in the group, the aim of British naval architects is to design all the battleships to go at approximately the same speed, and similarly for the cruisers. A special feature of all British warships is the large coal supply carried, in view of the fact that they may be required to operate in any part of the world. For this reason the armour in our ships is sometimes not so thick as in some foreign ships, which sacrifice coal supply and radius of action to obtain better protection. In other respects our ships are second to none.

The British battleship of to-day varies from 12,000 up to 15,000 tons in displacement, and has a maximum speed of fully 18 knots, or about twenty-one miles an hour. They are armoured from end to end, and are provided with two protective decks; the lower one, about the level of the water-line, being to protect the "vitals"; the upper one, to prevent the fragments of shells from above penetrating to the batteries below. Forward and aft are the two barbettes, each carrying a pair of long 12-inch 50-ton guns, firing 850-pound shot, capable of penetrating 28 inches of wrought iron at a range of two miles. The secondary armament of 6-inch or 7.5-inch guns is mounted in "casemates," or armoured chambers, so disposed that two of them can also fire straight ahead, and the other two straight astern. The most recent ships have these ahead or astern guns mounted in turrets, and in the largest ships of all, some of which are of 18,000 tons, these guns are 9.2-inch 380-pounders.

After the battleships come the cruisers, corresponding to the frigates of olden days, — ships whose functions correspond to that of the cavalry of land forces, having to act as scouts, carry messages, intercept the enemy's ships, and capture his mercantile ships, or protect their own merchant convoys. To perform these varied functions, one of the chief requirements is speed, rather than heavy armament, so that it can run, if need be, if it should happen to encounter a ship of greater power. Accordingly the best cruisers are given the high maximum speed of 23 to 25 knots.

Cruisers are divided into two classes: armoured and unarmoured. The former are really modified battleships, with thin armour and somewhat lighter armament, to enable the necessary engine power and coal supply to be provided. Armoured cruisers of this description could, at a pinch, take part in fleet actions — even against ironclads, as shown at the battle of the Yalu, between the Chinese and Japanese, when the latter, with protected cruisers and one or two armoured cruisers, defeated a fleet in which there were several ironclads much larger and better protected than themselves.

TYPES OF MODERN WARSHIPS.—FAST CRUISER, BATTLESHIP, DESTROYER.
(Reproduced by courteous permission of " The Engineer.")

The most recent armoured cruisers are ships of 13,000 to 14,000 tons displacement, and are protected by a belt of 6-inch armour, in addition to protective decks. They are armed with two or four 9.2-inch 380-pounder guns, mounted in barbettes of thick armour, and with a number of 6-inch 100-pounders; a number of 12-pounders and 3-pounders are also carried. Some ships of this description can spurt up to 25 knots — not so long ago considered a high speed even for a torpedo boat destroyer.

The unarmoured cruisers are intended chiefly for scouting purposes, or for capturing or protecting commerce. As they are only intended to fight with ships similar to themselves, which may attempt to make havoc among our merchantmen, their only protection is a protective deck which covers the vitals. The first-class unarmoured cruisers have an armament and speed similar to those of the armoured type, and may have casements for their broadside guns, and barbettes for the heavy ones; the second-class cruisers are armed with 6-inch and 4.7-inch guns, protected by simple shields only, and they have a speed of from 19 to 20 knots.

In a previous chapter, the torpedo boats used in the American Civil War were mentioned as being simply fast launches, and little progress was made in their construction, until the Russo-Turkish war taught that their value was much greater than had been supposed. From that time onwards, larger and faster boats began to be built, and even a certain amount of protection began to be given them, consisting of 1-inch iron plates round the boilers and engines, which was proof against small-arms, and even against the heavier Nordenfelt machine guns, except at the closest quarters. Boats of this type were from 130 to 170 feet long, and went at a speed of 22 knots. As speeds increased, there was less risk for the torpedo boat, and greater risk for her enemy, and it became plain, that some means of averting torpedo boat attack must be devised, else it would be absolutely impossible for a fleet to blockade an enemy's coast without grave risk to itself. Torpedo boats were essentially for coast defence, as they could only venture out in calm weather. It was therefore seen that a new type of boat was required, capable of keeping the sea in all weathers. Accordingly, the "torpedo boat destroyer" was designed with this object, and which, possessing superior speed, and an armament sufficiently powerful, could run down and destroy existing torpedo boats, would safeguard the fleet, and enable it to keep comparatively near the blockaded coast. These boats were also furnished with a torpedo equipment, so that they could be used as torpedo boats in connection with a fleet.

In these "destroyers," as they are called for short, everything must be sacrificed to save weight; the hull must be a mere shell, and the engines and boilers reduced to the very minimum of weight that can be expected to stand the strain of the power developed. When we know that the sides of a destroyer are only 0.3-inch thick, and that her engines and boilers only weigh 50 pounds for each horse-power they give out, while those of a mail steamer weigh 280 pounds, and those of a cargo steamer 440 pounds, per horse-power developed, we can hardly wonder that these boats have frequent breakdowns.

Present day destroyers are boats of 200 to 300 tons displacement, and are about 227 feet long. They attain a maximum speed of about 33 knots, or 37 miles an hour, which is produced by engines of 6,000 to 8,000 horse-power. They carry two swivel torpedo tubes on deck, and an armament of one 12-pounder gun and six 3-pounders. They are also fitted with search lights. To prevent the sea from breaking over the bows, it is raised somewhat higher than the rest of the deck, and is curved at the sides, so that waves breaking over it are diverted to the side, instead of sweeping aft over the deck. The bridge is placed at the rear of this hood, and carries the 12-pounder gun. These boats carry 80 tons of coal, and have a crew of 60 men. The accomodation for the crew, however, is very cramped, and those who work them have to put up with a good deal of discomfort.

Like the torpedo boats, destroyers are low in the water; with their short dumpy funnels, short mast, and inky hue, they have a peculiarly "wicked" appearance.

A new departure in these boats has been made by the introduction of "turbine" engines, which are much lighter and take up less room than engines of the ordinary type. These engines go at such a high rate of speed that four screw-propellers have to be provided to transmit the power efficiently. Turbine destroyers have attained a speed of 35 and a half knots, or nearly 41 miles per hour. One more type of vessel remains to be mentioned, which is receiving a good deal of attention at present. These are the "submarines," or boats designed to navigate under water. Their use, however, is largely discounted by the fact that it is impossible to see to any distance under water — in fact, a well-known submarine expert has said that the navigation of a submarine, even under the best conditions, presents exactly the same difficulties as that of an ordinary ship sailing in a fog. Hence a submarine must frequently rise to the surface to ascertain the distance traversed, and see that the proper course has been kept, and until some satisfactory means of avoiding this has been discovered, submarines will probably remain of comparatively little value for purposes of war.

The submarines made for the Navy are, 63 feet long, by 11 and 3 quarters feet broad. When running "awash" — that is, with a small part of their upper works above water, they are driven by a gasoline engine at a speed of over 10 miles an hour. Sufficient gasoline is carried to take them over 400 miles at this speed. When submerged, the speed is naturally glower; the gasoline engines are stopped, all openings are closed, and electric storage batteries are put in operation. These drive the boat at the rate of eight miles an hour, but for a run of four hours only, after which the batteries require recharging. For this reason submarines always require to act in concert with what has been called a "mother ship."

The most important types of vessels composing the British Navy have now been described. There are many others — sloops, gunboats, transports, despatch-boats, coal ships, hospital-ships, etcetera, which need not be more than mentioned. What warships will be like in the future it is impossible to forecast, as will be seen from what has been already said. Improvements in armour and guns, as well in machinery, are ever being made, which may alter the present type of ship altogether. Sad it is to think of the enormous expenditure of money and ingenuity in providing means of destroying our fellow-men with the greatest facility, and what a relief it would be to everybody if only the nations could agree to disarm — and keep disarmed! But as this may not be, for the present at any rate, we must be content to bear the burden of our national insurance policy, and, however much we may grudge its necessity, see that our naval power is sufficient to keep the command of the sea, on which our very existence as a nation depends. Of one thing we may rest certain, that the same spirit, the same indomitable courage and readiness to sacrifice their lives in defence of their country, exists among our officers and men in not less proportion than it did before England was engaged in that glorious struggle, with the world in arms against her, for her liberties and independence, the successful termination of which secured for her that peace which has now endured, with few interruptions, for well-nigh a century. That peace it will be our wise policy to maintain while we can do so with honour; at the same time guarding ourselves by every means in our power against the assaults of envious foes who may venture to attack us.